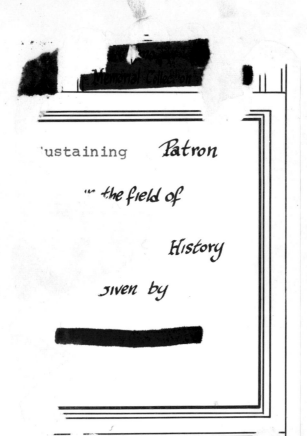

Memorial Collection

'ustaining *Patron*

" the field of

History

given by

OXFORD MEDIEVAL TEXTS

General Editors
V. H. GALBRAITH   R. A. B. MYNORS
C. N. L. BROOKE

DOCUMENTS OF THE
BARONIAL MOVEMENT
1258-1267

DOCUMENTS OF THE BARONIAL MOVEMENT OF REFORM AND REBELLION

1258-1267

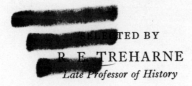

SELECTED BY

R. E. TREHARNE
Late Professor of History

EDITED BY

I. J. SANDERS
Reader in History
University College of Wales
Aberystwyth

OXFORD
AT THE CLARENDON PRESS
1973

Oxford University Press, Ely House, London W. 1

GLASGOW NEW YORK TORONTO MELBOURNE WELLINGTON
CAPE TOWN IBADAN NAIROBI DAR ES SALAAM LUSAKA ADDIS ABABA
DELHI BOMBAY CALCUTTA MADRAS KARACHI LAHORE DACCA
KUALA LUMPUR SINGAPORE HONG KONG TOKYO

*Printed in Great Britain
at the University Press, Oxford
by Vivian Ridler
Printer to the University*

PREFACE AND ACKNOWLEDGEMENTS

THE late Professor R. F. Treharne, whose death on 3 July 1967 was a great loss to the world of historical scholarship, concentrated his studies upon the latter half of the reign of Henry III. His book *The Baronial Plan of Reform* and the numerous articles which he published won for him recognition as a leading authority on the constitutional conflicts arising from the demand that the nobility should have greater influence in the administrative machinery of the realm. Among his many activities at the University College of Wales, Aberystwyth, he taught a detailed course in English history, covering the years 1250–72, and I was one of the students who, before World War II, enjoyed the privilege of his guidance. When I joined the staff at Aberystwyth after the war I co-operated with Professor Treharne in the teaching of this period of English history. My work on this book is explained by my long association with Professor Treharne who, before he died, had selected the documents, the majority of which he had translated. Mrs. Treharne invited me to complete the task which her husband had begun. I was very willing to do this because of the historical value of the documents and, more especially, in recognition of my great debt to Professor Treharne, both as a teacher and as a friend.

I have received aid from many sources. The University College, Aberystwyth, helped me meet the expense both of a summer vacation in Oxford, Cambridge, and London, consulting the manuscripts of the selected documents, and of photostats from the Bibliothèque Nationale and the Archives Nationales, Paris. The members of the Classics and French Departments at Aberystwyth have helped solve problems of medieval Latin and Anglo-Norman French. Professor W. Ullmann, Trinity College, Cambridge, has been most kind, and Dr. C. Knowles, University College of South Wales, Cardiff, has placed me in his debt for his careful and detailed work on the text of the Dictum of Kenilworth. Finally my most special thanks are due to Professor C. N. L. Brooke, Westfield College, University of London, whose guidance, help, and advice have only been exceeded by his patience and kindness in dealing with all the problems arising from the preparation of the manuscript for the press.   I. J. S.

CONTENTS

CONTENTS

INTRODUCTION

THE baronial movement which began in 1258 effected a political and constitutional revolution in order 'to reform the state of the realm' by a programme of legal, judicial, and administrative reforms coupled with radical changes in both the control and the framing of national policy. Its leaders, the greatest men of the land, had a fairly clear picture, from the beginning, of the changes which they intended to make, and although eventually the political movement of reform became a military rebellion and a civil war, at no stage did the control of its course and programme escape from the hands of the men who had begun it. Unlike those vast upheavals which spring from economic distress or social dissatisfaction, the movement of 1258–65 remained essentially to the end what it had been from the first in its aims. Furthermore, though growth and development can clearly be traced in its successive stages, at no point were its objectives other than those which its leaders declared, and sought to achieve by legislation and administrative action. Thus the official documents in which they published and sought to realize their purpose reflect the issues of the struggle with singular and faithful completeness: they are not a mere outward shell, concealing with superficial irrelevance hidden motive forces and deeper changes barely realized even by the actors themselves in the grip of social forces beyond their own control. When the documents which this movement produced are studied the mainsprings of human action are revealed: the essence of the movement, and not misleading superficialities, comes to light. This is not to say that economic forces counted for nothing in bringing about the situation which made possible the revolution of 1258 and its continuance in the rebellion of 1263, nor is it to suggest that the struggle had no fundamental social implications. Both economic and social forces were powerfully at work; without them the whole movement would have been inconceivable. But it does mean that from first to last the struggle was waged in terms of political and constitutional revolution, aimed at strictly practical reforms in law and government, and that it never got out of the control of men who knew what they wanted and how it could be achieved.

It is not intended to tell the story of the movement in this introduction; that has been done many times before, and will be done again elsewhere. The purpose here is to introduce the documents which have been selected. Exigencies of space have severely restricted the choice. All of the documents embodying constitutional change, and all of the ordinances of legal, judicial, and administrative reform at present known are included, as are also the unique series of *ex parte* statements made by both reformers and royalists in the remarkable succession of trials and arbitrations which characterize this episode of our history, and which were largely the result of the desire of the reformers to find a reasonable basis of settlement in compromise based on independent arbitration, after a hearing of the freely expressed views of both parties. Only a very few, however, of the most important letters of the period could be included; they will at least serve to show what a vivid light the official correspondence of the age throws on the events of the time, illuminating not only situations of intensely dramatic quality, but also the characters and motives of the actors themselves. Even to have skimmed the cream from this great store of material would unfortunately almost have doubled the size and the cost of this book. What is given here, then, is very much the bones of the matter, but, at least, they are not dry bones —there is plenty of marrow in them for anyone who wants to crack them open and find what is inside. The translation has kept very close to the original.

A. *Proposals for Reform*

The foundation documents of the whole period are the two declarations, dated 2 May 1258, whereby Henry III 'put himself in the counsel of his barons'. That supreme monument of his political folly, the 'Sicilian Affair', into which he had entered as far back as 1252, had become his ruination: not only had he gained no fraction of a foothold in that *damnosa hereditas*, but the mountain of debt which he had piled up in vain pursuit of the absurd scheme had led Pope Alexander IV to present him in March 1258 with an ultimatum. Henry must pledge himself to pay off speedily a debt which was the equivalent of about four years' normal income, and must undertake to appear in Sicily in 1259 with an army at least twice as big as England's entire feudal force, otherwise he would be excommunicated. Not daring to face such a

sentence, Henry, as the pope had bidden, appealed to the barons
to save him from so desperate a plight. A council, summoned to
London, met *circa* 7 April and discussion lasted for more than three
weeks; the Tewkesbury annalist states that the nobles demanded
the expulsion of aliens and reform of the realm by Englishmen
as a condition for an aid, if the pope reduced his demands.[1] The
agreement reached in the negotiations between the king and those
whom he met at the council is recorded in document 1. If the pope
would modify the terms of his ultimatum, in such a way as to
allow the king to fulfil his promise effectively, the barons would
strive to induce 'the community of the realm' to grant Henry a
common aid. In return the king promised that, before Christmas,
he would reform the state of the realm by the counsel of his proved
faithful men of England, together with the advice of a papal
legate should one come to England; he and the Lord Edward
bound themselves by a most solemn oath to fulfil this promise.
In addition Henry accepted the possibility of papal coercion should
he fail to fulfil his promise of reform. The importance of the
legates Guala and Pandulf during the king's minority had not been
forgotten, while Edward's oath to accept the reforms was important both because he was heir to the throne and because the
king, who was fifty years old, might die. This precaution was also
taken in cl. 8 of document 5 when the castellans were bound, for
up to twelve years, by the terms of the commission enforced by
the nobles. The baronial offer was doubly uncertain: their help was
conditional upon a modification of the papal terms sufficient to
enable Henry to fulfil his promise; but who was to judge that ill-
defined degree, even supposing the pope could be induced to
modify his demands? When these uncertain stipulations had been
fulfilled, the barons promised not the outright grant of an aid at
once, but only their good offices in persuading 'the community
of the realm'—clearly a larger and wider body than the baronage—
to grant an aid. The truth was that the barons had, to a man,
denounced the whole Sicilian bargain, ever since it had been made
public; they had never shown the least sympathy for Henry in
the increasing difficulties which he had faced, and they had constantly rejected any hint of responsibility for helping the king to
carry out the agreement. It is very hard to believe that they had
any intention of giving Henry any help, military or financial,

[1] *Ann. Mon.* i. 163.

which would have sufficed to win control of Sicily, and so their side of the bargain looks to us very disingenuous. Perhaps they counted on papal obstinacy to save them from the need to carry out their side of the bargain; perhaps they thought that some token grant would salve their consciences and keep both Henry and the pope quiet for long enough. However, whether they did, or did not, anticipate fulfilling their promise they could not look on with folded arms while their lord, the king, suffered excommunication and the land an interdict; and so they offered to rescue the king on terms. On the same day, 2 May 1258, Henry announced that Robert Walerand had sworn on the soul of the king that he (the king) would accept the reforms which were to be initiated by a committee of twenty-four—twelve to be chosen by the king and twelve to be nominated by the 'leading men', presumably those who had led the opposition to Henry at the council in London.

It is evident that the barons were determined to gain more success than had been achieved by the attempts at reform in 1227, 1232–4, 1238, 1242, and 1244; for on 12 April, within one week of the council meeting in London, the earls of Gloucester, Norfolk, and Leicester, together with Hugh Bigod, John fitz Geoffrey, Peter de Montfort, and Peter of Savoy had formed a pact to demand reform and render mutual aid.[1] All of these, except Peter of Savoy, the queen's uncle, were among the twelve chosen by the 'leading men', all, except Hugh Bigod, who became justiciar, were members of the Council of Fifteen.[2] The decision to choose a council of twenty-four to reform the state of the realm must have been taken as part of the negotiations between the king and the barons in April, for the words *iam electos* in document 2 suggests that the royal twelve had been chosen by 2 May. It is not known when the twelve were chosen by the barons, but they must have met soon in May as the third document, the *Petitio Baronum*, is probably the result of their consultations.

The parliament forecast in document 2 met at Oxford on 9 June, in the words of the Burton annalist *cum equis et armis*. The venue was Oxford, possibly because both the king and the nobles feared the influence of London, a power which became very evident

[1] Bémont, *Simon de Montfort*, p. 327, n. 30.
[2] Docs. 4, 5. Bigod, by right of his office, could attend the meetings of the Council of Fifteen.

in 1261, 1264, and 1267, and because this was the muster point for the expedition planned against Wales in July.[1] There can be little doubt that the Welsh campaign only partly explains why the barons mustered under arms; the real reason was undoubtedly their determination to force the king to accept their decisions and fear of the aliens—memories of the troubles in the years 1232–3 still lived. To this parliament, called the mad parliament of Oxford,[2] came the chosen twenty-four and many other supporters of both the king and the reformers.[3] Here the nobles presented the *Petitio Baronum*, which is a statement of grievances, not a programme of reform. The contents of the petition show that the reformers were not a faction seeking their own interest, for complaints against the nobles appear as well as those made by the nobles. In addition complaints were made covering a wide field of administrative and economic affairs. The twenty-nine clauses into which the petition is divided touch upon thirty-two different topics, which can be grouped into seven main categories: (i) tenure of land and the service due from it,[4] (ii) tenure of castles and aliens,[5] (iii) forests,[6] (iv) problems associated with the Church,[7] (v) administration of justice,[8] (vi) complaints against sheriffs and other royal officials,[9] (vii) economics.[10]

The contents of this document are of key importance as a guide to the future activities of those who claimed to be reforming the state of the realm. An examination of the future enactments of the 'reformers'[11] shows that the matters raised in the *petitio* formed the basis of much future legislation.[12] As far as is known only the matter of relief (cl. 1) does not reappear; even the problem of prise

[1] *Baronial Plan*, p. 69.
[2] This title is derived from the word *insane* written over an erasure, possibly *insigne* (*Liber de Antiquis Legibus* f. 75ᵛ; R. L. Poole, *E.H.R.* xl (1925), 402; E. F. Jacob, *History*, ix (1924–5), 189, n. 3; Treharne, ibid., xxxii (1947), 108–11).
[3] Richardson and Sayles, in *B.J.R.L.* xvii (1933), 298–9, discuss the personnel of such meetings.
[4] Cls. 1, 2, 3, 12, 27.
[5] Cls. 4, 5, 6, 15. The phraseology in cl. 15 is of interest as the words *de consensu consilii tocius regni Anglie* indicate that the barons were opposing independent royal decisions. A similar attitude appears in document 4 where Hugh Bigod is called *iusticiarius Anglie* not *iusticiarius regis*.
[6] Cls. 7–9.   [7] Cls. 10, 11.
[8] Cls. 13, 14, 19, 21, 24, 28, 29.   [9] Cls. 16–18, 20.
[10] Cls. 22, 23, 25, 26.   [11] Documents 9–12.
[12] See appendix 1.

(cls. 22, 23) received recognition in London in August 1258,[1] although it is not mentioned in later legislation.

A vivid picture of the activities of the nobles at Oxford is supplied by the fourth document, *Litera cuiusdam de curia regis de parliamento Oxonie*.[2] The office of justiciar, who was regent in the king's absence and chief deputy when the king was in the kingdom, had lapsed in 1234 when Stephen Segrave, who had succeeded Hubert de Burgh, earl of Kent, in 1232, was dismissed. The king, who had been declared of full age to govern in January 1227, had desired to restore the royal power to the level of that exercised by Henry II. He had found his aims thwarted by the great officers of state, justiciar and chancellor, and by baronial officials. Aided by Peter des Roches and Peter des Rivaux Henry directed his attention to the removal of these obstacles, and one of the first barriers to fall was the justiciar.

Thus the appointment of Hugh Bigod, brother of Roger Bigod, earl of Norfolk and marshal of England, to the office of justiciar marked the determination of the barons to re-establish barriers to absolute royal rule. This is shown by the fact that Hugh is called *iusticiarius Anglie*, rather than *iusticiarius regis*, and by his oath to administer justice, biased by neither influence nor bribery.[3] The problem of the castles was tackled and native constables were appointed.[4] The author of the letter from Oxford continues by stating that, 'after the articles noted above'[5] had been brought forward, the twenty-four 'sworn men'[6] considered means of improving royal revenue by restoring to the crown lands and castles which the king had alienated,[7] an action which struck at the very foundations of those to whom Henry had shown great favour.[8] The feeling of enmity toward the aliens caused the Lusignan brothers, together with their brother-in-law earl

[1] *Lib. de Ant. Leg.* p. 39.

[2] Many of the most valuable documents for the years 1258–9 are preserved in the Burton annals. It is possible that John Clarel, whose family came from the neighbourhood of Burton, the confidential clerk of John Mansel, was the source of these. As the words *articulis prenotatis* in the letter refer to the *Petitio Baronum* (doc. 4, n. 4), which immediately precedes the letter in the Burton annals, it is possible that Clarel wrote the letter to send to Burton with a copy of the *Petitio*.

[3] See doc. 5, cl. 6.   [4] Doc. 5, cls. 8, 24.

[5] This alludes to the petition (doc. 3) which immediately precedes the letter in *Ann. Mon.* i. 443.

[6] Doc. 5, cl. 5, records the oath of the twenty-four.

[7] Doc. 12, cls. 8, 14, 17, 27; doc. 29, n. 7; doc. 30, cl. 24; doc. 31, cl. 12.

[8] Doc. 1, nn. 2, 3.

Warenne, to flee from Oxford to Wolvesey castle, in Winchester, of which Aymer de Lusignan was bishop-elect.[1] This event, which took place *circa* 28 June, caused the meeting at Oxford to break up, for the barons followed the Lusignans to Winchester where negotiations began. The author of the letter states that the foreigners took the first step, offering full obedience to the enactments of the reformers. Doubt was felt by the barons about the sincerity of this offer, and consequently the reformers demanded that the Lusignans and their followers should leave the realm until such time as the king, advised by the barons, should decide about their future. When the king intervened, offering to guarantee the good behaviour of the foreigners, the reformers answered by offering two possible schemes. Either all should leave the land, as had already been demanded, or Guy and Geoffrey de Lusignan should leave, never to return, while their brothers, William de Valence and Aymer de Lusignan, who held lands in England, would remain in the realm under safe custody until reforms had been completed. Further negotiation must have taken place until it was finally agreed that all would leave the realm provided they could have the profits of their lands, a condition which the nobles defined as fitting maintenance. The balance of their wealth, which was to be kept for them, would be restored when they returned to England, but they were allowed to take 6,000 marks of their treasure with them.[2] Following this agreement the Lusignans left the country on 14 July.[3] The conduct of these negotiations, the truth of the account of which there is no reason to doubt, shows the determination of the barons to expel the aliens, but at the same time there is a commendable absence of vindictiveness and hatred in the solution which was finally reached. Also at Winchester, on 10 July, the Lord Edward gave the promise which his father had guaranteed in document 1, while a group of four councillors was appointed, both to advise the prince and to reform the households of the king and Edward.[4] The letter from Oxford ends with a report that the king had requested that only native-born Englishmen should be in his household, a royal gesture to placate the reformers.

[1] Doc. 4, nn. 7, 14.
[2] All their debts were to be paid from this treasure; any balance was to be held until their return.
[3] Doc. 4, n. 7. See doc. 24, n. 2 for date of their return.
[4] Doc. 4, nn. 11, 12; doc. 5, cl. 20. No mention is made here of reforming Edward's household.

In addition we are told that the barons faced many difficult decisions, an outline of which may be seen in document 5, that they intended to repair to London to make regulations about aliens, Romans, and money-changers, and that they were planning to take control of Winchester, since its bishop-elect had left England.[1]

B. *Enactments to Achieve Reform*

The fifth document, *Provisio facta apud Oxoniam*, is known in three texts and there is reference to a fourth.[2] Variations in details recorded in these texts result from the fact that each text, consisting of notes made of decisions taken on different occasions, probably belonged to different members of the Council of Fifteen. Some texts are a more accurate record than others, as there is evidence in some cases of attempts to make alterations reflecting changed decisions.[3] The informal aspect of the texts is also shown by the fact that none of them was enrolled or circulated. All were in French,[4] except for clause 1 which provided for the appointment of four knights in each shire to record complaints touching all sides of royal and baronial administration.[5] The origin of the *Provisio facta apud Oxoniam* is disputed. Treharne has suggested that they record the decisions of the twenty-four, whereas H. G. Richardson and G. O. Sayles believe that they were the enactments of the parliament which accepted or rejected the proposals of the twenty-four. This latter suggestion would explain the existence, in the *Provisio*, of two or three clauses on the same topic. Thus clause 6 mentions the oath of the justiciar and his obligation to obey the decisions both of the twenty-four and of the king's council, while clauses 13 and 16 elaborate the powers which the justiciar could exercise.[6] The origin suggested by Richardson and Sayles may explain why the oath of the castellans forms clause 8 whereas the names of these officials is left to the

[1] Doc. 4, nn. 13, 14.
[2] See doc. 5, n. 2, and doc. 11, n. 1, where the varied meanings of the term Provisions of Oxford are discussed.
[3] This topic is fully discussed by Richardson and Sayles, *B.J.R.L.* xvii (1933), 291–317.
[4] The Provisions of Oxford may be compared with the Provisions of Westminster (doc. 11) which were enrolled. The Oxford decisions resemble those made at Westminster and recorded in doc. 12.
[5] See docs. 6 and 8 for the enactment of this clause.
[6] Similarly the oath and power of the chancellor appear in clauses 7 and 15.

end of the document. Furthermore, clause 4, 'the oath of the community of England', obviously records an event taking place in parliament rather than a decision of the twenty-four.

The picture conveyed by the *Provisio* is of a gathering determined to effect serious reform rather than of a headstrong disorganized collection of rebels. The leaders were obviously men who were politically mature, understanding and accepting the tradition of administration which had developed in thirteenth-century England. Thus, in clause 18 there are three references to the charter of liberties as a guide to action, while the description of the negotiations with the Lusignans in document 4 confirms this picture of a politically mature gathering. The first clause of document 5, that which provides for the appointment of four knights in each county to record abuses, shows that the leaders of the reform movement could create administrative machinery to achieve their aims. More important still, the reformers, by stating that complaints against sheriffs, bailiffs, or any other person were to be enrolled, showed a desire for reform even in the sphere of feudal administration.[1] Unfortunately this desire for reform in a wide field did not last. Although weakened as early as October 1258, when the language of document 8 is less radical than clause 1 of document 5, the desire for reform in baronial as well as in royal administration still remained alive enough to find expression in February 1259, despite increased conflict in the ranks of the reformers.[2] However, the failure of the nobles to fulfil their promises found expression in October 1259 when a group of young men, whom the Burton annalist calls *communitas bacheleria Anglie* voiced their complaints.[3] Nevertheless, the early decision to inquire concerning complaints in royal and feudal administration bore results, as Hugh Bigod, the justiciar, went on circuit early in 1259 and the special eyre, organised in November and December 1259 was only cancelled in June 1260 as a reward for the support which the king had received from the earl of Gloucester.[4]

The steps taken to exercise permanent control of the administration show a growth in political understanding as compared with

---

[1] A similar decision appears in clause 16.
[2] Doc. 10, n. 4.
[3] *Ann. Mon.* i. 471; T. F. Tout, *E.H.R.* xvii (1902), 89–95; *Baronial Plan*, pp. 160–4; *Reform and Rebellion*, pp. 126–43.
[4] Docs. 13, 27; *Baronial Plan*, pp. 108–16, 145–56, 185–9; *Reform and Rebellion*, pp. 19–125.

the efforts of those who enforced Magna Carta.[1] The earl of
Warwick and John Mansel, royalists chosen by the baronial twelve,
together with Roger and Hugh Bigod, chosen by the royal twelve,
nominated, subject to the assent of the twenty-four,[2] the Council of
Fifteen which was in existence by 28 June.[3] The composition of the
Council once again shows the determination of the nobles to control
the crown, for nine of the baronial twelve appear. Only three
of the royal twelve (the archbishop of Canterbury, the earl of
Warwick and John Mansel) are named. The additional three were
Peter of Savoy, brother of the archbishop, the earl of Aumale,
grandson of a Norman who had married the heiress of the earldom,
and James de Audley, husband of Ela daughter of William de
Longespée, d. 1250, a cousin of the king. Thus there came into
existence a group of the greatest nobles and members of the royal
circle forming the first king's council,[4] as distinct from counsel,
a fixed group rather than an amorphous assembly. This Council
of Fifteen probably took an oath, similar to that of the twenty-
four,[5] the terms of which stressed obligation to the realm, whereas
the oath of the counsellors in 1257 placed the king in supreme
position.[6] Furthermore, the Council, which was to be in permanent
session at court, claimed power to advise the king in all matters
touching the king and the kingdom, taking decisions on a majority

[1] *Magna Carta*, pp. 334–7.   [2] Doc. 5, cls. 9, 23.

[3] *C.R. 1256–59*, pp. 315–16. There is no evidence of the relationship between
the twenty-four and the Council of Fifteen. The twenty-four split into various
administrative groups. Twelve of them were on the Council of Fifteen; two
(Hugh Bigod and Henry de Wingham, justiciar and chancellor) attended the
meetings of the Council by right of their office. Two (the bishop of London and
Hugh Despenser) were among the twelve representing the *commun* (doc. 5,
cl. 10); three (William de Valence, Aymer and Guy de Lusignan) left the realm.
The others (William Bardolf, Henry of Almain, earl Warenne, John Darlington,
and Richard de Crokesley) held no further office. The indefinite relationship
between the twenty-four and the Council of Fifteen is shown by the fact that
although the Council was in existence on 28 June the *Lib. de Ant. Leg.* p. 38
says that on 23 July *quidam de predictis duodecim baronibus* came to the Guildhall
in London for negotiations. Although these words do not prove the continued
existence of the twenty-four, as an administrative body, the reference to the
baronial twelve suggests that that group still existed. On the other hand the use
of the word *quidam* may mean that the Council of Fifteen came to the Guildhall,
as nine of the baronial twelve were members of the Council. The twenty-four
did not officially cease to exist until 4 Aug. 1258, when a proclamation in French
was issued binding the king to obey the Council. (*C.P.R. 1247–58*, pp. 644–5;
Royal Letters, ii. 129. See doc. 7.)

[4] *English Baronies*, p. 112; *G.E.C.* i. 354. Stephen de Longespée, one of the
guardians of the Lord Edward, was William's brother. See doc. 4.

[5] Doc. 5, cl. 5.   [6] *Ann. Mon.* i. 395.

vote. In addition the Council asserted that it could attend parliament, even if not summoned to do so by the king, and, in addition, the justiciar, chancellor, treasurer, and castellans were to be under its control. All these powers were to be exercised for possibly as long as twelve years.[1] In addition the 'community' named twelve who were to represent the *commun* at the parliaments which were to meet regularly on 3 February, 1 June, and 6 October.[2] The claims of Bémont,[3] Powicke, Stubbs, Ramsay, and Davis that parliaments consisted only of the Council of Fifteen and the twelve representing the *commun* have been proved incorrect.[4] Lastly there were named twenty-four who were to grant an aid to the king, the reward which the nobles had promised if Henry allowed them to reform the realm.[5] It is impossible to say if this action was evidence of a sincere desire to aid the king financially, or it may merely have been done as a formal gesture, for no aid was granted to Henry, although the Council of Fifteen could have done so.

Having established machinery to control the central administration, the twenty-four turned their attention to the sheriff. It was ordered that sheriffs were to be landowners in the counties over which they held office, and that they were to hold office for one year, at the end of which they were to answer to the exchequer. They, and other officials, were to be punished if they took bribes, while the sheriffs were to be paid a salary which would allow them to administer their counties justly. Thus the sheriff becomes a keeper and not a farmer of the county, he is to be a local landowner and not a careerist.[6] Similar detailed regulations to control

[1] Doc. 5, cls. 6–8, 13–15, 21, 23.

[2] Doc. 5, cl. 10 and n. 21. The demand by Simon de Montfort that the parliaments should meet at the stated times, independently of the king's wish, was one of the points of difference between him and Henry III. Although the names of the twelve chosen in 1258 are known, there is no reason to believe that they held office permanently, they may have changed for each parliament.

[3] *Simon de Montfort*, p. 170.

[4] Richardson and Sayles, *B.J.R.L.* xvii (1933), 296; *Lib. de Ant. Leg.* p. 20.

[5] Doc. 5, cl. 11; doc. 1. The twenty-four consisted of ten from the Council of Fifteen, nine from the twelve representing the *commun* and five new people: the bishop of Salisbury, the earl of Oxford, Giles de Erdington, judge and baronial sheriff of Cambridge and Huntingdon, Fulk de Kerdiston, one of the four knights recording complaints in Norfolk, and John Criol, a small landowner in Kent whose son married Eleanor, coheiress of the barony of Folkestone, Kent (*Baronial Plan*, p. 198, nn. 3, 8, pp. 226, 267, n. 5; *C.P.R. 1247–58*, pp. 520, 648; Foss, p. 234; *English Baronies*, p. 46; doc. 12).

[6] Doc. 3, cl. 16; doc. 5, cl. 17. See also doc. 8; doc. 12, cl. 22; doc. 31, cl. 3; docs. 37A, 37B, 37C; *Baronial Plan, passim*.

escheators, which office had been established in 1232, were enacted.[1] These officials were to be honest and trustworthy, they were not to take anything from the property of the dead man, they were to administer the goods of the deceased until any debts due to the king were paid. All their actions must accord with the charter of liberties.[2] As sanctions for the enforcement of these enactments the twenty-four appointed new castellans to administer royal fortresses and made it a condition that the keepers should surrender the castles only to the king or his heirs on the advice of the Council, a rule which was to last for twelve years.[3] Mentioned in document 5 as topics for further consideration are the reform both of the Church and of the royal household.[4] In addition the mint of London was to be reformed, the state of the city of London and of all other cities was to be examined as also was the position of the Jews in the realm.[5]

In the summer of 1258 the Council of Fifteen exercised complete control over the government and administration of the realm. The royal household was reformed and steps were taken to stop the abuse of prise. Between 28 July and 4 August letters patent were issued nominating the four knights who were to inquire concerning abuses in each of the thirty-eight counties of England.[6] Document 6, which contains instructions to the knights, states that they should swear before the county court, or before the sheriff and coroners if the county court would not be meeting soon, that they would make a full and true inquiry. The men of the shire were bound under oath to reveal all abuses, both by royal and feudal officials.[7] Information so gathered, authenticated by

[1] Doc. 5, cl. 18. Before the office of escheator was created sheriffs controlled escheats in their counties. In 1232 two escheators for each county were appointed; in 1234 there were two escheators south of the Trent and in 1236 one such official acted north of the Trent. Later there was one escheator north and one south of the river (*English Government at Work*, ed. W. A. Morris and J. R. Strayer, ii (1947), pp. 115–16. Mistakes on p. 116: William should read Adam son of William; n. 3 should be 135).

[2] This refers to clause 26 of Magna Carta (*Magna Carta*, pp. 324–5).

[3] Doc. 5, cls. 8, 24. A letter dated 8 Aug. 1261 states that Hugh Bigod refused to surrender Scarborough and Pickering castles without sanction of the Council (*Foedera*, I. i. 408).

[4] Doc. 5, cls. 12, 20. The text of the *Provisio* published by Richardson and Sayles gives evidence of the royal household being changed (*B.J.R.L.* xvii (1933), 321, cl. 33).

[5] Doc. 5, cls. 17, 19.   [6] *C.P.R. 1247–58*, pp. 645–9; doc. 5, cl. 1.

[7] Acting sheriffs were excused from this inquiry, but if they had previously held office in the county where they were officials in 1258 their actions could

the seals of the knights and of those who had supplied evidence, was to be delivered to the Council at Westminster on 6 October 1258.[1] Sheriffs were to give full aid to the knights and the document closes with the statement that matters which had already been reported or judged were not to be recorded in this inquiry.

In addition to being occupied with the problems arising from their seizure of power the reformers were faced with the necessity of negotiating with the pope and with Llywelyn ap Gruffydd, the leading Welsh prince. In a letter to the pope the reformers stated that, in the matter of Sicily, the king had acted without advice, and John Clarel, clerk of John Mansel, went to Rome to negotiate with Pope Alexander IV.[2] The threatened campaign against the Welsh was cancelled and envoys were named, on 27 July, to negotiate with the Welsh at Montgomery ford, in order to prolong the truce.[3] In addition, correspondence was opened with the King of Castile, whose daughter had married the Lord Edward, while the long series of discussions which culminated in the Peace of Paris in 1259 were under consideration.[4]

The first parliament to meet, under the terms of clause 21 of document 5, seems to have assembled at Westminster a week late, on 13 October 1258,[5] and on 18 October the king once again issued a proclamation, sent to every county, confirming his support for the Council of Fifteen and sanctioning its actions.[6] Texts of this document (no. 7), which was published in French and English, have survived, but no copy of the Latin text, which the Burton annalist claims was issued,[7] remains. In addition, in the same proclamation, all were ordered, under threat of extreme royal displeasure, to obey the enactments of the Council and to oppose those who accepted bribes or seized property. The sixteen

be reported (*Baronial Plan*, p. 121). *Reform and Rebellion*, pp. 19–35, examines the inquiries.

[1] This is the date when parliament was due to meet. Doc. 5, cl. 21.
[2] *Ann. Mon.* i. 170–4, 457–60, 461–8; *Chron. Maj.* vi. 400–5; *Baronial Plan*, pp. 104–6.
[3] *C.R. 1256–59*, pp. 242–3, 320.
[4] Ibid., pp. 314–15; *Peace of Paris*; I. J. Sanders, 'The Texts of the Peace of Paris', *E.H.R.* lxvi (1951), 81–97.
[5] *British Chronology*, p. 502; *Baronial Plan*, pp. 117–32, discusses the work of this parliament.
[6] The first proclamation of support is dated 4 Aug. 1258 (*C.P.R. 1247–58*, pp. 644–5; *Royal Letters*, ii. 129).
[7] *Ann. Mon.* i. 453. See introduction to doc. 7.

witnesses of the document include fourteen of the Council of
Fifteen and two of the twelve who were to represent the *commun*,
an indication that the scheme advanced in document 5, cl. 22
was working.[1] The decision for parliament to assemble on 13
October was probably made after it was ordered, in document 6,
that the knights should be at Westminster on 6 October. This
change is possibly linked with clause 29 of the text of the *Provisio*
published by Richardson and Sayles,[2] for it is here stated that
judges and wise men were to meet eight days before the next
parliament, at the place where parliament assembled, to consider
'of what ill Lawes and need of reformation there were'. The
reformers, believing that the knights would appear on 6 October
with their report on abuses, probably planned that the information
should be analysed by 'the judges and wise men' to prepare the
way for reforms to be enacted in the coming parliament.

There is evidence which suggests that at least fourteen, and
probably more, groups of knights appeared at Westminster.[3]
However, the ordinance issued on 20 October,[4] in Latin, French,
and English the Burton annalist says, and sent to each county to be
read in the county court, suggests that the inquiry by the knights
was not progressing as speedily as had been hoped. The document opens with an expression of the king's desire for the redress of all evils. However, great difficulties had, in some cases,
hindered both the visit of the knights and the needed reforms, but
it is promised that the plan for redress will be fulfilled. Since the
sheriff and the sheriff's officials were the chief instrument of the
government in the shires the majority of the complaints of abuses
must have been directed against these people. The reformers
obviously wished to reassure the community about the behaviour
of sheriffs in the future, for the ordinance continued with a full
statement of the duties and obligations of these officials. They
were to administer justice uninfluenced by bribes or threats, while
they were forbidden to let any district out to farm. The size of

[1] John Mansel was omitted from the fifteen. *Baronial Plan*, p. 119 mistakenly
claims that only twelve of the fifteen were present. The two from the twelve
were Hugh Despenser and the earl of Winchester. See also introduction to
doc. 8.

[2] *B.J.R.L.* xvii (1933), 317–21.

[3] H. M. Cam, 'The Parliamentary Writs *de expensis* of 1258', *E.H.R.* xlvi
(1931), 630–2.

[4] *Ann. Mon.* i. 453. Copies of the English and Latin texts have survived. See
doc. 8 introduction.

their following and the sustenance due to them was regulated, the frequency of their visits and those from whom they could demand hospitality was stated. Sheriffs' sergeants were to be trustworthy men who were not to make undue demands on the community. Furthermore, anyone who broke these rules was to suffer speedy and severe punishment. In future sheriffs were to receive from the issues of the county money to cover all expenses of their office, while neither sheriffs nor sergeants were to hold office for more than one year. Lastly, all were urged to report the wrongdoings of these officials.

The terms of this ordinance indicate that the Council of Fifteen was still intent upon reforming local administration, although there is a hint of a wish to act less drastically than was originally planned, for no mention is made of reporting the misdeeds of feudal officials. Nevertheless, the good intentions of the reformers found expression in the fact that between 23 October and 3 November nineteen sheriffs were appointed to control twenty-eight counties,[1] while Philip Lovel, treasurer since 27 August 1252, was replaced on 2 November by John Crakehall, formerly steward of Robert Grosseteste, d. 1253, bishop of Lincoln and one of the leading proponents of reform. Henry de Wingham, chancellor since 5 January 1255, remained in office.

Friction between the more advanced reformers and the more conservative group led by Richard, earl of Gloucester, was threatening to develop, and forms the background for document 9. There is considerable controversy among scholars about the date of this ordinance, which is headed *Prouidencia baronum Anglie anno regni regis Henrici xl secundo de sectis curiarum*. Although 42 Henry III ends on 27 October 1258 Sir Maurice Powicke has claimed that this document arose out of the deliberations of the parliament which met in February 1259, and, although the evidence which he cites is faulty,[2] it is possible that the regulations were compiled in March 1259. Professor E. F. Jacob, on the other hand, suggests that the MS. records decisions made in the summer of 1258 and recorded in March 1259,[3] while Richardson and Sayles

---

[1] *Baronial Plan*, p. 121.

[2] *Baronial Council*, p. 126, n. 4. Sir Maurice Powicke states that the date at the head of the document was *anno regni regis Henrici xlii* and claims that this is a scribal error for *xliii*. The date, however, is as above. See doc. 9, n.a. for evidence to support March 1259.

[3] *Reform and Rebellion*, p. 72.

claim that it comes from the deliberations of the parliament which sat in October 1258.¹ The contents of the manuscript, to be considered later, may have originated in the autumn of 1258, before the rift between the right and left wing of the reformers took place. Furthermore, it may have been the cause of the rift, leading to open hostility between Clare and Montfort, and resulting in an alliance between the Lord Edward and Richard de Clare, together with arrangements for arbitration in the quarrel between the earl and the prince.² Whatever the date of document 9 the phraseology suggests that it records a debate in council concerning planned reforms, touching upon problems arising from suit of court. Furthermore, the phrasing of the clauses indicates the influence of expert legal opinion, especially in clauses 24 and 25. The first thirteen clauses deal with problems arising between lord and tenant in matters of suit of court. Tenants are bound to suit of court according to the terms of their charter of enfeoffment, but those whose charters mention a fixed service in place of all other obligations are free of suit. Those who had done suit of court from time immemorial, and had no quittance from this service, must continue to serve, but those who were forced to perform suit of court despite the fact that this obligation was not in their charter of enfeoffment, or sanctioned by custom, were free of further suit. A tenement owing service of one suit of court continued to owe only one suit after it had been divided between coheirs. This first section of the document ends by mentioning both the methods by which those who were coerced to perform suit of court could obtain redress in the king's court and the manner by which those who did not fulfil their duties could be punished. Problems arising from demands for attendance at the sheriffs' tourn, to hold view of frank-pledge,³ occupy clauses 14–16. Bishops, abbots, priors, earls, and barons were excused attendance, those with extensive holdings 'where peace and law are satisfactorily preserved' need not be present unless they are summoned personally, and the

¹ B.J.R.L. xvii (1933), 296. Richardson and Sayles have suggested that the MS. may record the decisions of the judges and wise men who were to meet eight days before the October parliament. See above p. 14.

² Hist. MSS. Comm. Lord Middleton, Wollaton Hall, pp. 67–9; translated Hennings, pp. 93–5. The document mentions twelve of Edward's followers and nine of the Gloucesters'. The earl and prince possibly reached a temporary understanding on 28 Mar. 1259. See Baronial Plan, p. 140, for reason of quarrel.

³ W. A. Morris, Frankpledge System (1910); R. Steward-Brown, Sergeants of the Peace in Medieval England (1936).

demands for attendance to hold inquisitions were limited to comply with the terms of Magna Carta. Those who failed to attend when they should be present were to be punished, according to the terms of Magna Carta.[1] The remaining clauses of the *Prouidencia* deal with points of legal detail—fines for *beau plaider* are to be abolished,[2] actions of dower called *unde nichil habet*, assizes of *darrein presentment*, and pleas called *quare impedit* were to be held each three weeks.[3] Privileges given by writs of exemption from service on juries and inquisitions are limited by the needs of the administration of justice,[4] while there is detailed discussion of writs of entry, writs of *mort d'ancestor*, and of essoins.[5]

There is no evidence of this document being published, and its importance lies in the evidence which it supplies of the preliminary discussions which took place to draw up the Provisions of Westminster which appeared after the October parliament in 1259.[6] Furthermore, the attention shown in the *Prouidencia* to protecting the rights of the small man from the power of the nobility was an additional source of conflict between the more advanced and more conservative reformers.[7]

Of more definite date is document 10, the *Ordinationes Magnatum*, published on 22 February 1259 and sanctioned by the king on 28 March, when orders were issued that the French texts should be sent to each county to be read in the county and hundred courts.[8] The gap between the date of the issue of the document, 22 February, and the royal sanction on 28 March is possibly explained by the quarrel between the earls of Gloucester and Leicester. This quarrel, which may have been caused by

---

[1] Clause 20 of Magna Carta orders that fines be levied according to the seriousness of the offence (*Magna Carta*, pp. 332–3). The 1215 issue of the charter does not mention the tourn which appears in clause 42 of the 1217 issue in a context irrelevant to the *Prouidencia*. The allusion to Magna Carta, which is also mentioned on other occasions, is a good example of the way in which that document had already become the palladium of English liberty (Stubbs, p. 343).

[2] These were fines levied for faults in legal terminology during the hearing of a suit. See doc. 3, cl. 14; doc. 11, cl. 5.

[3] Hundred courts met each three weeks. See doc. 11, cls. 6, 7; *Baronial Plan*, pp. 134, 174, nn. 5, 199, 201, 389, 390 *et alibi*.

[4] Doc. 3, cl. 28.   [5] Doc. 9, n. 6.

[6] The close resemblance between the contents of the two documents is shown in appendix 1. See also introduction to document 9.

[7] *Baronial Plan*, pp. 136–7.

[8] Richardson and Sayles, *B.J.R.L.* xvii (1933), 320, cl. 24.

the terms of the *Ordinationes*, possibly ended on 28 March.[1] The document is a proclamation by the Council and the twelve elected to represent the *commun*,[2] promising that the wrongs done by the nobles and their officials would be corrected by the king and the justiciar. Such complaints could be heard as *querulae*, but it was stipulated that cases usually needing writs should follow the usual procedure.[3] Furthermore, all the liberties which had been granted by the king to his tenants-in-chief in Magna Carta were to be granted by the nobles to their tenants, while all regulations concerning suit of court and other details of feudal rights, to be reviewed by the council before 1 November, would be accepted by the nobles for their tenants.[4] Officers of the nobles were to take an oath, details of which are recorded, similar to that which was taken by the sheriffs,[5] and this obligation was to be enforced when new appointments were made; baronial officials who broke their oath were to be punished in their lord's court. Lastly, the Council and the twelve promised that no nobleman would avow any man who was not his own. Thus the reformers were still prepared to honour the terms of clause 1 of document 5 and had placed baronial officials under the same scrutiny and obligations as that which rested on royal officials.

During the summer of 1259 the truce which had been made between the earls of Gloucester and Leicester was strained. The controversy arising from the *Ordinationes* (doc. 10), which had divided the February 1259 parliament, was one of the factors which led Simon de Montfort to leave England, probably early in March, and he did not return until shortly before the parliament which met on 13 October 1259. Both the earls were engaged in negotiations with the French to complete the Peace of Paris, and Gloucester accused Simon de Montfort of maliciously hindering negotiations by his demands for the recognition of Countess Eleanor's claims to dower from the Marshal lands.[6] In addition,

---

[1] *Baronial Plan*, pp. 140–1. Clauses 31 and 32 of the text of the *Prouisio* published in *B.J.R.L.* xvii. 321, record a compact between the earls of Leicester and Gloucester, representing the Council of Fifteen, Thomas de Grelley and the earl of Winchester, representing the twelve, and the bishops of Worcester and Salisbury for the government of the realm.

[2] Thus the scheme mentioned in doc. 5, cls. 21, 22 was still working in Feb. 1259.

[3] This point is discussed in document 11; see doc. 12, cl. 18.

[4] The autumn parliament was due to meet on 6 Oct. 1259.

[5] See doc. 8; *Baronial Plan, passim.*

[6] Sanders, *E.H.R.* lxvi (1951), 81–97; doc. 29, *passim.*

difficulties arose from the fulfilment of the obligations which the king had undertaken when he had accepted the crown of Sicily for his son Edmund; in the middle of 1259 the Council stopped the collection of the Sicilian tenth until the whole problem could be solved.[1] The nobles were also in conflict with the papacy about Aymer de Lusignan, bishop-elect of Winchester, who had left the realm in July 1258. It was assumed by the reformers that the see of Winchester was vacant, but the pope refused to sanction this, and in August 1259 Velascus, a papal envoy, arrived in England with a bull affirming Aymer's tenure of Winchester. Church finances also caused problems, for in the middle of 1259 Italian merchants complained because the English clergy and laymen refused to refund the money which the pope had borrowed on their security. Conditions in the country were also disturbed by the conflict which developed between the earl of Gloucester and the Lord Edward who had made a pact of mutual support on 14 March 1259.

There is little direct evidence to explain the estrangement between the Lord Edward and Gloucester but suggestions may be made. There was conflict concerning the town and castle of Bristol, where the earl had interests and in which Edward had a chancery and an exchequer,[2] while the agreement between the earls of Gloucester and Leicester, on 28 March 1259, may well have annoyed Edward who must have felt that little trust could be placed in the earl of Gloucester, who could change sides in two weeks. In addition, the justiciar Hugh Bigod was on eyre administering justice and doing what he could to remedy the complaints recorded by the four knights who had been visiting the shires. The publication of document 10, on 28 March 1259, and the work of the justiciar must have raised high the hopes of those who felt aggrieved, hopes which became more important with the passage of time. This impatience, which had already found expression in the opening sentences of document 8, dated 20 October 1258, made itself manifest in the early part of October 1259 when London was crowded in preparation for the parliament which assembled

[1] W. E. Lunt, *The Valuation of Norwich* (1926), and *Financial Relations of the Papacy with England* (1939).

[2] Bristol, with its castle, was among the lands granted to Edward on 14 Feb. 1254 during the negotiations for his marriage to Eleanor of Castile, but difficulties arose because the court of the honour of Gloucester also met in Bristol (*King Henry III*, p. 233; *English Baronies*, p. 6, n. 4).

on 13 October. The Burton annalist states that the *communitas
bacheleria Anglie* announced to the Lord Edward, to the earl of
Gloucester, and to others of the council who had been chosen at
Oxford, that the king had met all the demands of the barons. In
contrast, claimed the *communitas*, the barons had failed to fulfil
their promises and the *communitas* demanded that some other
means of reform be found. The Lord Edward answered by saying
that although he had unwillingly taken the oath at Oxford he would
do all he could for reform, thus fulfilling the oath. Edward then
called upon the nobles to honour their oaths, threatening to
support the *communitas* if they did not do so. The annalist ends
his account by stating that the barons, seeing that they must fulfil
their promises caused the 'following provisions' to be published.[1]

The 'following provisions' are the French text of what came to
be known as the Provisions of Westminster.[2] The link between
the protest of the *bacheleria* and the publication of document 11
is not as close as the Burton annalist suggests. The close resemblance between the topics mentioned in document 9, possibly
dating from March 1259, and those which appear in the Provisions
of Westminster indicate that there had been considerable discussion of the contents of the latter document, discussion which
dated from a long time before October 1259. It is, however,
possible that the action of the *bacheleria* forced the hand of the
more conservative reformers, with the result that they could
no longer delay the publication of the Provisions. Furthermore,
it is very probable that some of the administrative measures
which appear in document 12, and which were of great interest to
the small tenant, were the result of the agitation. The statement of
the Burton annalist is also of interest, revealing the trust felt in

---

[1] *Ann. Mon.* i. 471. This gathering in London was in no way a national up-
rising. It was merely a protest meeting and the Burton annalist is the only writer
to mention the event. Bishop Stubbs and other scholars who were his con-
temporaries have suggested that the words *communitas bacheleria Angliae* meant
a group of knights. Professor Tout claims that the *bacheleria* were young men
being trained for knighthood in the households of the nobles. He suggests that
on this occasion the phrase meant a group of enthusiastic young men, many of
whom may have been tenants of the nobility, who felt that they had most to gain
from the suggested reforms and investigations by the knights in the shires (T. F.
Tout, '*Communitas bacheleria Angliae*', *E.H.R.* xvii (1902), 89–95).

[2] *Ann. Mon.* i. 471. For an unknown reason H. R. Luard, the editor of this
volume, states in the margin that these are the 'provisions of the twelve barons'.
See the introduction to document 11 for a discussion of the title Provisions of
Westminster.

the monarchy and the popularity of the Lord Edward, a popularity possibly based on a belief that he favoured the reform movement because he was no longer an ally of the earl of Gloucester, the recognized leader of the conservative reformers. Edward's action at this time is difficult to explain. He may have been a youthful enthusiast for reform—his twentieth birthday was in June 1259—or he may have already become an astute politician who saw a chance of causing a rift in the ranks of the reformers. The latter suggestion finds support from the fact that Edward joined Simon de Montfort, the leader of the radicals, on 15 October in an alliance which was to continue until April 1260.[1] The action of the *bacheleria* is also one of the first signs of the growing importance of the small landowner at this time. Several clauses in documents 3, 9 and 11 show that the reformers recognized the need to change conditions for the county class. These small landowners felt the wind of change and were to become an increasingly important force during the years of unrest in the realm.[2]

The regulations enacted in October 1259 may be divided into two groups, those dealing with legal matters (doc. 11) and those touching questions of politics and administration (doc. 12).[3] Both groups of clauses were probably originally written in French, but whereas the political and administrative group remained in that language the legal clauses were translated into Latin, probably for publication in the eyre, the regulations for which were drawn up late in November 1259 (doc. 13).[4] The official text of the legal clauses is the one recorded on the close roll. Furthermore, as the changes in the law were to be enacted by the judges, who were to go on eyre at the end of 1259, it is very probable that each group of judges was given a copy of the new laws for them to be read

[1] *Baronial Plan*, pp. 163–4.
[2] N. Denholm-Young, 'Feudal Society in the Thirteenth Century, the Knights', *History*, xxix (1944) and *Collected Papers on Medieval Subjects* (Oxford, 1946); R. F. Treharne, 'The Knights in the Period of Reform and Rebellion, 1258–67, a critical phase in the rise of a new class', *B.I.H.R.* xxi (1946).
[3] The distinction between these is made in 'Baronial Council', p. 130. Just as there is evidence to show that the legal clauses had been discussed before Oct. 1259 there is similar evidence for some of the administrative clauses.
[4] The French legal clauses are in *Ann. Mon.* i. 471–6 and in *Reform and Rebellion*, pp. 375–6. Latin texts appear in *Ann. Mon.* i. 480–4, a poor attempt to translate the French, in *C.R. 1259–61*, pp. 146–50, in Cambridge U.L., MS. Mm. 1. 27, ff. 75–6. See introduction to document 11 for full discussion. The practice of translating French into Latin for publication in the law courts may be seen in document 5 where only clause 1 is in Latin.

out in the county courts. The clauses of document 11, which show the influence of documents 3 and 9,[1] may be divided into three main groups, (a) those which guard the rights of mesne tenants, (b) those which reform court procedure, (c) those which abolish abuses in the administration of justice.

The first section of clauses—those which guard the rights of mesne tenants—opens with clause 1 which defines obligations of suit of court. The second clause deals with suit due from a divided inheritance while clause 3 protects the mesne tenant from wrongful distraint. Clauses 9, 10, and 12 protect the rights of heirs while clause 16 allows a sub-tenant who feels that he has not received a just judgement in a feudal court to appeal to the king. Lastly, clauses 11, 17, and 18 restrict power of distraint, a threat which an overlord could use against his tenants. The second section, that which deals with reforms in court procedure, increases the time for hearing pleas of dower, *darrein presentment*, and *quare impedit* (cls. 6, 7). Clause 8 removes the inconvenience caused by royal grants of exemption from jury service and clause 15 minimizes the difficulties arising from essoins. The last section, which deals with abuses in the administration of justice, cancels, in clause 4, abuse by the sheriffs of their power to enforce attendance at the tourn while clause 5 abolishes fines for *beau plaider*. Power to fine for default of common summons is restricted (cl. 13) while clauses 21, 22, and 23 provide remedies against unjust fines. Those who are pledges for a clerk to appear in a lay court are excused liability if the clerk claims the right to answer in a court Christian (cl. 24). Three clauses do not fit into any of these groups. Clause 14 forbids the granting, by sub-tenants, of lands to monasteries without permission of the overlord from whom the monastery was to hold any such lands,[2] aid is given to those lords whose bailiffs default (cl. 19) and the actions of those who hold lands at lease are controlled (cl. 20). This document, number 11, marks the climax of the reform movement and the apex of the power of the Council of Fifteen.[3] It was a serious attempt to remedy abuses which had long tormented the realm, some of which had probably been revealed by information collected in the counties by the four knights, or

---

[1] See appendix 1.
[2] See 1217 issue of Magna Carta, cl. 43; doc. 3, cl. 10; Statute of Mortmain (Stubbs, pp. 343, 451).
[3] *Baronial Plan*, pp. 157 f.

which had come to light during the period when Hugh Bigod was in circuit. Furthermore, the steps taken to protect the small tenant from the power of the barons show the reformers making a serious effort to fulfil their promises.

The political and administrative clauses, which form document 12 and are only known in a French text,[1] record the problems which had been discussed both before and during the meetings of October 1259. As in document 11 the clauses in document 12 can be divided into three main groups, (a) decisions to complete political affairs already in hand, (b) articles to begin inquiries for the consideration of problems of local and central administration, (c) ordinances to facilitate the working of reforms already published. The first section touches on negotiations with the Welsh (cl. 11), the appointment of messengers to Rome (cl. 13), arrangements for the king to go to France,[2] and for the governance of the realm during his absence (cls. 10, 26). The second group of clauses, those which institute inquiries and commissions, is by far the largest. A special eyre was to be appointed to supervise the administration of justice (cl. 1)[3] and some aspects of the power of justices in eyre were defined (cl. 7). Arrangements were made for the court of common pleas and the exchequer (cl. 19, 28) while reforms of the exchequer and of the exchequer of the Jews were to be considered (cl. 23). Control of the wardships was organized (cls. 8, 14) and the judicial procedure for trial of cases involving wardship, escheat, warranty of charter, covenant, writs of trespass, and pleas of customs and services was to be amended (cls. 16, 17). Inquiry was to he held concerning the burdens of tallage (cl. 15),[4] castellans were to receive allowances for expenses (cl. 27), and an inquiry into the forests was planned (cls. 24, 25). Problems concerning sheriffs loom large. It was planned that sheriffs should hold office for only one year,[5] and as nineteen sheriffs had been appointed, between 23 October and 3 November 1258, to control twenty-eight counties the time had arrived for the appointment of new officials. The problem of choosing sheriffs

---

[1] *Ann. Mon.* i. 476–9; *Reform and Rebellion*, pp. 372–4.
[2] The king left England on 14 Nov. 1259 and did not return until 23 Apr. 1260. Negotiations with Rome were about Aymer de Lusignan. On Wales see *Baronial Plan*, pp. 194–5.　　　　　　　　　　　[3] This clause led to document 13.
[4] This involved a much closer supervision of royal revenue than was envisaged in doc. 5, cl. 17. See doc. 30, cl. 24; doc. 31, cl. 12.
[5] Doc. 5, cl. 17.

is mentioned in clause 9, while the final decision appears in clause 22. Each county was to choose four men at the meeting of the last county court before Michaelmas (29 September).[1] These four men were to appear before the exchequer at Michaelmas and the barons of the exchequer would choose the best man.[2] Clause 17 in document 5 had demanded that sheriffs should be vavasours of the county to which they were appointed, but left appointment to the king. This new clause in document 12 gives the counties a share in the choice of their sheriffs and is a step toward the election of that official in the county court: in 1265 the sheriff of Here-fordshire was chosen by election. Furthermore, these new rules made it possible for the small county squire to become the chief royal representative in the shire. The reformers were also deter-mined to maintain control of the sheriffs. Four knights were to be appointed to record wrongs done by the sheriffs (cls. 5, 20) and steps were taken to organize machinery to deal with *querulae* (cl. 18). There is also evidence that the more liberal reformers still exercised some influence, as clause 6 ordered inquiry into the actions both of great men and of their officers. Lastly, it was ordered that the rules which had been enacted were to be published and enforced (cls. 2, 12), Magna Carta and the charter of the forest were also to be enforced (cl. 3). The last group of clauses, those aimed at facilitating the working of the reforms, is small. Clause 4 forbids unsanctioned attendance under arms at parliaments, clause 7 orders that two or three councillors of middle rank should be in constant attendance on the king, a rota of service was to be organized, and arrangements were made to summon all the councillors if any problem arose. Once again, the influence of the more radical reformers may be seen: the great councillors were not to monopolize power, and a close scrutiny of the royal court was to be maintained. It was also enacted that the justiciar, chancellor, and treasurer should remain in power until the next parliament, February 1260.[3] The last clause of document 12 also

---

[1] This clause is evidence that the political and administrative problems had, like the legal problems, been considered before the October meeting.

[2] See doc. 12, n. 4.

[3] Doc. 12, n. 9; doc. 5, cls. 13–15 had ruled that these officials should remain in office for only one year. Bigod, the justiciar, continued in office until Oct. 1260, Wingham, the chancellor, continued until the same time. Lovel, the treasurer, was dismissed in Oct. 1258, his successor John Crakehall died in office in Sept. 1260.

supplies evidence of the continued existence of the government machinery planned in clause 22 of document 5. Just as document 10, dated February–March 1259, is an announcement 'by the king's council and the twelve elected by the community of England', so these regulations were made by the king and his council 'et les xii. par le commun conseil esluz par devant le communance de Engleterre'.[1]

As has been mentioned above, the administrative and political clauses were obviously not all compiled during the meeting of October 1259, for internal evidence shows that they originated in notes made during discussions at many meetings. The same topic appears in widely separated clauses. The royal visit to France appears in clauses 10 and 26,[2] wardships are mentioned in clauses 8, 14, and 17, sheriffs appear in clauses 9, 20, and 22, the court of common pleas and the exchequer occupy clauses 19 and 28, while plans for the administration of justice are scattered through clauses 1, 5, 16–18. Thus document 12 is a record of discussions by the Council of Fifteen, discussions which show that problems were being fully considered and that solutions were not being hastily improvised. The intention to continue to control the realm is evident and the interests of the small man, which had been recognized in document 11, were also being respected.

In the autumn of 1259 the Council of Fifteen was at the climax of its power. Steps were taken to implement decisions which had been finalized in the October parliament. On 4 November the appointment of Thomas de Grelley to keep the forests south of the Trent was confirmed, the castle of Rockingham, Northants., was placed in his care whilst the Council continued to exercise control over castles.[3] Sheriffs for 1259–60 were appointed by the

---

[1] Clause 22 of document 5 says that 'le commun elise xii prodes homes' and document 10 reads 'les duze esluz par le commun d' Engleterre.' The words used in document 12 are not exactly the same as those used on the former occasions. The statement 'par le commun conseil eluz' is a puzzle. *Le commun conseil* is obviously not the Council of Fifteen; it can only be assumed that it was a group distinct from the general mass of those who attended the parliament. The difficulty may arise only from loose phraseology as clause 28 speaks of the twelve elected by the *commun*. In any case the main point of interest is the fact that the practice of choosing twelve to represent the *commun* was still followed.

[2] References to the royal visit appear in letters dated in Aug. 1259 (*C.R. 1256–59*, p. 423; *C.P.R. 1258–66*, p. 39).

[3] *Baronial Plan*, pp. 192–4; *C.P.R. 1258–66*, p. 58. Grelley replaced Robert Walerand as one of the king's clerks. He had been appointed to control forests sometime before 23 Sept. 1259 (*C.R. 1256–59*, pp. 486–7). See doc. 12, cl. 24.

method described in clause 22 of document 12, all those who had
held office in 1258–9 being changed in obedience to clause 17
of document 5. Both the legal and administrative provisions were
enforced.[1]

The big task at this time was the organization of the eyre ordered
in clause 1 of document 12. Seven circuits were planned but the
whole of the realm was not covered. Counties north of the Trent
were excluded as were Surrey and Kent which had been visited
by Hugh Bigod between November 1258 and January 1259.[2]
The rule that 'one of the twelve or of the rest of the community'
should be on each circuit is changed in the opening clause of
document 13 which states that it had been provided that members
of the council should go on eyre. Furthermore, document 13
states that each of six circuits should be visited by one of the
council, one of the twelve, and a justice—the seventh circuit
covering south-east England was visited by Hugh Bigod alone.
The rule about councillors and one of the twelve was not fully
enforced. The eastern circuit was to be visited by a judge and
Philip Basset, one of the Council of Fifteen in 1259, but Basset
was replaced by a judge. One midland circuit was to be visited by
a judge and Hugh Despenser, one of the twelve, but Despenser
also was replaced by a judge, another midland circuit was to receive
a judge and James de Audley, a member of the Council of Fifteen,
but he was replaced by Philip Marmion. The counties of Gloucester, Hereford, and Worcester were to be the circuit of a judge
and the earl of Hereford, one of the Council of Fifteen, whilst
the south-west circuit was fully manned with a judge, the earl of
Warwick, one of the council, and John de Grey, one of the twelve.
Lastly, a circuit in the north was the province of a judge and two
of the twelve.[3] Thus on the six circuits four of the council were
nominated, but two were replaced, whilst of the four of the twelve
named one was excused. Nevertheless, except for the eastern
circuit which was visited by two judges, there was other representation on all the circuits. The absence of members of the council is
explained by the fact that six were with the king in France and
six were to be with the justiciar during the king's absence,[4] but
no reason can be given for the failure to appoint one of the twelve
to each of the six circuits.

---

[1] *Baronial Plan*, pp. 204–12.   [2] See notes to doc. 13.
[3] See ibid.   [4] Doc. 12, cl. 26.

The eyre which was instituted by letters dated 28 November—fourteen days after Henry III had left England and Hugh Bigod was regent—was to inquire into specified trespasses and to consider pleas which had been named in the legal provisions.[1] Sheriffs were to proclaim that all who wished to complain of trespasses suffered in the past seven years, which could be determined without writ and which were not pleas of the crown, should meet the justices at times and places to be announced. This is the first time that proceedings by *querulae* were authorized in an eyre. The community was to aid in the administration of justice, for twelve knights or other worthy men of each hundred were to inquire concerning the specified trespasses and report to the judges in January. Those who were accused were to appear before the judges at a time and place where the twelve who had conducted the inquiry could attend. All who had hindered justice by gifts to the king's officers were to admit their acts or suffer punishment when their actions were exposed. Those who had been royal or baronial officers during the past seven years were to appear before the judges at the same time as the twelve men from each hundred presented their report of trespasses committed in the past seven years, which could touch the actions of these officers. Complaints against royal and baronial officials were to be righted—the radical reformers still managed to press their demand that baronial officials should be treated in the same way as were royal officials. The justices were to ensure that the oath demanded from sheriffs and other royal officers had been taken from the bailiffs of nobles who had been granted charge of hundreds.[2] The instructions for the eyre ended with orders to inquire into matters which were usually only considered in a general eyre. Information was to be obtained about any rights which had been withdrawn from the king, about any wrongdoers and those who sheltered them. Inquiry was to be made to find if anyone had, since 2 February 1259, taken persons under their avowry[3] against the will of the lords of these persons. As far as is known business began in all the circuits, much against the will of the right wing of the Council of Fifteen many of whom were in France with the king.[4]

---

[1] Doc. 11, cls. 6, 7.
[2] Doc. 8.
[3] Avowry was forbidden in document 10.
[4] See doc. 12, cl. 26; doc. 26.

C. *The Revival of the King's Power*

Henry was absent from the realm between 14 November 1259 and 23 April 1260. On the surface the position of the Council of Fifteen seemed secure but the foundations of its power were being undermined. The king's departure weakened the machinery of administration—the chancery lost some of its key men and the Council was divided. Six of the Council and three of the twelve were with the king. Of these nine only three were left-wing reformers, Leicester, Giles de Argentin, and Peter de Montfort, the others were royalists, Peter of Savoy and John Mansel, or right-wing like the earl of Gloucester. Attendance at the king's court subjected the councillors to strong royal pressure which was strengthened by the influence of the French king whose wife was sister of the English queen. The strained relations between Gloucester and Leicester continued, with the influence of Henry III and Louis IX being thrown against de Montfort, a factor which weakened the position of the left-wing reformers of whom he was the leader.

Meanwhile the king was determined to regain power. In January 1260 he reopened negotiations with the papacy hoping to renew the claim of his son Edmund to the Sicilian crown. Furthermore, Henry prolonged his stay in France for reasons which he gave in document 14, a letter written to Hugh Bigod. The king states that the death of Louis, eldest son of the king of France, had hindered the marriage of Beatrice, Henry's daughter, while problems arising from the fulfilment of the Peace of Paris, completed on 3 December 1259, were causing difficulty. Mention is made of Welsh attacks in south-east Wales before the king comes to a point of supreme importance. No parliament, which according to clause 21 of document 5 should assemble on 3 February, was to meet during the king's absence from the realm. Similar letters were written to the Lord Edward who at this time supported the more radical reformers, and to Richard of Cornwall.[1] It cannot be proved that Henry was deliberately delaying his return to England in order to increase the difficulties of the radical reformers but the demand that no parliament should meet in his absence was a blow which struck at the very foundations of the plan to control the government of the realm. The reformers at Oxford in 1258 had planned

[1] This is stated at the end of document 14.

the creation of machinery which could act independently of the royal whim. Parliament was to meet three times a year, needing no royal summons and thus creating a link between the Council of Fifteen and the nation. The king's letter reduced parliament to the position which it had occupied before 1258—to being an assembly which met and dispersed at the royal will; the link between the reformers in London and the nation was to be broken. Simon de Montfort saw the implications of the royal command and forcefully expressed his opposition. He returned to England about the middle of January and on 3 February, when parliament should meet, Simon and 'other sound councillors' came to London where they met the justiciar who told them of the royal command. Furthermore, Hugh Bigod, the justiciar, stated that as the king planned to return to England within three weeks the assembly of parliament was adjourned for that time.[1] On 10 February at St. Albans the earl of Leicester strongly demanded that parliament should meet, asserting that parliament was being reduced to a feudal council, that the very foundations of the plan for reform were being destroyed. In addition he protested against sending any money to Henry, and there was a hint of possible armed opposition to the king. De Montfort's activities in England probably influenced document 15, a letter written on 19 February 1260 by the king[2] to those nine members of the Council of Fifteen who were in England. Henry expressed his thanks for the good will of those to whom he had written and his pleasure on hearing of the peaceful state of the realm. He explained his continued absence from England and repeated the order that parliament should not meet in his absence. In July 1260, when accusing Simon of disloyalty and sedition, the king claimed that the earl had held a parliament, thus disobeying the royal command.[3] De Montfort denied the charge and as there is no other evidence of such an assembly it would seem that this, like many others of Henry's accusations, was baseless. A letter from the councillors urged the king to return to England and in his reply, dated 1 March 1260 (doc. 16), the king mentioned the difficulties arising from the Peace of Paris, asked for advice and money, and promised a speedy

[1] Doc. 29, cl. 31.
[2] This was an answer to a letter dated 7 Feb. which Philip Marmion and Simon Passelewe had brought from England.
[3] Doc. 29, cls. 35, 36.

return. A letter of the same date, to the Lord Edward (doc. 17), says that John de Darlington had brought the prince's letters to the king. Henry says that he was pleased to hear of Edward's activities and intentions which had been puzzling. The prince had supported the *bacheleria* in October 1259, he had quarrelled with the earl of Gloucester, the leading royalist among the reformers, and had become friendly with de Montfort. Nothing is known of what was reported to the king about Edward's intentions. The prince may have promised to mend his ways, and may have explained his actions as part of a scheme to divide the ranks of the reformers.

Henry's request for advice and money appears to have been in vain, for on 6 March the king wrote to the earl of Norfolk and other strong royalists (doc. 18) asking about the state of the realm and the possibility of his safe return to England. News of unrest in the country must have reached the king. The earl of Leicester was in London, Peter of Savoy, the queen's uncle, resigned from the Council of Fifteen,[1] and there is evidence that the Lord Edward was still supporting Leicester. Those who demanded that a parliament should assemble despite the king's absence announced that such an assembly would meet on about 18 or 25 April, ample warning to the king. On 9 March Henry received £1,000, and throughout March his demands for money increased.[2] The king had decided that it was necessary to assemble a force of Flemish and French mercenaries to accompany him to England.[3] The nineteenth document is a letter from the king repeating his request for information about the state of the realm and for advice about returning to England; on the same day Hugh Bigod and others were ordered to 'treat with magnates of the realm'. In addition Bigod was to summon named people to be in London three weeks after Easter (25 April).[4] On 1 April the king wrote to the earl of Gloucester (doc. 20) stating that although he had received permission from Louis IX to muster knights in France

---

[1] The king claimed that Peter had been expelled by De Montfort. The earl claimed that he had resigned voluntarily but admitted that the council had considered replacing Peter (doc. 29, cl. 33).

[2] *Baronial Plan*, p. 221, n. 6; *C.R. 1259–61*, pp. 240, 244, 246; *C.P.R. 1258–66*, pp. 119, 121–3.

[3] *Baronial Plan*, pp. 227–8. Much of the money which Henry received from Louis IX under the terms of the Peace of Paris was used to hire mercenaries (doc. 29, cl. 39; *Peace of Paris*, p. 57).

[4] *C.P.R. 1258–66*, p. 123; doc. 21.

few or none would come to England without him. Henry said that he was ashamed at his long absence, promised to return soon to aid Gloucester. Steps were taken to fulfil this promise, as the king announced that he would attend the assembly called to London for 25 April, and shipping was to collect to bring the king from Wissant on 18 April.[1] Meanwhile the situation in England was deteriorating. The earl of Leicester's opposition to the king found expression in increased opposition to sending money to France, and it was rumoured that he threatened to stop Henry from entering England if mercenaries were with the king.[2] De Montfort's forces were mustering, and together with the Lord Edward they were camped to the north of the Thames while the followers of the earl of Gloucester gathered to the south of the river. In addition Leicester was summoning aid from France.[3] The king believed that his enemies were preparing to hold a parliament and that the Lord Edward planned to seize the houses of the bishop of London near St. Paul's cathedral. In order to save London from attack, Henry, in 10 April, wrote both to Hugh Bigod and to the mayor and community of London (doc. 22) ordering them to forbid anyone suspected of plotting against the realm—the Lord Edward is especially named—to stay within the city walls. On the other hand Earl Warenne, husband of Alice de Lusignan, was to be given accommodation at the New Temple or at Clerkenwell. The following day, 11 April, the earl of Gloucester and others were called upon to muster men from the county of Kent to meet the king when he arrived at Dover (doc. 23). Threats of civil war and attacks on England were rumoured. The vicomte of Limoges, aided by the king's half brothers, the Lusignans, was believed to be planning to land in Cornwall to assert claims on that county. Richard of Cornwall was asked to resist this attack (doc. 24), while letters were sent to the duke of Brittany and to Louis IX asking for their aid.[4]

The impending muster at London, called for 25 April 1260 (doc. 21), increased the tension in the city. On 10 April the king had ordered Hugh Bigod and the mayor of London to refuse entry to anyone whom they suspected of evil intent. When he

---

[1] *C.R. 1259–61*, pp. 250–1.   [2] Doc. 29, cl. 39.
[3] *C.R. 1259–61*, pp. 277, 283; doc. 25. It should not be forgotten that Simon was by birth a Frenchman himself.
[4] Doc. 25; *C.R. 1259–61*, p. 286. Henry's daughter Beatrice had married the son of the duke (doc. 14).

arrived at Dover on 23 April Henry took further precautions to ensure that London would not fall into the hands of his enemies. The mayor and citizens were ordered to allow entry and accommodation only to those named by Philip Basset and Robert Walerand.[1] Reassured, Henry approached London cautiously, reaching the city on 30 April and occupying the palace of the bishop of London near St. Paul's. De Montfort and the Lord Edward were still under arms, tension continuing for a few days until Richard of Cornwall and Boniface of Savoy, archbishop of Canterbury, mediated and Edward was reconciled with his father. The king, determined to reassert his authority, summoned a parliament to meet at St. Paul's probably in the first half of May. Flushed with his initial success the king was determined to attack de Montfort, who had been deserted by the Lord Edward, but for unknown reasons Henry was persuaded to delay action against the earl until the parliament, the meeting of which had been postponed until July.[2] Meanwhile, although the authority of the Council of Fifteen was, in theory, recognized there is much evidence to show that only the royalist members of this group were active. An increasing number of writs were issued solely on the authority of the crown, or of the chancellor alone, while the power of the wardrobe was reviving.[3] Henry's power was growing, he dismissed the mercenaries whom he had brought from France, gifts were made to favourites, and on 5 June he cancelled the special eyre which had been set up in November 1259,[4] the claim that this was done because of distress resulting from famine being, doubtless, only an excuse. A more valid reason for cancelling the eyre was to reward those who had supported him in the spring of 1260; such men, royalist and right-wing reformers, were opposed to the plan to inquire into the activities of baronial officials. Furthermore, the stopping of the eyre was a decisive stroke against the implementation of the plan of reform and a blow to destroy the morale of the left-wing reformers. Meanwhile, although the quarrel between the earl of Gloucester and the Lord Edward had been healed,[5] the king took special precautions to ensure the peace of the realm during the coming parliament in July 1260. The barons and bailiffs

[1] Doc. 26; *Baronial Plan*, pp. 229–30.
[2] Ibid., p. 233. The date fixed in doc. 5, cl. 21, 1 June, was too soon.
[3] Doc. 5, n. 17.   [4] Doc. 27. See docs. 12, 13.
[5] *C.P.R. 1258–66*, p. 79.

of Dover, together with 'the barons of all the ports', presumably the Cinque Ports, were ordered to ensure that no papal bulls prejudicial to the king entered the realm. The landing of armed men was to be opposed, and any who arrived were to be arrested and held, pending orders from the king.[1]

D. The King, Supported by the Pope, Asserts his Power

Preparations began to bring de Montfort to trial in the July parliament. A committee consisting of the archbishop of Canterbury, the bishops of London, Lincoln, Worcester, Norwich, and Exeter, or any four of them, was to hold a preliminary inquiry and report to the Council. The Council, together with an unspecified number of earls and barons, would then decide the amends to be made by Simon for any transgressions of which he was found guilty.[2] The document resulting from this investigation has survived (doc. 29). Clauses 1–22 refer to difficulties between the king and Simon, and their influence on the negotiations for the Peace of Paris of 1259. De Montfort's part in initiating and continuing negotiations with France, and Countess Eleanor's demands appear in the first three clauses, while the difficulties arising from Eleanor's refusal to renounce her claim to lands in France are mentioned in many clauses.[3] The king's claim that he had met Eleanor's demands for dower from the Marshal lands was not fully accepted by Simon[4] and the difficulties arising from Bigorre appear in clauses 12, 16, 17. The rest of the document, clauses 23–39, touches on varied topics. The earl was accused of trying to stop the marriage of the king's daughter (cl. 23), of being the leader of the movement forcing the Lusignans to leave England (cl. 24),[5] and of causing the expulsion of Peter of Savoy from the council (cl. 33). Henry continued his attack by asserting that Leicester had held a parliament in February 1260, that he had

[1] Doc. 28; *Baronial Plan*, pp. 238–9.
[2] The arrangements for this inquiry are printed by E. F. Jacob under the title 'A proposal for arbitration between Simon de Montfort and Henry III in 1260', *E.H.R.* xxxvii (1922), 80–2. Treharne criticizes many of Jacob's statements (*Baronial Plan*, p. 239, n. 1).
[3] Cls. 4–7, 13, 19, 20, 22. Louis IX's refusal to pay 15,000 marks is mentioned in cl. 21.
[4] Cls. 8, 10, 11, 14–16, 18. Problems arising from the Council's control of the royal demesne are mentioned in cl. 9.
[5] On the other hand the king accused Simon of having secretly made peace with the Lusignans (cl. 25).

attended this assembly under arms despite the fact that this had
been forbidden.[1] The king complained because de Montfort
had left France before him (cls. 27, 28), and accused Simon of
plotting to threaten the peace of the realm and of stopping Bigod
from sending money to France. Lastly the earl's actions had forced
the king to bring a large force of mercenaries to England.[2] De
Montfort's answers were skilful and, at times, counter-attacked
the king. Difficulties from Eleanor's claims arose, Simon said,
from the king's failure to fulfil his side of the bargain (cl. 19).
Doubts were cast on the truth of some of Henry's statements,
responsibility was denied and, on several occasions, the king was
said to be in error.[3] On many occasions the earl's answers involved
the Council,[4] so that if the king wished to press the attack the
whole Council would be included.

The attack on Simon failed, for the Council refused to condemn
him and he was acquitted by parliament. On the other hand, despite
this defeat, the king was, by the middle of 1260, in a strong position.
A powerful group of councillors were his allies, while the rest of
the baronage was divided into loyalists and a few Montfortians.
Threats from the Welsh turned attention to the west. A twofold
attack was planned for September, Simon was to be occupied by
being in command of the army assembling at Chester.[5] Nothing
came of the proposed expeditions, as peace was made before 1 September when the musters were cancelled and the earl left England
before the parliament which assembled *circa* 13 October 1260.

In the early summer of 1260 it is very probable that real power
in the realm rested with those few right-wing councillors who were
permanently in attendance at court.[6] Consequently the king's
wishes were respected, the vacant see of Durham was placed in
the care of John Mansel, a leading 'civil servant', wardships were
granted, and the wardrobe was active in finance. However, the
October 1260 parliament reminded the king that the scheme of
government planned at Oxford in 1258 still existed, for the
assembly was less under royal influence than were the councillors.
The royalist justiciar Hugh Bigod was replaced by Hugh Despenser,
a friend of the earl of Leicester with whom he died at Evesham in

[1] Cls. 26, 29–32, 35, 36; doc. 12, cl. 4.   [2] Cls. 34, 36–9.
[3] Cls. 5, 19, 20, 32, 34–6.   [4] Cls. 1, 23, 24, 31, 33, 39.
[5] *Baronial Plan*, p. 243; Lloyd, *History of Wales*, ii. 727–8.
[6] Doc. 12, cl. 7.

1265. Henry de Wingham, chancellor since 1255, gave way to Nicholas de Ely while John de Crakehall, who had died in September 1260, was succeeded by John de Caux, abbot of Peterborough. Although the three new officers may not be called partisans in 1260, the king had lost the official support of Bigod and Wingham, staunch royalists. The actions of the parliament, however, did not stop the steady trend toward the king. There is a noticeable lack of drive to effect reforms. Thus the annual change of the sheriffs, which had been ordered at Oxford in 1258, did not take place although it was due. In addition there is evidence that the earlier work of the reformers was being undone. On 20 October Richard of Cornwall was allowed 'in pursuance of an ordinance made by the whole Council that every magnate of the realm shall have the power of correcting the excesses of his bailiffs and sergeants when complaint is made to him of their trespasses' to take steps 'touching the excesses and trespasses of his . . . bailiffs . . .' On 21 January 1261 the justiciar and justices were ordered not to hear complaints against Richard of Cornwall's officers, who were to appear before him.[1] Thus one of the most important decisions of the reformers, to make baronial officials answer for their misdeeds before royal judges, was set aside. Furthermore, when in November and December 1260 an eyre was ordered for January 1261 the articles were of the pre-1258 type. No investigation of grievances against royal or baronial officials was ordered, only two circuits were planned, and none of the Council of Fifteen or of the twelve representing the *commun* were named, as had been the case in November 1259 (doc. 13). In addition, the king's power had become great enough for him to dispense with the Council. Although the last formal order by the Council of Fifteen is dated 28 December 1260, and there is some evidence that it and the twelve continued until the March parliament of 1261,[2] both groups disappear after this and the king was free to act alone.

Henry took active steps to rule as he wished. He was in negotiations with the papacy to be freed from his oaths to obey the Council, negotiations which bore fruit with the bull of absolution

---

[1] *C.P.R. 1258–66*, p. 97; *C.R. 1259–61*, p. 335. Misprint in *Baronial Plan*, p. 246.

[2] *C.Ch.R.* ii. 35; *C.P.R. 1258–66*, pp. 142, 149; Richardson, *T.R.H.S.* 4th ser. v (1922), 61; doc. 31, cl. 19 *et passim*.

issued on 13 April 1261 (doc. 32). To ensure his control of London the king left Windsor on 8 February 1261 and took up residence in the Tower of London where he remained until 24 April. On 13 February all Londoners above twelve years of age were ordered to take an oath of fealty to the king. The city gates were specially guarded, while on 17 February twenty-seven nobles were summoned to London under arms as rumour made these precautions necessary.[1] When a parliament assembled, probably at the beginning of March 1261,[2] the king acted independently. New keepers were appointed to royal castles, sheriffs were summoned to London for Henry to assure himself of their loyalty, and all possible sources were tapped for money. The king's actions alarmed the nobles, who asked him to state his complaints so that they could take steps to remove those things which annoyed him. After some controversy it was agreed that a board of three arbitrators should be appointed to hear Henry's complaints and receive the replies of the council. Henry, in the words of Thomas Wykes, 'began to frame vigorous articles against the barons with reasons to show that he was not bound by the Provisions'.[3]

The arguments and claims expressed by both sides at the meeting held before the arbiters are preserved in document 31, written in Norman French; document 30 is a Latin text of some of the king's complaints. N. Denholm-Young, who has published document 30,[4] has claimed that the manuscript dates from March 1260 but F. M. Powicke has argued that it is contemporary with document 31.[5] The more interesting of the two is document 31 which records the Council's answers to the king's complaints. Henry asserted that his status and dignity were degraded; he lacked money, could not choose officials, the royal castles were neglected, he was scorned.[6] Justice was not administered, lawlessness and the misdeeds of officials were unpunished, while the Council was

---

[1] C.R. 1259–61, p. 457; Baronial Plan, p. 251.

[2] Ibid. Evidence upon which Treharne claims that the king summoned parliament to meet on 23 Feb. is faulty. British Chronology, p. 503, quotes Treharne.

[3] Ann. Mon. iv. 125. This appears under 1259 but Wykes is very muddled at this point. He confuses events of 1259–60 with those of 1260–1 and runs the two narratives into a single year.

[4] E.H.R. xlviii (1933), 572–5; Collected Papers, pp. 127–9.

[5] King Henry III, p. 421, n. 3. See doc. 30, introduction, for discussion of the relationship between the two documents.

[6] Cls. 1, 4, 7–9, 12, 16, 17.

blamed for difficulties arising from the Sicilian negotiations, for trouble in completing the business of the Peace of Paris, and for losses in Wales.[1] The complaints about France were answered in a significant phrase: it was stated 'let the Council come together in one place' and they will consider the problem. This suggests that the Council had met in March 1261 only at the king's pleasure. It may even mean that the Council itself did not all meet at this time, and that the answers were given by a few representatives.

The royal complaints, true or false, which were raked up from every possible corner, are an outward sign of Henry's determination to be rid of the whole system of control which had been created since the meeting at Oxford in June 1258. The answers which were given vindicated the actions of the Council,[2] but this did not change Henry's will to regain complete freedom of action. He had agreed to arbitration as a means of gaining time in order to establish his power more firmly. Ever since 1259 Henry had been in secret negotiation with the papacy concerning Sicily, promising to pay his debts to Rome, and seeking support and absolution from his oaths. On 13 April 1261 a papal bull granted absolution from Henry's oath to 'observe certain statutes, ordinances and other things' (doc. 32). Toward the end of the same month a papal bull allowed Boniface of Savoy and others to absolve clergy and magnates from similar oaths with a threat of ecclesiastical censure against all opponents (doc. 33). A third bull, issued on 7 May, gave power to the archbishop and others to warn all who had been bound by oaths to be faithful and dutiful subjects of the king, once again excommunication or interdict being used as a threat (doc. 34). The three bulls were published at Winchester on 12 June 1261, and at the same time the king was working to increase his power.

On 24 April 1261 the Lord Edward, who had been abroad since November 1260, returned to England accompanied by William de Valence, one of the Lusignans who had been expelled in July 1258; and other aliens were allowed to return.[3] At the beginning of May royal constables were appointed to castles in southern England and on 25 May John Mansel was placed in control of the Tower of London. Royal sheriffs were appointed on 8–9 July and the administrative power of the royal household was being

---

[1] Cls. 2, 3, 10, 11, 13–15, 18–29.   [2] *Baronial Plan*, pp. 253–6.
[3] *Baronial Plan*, p. 256.

restored. Hugh Despenser, who had succeeded Hugh Bigod as justiciar in October 1260, was replaced in June 1261 by Philip Basset while the chancellor Nicholas of Ely, also appointed in October 1260, gave way to Walter de Merton formerly temporary keeper of the seal.[1]

The rapid growth of the royal power made the nobles realize that all their work for reform was in danger. On 5 July 1261 a suggested board of arbiters was appointed to consider the quarrel between the king and Simon de Montfort; the duke of Burgundy and Peter the Chamberlain were to mediate if agreement could not be reached.[2] On 20 July Henry announced that the attempted arbitration had failed and asked the queen of France, his wife's sister, to consider the conflict between him and the earl.[3] On the other hand the bishop of Worcester, the earls of Leicester, Norfolk, Gloucester, Warenne, and Hugh Bigod asked Louis IX to intervene. The growing power of the king was certainly reuniting those who had followed very different paths since early in 1259. Henry was not to be restrained; on 16 August he issued a letter justifying his actions.[4] This forced the nobles to more drastic action for they summoned three knights from each shire to meet them at St. Albans on 21 September 1261.[5] Thus the nobility opposed to the king sought the support of the county class which had been growing in importance since 1258. The revolutionary step of calling an assembly without the king's assent was possible because when Henry, early in July, changed the sheriffs many of those who had been appointed in the autumn of 1259 refused to surrender office to the royal appointees. Thus the reformers had supporters in the counties to execute the commands which they issued. In order to forestall the meeting which the reformers had called to St. Albans for 21 September the king announced that he would be meeting the nobles at Windsor on that day to negotiate an

---

[1] See docs. 21, 31, 37B.

[2] *C.P.R. 1258–66*, p. 162. See docs. 14, 15 for Peter the Chamberlain. Hugh IV, duke of Burgundy accompanied Simon on crusade in 1239–40 (*Simon de Montfort*, p. 65; A. Kleinclausz, *Histoire de Bourgogne* (1909)).

[3] *C.P.R. 1258–66*, p. 169; Bémont, *Simon de Montfort*, pp. 331–2. The initial of the Christian name of the duke of Burgundy is wrongly given as B. in *C.P.R.*, loc. cit. The queen of France had been considered as a possible arbiter early in 1261.

[4] *C.P.R. 1258–66*, p. 173. Full text *Foedera*, i. i. 408–9.

[5] This information is contained in a letter issued by the king (doc. 35). There is no other evidence of the truth of this statement.

agreement. The knights who had been chosen to go to St. Albans were to come to Windsor. Henry's action was successful, the meeting at St. Albans did not take place and there is no evidence of an assembly at Windsor: the king's summons had killed St. Albans but opposition in the land was strong enough to stop an alternative meeting.

Those who had united against Henry in July 1261 could not remain allies, despite the growing royal power. In the middle of October 1261 the earl of Gloucester was in negotiation with the king, while Simon de Montfort had left England disgusted at the fickleness of those who had joined him three months earlier. Henry summoned a large number of his followers to muster in London on 29 October, and steps were taken to collect a large force of mercenaries who were to land at ports controlled by Richard of Cornwall if they were opposed at the Cinque Ports.[1] At the same time opposition to the king in the counties, which had hindered the royal appointees in July 1261, found expression in the dismissal of the king's sheriffs and the appointment of county wardens.[2] The country seemed to be on the verge of civil war but negotiations took place. On 20 October 1261 the king issued a safe conduct, lasting until 1 November, for those nobles who were coming to Kingston-on-Thames on 29 October to make peace; later letters extended the safe conduct until 13 November.[3] On 21 November an agreement called the Treaty of Kingston was made; six arbiters, three royal and three baronial, were to discuss grievances arising from the Provisions of Oxford (doc. 5).[4] Richard of Cornwall was to arbitrate in cases of disagreement. In addition, the problem of the appointment of sheriffs (the royal nominees of July 1261 having been opposed by county wardens) was to be considered and Richard of Cornwall or Louis IX was to arbitrate if no agreement could be reached.[5] It was also stated that any opposition to the agreement must end by 6 January 1262; in fact the terms of the agreement were ratified on 9 December 1261. The king remained in control. De Montfort was in France, the king's opponents were divided, the Council of Fifteen had not

---

[1] C.R. 1259–61, pp. 495–7; Royal Letters, ii. 193–4.
[2] C.P.R. 1258–66, p. 178.   [3] Ibid., pp. 179, 189, 190.
[4] Baronial Plan, p. 279; Foedera, 1. i. 415.
[5] C.R. 1261–64, p. 126; Royal Letters, ii. 174–5, 197–8; Baronial Plan, pp. 272, 279, n. 5. Mistake in editing, Royal Letters, ii. 174–5; mistake Baronial Plan, p. 272, November 1 not 8.

been restored, baronial county wardens were dismissed, and royal sheriffs were in control. Lands and money were given to foreign favourites, and although the 1261 eyre was renewed[1] no provision was made for *querulae*—cases which could be heard without writ —the main channel by which complaint could be made against officials. Thomas Wykes says that a parliament met in London *circa* 2 February 1262 when the king and nobles appealed to Richard of Cornwall and Louis IX to act as arbiters.[2]

Henry's power continued to grow. Alexander IV, the pope who had issued the three bulls in April and May 1261 (docs. 32–4), had died on 25 May 1261; he was succeeded by Urban IV. The king was once again in touch with Rome[3] and on 25 February 1262 a bull was issued ordering that the terms of the three previous documents should be obeyed (doc. 36); the bull was published in London some time in March 1262.[4] On 2 May 1262 Henry announced that although the Charter of Liberties and the charter of the forest would be respected all enactments since the time of the Provisions of Oxford were cancelled; sheriffs were to arrest those who did not accept this ruling.[5] On 20 May Richard of Cornwall ruled, and on 28 May the king announced, that the Provisions of Oxford were cancelled, a statement, according to the Osney Chronicler,[6] accepted by the nobles but not by the earl of Leicester who was in France.

E. *The Threat of Civil War; Arbitration by Louis IX*

Henry now felt secure enough to leave England on 14 July 1262, and go to France; the justiciar Philip Basset was regent. In contrast to his visit to France from November 1259 to April 1260, none of the important nobles now accompanied him. The king, who was determined to discredit the earl of Leicester, tried to find evidence while he was in France.[7] Henry's confidence in his power proved to be excessive. On 15 July 1262 Richard, earl of Gloucester, the leader of the royalist reformers and main opponent of de Montfort, died. The royal administration was unbelievably foolish in its treatment of Richard's heir Gilbert, who was not quite nineteen

---

[1] *C.P.R. 1258–66*, pp. 200, 227.
[2] *Ann. Mon.* iv. 130. Wykes also records meetings in London in Apr. and May 1262 to discuss topics arising from the Treaty of Kingston (ibid., pp. 130–1).
[3] *Baronial Plan*, pp. 275–9.   [4] *Lib. de Ant. Leg.* p. 49.
[5] *C.R. 1261–64*, p. 123.   [6] Ibid., p. 126; *Ann. Mon.* iv. 130.
[7] *Baronial Plan*, pp. 280–4.

years old. Although the crown acted within its rights, the granting of the heir's estates to keepers was not a tactful way to treat the most powerful and richest of all the feudal lords. Other acts of the crown so annoyed Gilbert de Clare that he became a very active centre of unrest. Trouble also arose in the household of the Lord Edward, who made demands upon his steward Roger de Leybourne. Roger, whose lands were seized by Edward,[1] obtained the support of his brother-in-law Roger Clifford, Lord of Clifford in Herefordshire and half the barony of Appleby, Westmorland,[2] together with many of the Marcher lords. Unrest developed and on 25 August 1262 the justiciar took the precaution of forbidding the holding of tournaments which, because of the assembly of armed men, could become centres of unrest. These difficulties were increased by a threat from Wales, for the truce which had been made in August 1260 had ended. Attempts to renew the agreement failed, the storm broke, and in November 1262 the Welsh seized much of Roger Mortimer's lands.[3] This event increased the Marcher lords' enmity towards the king as Peter d'Aigueblanche, a Savoyard and bishop of Hereford, favourite of Henry, was blamed for the troubles. Meanwhile the royal household in France was smitten, early in September, with an epidemic which struck down and killed some sixty of the English court. Both the king and the queen fell ill; when he recovered Henry decided to go on a pilgrimage to Burgundy although his business in France was finished and despite the news which came from England.

The unrest in the realm, arising from troubles in the Marches and the conflict between the Lord Edward and de Leybourne, grew as many had been alienated by the king's actions. In October 1262 Simon de Montfort appeared in London before an assembly of nobles. He claimed to be in possession of a papal bull which cancelled the document which Urban IV had issued in support of the king.[4] Having produced this bombshell the earl withdrew to France. On 20 December 1262 Henry returned to the turmoil which tore England apart. In addition the Welsh were devastating the present-day counties of Hereford, Brecon, and Radnor.[5] To

---

[1] *C.R. 1261–64*, pp. 117, 171.   [2] *English Baronies*, p. 104.

[3] *Baronial Plan*, pp. 291 f.

[4] Bémont doubts the truth of Leicester's claims (*Simon de Montfort* (Paris, 1884), p. 198, n. 1). Treharne believes that Simon was speaking the truth (*Baronial Plan*, p. 289, n. 9).

[5] *Baronial Plan*, pp. 291–9.

win support Henry announced on 12 January 1263 that he had
reissued the Provisions of Westminster (doc. 11) with some added
clauses.[1] In addition the Lord Edward was sent to France to
collect a military force. The situation in England was made more
explosive by the fact that some of those who had taken the lead
in 1258, the earl of Gloucester, the earl of Warwick, John fitz
Geoffrey, and the bishop of London had died. These men had
been succeeded by younger men, such as Gilbert de Clare, who
were impatient and demanded action. The earl of Leicester had
not interfered in England since he left in October 1262, and waited
his time to act. Late in April 1263 Simon returned, and at the
start of May met Gilbert de Clare and other nobles at Oxford.
Here the oaths of 1258 (doc. 5, cls. 4, 5) were renewed, and all
promised to treat as enemies those who opposed the Provisions
of Oxford. Henry refused a demand that he observe the Provisions,
so the Oxford nobles joined the Marchers and others who were
under arms. The earl of Leicester made his headquarters in
Gloucester and reached an agreement with the Welsh leader
Llywelyn for co-operation against the king.[2]

The king's opponents were strong enough in June to occupy
Bridgnorth and Worcester, while a detached group seized control
of Salisbury. The Lord Edward occupied the town and castle of
Dover in the middle of June in order to keep open a road to
France. Henry went to the Tower of London but the administration of the city had collapsed, leaving bands of lawless men in
control. Having refused the attempts of Richard of Cornwall to
arbitrate the earl of Leicester left the town of Gloucester at the
end of June. He moved to south-east England, gained control of
the area, and on 12 July 1263 Henry was forced to seek peace.
Meanwhile de Montfort had announced his plans. The Londoners
were asked to declare for or against the Provisions of Oxford;
any rules harmful to the king or the realm were to be amended,
Henry must accept the enactments which had been made by the
former Council of Fifteen, and the king must govern only through
Englishmen. On 16 July Henry surrendered,[3] Simon occupied the
city on 22 July, and the king returned to Westminster whilst the

---

[1] C.P.R. 1258–66, p. 253. All the chroniclers call these the Provisions of
Oxford. See doc. 5, n. 2 and Baronial Plan, p. 296, n. 6.

[2] Lloyd, History of Wales, ii. 732–3.

[3] C.P.R. 1258–66, pp. 269–70. The king's acceptance of the Provisions and
the oaths of obligation was sealed with the seal of Richard of Cornwall.

Lord Edward was forced to surrender Windsor castle—an insult which he never forgot or forgave. Simon was now in full control, so it seemed.

The earl of Leicester sought to rebuild the former machinery of administration which had been created by the reformers. As in the years 1258–60, when the reformers exercised power, a parliament met in London on 13 October 1263, but no decisions or action of any importance resulted. An attempt was made to revive the Council of Fifteen but Simon found little support for this plan. Because the shires were in the hands of royal sheriffs, wardens were appointed to co-operate with them. The greatest need, however, was to enforce peace and reach an agreement with the king. Both these problems proved to be insoluble. Those who had suffered at the hands of the supporters of Roger de Leybourne, and of other marauders since the middle of 1262, opposed de Montfort who, in their eyes, was the leader of these lawless men, while the Marchers were alienated by the earl's agreement with Llywelyn. Gilbert de Clare, who had been alienated from the crown, was becoming jealous of de Montfort's power, and the Lord Edward, ever seeking revenge, won the support of Henry of Almain and of Earl Warenne, husband of a Lusignan. Additional troubles were caused by bands of armed men who attacked and seized some towns such as Bury St. Edmunds. Simon tried to reach an agreement with the king. On 9 September 1263 a 'general peace' between the two men was ratified and later in the same month they met Louis IX at Boulogne in an effort to settle their differences.[1]

During all this time de Montfort was exercising only a shadow of power. The first blow fell when the Lord Edward regained control of Windsor castle where he was joined by his father on 16 October. On 17 October the king announced, in order to win public support, that he had no intention of infringing the Provisions of Oxford. He gained full control of the chancery and the exchequer, sheriffs were ordered to ignore the wardens whom de Montfort had appointed, and counties were organized in groups, each group being controlled by a peace custodian who had military responsibilities. Armed forces were mustered and an attempt was made to control Dover castle which was in the hands of Richard de Grey, a faithful Montfortian. In September absolution from

[1] C.R. 1261–64, p. 312.

the oaths which Henry had taken was granted by the pope and in December 1263 Guy Foulques, servant of the French royal family, cardinal-bishop of Sabina, later Clement IV (1265–9), was appointed papal legate to England with orders to restore the king's power. The royalists mustered, many of Simon's tepid supporters deserted him, and the possibility of civil war developed.

Richard of Cornwall tried to arbitrate. The earl of Leicester, who came to London from Kenilworth, was nearly seized by royal plotters. This did not create a good atmosphere for agreement, but in the middle of December both sides agreed to allow Louis IX to arbitrate.[1] Henry III reached Amiens where he was to stay 12–27 January 1264; an accident stopped Simon from going to France where the reformers were represented by Peter de Montfort and others.[2] The royal case is presented in document 37A[3] which may be divided into eight clauses complaining of the actions of the reformers and requesting a cancellation of 'all ordinances, statutes, and obligations'. The king expressed opposition to the reformers appointing his officials, great and small, and members of his household (cls. 1–5). He asserted that he had been robbed of the power to control his ministers (cl. 6), that his opponents had ravaged the lands and property of the crown and of those faithful to the king (cl. 7). Furthermore, there were other reasons for conflict, to be revealed later, which had caused damage for which the king demanded £300,000 compensation and an additional 200,000 marks (cl. 8). Henry asked Louis to cancel all provisions, statutes, and obligations, especially as those had been quashed by the pope, and to restore the royal power to the full. Document 37B states the barons' case in three sections. They explain their actions in 1258 and describe the appointment of the Council of Twenty-Four whose actions are stated. The fact that the king had accepted the actions of the twenty-four is stressed (cls. 1–3). In addition they ask that the arbiter should consider all points of difference between the two sides, and assert that they have an 'infinite multitude' of supporters (cls. 4–6). The second section of document 37B

[1] *C.P.R. 1258–66*, pp. 303–4. Text in full in *Royal Letters*, ii. 251–2 and *Foedera*, I. i. 433–4. There are mistakes in both these texts. See doc. 38 where this document appears.

[2] *Baronial Plan*, pp. 337–8.

[3] Powicke, *Thirteenth Century*, p. 179, n. 2, claims that this document was presented to Louis IX in Sept. 1263 at Boulogne.

recalls much of document 5 and answers the king's complaints made in document 37A. The need for a justiciar appointed by the Council is stressed, the bad royal finances demand a good treasurer, and the failure to issue writs correctly calls for a new chancellor (cls. 7-9). Stress is laid on the need for good sheriffs and the appointment of councillors is justified (cls. 10-12). This section ends with a claim (cl. 13) that the terms of the Provisions of Oxford were fully justified and asserts that those who opposed them were trying to ruin the realm. The third section of the document answers the accusations of ravage and rapine made in clause 7 of document 37A. Royal actions which have broken the peace and the agreement made on 16 July 1263 are recorded: the seizure of Winchester castle, causing trouble in the Cinque Ports (cls. 14 and 17), the actions of Roger Mortimer, and the appointment of royal officials after the compromise of July 1263 (cls. 15, 16, 18, 19).

Document 37C appears to be a continuation of 37B, stating the more general and enduring causes of difficulty between the king and his subjects. Henry is accused of having abused his power over the Church, of having transgressed the charter of liberties, and of having wasted lands which were escheats or in wardship (cls. 1, 2). Justice had been abused because of favouritism to aliens whose privileges were sought by the strong to crush the weak (cls. 3, 4). Merchants no longer came to England because of unjust prises. The sheriffs, because the farm had been increased, were extortionate and untrustworthy (cls. 5, 6). The royal finances were crippled by grants to courtiers and aliens. Demands arising from the planned crusade, from Sicily, and from the tenth had impoverished the land. The money so collected was wasted and churchmen had, unknowingly, been committed as pledges to pay money for the Sicilian business (cls. 7, 8).

This is the case which was placed before Louis IX who, on 23 January 1264, announced his decision which is known as the Mise of Amiens (doc. 38). King Henry's petition was accepted in every detail except for his financial demands of £300,000 and 200,000 marks. The king of France was a firm believer in the rights and power of a monarch who was, in his eyes, appointed by God to rule the people. These beliefs were strengthened by those who surrounded Louis. Eleanor of England, sister of Margaret of France, had spent much time at the French court

working for her husband. The papal bulls which absolved Henry from his oaths, together with the support which the pope had given to the king from the middle of 1263, when Henry had been forced to submit to Simon, undoubtedly influenced St. Louis.[1] Thus, because the French king had been subjected to all these forces it may be claimed that he was not a truly impartial judge in the case submitted to him; on the other hand he may have been expressing an honest unbiased judgement. Whatever one may say, the award swept away all the work of the reformers. The French king's decision is preceded by letters from the king, the Lord Edward, and the barons announcing their willingness to abide by the judgement of St. Louis. There is a statement confirming that this agreement had been made (cls. 1–8), the meeting at Amiens is described (cl. 9), and this is followed by the Mise itself. All provisions were cancelled, no new statutes could be made, and all relevant documents were to be surrendered to the king (cls. 10–12). Castles were to be restored to the king, the royal power of appointing to all offices was restored, all acts against, and restrictions on, aliens were to end (cls. 13–16). Royal privileges were completely restored, saving all liberties which had existed before 1258, and neither side was to bear rancour (cls. 17–19). Thus Henry's complaints were all remedied; as the late Professor Treharne said, 'in effect Henry III had written the Mise of Amiens himself and Louis adopted it'.[2]

F. *Civil War: Government after the Battle of Lewes*

The award was so drastic that those who wished to reform the realm could only refuse to accept it. Simon de Montfort asserted that the king of France had acted outside the terms of reference, for he had not arbitrated on the Provisions, rather he had cancelled them. The words of the letters of the king, the Lord Edward, and the barons indicate that this was an unwarranted attack on Louis IX, who had been given a free hand. However, Simon remained opposed to the Mise; his most immediate hope of aid was Llywelyn, the enemy of the Marcher lords who had become allies of the king. Active hostilities developed in the March: Llywelyn, supported by the earl's sons, attacked Roger Mortimer, who was

[1] On 14 Mar. 1264 the pope congratulated Louis on his pronouncement (*Simon de Montfort*, p. 207, n. 1).
[2] *The Battle of Lewes*, p. 88.

supported by the Lord Edward. The earl of Derby, who had captured the town of Worcester on 29 February 1264,[1] came to help the Montfortians besiege Edward who was holding Gloucester castle. A truce, signed on 10 March, allowed the prince to withdraw and he joined his father at Oxford. Attempts to find agreement between Henry and de Montfort failed; the king ordered a muster at Oxford. Late in March a group of Montfortians, led by Simon junior and Peter de Montfort assembled at Northampton where on 5–6 April they were surrounded and forced to surrender to royal forces.[2] This battle, which in later days was considered in the law courts to mark the beginning of the period of war, gave the crown control of the east Midlands. About eighty knights and nobles were captured, some were imprisoned in royal castles, Windsor and Norwich, some were taken by the Marchers to the Welsh border.[3] Simon, who was at London, determined to control the Cinque Ports to stop royal reinforcement arriving from France. Gilbert de Clare, the young earl of Gloucester who still remembered the treatment which he had suffered at the hands of the crown in 1262, at this time a supporter of the earl of Leicester, was at Tonbridge, the centre of lands which he held of the archbishop of Canterbury. On 18 April Simon and Gilbert captured Rochester, and shortly after this Tonbridge and Rochester fell to the royalists, who soon gained control of south-east England, except for Dover castle. On 6 May the king's forces were at Lewes, Simon was camped near by. Attempts at arbitration failed and on 14 May the battle of Lewes was fought. The king and his brother Richard of Cornwall were captured, and the Lord Edward was forced to accept a truce. He and his cousin, Henry of Almain, became hostages, being sent initially to Dover castle. The king and Richard of Cornwall were taken to London with de Montfort. An agreement, to which allusion was made on 17 May 1264 in a letter patent,[4] was made between the king and Leicester.[5] The terms of this agreement, suggested by

[1] *Ann. Mon.* iv. 448.
[2] R. F. Treharne, 'The Battle of Northampton', *Northamptonshire Past and Present*, ii (1955), 13–30.
[3] After the battle of Lewes, 14 May 1264, the majority of the Northampton prisoners were freed. On the other hand, despite orders and promises, the Marchers held their prisoners even as late as Dec. 1264.
[4] *C.P.R. 1258–66*, p. 318.
[5] Stubbs, *Constitutional History*, ii. 93 and Jacob, *Simon de Montfort*, pp. 214, 222 are mistaken in claiming that the *Compositio pacis post bellum de Lewes*

Denholm-Young,[1] were (a) the surrender of the Lord Edward and Henry of Almain as hostages, (b) the release of those who had been captured at Northampton, (c) only those who had captured royalists at Lewes were to control the lands of their prisoners from whom they could collect a ransom, (d) a committee of French clergy and nobles was to arbitrate.

On 26 May a letter was sent to the king of France with a copy of the agreement. The *Flores Historiarum* states that three French nobles and three French clergy were to nominate two Frenchmen who, on coming to England, would choose one Englishman thus creating a board of three arbiters.[2] The letter sent to the king of France does not appear to have been answered, and new letters were sent from England on 6 and 10 July.[3] While these negotiations were taking place the earl of Leicester had to control the realm. Royal constables still held the castles, the Marchers and some northern nobles were actively hostile; an expedition forced the Marchers to sue for peace on 25 August. Queen Eleanor and other royalists were in France; the papal legate, refused entry into England, threatened excommunication and interdict. To protect the realm Simon placed his sons in control of the coasts of Norfolk, south-east and south-west England; levies were mustered, and on 4 June keepers of the peace were appointed in each county 'for the protection and safety of these parts' (doc. 39). Attempts were made to raise money, Flemish cloth was banned as Queen Eleanor was at Damme, a port near Bruges. On 4 June four knights from each shire were to meet in London on 22 June (doc. 39); the earl of Leicester was turning to that section of the community which in future was to be his strongest support. The failure of St. Louis to answer the letter sent to him on 26 May may possibly be explained by the fact that the French king considered that his pronouncement at Amiens was the solution to the conflict between Henry and the English rebels. Louis could see

(*Chronicon de Duobus Bellis*, Camden Soc., old series, xv. 37) together with *C.P.R. 1258–66*, pp. 370–1 record the agreement. B. Wilkinson, *Constitutional History of England*, i. 155–60 mistakenly claims that there were two texts of the *Compositio*, makes no mention of the September negotiations (*C.P.R. 1258–66*, pp. 347–8, 370), and fails to note that the *Forma Pacis* (doc. 40) is formed of two sections dated June and Aug. 1264.

[1] 'Documents of the Barons' War', *E.H.R.* xlviii (1933), 558–75.
[2] *Flores Historiarum*, iii. 360–1.
[3] *C.R. 1261–64*, pp. 389, 390–1; *Royal Letters*, ii. 257–8 is badly edited.

no reason to intervene in a situation which arose because of the rebels' victory. The letter sent to France on 26 May contained the words 'if any other shorter way to peace can be found for us and our kingdom we and our barons propose to take it to obtain a good peace more quickly'.[1] This 'shorter way' was the first half of document 40, accepted by the gathering in London on 22 June.

The preamble to document 40, obviously written at the same time as the August section, states that the ordinances which had been made in the June parliament were to remain in force 'until the peace between the lord king and the barons, promised at Lewes . . . should be completed'. These ordinances, which formed the first half of document 40, established machinery to control the central administration. As the Council of Fifteen no longer existed a new council had to be created. Three faithful subjects were to be chosen, but nothing is said of who does this. The three, who were Leicester, Gloucester, and the bishop of Chichester, were to nominate a Council of Nine, three of whom were to be constantly in court.[2] This Council of Nine were to choose all officials and advise the king in all matters.[3] Councillors and all officials were to be bound by oath to act in an upright way; councillors could be dismissed by the king on the advice of the three who nominated them, and officials who erred would be removed on the advice of the nine. Disagreement among the three or the nine was to be decided by a two-thirds vote, provided a churchman was among the two-thirds in matters which touched the Church; if the nine could not agree the three or the majority of them would decide.[4] If the barons and prelates wished to remove all or one of the three the king could act on the advice of the counsel of the barons and prelates, a clause which was merely of theoretical importance in June 1264. The document continues with the statement that 'the

[1] *C.R. 1261–64*, p. 386.

[2] See notes to doc. 40 for names of these nine.

[3] Thomas Cantilupe, nephew of the bishop of Worcester, was chancellor between 25 Feb. and 7 May 1265 and was replaced by Ralph de Sandwich, keeper of the wardrobe (*C.P.R. 1258–66*, pp. 410, 423). *Simon de Montfort*, p. 231 and *British Chronology*, p. 83 are mistaken on the date of appointment of Thomas. Ralph was a layman; it was not until the end of the fourteenth century that a non-cleric was again head of the chancery. The royal household was controlled by Adam de Newmarket and Walter de Crepping (*C.P.R. 1258–66*, pp. 331, 389, 404, 427; Tout, *Administrative History*, i. 310 and n. 2; 311, n. 2; 314 and n. 2).

[4] This gave de Montfort and his ally the bishop of Chichester complete control.

king shall do all these things by the counsel of the nine . . . or
they shall do them in place of, and on the authority of, the lord
king' and ends by enacting that the ordinance should last until
the agreement made at Lewes was completed.

The delay by Louis IX to act as arbiter continued. The arrangements which were made in July for the English and French courts
to be at Dover and Boulogne to aid communications bore no
results.[1] On 12 August the English court was at Canterbury; three
days later a mission was sent to Louis with a letter beginning with
the words 'As the king and Edward his son and his barons have
agreed upon a form of peace, to show which the king is sending
Robert de Ver . . . to the king of France'. The king of France was
asked to accept the peace and cause it to be accepted by Henry's
friends abroad.[2] This peace, later called 'the peace lately provided
at Canterbury',[3] consisted of the *Forma Pacis* of June 1264
together with additional clauses touching topics not mentioned
in the *Forma*. In addition it was stated that the terms of the peace
were to last during the life time of King Henry and during the
reign of King Edward 'to a date which shall be settled hereafter'.[4]

The continued failure to reach a final settlement with the king,
and the absence of French arbitration, forced de Montfort to
take further steps to administer the realm. These plans form the
second part of document 40 which begins with the words 'It is
also ordained', stating some very general intentions of future
action. The Church was to be reformed, the Three, the Nine and
all officials were to be natives, but aliens and merchants were
promised freedom of movement. The charter of liberties and the
charter of the forest were confirmed as were all past enactments
of reform.[5] Neither side, king or reformers, was to bear rancour.

The opposition of Louis IX, aided by the legate, forced Simon
to seek further negotiations with France. Missions were named,
on 11, 13 and 15 September, to meet French representatives; the
result was the *Compositio* mentioned in the *Chronicon* and on

---

[1] *C.R. 1261–64*, pp. 390–1, 396; *Royal Letters*, ii. 263 has mistakes in editing.
During May–August Simon was negotiating with the papacy.

[2] *C.P.R. 1258–66*, p. 366.   [3] Ibid., p. 370.

[4] In Aug. 1264 Henry III was 56 years old—a good age for a man in the
thirteenth century. Edward, aged 25, was violently opposed to the reformers.
It was therefore necessary to create machinery of government which would survive Henry and control an autocratic successor. A similar situation was envisaged
in 1258. See doc. 5, cl. 8.

[5] See notes to doc. 40.

the patent roll.[1] Arbiters with restricted powers were named, the royal household was to be controlled, and, under certain circumstances, the Lord Edward and Henry of Almain would be released. The resulting situation was to be less radical than the terms of the Peace of Canterbury.

Simon was making every effort to secure peace as unrest within the realm continued. During October–November 1264 the Marchers captured Gloucester and Bridgnorth. Carmarthen and Chester were held for the crown while a royalist force from Bristol tried to rescue the Lord Edward from Wallingford castle. De Montfort, determined to crush the Marchers, mustered an army and early in December he and the king were at Worcester. The Marchers immediately negotiated, for they were also being threatened by Llywelyn. On 12 December it was agreed that the leading Marchers should go to Ireland for a year and a day, that Chester, Bristol, and Edward's lands in Wales would be surrendered to Simon. On 14 December, at Worcester, the 1263 text of the Provisions of Westminster was reissued with the final clause as in the Cambridge text of the Provisions in 1259.[2] Summonses were issued on 14 and 24 December[3] for a parliament to meet in London on 20 January (doc. 41, A–D). Besides nobles and clergy two knights were summoned from each shire and two burgesses from each borough. This marks a great step forward to the final formation of parliament. The number of knights summoned from the shires varied between three and four in 1213, 1261, 1264 and 1275, the number in later parliaments was two. Furthermore, the summoning of knights in 1261, 1264 and 1265 is a good indication of the importance of that section of the community to the reformers. Even more important is the fact that this is the first parliament to which borough representatives were called. Later practice was to order sheriffs to send two representatives

---

[1] *C.P.R. 1258–66*, pp. 345, 369, 370–1; *Rishanger's Chronicle*, pp. 37–8. The *Chronicon* text seems to be a précis of the patent roll. Denholm-Young (*E.H.R.* xlviii. 564) is mistaken in claiming that the *Compositio* dates from 15 Aug. to 11 Sept.

[2] British Museum, Cotton MS. Claudius D. ii, f. 125ᵛ. Text printed in *Registrum Malmesburiense* (R.S. 1879–80), i. 50.

[3] *Reform and Rebellion*, p. 77; *C.R. 1264–68*, p. 85 in error prints 13 Dec., the close roll MS. reads xiiii. Stubbs, p. 403, Hennings, p. 181, *Dignity of a Peer*, iii, App. i. pt. i. 33, *Foedera*, i. i. 449 give date as 14 Dec. Stubbs's list of those summoned is misleading as he omits nine bishops, one bishop-elect, and four deans.

of each city and borough to parliament,[1] but on this occasion
the writs were addressed to the citizens, an appeal directly to the
urban communities in which de Montfort found much support.
On this occasion the writ was addressed to the 'citizens of York,
Lincoln, and other boroughs', a general term which was to cause
much trouble in the future. The writ issued to Sandwich (doc.
41B) is the only known full text of the writ which was sent to the
boroughs. Not all the writs can have been exactly the same as that
which went to the Cinque Ports, who were each ordered to send
four representatives, an indication of the importance attached to
them by de Montfort.[2] Furthermore, the fact that the writ to
Sandwich was issued on 20 January, when parliament was meant
to be meeting, is an indication of the disorganized state of the
realm. This condition is also shown in document 41D which
refers to the failure to appear of the knights from Staffordshire
and Shropshire, counties which were in the hands of the Marchers,
who had neither withdrawn to Ireland nor made peace with the
earl of Leicester. The order summoning the representatives of
these shires to appear before the king on 8 March was an attempt,
made after parliament had dispersed, to enforce obedience.

Subjects discussed at the parliament are not known. The London
chronicler states that on 14 February parliament was told that the
king had promised that neither he nor the Lord Edward would
in future bear malice against London or the earls of Leicester and
Gloucester, also the king was willing to observe the charters of
liberty and the *Forma Pacis* of June 1264.[3] A statement in the
writ of summons gives some indication that matters touching the

---

[1] The fact that the cities and boroughs were not named led to great difficulty,
as there were no criteria by which it could be decided if a community was a
borough. Except for the most important communities all depended on the
sheriff and the arrangements which the communities, who did not wish to bear
the expense of representation, could make with him. The indecision in deciding
which communities were boroughs also caused difficulty in taxation, as borough
dwellers were taxed more heavily than were others. The task of avoiding borough
status in taxation involved negotiations with the chief taxers of the counties.
Thus there arose the strange situation that in the same county, except for the
large communities which could not avoid borough status, taxation boroughs
need not be the same as parliamentary boroughs (J. Tait, *The Medieval English
Borough* (1936); J. F. Willard, *Parliamentary Taxes on Personal Property*,
1290–1344 (1934); C. Johnson, 'The Collection of Lay Taxes', in *The English
Government at Work*, ii (1947).
[2] K. M. E. Murray, *The Constitutional History of the Cinque Ports* (1935).
[3] *Lib. de Ant. Leg.* p. 71. This is the first part of doc. 40.

peace of the realm were to be discussed, while the London Chronicle and the writ to the sheriff of Yorkshire (doc. 41C) show that the assembly lasted until the middle of February.[1] The summons which de Montfort issued to all classes of the realm is an indication of the wide meaning which he attached to the words 'community of the nation'. He was not to live to meet another parliament but he had laid the foundation upon which Edward I was to build.

The earl's hopes of finding a settlement were still unfulfilled. The Marchers, who had not retired to Ireland, still held those whom they had captured at Northampton in April 1264. Divisions were even appearing in the ranks of the Montfortians. John Giffard had to be reprimanded for illegally seizing lands, while Gilbert de Clare, the most powerful lord in the kingdom, was annoyed because Bristol, which had been a cause of quarrel between his father and the Lord Edward, had passed into Simon's hands. Furthermore, the earl of Gloucester was jealous of de Montfort's monopoly of power and annoyed because his followers had been stopped from occupying lands. Consequently early in 1265 de Clare withdrew to the Welsh March—the home of de Montfort's most intractable enemies. As if this were not enough, the earl of Derby, a firm supporter of Leicester, who had captured Worcester on 29 February 1264 was arrested because he was waging private warfare. So much unrest was rife in the land that on 17 February 1265 de Montfort banned a tournament at Dunstable for fear of conflict between his men and the followers of Gilbert de Clare. In a final attempt to win support Leicester reissued on 8 March the first part of the *Forma Pacis* (doc. 40) together with a statement that the king pardoned enemies, that the Lord Edward, who was to be released from prison, would not attack the Montfortians, and the earl's tenure of Bristol and Chester was confirmed.[2] On 10 March the Lord Edward, who promised to recognize the *Forma Pacis* and to accept further restrictions,[3] was allowed to join his father, both being under house arrest in the entourage of Simon de Montfort. The climax

---

[1] D. Pasquet, *An Essay on the Origins of the House of Commons* (1925), pp. 166 f. and M. McKisack, *The Parliamentary Representation of the English Boroughs in the Middle Ages* (1932), ch. 5 give details of the financial burden of attendance at parliament.

[2] *C.Ch.R.* ii. 54; *Foedera*, 1. i. 451–2.

[3] *Foedera*, 1. i. 452; *Lib. de Ant. Leg.* pp. 71–2.

of the attempts to reach a settlement came on 14 March when document 42 was issued. The king announced his acceptance of the *Forma Pacis*, promised both not to bear malice and 'to observe all those things which were provided for the release of our son and nephew'. If the king or Edward broke their oaths they could be resisted and their supporters outlawed. In addition Henry bound himself to observe the charters of liberty and of the forest, together with the Provisions of Westminster which had been reissued at Worcester on 14 December 1264. All royal officials were to be bound in the same way under threat of excommunication and punishment, saving the privilege of clergy. Copies of the documents mentioned above, together with document 42, were to be kept in each county and read in the county court at least twice a year. Lastly, the king renounced all privileges which had been or might in the future be granted by the pope.

De Montfort's efforts to win the support of the Marchers and of the royalists failed. On 19 March Peter of Savoy at Pevensey, John de Warenne at Lewes, Hugh Bigod at Bosham, Sussex, and William de Valence at Brickendon, Herts., were summoned to a parliament which Simon planned to hold on 1 June 1265[1] (doc. 43). Unlike the January parliament town representatives were not summoned, probably because unrest in the realm precluded the assembly of a large body of people. Simon, accompanied by the king and the Lord Edward, moved to Gloucester on 28 April to be near the main source of trouble, the Welsh March. Several of de Montfort's former allies were in negotiation with Roger Mortimer, the leading Marcher, and all efforts to arrange a meeting between the earls of Gloucester and Leicester failed. Despite the fact that Simon's forces were to muster at Gloucester, that Valence and Warenne had landed at Pembroke on 10 May, the intention of holding a parliament continued as late as 15 May when the place of assembly was changed from Westminster to Winchester, nearer the Welsh border (doc. 43).[2] Toward the end of the third week of May, Simon, with Henry and Edward, moved to Hereford, and on 28 May Edward escaped to join Mortimer and Gilbert de Clare at Wigmore. On 8 June the forces from Pembroke joined Clare and Mortimer. Chester, Bridgnorth, and Worcester were seized by the royalists, and Gloucester

---

[1] *C.R. 1264–68*, p. 36.

[2] The crisis on the Welsh border meant that the parliament did not meet.

castle was besieged. Simon was being locked to the west of the river Severn. He summoned his young son Simon to bring aid from south-east England and signed the Treaty of Pipton with Llywelyn on 22 June. Gloucester castle fell to the earl of Gloucester and the Lord Edward on 29 June, Simon moved from Hereford to Monmouth, thence to Usk and Newport hoping to meet ships from Bristol. None appeared, and de Montfort withdrew to Hereford. The young Simon, who did not realize his father's danger, moved slowly. He occupied Winchester on 16 July but on the night of 31 July–1 August his forces were shattered, near Kenilworth by the Lord Edward, and Simon junior fled to that castle. The diversion of the Kenilworth encounter allowed the earl of Leicester to cross the Severn at Kempsey on 2 August. He moved to Evesham where on 4 August he was killed and his forces decimated.

G. *Conflict and Arbitration after the Battle of Evesham*

The royal victory at Evesham did not bring peace to the realm, as several centres of resistance remained. The isle of Axholme, in the Lincolnshire fens, fell in December 1265, unrest in the Midlands continued until a royal victory at Chesterfield on 15 May 1266, and the Cinque Ports resisted until March 1266. London, a strong supporter of de Montfort, faced the wrath of the Lord Edward. When the city surrendered in November 1265 important citizens were taken as hostages, rights of self government were forfeited and a heavy fine was levied. Despite this, unrest continued to such an extent that the royal administrative machinery withdrew, in April, from Westminster to St. Paul's.[1] These knots of opposition were merely concentrations of widespread unrest. The royalist victory and the collapse of the administrative machinery allowed feelings of greed, hatred, and revenge to find expression in widespread robbery, seizure of lands, and violence. The situation had been made worse by Henry's rashness after Evesham. The absence of Edward, Richard of Cornwall, and Henry of Almain from the royal court in August, and the fact that the legate Ottobuono did not meet the king until 1 November 1265 at Canterbury removed moderate elements from the presence of the king. The Marcher lords, and others inspired with greed and

---

[1] The exchequer worked in the bishop's chamber, the justices of the Bench in his hall.

revenge, were only too willing to profit from some rash words said to have been uttered by Henry on the battle field of Evesham. The king declared that the rebels had forfeited all lands and goods. Any royalist may keep what he seized from those who had opposed the king. This was sanctioned by the parliament which met at Winchester in September 1265.[1] In addition the Welsh captured Hawarden castle in the autumn of 1265, defeated Roger Mortimer in May 1266, and it was not until September 1267 that peace was made at Montgomery.[2]

Among all the centres of opposition the castle of Kenilworth, given to de Montfort by the king in 1244, was the most difficult to crush. The garrison was large, the castle was strong, unrest in the realm postponed attempts to muster an army to invest it until April 1266. The order to muster was poorly answered; the widespread unrest made people fearful of leaving their homes. It was not until the middle of June 1266 that the castle was surrounded, while on 9 August a rebel force seized the isle of Ely and threatened the rear of the royal army.[3] Furthermore, the Kenilworth garrison hoped to receive aid from France, to the sanctuary of which Eleanor de Montfort and her two sons, Guy and Simon, had fled. On 22 August 1266 a parliament met at Kenilworth,[4] the king asked the Church for financial aid, the papal legate Ottobuono demanded that negotiations be opened with the besieged rebels. The king announced on 31 August that the bishops of Exeter and Bath and Wells, together with the bishop-elect of Worcester,[5] Alan de la Zuche, Robert Walerand, and Roger de Somery, should choose six more (one prelate and five knights) to form a committee 'to procure what they understand to be necessary for the reformation of the peace of the land'.[6]

---

[1] *Simon de Montfort*, p. 246; *Reform and Rebellion*, p. 169.
[2] Lloyd, *History of Wales*, ii. 747–54; *King Henry III*, ii. 577–82, 637–45.
[3] Ely continued to be a source of trouble until July 1267, being aided by a rising in London, in Apr. 1267, which the earl of Gloucester supported. Clare, who had not become a reactionary royalist, had quarrelled with Roger Mortimer at the end of 1266 and favoured a less violent policy of repression. London capitulated in the middle of June 1267 when Clare retired and Edward occupied the city.
[4] This date is based on a statement made on 31 Aug. (*King Henry III*, ii. 532, n. 1).
[5] Called bishop in document 44.
[6] *C.P.R. 1258–66*, p. 672; *Ann. Mon.* iii. 243; *Chronicon de Duobus Bellis*, p. 555; *Flores Hist.* iii. 12; prologue to doc. 44. Wrong reference in *Simon de Montfort*, p. 253, n. 4.

Any disagreement within the committee of twelve was to be submitted to the arbitration of the legate and Henry of Almain, who were also to arbitrate if the named six could not agree upon the six whom they were to co-opt. If the committee were in accord their decisions needed the approval of the king and the two arbiters before action could be taken. It was also enacted that if one of the twelve died the others could fill the vacancy, provided the committee consisted of four bishops and eight knights. The committee of twelve would have power to take decisions up to 1 November 1266.

The twelve met in Coventry. In some cases their decisions called for arbitration by Henry of Almain and the legate whose rulings often modified toward leniency the original suggestion.[1] The final scheme, combining the ideas of the twelve, as modified by the arbiters, was proclaimed at Kenilworth on 31 October and announced by the legate at an ecclesiastical council in Coventry on 1 November.[2] The rebels, who had expected a better offer, rejected the terms of peace when they were published, but the approach of winter, sickness, and shortage of food forced them to reconsider their decision. They asked to be allowed forty days, hoping that aid might arrive, but on 14 December 1266 they were allowed to leave Kenilworth, still bearing arms; the sole obligation placed upon them was that of keeping the peace and answering to the terms of the *Dictum* when required by the king to do so.

The *Dictum*[3] of Kenilworth was not a negotiated settlement; it was an offer by the royalists to the besieged garrison. Initially the terms of the *Dictum* were not popular with either side. Those

---

[1] The decisions of the arbiters, called *Explanacio dicti* is printed in *S. of Realm*, i. 18. See document 44 for a full discussion. See also R. Graham, 'Letters of Cardinal Ottobuono', *E.H.R.* xv (1900), 109.

[2] *King Henry III*, ii. 533. The ecclesiastical council, originally called to Northampton for 27 Oct., moved to Coventry by 31 Oct. (C. R. Cheney, *Councils and Synods*, ii. 729; Jacob and Cam, *E.H.R.* xliv (1929), 104). Jacob (*Simon de Montfort*, p. 253) states that the plan was approved at Northampton on 20 Oct. No reference is given; presumably it is a mistaken copy of Bémont (*Simon de Montfort*, p. 247) who, without reference, gives the date as 26 Oct. Gervase of Canterbury, when mentioning the feast of Simon and Jude, says *in quo festo* a parliament of the king, the papal legate, churchmen, and magnates met at Northampton (*Chronicle*, ii. 245). Presumably Bémont used this statement but the feast is on 28 Oct. *Lib. de Ant. Leg.* pp. 84–6 speaks of a Northampton parliament *circa* 1 May 1266.

[3] So called by Robert of Gloucester (*Metrical Chronicle*, ed. W. A. Wright (1887), ii. 773).

who had obtained lands did not take kindly to the idea of surrendering them, while many of those opposing the king hoped that continued resistance would win better terms. The offer of redemption instead of forfeiture meant that it was planned to reverse the territorial revolution which had been legalized on 17 September 1265, at the Winchester parliament, when it was announced that the lands of rebels were to be confiscated. The grading of punishments, according to the violence of opposition offered to the crown, favoured the large number who had supported de Montfort without acting with violence. The fixed rates of payment to be made for redemption, together with schemes to meet the many varied situations which had arisen, allowed those who had lost their lands to plan means of meeting the demands to recover the estates. Reconciliation and rehabilitation opened a way which could bring the rebels to lay down their arms, return to the king's peace, and join the 'community of the realm'. At times it bore hardly on individual rebels, but it must be remembered that, in the eyes of the royalists, these were men who by the act of rebellion had forfeited all rights.

The *Dictum* falls into two parts, the political and the legal settlements. Politically no concession was made to the king's opponents. All restraints, except those which the crown had recognized before the Oxford parliament of 1258, were removed (cls. 1, 6, 7). The king was asked to appoint worthy men, to respect the charters and the liberties of the Church, and to confirm grants which 'he has made freely and not under compulsion'. (cls. 2, 3, 4, 10). This alludes to the legal clauses of the Provisions of Westminster (doc. 11) which Henry had confirmed in January 1263 in an endeavour to win support against the rising tide of opposition.[1] The changes resulting from document 11, which did not affect the constitutional position of the crown, were in some ways the most important achievement of the reformers; their mention in the *Dictum* and their re-enactment with slight modification in the Statute of Marlborough, issued on 18 November 1267, is witness of the crown's acceptance of this fact.[2]

[1] Reissued on 13–14 Dec. 1264.
[2] The Statute of Marlborough is printed in *S. of Realm*, i. 19–25 where it is divided into 29 clauses. Of these the first eight show the influence of the *Dictum*, the rest repeat the Provisions of Westminster, clauses 13, 28, and 29 recording the additions made when Henry III confirmed and reissued the document in Jan. 1263. The links between the *Dictum*, the Provisions of Westminster, and

The legal settlement is the much larger section of the *Dictum*. The king would not bear vengeance but those who continued to oppose the crown were to be outlawed (cls. 5, 20, 37–9). Those who had lost lands would be repossessed (cls. 30–2), in some cases a graded scale of payment was to be made either to the crown or to the new tenant (cls. 12, 14, 17, 18, 26, 27, 29). Care was taken to enforce the terms of the *Dictum* fairly (cls. 13, 19, 21, 23, 24, 30, 33, 35, 40).[1]

The meaning and purpose of the *Dictum* are clear enough, but its application raised difficulties and left cases where individuals felt sorely aggrieved. The enforcement of the terms of the *Dictum* transferred the civil war from the battle field to the law courts where it dragged on in some cases to the reign of Edward I. On the whole it succeeded remarkably well, displacing despairing enmity with the certainty of reconciliation within clearly known and reasonable limits of time, and avoiding a territorial revolution by indiscriminate confiscations. Furthermore, the *Dictum* fused two streams destined to merge into the legislation of Edward I at the end of the thirteenth century. The first stream is represented by the document taking the form of an award—a practice which became very popular during the period of unrest—the Mise of Amiens, the Mise of Lewes. The second stream forecast the legislation later in the century. Although disorderly, being the outcome of prolonged discussion and afterthoughts, the *Dictum* is an attempt to deal with one outstanding problem, the disinherited, but the wide sweep of topics considered make it comparable with the statutes of Edward I. Behind all the clauses of the *Dictum* may be seen ideas which mark a growth in constitutional ideas about the position of the king as ruler of the realm. The principle that there was a distinction between the civil war and rebellion was undermined. The conflict between the crown and Richard Marshal in 1234 could be called warfare between Henry and the earl of Pembroke, but no mention is made of warfare between the king and de Montfort. Civil war was now rebellion, those who surrendered after the battle of Evesham were rebels

the Statute of Marlborough are mentioned in *King Henry III*, ii. 547 and *Reform and Rebellion*, p. 124.

[1] See doc. 44, n. 32, for discussion of the jurisdiction of the Court of King's Bench, and of the eyre. Many other topics were considered; London, wardship, lands held at farm, castles, stolen property (cls. 11, 15, 16, 24, 25, 28).

not defeated enemy. Furthermore, the *Dictum* made a serious breach in the legal theory, upheld after the Treaty of Kingston in 1217, that no judicial action could be taken about acts done in time of war.[1] Much of the ordinance was devoted to the solution of actions which had taken place during the time of war—5 April 1264 (the attack on Northampton) to 16 September 1265.[2]

Practical solutions suggested to solve the many problems are very evident, while the wide sweep of topics which had to be considered often caused difficulties arising from conflict with rules established by the current law.[3] On the other hand the *Dictum* had very little effect on contemporary law, possibly for two reasons. In the first place it was concerned with only one section of the community—those who had been rebels. Secondly, the decisions reached were framed to deal with special problems of short duration. By July 1267 the bulk of the people had accepted the *Dictum* and the application of the document had been completed by 1280, except for some dower cases which occurred as late as the first years of the fourteenth century.

The years of reform and rebellion, although in theory the king's power had been restored to the position which it had held before 1258, left their mark on the economic, social, and constitutional life of the community. The crown was not to forget the lesson which could be learned from past events. Edward I was to see the value of parliament, which he adapted as an instrument to aid in the government of the realm, while on 18 November 1267 a series of provisions which came to be known as the Statute of Marlborough was issued. In the words of Sir Maurice Powicke 'The work of 1258–9 culminated in the Provisions of Westminster and the one great statute of Henry's later years, the Statute of Marlborough, was based upon the Provisions of Westminster. Just as a revised Magna Carta survived the war against King John, so the statute of 1267 gave permanence to the work done in 1259, when the king and barons were still allies, if not friends.'[4]

---

[1] *King Henry III*, ii. 555, n. 1.

[2] These dates were decided by the parliament which met at Winchester in Sept. 1265.

[3] See C. H. Knowles 'The Disinherited', iii. 32–6; iv. 75 for discussion of this.

[4] *King Henry III*, i. 394–5.

SELECT BIBLIOGRAPHY AND
LIST OF ABBREVIATIONS

ADAMS, G. B., and STEPHENS, H. M., *Select Documents of English Constitutional History* (New York, 1937).

ADLER, M., 'The Testimony of the London Jewry against the Ministers of Henry III', *Trans. of the Jewish Historical Society of England*, xiv (1935–9), 141–85.

A.H.R.: *American Historical Review*.

AINSLEY, H., 'The Problems relating to the Maintenance of Law and Order in Thirteenth Century England, with particular reference to the *custos pacis*', Ph.D. thesis, University of Wales (Aberystwyth, 1968).

Anglicarum Scriptores: *Rerum Anglicarum Scriptores*, i, ed. W. Fulman (Oxford, 1684).

Annales Cambriae: ed. John Williams ab Ithel (R.S., 1860).

Ann. Mon.: *Annales Monastici*, ed. H. R. Luard (R.S., 1864–9).

'Baronial Council': Sir F. M. Powicke, 'Some Observations on the Baronial Council (1258–60) and the Provisions of Westminster', *Essays in Medieval History presented to Thomas Frederick Tout*, ed. A. G. Little and Sir F. M. Powicke (Manchester, 1925), pp. 119–34.

Baronial Plan: R. F. Treharne, *The Baronial Plan of Reform, 1258–63* (Manchester, 1932).

Battle of Lewes: Sir F. M. Powicke, R. F. Treharne, C. H. Lemmon, *The Battle of Lewes, 1264* (Lewes, 1964).

BÉMONT, *Simon de Montfort*: C. Bémont, *Simon de Montfort, comte de Leicestre. Sa vie 120?–1265, son rôle politique en France et en Angleterre* (Paris, 1884).

—— See *Simon de Montfort*.

B.I.H.R.: *Bulletin of the Institute of Historical Research*.

B.J.R.L.: *Bulletin of the John Rylands Library*.

BLACKSTONE, W., *The Great Charter of the Forest with other authentic documents* (Oxford, 1759).

Book of Fees: *The Book of Fees*, 3 vols. (Public Record Office, 1921–31).

Bracton, Henry de, *De Legibus et Consuetudinibus Angliae*, ed. G. E. Woodbine (Yale U.P., 1915–42).

British Chronology: *Handbook of British Chronology*, 2nd edn., ed. Sir F. M. Powicke and E. B. Fryde (London, 1961).

CAM, H. M., *The Hundred and the Hundred Rolls* (London, 1930).

—— 'Studies in the Hundred Rolls', *Oxford Studies in Legal and Social History*, vi (Oxford, 1921).

—— 'The Parliamentary Writs *de expensis* of 1258', *E.H.R.* xlvi (1931), 630–2.

    and see Jacob, E. F.

A Catalogue of the Harleian Manuscripts in the British Museum, 4 vols. (Record Com. 1808–12).

C.Ch.R.: *Calendar of Charter Rolls*, 6 vols. (Public Record Office, 1903–27).

C. Docs. France: *Calendar of Documents preserved in France*, ed. J. H. Round (Public Record Office, 1899).

CHENEY, C. R., *Councils and Synods, with other documents relating to English Church History*, ii, 2 parts, ed. C. R. Cheney and Sir F. M. Powicke (Oxford, 1964).

Chron. Majora: Matthew Paris, *Chronica Majora*, ed. H. R. Luard, 6 vols. (R. S., 1872–83).

Chronicon de Duobus Bellis: see *Rishanger's Chronicle*.

C.Lib.R.: *Calendar of Liberate Rolls*, 6 vols. (Public Record Office, 1930–64).

C.Misc.Inq.: *Calendar of Miscellaneous Inquisitions*, i (Public Record Office, 1898).

Collected Papers: N. Denholm-Young, *Collected Papers on Medieval Subjects* (Oxford, 1946; Cardiff, 1969).

C.P.R.: *Calendar of Patent Rolls of the Reign of Henry III*, 4 vols. (Public Record Office, 1906–13).

C.R.: *Close Rolls of the Reign of Henry III*, 14 vols. (Public Record Office, 1902–38).

CRAMER, A. C., 'The Jewish Exchequer', *A.H.R.* xlv (1939–40), 327–37.
—— 'The Origins and Functions of the Jewish Exchequer', *Speculum*, xvi (1941), 226–9.

CUTTINO, G. P., 'The Process of Agen', *Speculum*, xix (1944), 168–78.

DENHOLM-YOUNG, N., 'The Merchants of Cahors', *Medievalia et Humanistica*, iv (1946), 37–44.
—— 'Feudal Society in the Thirteenth Century: The Knights', *History*, xxix (1944), 107–19; *Collected Papers*, 56–67.
—— 'Documents of the Barons' Wars', *E.H.R.* xlviii (1933), 558–75; *Collected Papers*, 155–72.
—— 'The Winchester-Hyde Chronicle', *E.H.R.* xlix (1934), 85–93.
—— 'Robert Carpenter and the Provisions of Westminster', *E.H.R.* l (1935), 22–35.
—— see also *Collected Papers*.

Diplomatic Documents preserved in the Public Record Office, 1101–1272, ed. P. Chaplais (Public Record Office, 1964).

Dignity of a Peer: *Reports from the lords committees appointed to search . . . for all matters touching the dignity of a peer* (London, 1820–9).

DOUGLAS: *English Historical Documents, 1042–1189*, ii, ed. D. C. Douglas and G. W. Greenaway (London, 1953).

DUGDALE, Sir W., *Origines Juridicales* (London, 1666).

E.H.R.: *English Historical Review*.

ELLIS, A. J., 'On the only English Proclamation of Henry III', *Trans. of the Philological Society* (1868), 1–135.

ELMAN, P., 'Jewish Finance in Thirteenth Century England', *B.I.H.R.* xv (1938), 112.

English Baronies: I. J. Sanders, *English Baronies, a study of their origin and descent* (Oxford, 1963).

Flores Historiarum, ed. H. R. Luard, 3 vols. (R.S., 1890).

Foedera: *Foedera, Conventiones, Litterae*, ed. T. Rymer, new edition, 3 vols. in 6 (Record Com., 1816–30).

Foss, E., *A Bibliographical Dictionary of the Judges of England from The Conquest to the Present Time, 1066–1870* (London, 1870).

G.E.C.: G. E. Cokayne, *The Complete Peerage*, 13 vols. (London 1910–59).

Gibbs, M., and Lang, J., *Bishops and Reform, 1212–72* (Oxford, 1934).

Gilson, J. P., 'An unpublished notice of the battle of Lewes', *E.H.R.* xi (1896), 520–2.

—— 'The Parliament of 1264', *E.H.R.* xvi (1901), 499–500.

Graham, R., 'Letters of the Cardinal Ottobuono', *E.H.R.* xv (1900), 109.

Green, F., *Menevia Sacra* (Cambrian Archaeological Association, 1927).

Gwynn, A., 'Some unpublished texts from the Black Book of Christ Church, Dublin', *Analecta Hibernica*, no. 16 (Dublin, 1946), 281–337.

Harding, A., 'The Early History of the Keepers of the Peace', *T.R.H.S.* 5th ser. x (1960), 85–109.

Hennings: M. A. Hennings, *England under Henry III* (London, 1924).

Historical MSS. Commission: *MSS. of Lord Middleton preserved at Wollaton Hall, Notts.* (1911).

Holmes, T. S., *Wells and Glastonbury* (London, 1908).

Hoyle, M., 'Judicial Proceedings under the Dictum of Kenilworth', Ph.D. thesis, University of Manchester, 1934.

Jacob, E. F., 'What were the "Provisions of Oxford"?', *History*, ix (1924), 188–200.

—— 'A proposal for arbitration between Simon de Montfort and Henry III in 1260', *E.H.R.* xxxvii (1922), 80–2, 320.

—— 'Complaints of Henry III against the Baronial Council in 1261', *E.H.R.* xli (1926), 559–71.

—— and H. M. Cam: 'Notes on an English Cluniac Chronicle', *E.H.R.* xliv (1929), 94–104.

—— see *Reform and Rebellion*.

—— see *Simon de Montfort*.

Jacob, G., *A New Law Dictionary* (London, 1772).

James, M. R., *The Western Manuscripts in the Library of Trinity College, Cambridge. A Descriptive Catalogue*, 3 vols. (Cambridge, 1902).

Jenkinson, C. H., 'The First Parliament of Edward I', *E.H.R.* xxv (1910), 231–42.

Johnson, C., 'The Collection of Lay Taxes', in *English Government at Work*, ii (Cambridge, Mass., 1947).

Jones, P. E., and Smith, R., *A Guide to the Records in the Corporation of London Records Office and in the Guildhall Library Muniment Room* (London, 1951).

King Henry III: Sir F. M. Powicke, *Henry III and the Lord Edward* (Oxford, 1947).

Kleinclausz, A., *Histoire de Bourgogne* (Paris, 1909).

KNOWLES, C. H., 'The Disinherited, 1265–80', Ph.D. thesis, University of Wales (Aberystwyth, 1959).

LAPSLEY, G., 'Buzones', *E.H.R.* xlvii (1932), 177–93, 545–67.

LAWLER, H. J., 'A Calendar of the Liber Niger and Liber Albus of Christ Church, Dublin', *Proc. of the Royal Irish Academy*, xxvii (1908–9), 1–93.

LEGG, L. G. W., *English Coronation Records* (London, 1901).

LEWIS, A., 'Roger Leyburn and the pacification of England', *E.H.R.* liv (1939), 193–214.

LEWIS, F. R., 'William de Valence, *c.* 1230–1296', *Aberystwyth Studies*, xiii (1934), 11–35; xiv (1936), 69–92.

Lib. de Ant. Leg.: *De Antiquis Legibus Liber*, ed. T. Stapleton, Camden Soc., old series, xxxiv (London, 1846).

Lists and Indexes published by the Public Record Office: vol. ix: *List of Sheriffs for England and Wales from the earliest times to A.D. 1831* (1898).

LLOYD, J. E., *A History of Wales from the earliest times to the Edwardian Conquest* (London, 1939).

LUNT, W. E., *The Valuation of Norwich* (Oxford, 1926).

—— *Financial Relations of the Papacy with England to 1327* (Cambridge, Mass., 1939).

MADAN, FALCONER, et al., *A Summary Catalogue of the Western Manuscripts in the Bodleian Library at Oxford*, 7 vols. (Oxford, 1895–1953).

Magna Carta: J. C. Holt, *Magna Carta* (Cambridge, 1965).

MANSI, J. D., *Sanctorum Conciliorum nova et amplissima collectio*, 56 vols. (Florence, Venice, Pisa, Arnhem, and Leipzig, 1759–1962).

MAS-LATRIE, L. de, *Trésor de Chronologie* (Paris, 1889).

MAXWELL-LYTE, Sir H. C., *Historical Notes on the use of the Great Seal of England* (London, 1926).

MCKISACK, M., *The Parliamentary Representation of the English Boroughs During the Middle Ages* (Oxford, 1932).

MOORMAN, J. R. H., *Church Life in England in the Thirteenth Century* (Cambridge, 1946).

MORRIS, W. A., *English Government at Work*, ii, ed. W. A. Morris, J. R. Strayer (Cambridge, Mass., 1947).

—— *The Frankpledge System* (Harvard Historical Studies, xiv, 1910).

MURRAY, K. M. E., *The Constitutional History of the Cinque Ports* (Manchester, 1935).

—— 'Faversham and the Cinque Ports', *T.R.H.S.* 4th ser. xviii (1935), 53–84.

New Palaeographical Society, 1 ser. (1905–6), (London 1914). Plate 73 is facsimile of the English and French texts of document 7.

OGLE, O., ed., *Royal Letters addressed to Oxford* (Oxford, 1892).

Parl. Writs: *Parliamentary Writs and Writs of Military Summons*, ed. Sir F. Palgrave, i (Record Com., 1827).

PASQUET, D., *An Essay on the Origins of the House of Commons* (Cambridge, 1925).

Peace of Paris: M. Gavrilovitch, *Étude sur la traité de Paris de 1259* (Paris, 1899).

PLANTA, J., *A Catalogue of the Manuscripts in the Cottonian Library deposited in the British Museum* (Record Com., 1802).

PLUCKNETT, T. F. T., *Legislation of Edward I* (Oxford, 1949).

—— ed. Taswell Langmead, T. P., *English Constitutional History from the Teutonic Conquest to the Present Time* (London, 1960).

POOLE, R. L., 'The "Mad" Parliament, 1258', *E.H.R.* xl (1925), 402.

POWICKE, M. R., 'Distraint of Knighthood under Henry III', *Speculum*, xxv (1950), 457–70.

P.R.: Patent Rolls of the reign of Henry III, 2 vols. (Public Record Office, 1901, 1903).

P.R.O.: Public Record Office.

PRYNNE, W., *The History of King John, Henry III and Edward I* (London, 1670).

RAMSAY, J. H., *The Dawn of the Constitution* (Oxford, 1908).

Reform and Rebellion: E. F. Jacob, *Studies in the period of Baronial Reform and Rebellion, 1258–1267* (Oxford, 1935).

Registrum Malmesburiense, ed. J. S. Brewer, 2 vols. (R.S., 1879–80).

RENOUARD, Y., 'Les Cahorsins, hommes d'affaires Français du XIIIᵉ siècle', *T.R.H.S.* 5th ser. xi (1961), 43–67.

RICHARDSON, H. G., 'Year Books and Plea Rolls as sources of Historical Information', *T.R.H.S.* 4th ser. v (1922), 28–62.

—— 'The English Coronation Oath', *T.R.H.S.*, 4th ser. xxiii (1941), 129–58; *Speculum*, xxiv (1949), 44–75.

RICHARDSON, H. G., and SAYLES, G. O., *The Governance of England* (Edinburgh, 1963).

—— *Law and Legislation from Aethelbert to Magna Carta* (Edinburgh, 1966).

—— 'The Provisions of Oxford', *B.J.R.L.* xvii (1933), 291–321.

—— 'Early Coronation Records', *B.I.H.R.* xiii (1936), 129–45; xiv (1937), 1–9, 145–8.

—— 'The Early Statutes', *Law Quarterly Review*, l (1934).

RILEY, H. T., ed. *Munimenta Gildhallae Londoniensis* (R.S., 1859–62).

Rishanger's Chronicle, ed. J. O. Halliwell, Camden Soc., old series, xv (1840).

Robert of Gloucester, the Metrical Chronicle of, ed. W. A. Wright (R.S., 1887).

Rot. Litt. Claus.: Rotuli Litterarum Clausarum, ed. T. D. Hardy (Record Com. 1833–4).

ROTH, C., *A History of the Jews in England* (Oxford, 1941).

Rotuli Selecti, ed. J. Hunter (Record Com. 1834).

Royal Letters: Royal and other letters illustrative of the reign of Henry III, ii, ed. W. W. Shirley (R.S., 1866).

R.S.: Rolls Series.

SANDERS, I. J., *Feudal Military Service in England* (Oxford, 1956).

—— 'The Texts of the Peace of Paris, 1259', *E.H.R.* lxvi (1951), 81–97.

SAYLES, G. D., *Select Cases in the Court of King's Bench*, Selden Society, lvi–viii (1936–8).

SCHRAMM, P. E., *A History of the English Coronation* (Oxford, 1937).

Simon de Montfort: *Simon de Montfort, earl of Leicester, 1208–1265* (ed. E. F. Jacob, Oxford, 1930). Translation of Bémont, *Simon de Montfort*.

SKEAT, W. W., 'On the only English Proclamation of Henry III, 18 October 1259', *Trans. of the Philological Society* (1880–1), app. vi, p. 169.

S. of Realm: *The Statutes of the Realm*, i, ed. A. Luders et al. (Record Com. 1810).

STEWART-BROWN, R., *Serjeants of the Peace in Medieval England* (Manchester, 1936).

STONES, E. L. G., *Anglo-Scottish Relations, 1174–1328, Some Selected Documents* (Nelson's Medieval Texts, 1965; repr. Oxford Medieval Texts, 1970).

STUBBS: *Select Charters Illustrative of English Constitutional History*, ed. W. Stubbs, 9th ed. (Oxford, 1913).

STUBBS, W., *The Constitutional History of England in its origin and development*, 3 vols., 6th ed. (Oxford, 1903–6).

TAIT, J., *The Medieval English Borough* (Manchester, 1936).

Taxation: S. K. Mitchell, *Studies in Taxation under John and Henry III* (New Haven, 1914).

The Thirteenth Century: Sir F. M. Powicke, *The Thirteenth Century, 1216–1307* (Oxford, 1953).

TOUT, T. F., 'Communitas bacheleria Angliae', *E.H.R.* xvii (1902), 89–95.

—— *Chapters in the Administrative History of Medieval England*, 6 vols. (Manchester, 1920–33).

—— *A Political History of England, 1216–77* (London, 1920).

Treaty Rolls preserved in the Public Record Office, i, *1234–1325*, ed. P. Chaplais (London, 1955).

TREHARNE, R. F., 'An unauthorised use of the Great Seal', *E.H.R.* xl (1925), 403–11.

—— 'The Nature of Parliament in the Reign of Henry III', *E.H.R.* lxxiv (1959), 590–610.

—— 'The "Mad" Parliament of Oxford, 1258', *History*, xxxii (1947), 108–11.

—— 'The Knights in the period of Reform and Rebellion, 1258–67', *B.I.H.R.* xxi (1946), 1–12.

—— 'The Role of Simon de Montfort in the period of baronial reform and rebellion, 1258–65', *Proc. of the British Academy*, xl (1954), 75–102.

—— 'The Battle of Northampton', *Northamptonshire Past and Present*, ii (1955), 13–30.

—— 'The Mise of Amiens, 23 January 1264', in *Studies in Medieval History presented to F. M. Powicke*, eds. R. W. Hunt, W. A. Pantin, and R. W. Southern (Oxford, 1948), pp. 223–39.

—— see *Baronial Plan*.

TREVET, N., *Annales*, ed. T. Hog (Eng. Hist. Soc., 1845).

T.R.H.S.: *Transactions of the Royal Historical Society*.

TURNER, G. J., *Select Pleas of the Forest*, Selden Soc. xiii (1901).

Urban IV, Les Registres d'Urban IV, ed. L. Dorez, J. Guiraud, 4 vols. (Bibliothèque des Écoles Françaises d'Athènes et de Rome, 2 ser. xiii (1892–1929)).

V.C.H.: *Victoria County History*.

WALNE, P., 'The Barons' Argument at Amiens, January, 1264', *E.H.R.* lxix (1954), 418–25; ibid. lxxiii (1958), 453–9.

WARD, L. P., 'The Coronation Ceremony in Medieval England', *Speculum*, xiv (1939), 160–78.

WATKIN, A. (ed.), *The Great Cartulary of Glastonbury*, 3 vols. (Somerset Record Soc. lix, 1947; lxiii, 1952; lxiv, 1956).

WHITE, A. B., *Self-government at the King's Command, a study in the beginnings of English Democracy* (Minneapolis, 1933).

WILKINSON, B., *The Constitutional History of Medieval England*, 3 vols. (London, 1948–58).

—— 'The Coronation Oath of Edward II and the Statute of York', *Speculum*, xix (1944), 445–69.

WILLARD, J. F., *Parliamentary Taxes on Personal Property, 1290–1334* (Cambridge, Mass. 1934).

WILLIAMS, G. A., 'Social and Constitutional Development in Thirteenth Century London', M.A. thesis, University of Wales (Aberystwyth, 1952).

—— 'London, 1216–1337', Ph.D. thesis, University of London, 1961.

—— *Medieval London, from commune to capital* (London, 1963).

WOOD, C. T., 'The Mise of Amiens and Saint Louis' theory of kingship', *French Historical Studies*, vi (1970), 300–10.

MANUSCRIPTS CITED, WITH SIGLA

Cambridge
M   Cambridge University Library MS. Mm. i. 27.
     Cambridge University Library MS. Ll. iv. 17.
     Cambridge University Library MS. Ll. iv. 18.
     Trinity College Library MS. O. 3. 20, no. 1192 in James's
       Catalogue.

Dublin
     Christ Church Cathedral, Dublin MS. Liber Niger.

Durham
     Muniments of the Dean and Chapter of Durham, Locellus, 1. 62.

London
A   British Museum, Cotton MS. Appendix xxv.
C   Cotton MS. Claudius D. ii.
                Cotton MS. Cleopatra E. i.
N   Cotton MS. Nero D. i.
T   Cotton MS. Tiberius B. iv.
                Cotton MS. Titus C. ix.
V   Cotton MS. Vespasian E. iii.
F   Harley MS. 1033.
R   Royal MS. 10. B. vi.
                Stowe MS. 1029.
H   Guildhall Record Office, Liber Horn.
     Inner Temple,   Petyt MS. 533/6.
     Public Record Office,   Charter Roll, C. 53/54.
                       Close Rolls, C. 54/75, 76, 77, 82.
                       Liber B (E. 36/275).
                       Liber X also called Statute Book of the
                          Exchequer (E. 164/9).
                       Papal Bulls, S.C. 7.3. (25) (29).
                            S.C. 7.33. (4) (5) (6) (9) (11).
                       Patent Rolls, C. 66/72, 73, 81, 82.

Oxford
B   Bodleian Library, Bodley MS. 91.
D   Dugdale MS. 20.
E   Rawlinson MS. C. 820.

Paris

K Archives Nationales, J. 654, no. 12. Transcript in Public Record
Office, London: P.R.O. Transcripts, 8/133, section 4, no. 37.

J Archives Nationales, J. 654, no. 17. Transcript in Public Record
Office, London: P.R.O. Transcripts, 8/133, section 6, no. 1.

Archives Nationales, J. 654, no. 29 *bis*.

Bibliothèque Nationale, MS. Latin 9016, no. 5.

DOCUMENTS OF THE
BARONIAL MOVEMENT
1258–1267

1

*Per regem et baronagium Anglie**

Rex omnibus, etc. Cum pro negotiis nostris arduis nos et regnum
nostrum contingentibus, proceres et fideles regni nostri ad nos
Londonias in quindena Pasche proximo preterite faceremus conuocari; et cum de negotiis supradictis et maxime de prosecutione
negotii Sicilie diligenter cum eisdem tractaremus; ac ipsi nobis
responderint quod si statum regni nostri per consilium fidelium
nostrorum rectificandum duxerimus, et dominus papa conditiones
circa factum Sicilie appositas meliorauerit, per quod negotium
illud prosequi possemus cum effectu, ipsi diligentiam fideliter
apponent erga communitatem regni nostri quod nobis commune
auxilium ad hoc prestetur;[1] nos eis concessimus quod infra
festum Natalis Domini proximo futurum per consilium proborum
et fidelium hominum nostrorum regni Anglie, una cum consilio
legati domini pape, si in Anglia medio tempore uenerit, statum
regni nostri ordinabimus et ordinationem illam firmiter obseruabimus: et ad hoc fideliter obseruandum, supponimus nos cohercioni
domini pape, ut nos ad hoc per censuram ecclesiasticam, prout
expedire uiderit, ualeat arctare: protestamur etiam quod Edwardus
filius noster primogenitus, prestito sacramento corporali, per
litteras suas concessit quod omnia superius expressa, quantum
in ipso est, fideliter et inuiolabiliter obseruabit et in perpetuum
obseruari procurabit. In cuius etc. Hiis testibus, Edwardo filio
nostro primogenito; Galfrido de Lezignan, Willelmo de Valencia,
fratribus nostris;[2] Petro de Sabaudia,[3] Iohanne de Plessetis comite

---

* *Text*: Rot. Pat. 42 Hen. III, m. 10. *Printed*: i. *C.P.R. 1247–58*, p. 626;
ii. *Foedera*, I. i. 370; iii. Stubbs, pp. 371–2. *See*: *Baronial Plan*, pp. 64–8.

---

[1] The last aid, granted in 1237, had been the cause of much controversy. The
aids in 1245 and 1253 had been for the marriage of Margaret to the king of
Scotland and for the knighting of the Lord Edward.
[2] Geoffrey and William were sons of Isabella of Angoulême, mother of
Henry III, by Hugh de Lusignan, count of La Marche. Their brother Guy was
in England and Aymer de Lusignan, bishop-elect of Winchester was another

1

From the king and the barons of England

The king to all men, etc. Since, for difficult business of ours, affecting both ourselves and our kingdom, we have caused the great and loyal men of our realm to be summoned to us at London in the quinzaine of Easter last [i.e. by 7 April 1258]; and since we were to negotiate diligently with them concerning these affairs, and especially about the furtherance of the Sicilian business; and since they have replied to us that, if we should be pleased to reform the state of our realm by the counsel of our loyal subjects, and provided that the lord pope would ameliorate the conditions which he has stated for the Sicilian affair in such a way that we might be enabled to take the matter up effectively, they would loyally use their influence with the community of the realm so that a common aid should be granted to us for that purpose;[1] we have granted to them that, before Christmas next, by the advice of our good and loyal men of the kingdom of England, together with the counsel of the lord pope's legate, if he comes to England in the meantime, we will make ordinance for the state of our kingdom and will firmly observe that ordinance; and for its faithful observance we will submit ourselves to the lord pope's coercion, so that he shall be empowered to compel us to it by ecclesiastical censure as he may see fit. We also declare that Edward, our eldest son, having given his personal oath, has granted in writing that, to the utmost of his ability, he will faithfully and inviolably observe all that is stated above, and will cause it always to be observed. In testimony of which, etc. These being witnesses: Edward, our eldest son; Geoffrey de Lusignan and William de Valence, our brothers;[2] Peter of Savoy,[3] John de Plessis, earl of Warwick,[4] John Mansel,

brother. A full account of William de Valence is given by F. R. Lewis in *Aberystwyth Studies*, xiii (1934), 11–35; xiv (1936), 69–92. Mistake on genealogical table facing p. 92: Alice, wife of John de Warenne, was sister and not niece of William de Valence.

[3] Peter was brother of Boniface of Savoy, archbishop of Canterbury. Their sister Beatrice, wife of Raimond-Berengar, count of Provence, was mother of Eleanor, wife of Henry III (*G.E.C.*, x. 805–9; C. W. Previté Orton, *The Early History of the House of Savoy, 1000–1233* (Cambridge, 1912), p. 392; F. Mugnier, *Les Savoyards en Angleterre au XIIIe siècle* (Chambéry, 1890)).

Warrewici,[4] Iohanne Maunsel thesaurario Eboracensi,[5] Henrico de Wingeham decano Sancti Martini, London;[6] Petro de Riuallis,[7] Guidone de Rocheford,[8] Roberto Walerand,[9] presentibus et multis aliis comitibus, baronibus regni nostri. Datum apud Westmonasterium, ii die Maii.

2

2 MAY 1258

Status regni nostri ordinetur*

Rex omnibus, etc. Noveritis nos concessisse proceribus et magnatibus regni nostri, iuramento in animam nostram per Robertum Walerand prestito, quod per xii. fideles de concilio nostro iam electos et per alios xii. fideles nostros, electos ex parte procerum ipsorum,[1] qui apud Oxoniam a festo Penetecostes proximo futuro in unum mensem conuenient,[2] ordinetur, rectificetur et reformetur status regni nostri secundum quod melius uiderint expedire ad honorem Dei et ad fidem nostram ac regni nostri utilitatem. Et si forte aliqui electorum ex parte nostra absentes fuerint, liceat illis qui presentes fuerint alios substituere loco absentium; et similiter fiat ex parte predictorum procerum et fidelium nostrorum. Et quicquid per XXIIII[o] utrimque electos

---

* *Text*: Rot. Pat. 42 Hen. III, m. 10. *Printed*: i. *C.P.R. 1247-58*, p. 626; ii. *Foedera*, I. i. 371; iii. Stubbs, p. 372. *See*: *Baronial Plan*, pp. 64-8; *B.J.R.L.* xvii (1933), 291-321; *E.H.R.* lxxiv (1959), 590-610.

---

[4] A royal favourite, husband of the heiress of the baronies of Hook Norton, Oxon., and Warwick (*English Baronies*, pp. 54, 94).

[5] A key civil servant. Chancellor, 1246-7, 1248; Chancellor of St. Paul's, London; Provost of the collegiate church of St. John the Evangelist, Beverley, Yorks.; Treasurer of York Minster (*Baronial Plan, passim*; *British Chronology*, p. 83; *D.N.B.* xxxvi. 84-6; *V.C.H. Yorks.*, iii. 354).

[6] A trusted civil servant. Chancellor, Jan. 1255-Oct. 1260; Bishop of London, June 1259-July 1262 when he died (*Baronial Plan, passim*; *British Chronology*, pp. 83, 239).

[7] A Poitevin, son or perhaps nephew of Peter des Roches, bishop of Winchester, 1205-38. Keeper of the Wardrobe, 1218, 1231-4, 1257; Treasurer of the Chamber and Wardrobe, 1231-4; Treasurer, 1233-4; Keeper of the Privy Seal, 1232-4 (*Baronial Plan, passim*; *British Chronology*, pp. 77, 99).

treasurer of York,[5] Henry de Wingham, dean of St. Martin's, London;[6] Peter des Rivaux,[7] Guy de Rocheford,[8] Robert Walerand,[9] in the presence of many other earls and barons of our realm. Given at Westminster, 2 May.

2

2 MAY 1258

That the state of our realm be reformed

The king to all men, etc. Know that we have granted to the chief men and the magnates of our realm, having taken, by the agency of Robert Walerand, an oath upon our soul, that the state of our realm shall be put in order, corrected, and reformed by twelve loyal men of our council, already chosen, and by twelve other of our loyal subjects, chosen by these leading men,[1] who shall meet at Oxford one month after next Whitsunday[2] [9 June], accordingly as they shall see to be most fitting to the honour of God, their fealty to us, and the good of our kingdom. And if by chance any of those chosen on our side shall be absent, those who attend may substitute others in place of the absentees, and the same shall apply to those chosen by the said leading men and faithful subjects of ours. And whatever shall be ordained on this matter by the twenty-four

[8] A Poitevin, bailiff of Colchester. Forced to leave England with other foreigners, but returned in 1261. Remained in royal service after the battle of Evesham (*C.P.R. 1258–66, passim*).

[9] A civil servant. Steward of the Household, 1250–70; Deputy Chancellor, 1262; Justice of the Forests South of the Trent, 1259; constable of many castles, 1259–61; Sheriff of Kent, 1263; Keeper of the Cinque Ports, 1261. Possibly a member of the Council of Fifteen after July 1260 (*Baronial Plan, passim; British Chronology*, p. 74).

[1] See doc. 5, cls. 2, 3 for the names of the royal twelve and the baronial twelve. The Latin word *concilio* has been translated council, rather than counsel, as there is evidence of the existence of a fixed group of men, bound by oath to the service of the king (*Ann. Mon.* i. 395–7). The words 'already chosen' suggest that the king had acted upon decisions, possibly born in the parliament which had met in London *c.* 7 Apr. (doc. 1), and expressed forcibly on 30 Apr. (*Baronial Plan*, p. 66). The 'leading men' were presumably those who had expressed opposition to the king in April.

[2] *C.P.R. 1247–58*, p. 626 wrongly states that the Oxford meeting took place on Whitsunday.

et super hoc iuratos, uel maiorem partem eorum, circa hoc
ordinatum fuerit inuiolabiliter obseruabimus;[3] uolentes et firmiter
ex nunc precipientes quod ab omnibus inuiolabiliter obseruatur
eorum ordinatio. Et securitatem omnimodam quam ipsi uel maior
pars eorum ad huius rei obseruationem prouiderint, uel prouiderit,
eis sine qualibet contradictione, plene faciemus et fieri procurabimus. Protestamur etiam quod Edwardus filius noster
primogenitus, prestito sacramento corporali, per litteras suas
concessit quod omnia superius expressa et concessa, quantum in
ipso est, fideliter et inuiolabiliter obseruabit et procurabit in
perpetuum obseruari. Promiserunt etiam comites et barones
memorati quod, expletis negotiis superius tactis, bona fide
laborabunt ad hoc quod auxilium nobis commune prestetur a
communitate regni nostri. In cuius sunt his testibus ut supra.
Datum ut supra [ii die Maii].

3

MAY 1258

*Petitio Baronum**

Domino rege Henrico apud Wodestok' existente, conuocatis et
conuenientibus apud Oxoniam totius regni magnatibus, cum
equis et armis maioribus et minoribus, una cum clero, ad
prouisionem et regni in melius reformationem et ordinationem
faciendam, sub fidei sacramento prolati sunt ibidem articuli qui
indigent in regno correctione subsequentes.

1. *a*Petunt comites et barones de successionibus, quod filius
natus et primogenitus uel filia post patrem libere ingrediatur
possessionem patris, ita quod capitalis dominus debet habere

---

a D *has* f. 281 *at this point.*

* *Text*: British Museum, Cotton MS. Vespasian E. iii, ff. 81–82ᵛ (old ff.
78–79ᵛ) (V). *Printed*: i. *Ann. Mon.* i. 438–43; ii. *Anglicarum Scriptores*, i. 407–10;
iii. Stubbs, pp. 373–8. *Additional Text*: Bodleian Library, Dugdale MS. 20,
ff. 138ᵛ–140 (D). This is possibly copied from a missing part of Cotton MS.
Titus C. ix (see doc. 30). Dugdale refers to ff. 281–4 of the source from which he
copied this document. See text notes. The wording is not identical with the
text in V and some clauses are omitted. *See*: *Baronial Plan*, pp. 70–1, 175–8.

chosen from both sides, and sworn to this purpose, or by the majority of them, we will observe inviolably;[3] and we will and firmly command, from this moment, that their ordinance shall be inviolably observed by all men. And whatever guarantee they or the majority of them shall stipulate for the observance of this matter, we will fulfil and cause it to be fulfilled to them without any opposition. We also declare [as in document 1]. The earls and barons have promised that when the business stated above has been completed, they will do their best, in good faith, to ensure that a common aid shall be granted to us by the community of our realm. Witnessed as above; dated as above [document 1].

3

MAY 1258

The Petition of the Barons

While the Lord King Henry was at Woodstock, the magnates of the realm, both high and low, together with the clergy, having been summoned to Oxford with horses and arms to make provision and ordinance for the reform of the kingdom, the following articles were brought forward, under an oath of fealty, as matters requiring correction in the kingdom.

1. In the matter of inheritance, the earls and barons ask that the firstborn son, or daughter, being of full age and having proved his right to do towards his lord what he ought to do, shall have free

---

The *petitio* is preceded in V with the statement that the document was produced at the Oxford parliament as a plan for reform. Topics mentioned in this document influenced later actions and enactments of the reformers. Only one matter, relief, mentioned in clause one, does not reappear. The MS. text is divided into paragraphs, the initial letters alternating in blue and red. The paragraphs have been numbered for ease of reference.

---

[3] These regulations are reminiscent of Magna Carta where the practices of co-option to fill vacancies and majority decision were mentioned (*Magna Carta*, pp. 334-5). See doc. 5, cls. 3, 11.

simplicem seisinam*b* per unum ex balliuis suis, ita quod nichil
capiatur per predictum balliuum de exitibus terre uel redditibus;
quando uero heres fuerit plene etatis, et prosecutus ius suum
fuerit, ad faciendum domino suo quod facere debet: et ita fiat
de fratre uel sorore et de auunculo seisito, si obierit sine herede,
ad nepotem suum filium primogeniti; et si frater non habeatur,
ad liberos fratris uel sororis, et sic deinceps, per rationabile
releuium[1] et homagium et releuia domino feodi facienda; ita
quod dominus feodi medio tempore nullum faciat uastum uel
exilium, uenditionem uel alienationem, de domibus uel boscis,
uiuariis, parcis siue hominibus uillenagium tenentibus. Quod si
hoc fecerit et inde conuictus fuerit, secundum quantitatem delicti
puniatur. Et omnia dampna que predictus heres ea occasione
habuerit, sine dilatione restituet. Et cum heres fecerit domino
regi rationabile releuium cum fuerit plene etatis, domina regina inde
petit aurum secundum estimationem decime partis, et uidetur
quod non debet habere nisi de fine.[2]

2. Item petunt remedium quod ubi aliquis infra etatem existens
tenet plures terras de pluribus et diuersis dominis, et idem teneat
aliquam quantitatem terre de domino rege in capite per seruicium
militare uel sergantiam, occasione cuius seruicii dominus rex
habet custodiam omnium terrarum et tenementorum predictorum
heredis, de quocumque tenuerit; si dominus rex eat in exercitu,
licet teneat in manu sua plura feoda militum de feodis aliorum,
sicut predictum est, nichilominus petit totum seruicium a predictis
dominis feodi qui de eo tenent in capite, nec eis uult quicquam
allocare ex hoc quod tenet custodiam predictorum feodorum in
manu sua.[3]

3. *c*Item petunt barones habere custodiam terrarum et tenementorum suorum qui sunt de feodis suis, et heredum usque ad
legitimam etatem ipsorum; ita quod dominus rex habeat maritagium
et custodiam corporis penes se: et hoc petunt de iure communi.

b D *has* f. 281ᵛ *at this point.*   *c* D *has* f. 282 *at this point.*

---

[1] Relief is not mentioned in any later enactments of the reformers or of the
king. Many unanswered questions surround the problems of the payment of
relief in the thirteenth century. See I. J. Sanders, *Feudal Military Service,*
pp. 98–107, for an examination of this topic.
[2] If a fine was paid for a concession one tenth of the fine was added to be paid
as a present to the queen. The petitioners are claiming that relief is not a fine,
consequently no queen's gold should be charged.

entry after his father to his father's possessions; and that the chief lord shall have only formal seisin, by one of his bailiffs, whereby nothing may be taken by the bailiff from the profits of the land or from the rents. And let this be done also when a brother, or a sister or an uncle has died in possession without any heir of his body and [succession goes] to his grandson, son of the firstborn son, or, if there is no brother, to the children of his brother or sister, and so on, by reasonable relief and by doing homage and [paying] relief to the lord of the fee,[1] always providing that, in the meantime, the lord of the fee shall make no waste, destruction, sale, or alienation of houses or of woods, stewponds, parks, or men holding in villeinage. And if the lord does any of these things and it is proved against him let him be punished in proportion to the offence; and let him at once make good all the losses which the heir may have suffered thereby.

And when an heir who is of full age has undertaken to pay a reasonable relief to the lord king, the lady queen demands queen's gold in consequence, calculated at the rate of one-tenth, whereas it would appear that she ought not to have it except when a fine is made.[2]

2. Further, they ask for a remedy in such a case as this: that, when a minor holds many lands from several different lords, and at the same time holds any land whatsoever from the lord king in chief by knight service or by serjeanty, by reason of which service the lord king has the custody of all the lands and tenements of the said heir, from no matter whom he holds them; then, if the lord king goes to war, for the reason stated, although he holds in his hand many knights' fees belonging to the fees of other lords, he nevertheless demands the full service from the said lords of the fee who hold of him in chief, nor will he make them any allowance in respect of the fact that he holds in his hand the custody of the said fees.[3]

3. Further, they ask that they may have the custody of their lands and tenements which belong to their fees, and of heirs until the heirs come of age, provided that the lord king shall have the right of marriage and the custody of the person of the heir: and this they ask as a matter of common right.

[3] A tenant who was a major, holding lands of the king and of other lords, paid scutage to the king for those lands which he held of the crown, and by reason of the writ *de scutagio habendo*, to the lords of the other lands which he held.

4. Item petunt quod castra regis committantur custodienda ad fideles suos et de regno Anglie natos, ob plures casus qui poterunt in regno Anglie euenire uel emergere.[4]

5. [d]Item petunt quod castra regis que sunt supra portus maris, ubi nauigia euenire possunt, committantur fidelibus hominibus de regno Anglie natis, propter pericula plurima euidencia que emergere possunt si aliis committerentur.

6. Item petunt de maritagiis domino regi pertinentibus, quod non maritentur ubi disparagentur, uidelicet hominibus qui non sunt de natione regni Anglie.[5]

7. Item petunt remedium quod bosci et terre infra metas foreste non existentes, qui per ambulacionem proborum hominum, et per quindecimam partem omnium bonorum hominum Anglie domino regi datam, deafforestati fuerunt, per uoluntatem suam reafforestauit.[6]

8. Item petunt de assartis factis infra metas foreste de terris suis propriis et tenementorum suorum de nouo arentatis, unde dominus rex uendicat sibi custodiam heredum talium, et nichilominus uendicat seruicium omne inde debitum.

9. Item petunt remedium quod foreste deafforestate per cartam regis et per finem eidem per communitatem tocius regni factam, ita quod quisque ubique possit libere fugare, dominus rex de uoluntate sua pluribus dedit de predicta libertate warennas, que sunt ad nocumentum predicte libertatis concesse.[7]

10. Item petunt remedium quod religiosi non intrent in feodum comitum et baronum et aliorum sine uoluntate eorum, per quod amittunt imperpetuum custodias, maritagia, releuia et eschetas.[8]

---

[d] D om. *this clause.*

---

[4] See doc. 4.

[5] This may be an allusion to the marriage of Joan, daughter of Warin de Montchenesy, to William de Valence, the king's half-brother. Joan's mother was Joan, sister and co-heir of Anselm Marshal, earl of Pembroke who d.s.p. 1245. One should not forget that Simon de Montfort, a foreigner, was married to Eleanor, sister of Henry III and widow of William Marshal, d. 1231, brother of Anselm and Joan (*English Baronies*, pp. 63, 111).

[6] Promises of deforestation were made in *Magna Carta*, cl. 47 and in the Charter of the Forest issued in 1217 (*Magna Carta*, pp. 328, 359). In 1225 the king had been granted a fifteenth as the price for the reissue of the charters (Stubbs, pp. 351–3).

[7] Right of free warren allowed the grantee to take beasts and fowl of the warren—rabbit, pheasant, quail, and others. Furthermore the grantee possessed

4. Further, they ask that the royal castles shall be committed to the custody of the king's faithful subjects born in the kingdom of England, on account of many dangers which might befall or arise in the realm of England.[4]

5. Further, they ask that royal castles situated on a harbour, into which ships might sail, should be entrusted to true-born Englishmen, on account of many evident perils which could arise were they entrusted to others.

6. Further, they ask in the matter of marriages pertaining to the lord king, that the [women] shall not be married in such a way as to disparage them—that is, to men who are not true-born English-men.[5]

7. Further, they ask for remedy of this: that whereas woods and lands lying outside the bounds of the forest were disafforested by a grant to the lord king of a fifteenth of all the goods of the men of England and by the perambulation of sound men, the lord king has now reafforested them arbitrarily.[6]

8. Further, they ask for redress in the matter of newly-arrented assarts made within the bounds of the forest on their own lands and of their own holdings, on account of which the lord king claims for himself the custody of the heirs of any such holdings, and nevertheless claims also all the service due in respect of them.

9. Further, they ask for redress in this: that whereas the forests were disafforested by royal charter and by a fine made between the lord king and the community of the whole realm, in order that everyone might be able to hunt freely everywhere, the lord king arbitrarily grants rights of warren to many persons from this liberty, which grants infringe the grant of the liberty.[7]

10. Further, they ask a remedy: namely that monks be not allowed to have entry into the fees of earls, barons, and other lords without their consent, whereby they would lose in perpetuity wardships, marriages, reliefs, and escheats.[8]

such powers of jurisdiction as were required to protect this right. See G. J. Turner, *Select Pleas of the Forest*, Selden Soc. xiii (1901).

[8] Restrictions on the tenure of land by the clergy were enforced by cl. 2 of the Constitutions of Clarendon, cl. 43 of the 1217 reissue of *Magna Carta*, cl. 14 of the Provisions of Westminster, and the *Statutum de Viris Religiosis* (Douglas, ii. 719, cl. 2; *Magna Carta*, p. 356, cl. 36; *S. of Realm*, i. 19; doc. 11, cl. 14; Stubbs, pp. 451–2; T. F. T. Plucknett, *Legislation of Edward I* (1949), pp. 94–102).

11. Item petunt remedium de abbatiis et prioratibus fundatis de feodis comitum[e] et baronum, unde dominus rex ad vacacionem dictarum domorum inde petit custodias, ita quod non possunt eligere sine uoluntate domini regis: et hoc est in preiudicium comitum et baronum, cum seruicia inde debita domino regi sustineant ut medii.

12. Item petunt remedium de hoc, quod dominus rex aliquando pluribus dat per cartam suam aliena iura, dicens illa esse escheta sua, unde tales dicunt quod non debent nec possunt respondere sine domino rege. Et cum iusticiarii hoc ostendunt domino regi, nichil iusticie in hac parte factum est.

13. Item petunt remedium, quod cum ipsi comites et barones habeant terras suas in pluribus comitatibus, et iusticiarii domini regis sint itinerantes uno tempore in omnibus comitatibus predictis, ad placitandum de omnibus placitis, et de foresta simul et semel, et nisi ipsi comites et barones compareant coram illis primo die communis summonitionis, amerciabuntur ad uoluntatem domini regis pro sua absentia, nisi habeant breue domini regis de acquietantia.

14. Item predicti iusticiarii capiunt finem grauem pro pulchro placitando[9] de quolibet comitatu. Ne occasionentur et non debent emere iura et de aliis pluribus occasionibus de placitis corone. Et si uillate quatuor propinquiores ad mortem hominis interfecti uel submersi non accesserint, omnes de aetate xii. annorum predictarum iiii. uillatarum grauiter amerciabuntur.

15. Item petunt[f] quod nullus possit firmare castrum supra portum maris, uel supra insulam infra inclusam, nisi sit de consensu consilii tocius regni Anglie;[10] quia plura pericula possent inde euenire.

16. Item de uicecomitum firmis et aliorum balliuorum liberorum qui capiunt comitatus et alias balliuas ad firmam, qui etiam habent comitatus suos ad tam altam firmam quod non possunt dictam firmam inde leuare; nec amerciant homines secundum quantitatem delicti, set ad redempcionem ultra uires eos arctant.

[e] D has f. 282[v] at this point.   [f] D has f. 283 at this point.

[9] Fair pleading, also called miskenning, was failure to plead using fixed legal terminology.

[10] The use of the term 'council of the whole realm of England', in contrast with 'the king's council', shows the development of the ideas of self-government which inspired the nobles in 1258. A similar terminology appears in doc. 4

11. Further, they ask for redress in the matter of abbeys and priories founded out of the fees of earls and barons, whereof, at the falling vacant of [the headships of] the said houses, the lord king demands custody, so that they cannot hold an election without the lord king's consent: and this is prejudicial to the earls and barons, since, as intermediate lords, they bear the service due from these houses to the lord king.

12. Further, they ask redress in this: that the lord king sometimes gives the rights of others to many persons by royal charter, stating that these rights are his escheats, on account of which the grantees declare that they cannot and should not answer [concerning these grants] without the lord king. And when the justices report this to the lord king, no justice is done in these cases.

13. Further, they ask for a remedy in this: that whereas the earls and barons hold their lands in many different counties, and the lord king's justices are on eyre in all the aforesaid counties simultaneously, to take all pleas, and those of the forest, at one and the same time, then unless such earls and barons appear before them on the first day of the common summons, they are amerced at the lord king's will for their absence, unless they hold the lord king's writ of quittance.

14. Further, the aforesaid justices levy a heavy fine for fair pleading[9] in each county court. They [suitors at the court] should not be prosecuted for this, and they ought not to buy justice and [pay money] on many other occasions for pleas of the crown. And if, at the death of a man slain or drowned, all four neighbouring townships do not attend, then all over the age of twelve in the aforesaid four townships are heavily amerced.

15. Further, they ask that no one shall be allowed to fortify a castle on a harbour, or upon an island enclosed within a harbour, unless by the consent of the council of the whole realm of England,[10] since many perils might arise therefrom.

16. Further, concerning the farms of sheriffs and of other free bailiffs, who take counties and other bailiwicks at farm, and who hold their counties at such high farms that they cannot recover these farms from them: for such officials do not amerce men according to the amount of their offences, but rather force them to pay ransoms beyond their means.

where Hugh Bigod is called 'justiciar of England' rather than 'justiciar of the king'.

17. Insuper dicunt quod uicecomites ad duos turnos[11] suos per annum demandant personalem aduentum comitum et baronum tenentium baronias suas in diuersis locis et comitatibus; et si non uenerint ibi personaliter, amerciant ipsos sine consideracione et iudicio. Et hoc quia quilibet uicecomes dicit quod in dictis turnis est iusticiarius.[g]

18. Item ubi aliquis habet aliquam partem terre, scilicet duas acras terre uel plus uel minus, sine mansione eidem adiacente, nisi racione illius terre ad turnos suos ueniat, tunc pro uoluntate sua amerciabitur.

19. [h]Item si aliqua iusticiaria mandata fuerit specialiter coram aliquo iusticiario assignato, uel de noua disseisina, uel de morte antecessoris, uicecomites clamare faciunt in mercatis, quod omnes milites et libere tenentes patrie ueniant ad certum diem et locum audituri et facturi preceptum regis, et cum ibi non uenerint eos amerciant pro uoluntate sua.[12]

20. Item petunt remedium de hoc quod si aliquis comes uel baro, uel balliuus, uel aliquis alius qui libertatem habeat, uel in ciuitate uel in uillata, ceperit aliquem malefactorem et illum optulerit uicecomiti uel suo balliuo, ad incarcerandum uel custodiendum quousque de eo fiat iudicium, uicecomes recusat admittere prisonem illum, nisi is qui ipsum ceperit finem faciat per sic quod ipsum recipiat.

21. Item de eo quod multi homines de diuersis partibus regni propter caristiam temporis uenientes, et per diuersas prouincias transitum facientes, fame et inedia moriuntur, et tunc per legem terre uisum factum est per coronatores, et quatuor villatas uicinas, et cum predicte uillate de ita mortuis nichil sciunt nec dicunt, nisi quod casu predicto moriuntur, et quia nichil de huthesia Engle-scheria assignatur, amerciatur patria coram iusticiariis tamquam de murdro.[13]

22. Item de prisis domini regis in nundinis et mercatis et ciuitatibus, uidelicet quod hi qui assignati fuerint ad predictas prisas[i] capiendas, eas rationabiliter capiant, scilicet quantum

---

[g] *The scribe adds the words* quo ad diem. D *adds* quantum ad diem illum *at the end of this clause.*   [h] D *om. clauses 19 and 20.*   [i] D *has f.* 283[v] *at this point.*

[11] The sheriff's tourn of the county was, among other things, to enforce view of frank-pledge (W. A. Morris, *The Frankpledge System* (1910)).
[12] Full attendance was only legally due at the times of a General Eyre.

17. Further, they say that the sheriffs, at their two tourns a year,[11] demand the attendance in person of earls and barons, who hold their baronies in different places and counties: and if they do not attend in person, the sheriffs amerce them without consideration and judgement, and they do this because every sheriff claims that, on the tourns, he is a justice for the occasion.

18. Moreover, where anyone has any scrap of land, such as two acres, or a little more or less, without any residence nearby, then unless he comes to the tourns on account of this holding, he will be arbitrarily amerced.

19. Further, if any court matter is specially ordered before any chosen justice, such as a case of *novel disseisin* or of *mort d'ancestor*, the sheriffs have proclamation made in the markets that all the knights and freeholders of the district shall come on a certain day to a certain place, to hear and to do the king's command, and if they do not come there, the sheriffs amerce them at will.[12]

20. They also seek a remedy for this: that if any earl, baron, bailiff, or any other having a liberty in a city or in a township, has arrested a malefactor and offered to deliver him to the sheriff or to his bailiff, to be imprisoned and held until judgement can be passed on him, the sheriff refuses to accept such a prisoner unless the person who has arrested him makes a fine so that the sheriff shall take custody of him.

21. Further in this: that many men coming, on account of the present famine, from different parts of the land, and making their way through the different counties, die of hunger and want; and then according to the law of the land, the coroners hold inquest with the four nearest townships; and when the townships say that they know nothing of the men who have died in this way, save that they have died of the aforesaid cause, since there is no presentment of Englishry, the district is amerced before the justices as in a case of *murdrum*.[13]

22. Moreover, in the matter of the lord king's prises in fairs, markets, and cities, they ask that those who are appointed to take the said prises shall take them reasonably—that is, as much as is

[13] See doc. 31, n. 4. The *murdrum* fine, which was enforced by William the Conqueror, was levied on the neighbourhood in which a dead body was found. It was assumed that the dead person was not English until the presentment of Englishry proved otherwise.

pertinet ad predictos usus domini regis; unde conqueruntur, quod dicti captores capiunt in duplo uel in triplo plusquam cedit ad usus domini regis: capiunt et totum illud superfluum ad opus suum, uel ad opus amicorum suorum retinent, et partem inde aliquam uendunt.[14]

23. Item conqueruntur quod dominus rex de prisis nullam fere facit pacacionem, ita quod plures mercatores de regno Anglie ultra modum depauperentur, et alii mercatores extranei ea occasione subtrahunt se deueniendi in terram istam cum suis mercibus, unde terra magnam incurrit iacturam.

24. Item petunt remedium de sectis de nouo leuatis in regno tam ad comitatus et hundreda, quam ad curias libertatis, que numquam aliquo tempore fieri consueuerunt.

25. Item petunt remedium de hoc, quod Iudei[15] aliquando debita sua et terras eis inuadiatas ⟨tradunt⟩ magnatibus et poten-tioribus regni, qui terras minorum ingrediuntur ea occasione: et licet ipsi qui debitum debent, parati sint ad soluendum predictum debitum cum usuris, prefati magnates negocium prorogant, ut predicte terre et tenementa aliquo modo sibi remanere possint, dicentes quod sine Iudeo cui debebatur debitum nichil possunt nec sciunt facere, et semper differunt solucionem dicte pecunie, ita quod occasione mortis uel alicuius alterius casus, euidens periculum et manifesta patet imminere exheredacio his quorum predicta tenementa fuerunt.

26. Item petunt remedium de Christianis usurariis, ut de Caursinis[16] qui degunt Lond(oniis), cum Christiane religioni contrarium uideatur manutenere uel fouere aliquos huiusmodi, saltim ex quo nomen Christiani induerunt. Et preterea per eorum usuras plures[j] depauperentur et destruuntur; et etiam plures mercandias uenientes uersus Lond(onias), tam per aquam quam per terram, occupant et emunt, ad magnum detrimentum

---

[j] D has f. 284 at this point.

[14] The *Lib. de Ant. Leg.* p. 39, states that on 5 Aug. 1258 laws were passed restricting prise in the city of London.

[15] This clause is evidence that the nobles were not interested only in their own class, for the burden of Jewish debts fell on the lower ranks of society. See C. Roth, *A History of the Jews in England*, Oxford, 1941; P. Elman, 'Jewish Finance in Thirteenth Century England', *B.I.H.R.* xv (1938), 112; M. Adler, 'The Testimony of the London Jewry against the Ministers of Henry III', *Trans. Jewish Historical Society of England*, xiv (1935–9), 141–85; articles by

required for the lord king's uses, for complaint is made that the said collectors take two or three times more than is actually handed over for the lord king's use, and that they take the whole of the surplus for their own profit, or keep it for the use of their friends, or even sell part of it.[14]

23. Moreover, complaint is made that the lord king scarcely ever pays for his prises, so that many English merchants are impoverished beyond measure, while alien merchants for this reason refuse to come with their goods into the kingdom, wherefore the land suffers grievous loss.

24. Further, they ask a remedy in the matter of suits newly raised, both in county and hundred courts and in courts of liberties, which were never before performed customarily.

25. Further, they seek a remedy in this: that Jews[15] sometimes [transfer] their debts, and the lands pledged to them, to magnates and other persons powerful in the kingdom, who on this pretext enter the lands of minors, and although those who owe the debt are ready to pay it, with the interest, the magnates put off the matter, in order that by hook or by crook the lands and holdings shall remain in their hands, saying that without the Jew to whom the debt was owed they cannot do anything, and that they know nothing, and thus they continually put off the repayment of the borrowed money so that, by the intervention of death or of some other mischance, evident peril and manifest disherison plainly threaten those to whom the holdings belonged.

26. Further, they ask for a remedy in the matter of Christian usurers, such as the Caursini[16] who dwell in London, since it seems contrary to Christian religion to maintain and favour men of this kidney, especially as they profess and call themselves Christians. And, moreover, many are impoverished and ruined by their usuries; and they also buy up and corner much merchandise on its way to London both by water and by land, to the great loss of the

A. C. Cramer on the Jewish Exchequer, *Speculum*, xvi (1941), 226–9; *A.H.R.* xlv (1939–40), 327–37.

[16] In the middle years of the thirteenth century the merchants of Cahors became so active in financial dealings that the term Cahorsin assumed the meaning of usurer or moneylender (N. Denholm-Young, 'The Merchants of Cahors', *Medievalia et Humanistica*, iv (1946), 37–44; Y. Renouard, 'Les Cahorsins, hommes d'affaires Français du xiiie siècle', *T.R.H.S.* 5th ser. xi (1961), 43–67). See doc. 4.

mercatorum et omnium predicte ciuitatis, et ad magnum dampnum domini regis, quia cum dominus rex talliat predictam ciuitatem, in nullo participant nec participare uolunt cum predictis ciuibus in tallagiis et aliis domino regi faciendis.

27. Item petunt remedium de maritagiis alienatis, uidelicet in tali casu; si aliquis dederit alicui unam carucatam terre in maritagio cum filia uel sorore habendam et tenendam eis et heredibus de predictis filia uel sorore exeuntibus, ita uidelicet quod si predicta filia uel soror obierit sine herede de corpore suo, terra cum pertinentiis integre reuertatur ad ipsum qui terram dederit in maritagium uel ad heredes suos; et cum predictum donum non sit absolutum set conditionale, tamen mulieres post mortem uirorum suorum in uiduitate sua dant uel uendunt predicta maritagia et infeodant pro uoluntate sua, licet heredes de corpore suo non habuerint, nec huiusmodi feofamenta hucusque aliquatenus fuerunt reuocata. Vnde petunt quod ex equitate iuris, ratione predicte condicionis, siue per breue de ingressu uel aliquo alio modo competenti prouideatur remedium ad reuocandum huius modi feofamenta, et quod in tali casu procedatur ad iudicium pro ipso petente.^{k}17

28. Item petunt remedium de hoc, quod dominus rex large facit militibus de regno suo acquietanciam, ne in assisis ponantur, iuramentis uel recognicionibus, propter quod in pluribus comitatibus pro defectu militum non potest capi aliqua magna assisa, et ita remanent huiusmodi loquele ita quod petentes nunquam iusticiam consequntur.[18]

29. Item in pluribus comitatibus usitatum est, quod si aliquis defert breue de recto directum proximo capitali domino feodi, et petens probauerit defaltam curie ipsius capitalis domini pro consuetudine regni, et post eat ad comitatum et petat quod aduersarius suus summoneatur quod sit ad proximum comitatum, ueniet superior capitalis dominus feodi eiusdem et petit suam

---

^{k} D ends per ipso pe (ceterum deest) [sic]. Clauses 28 and 29 are omitted.

[17] This foreshadows the enactment De Donis Conditionalibus, part of the Statute of Westminster ii, 1285 (Stubbs, pp. 462–3; Plucknett, op. cit., pp. 131–5).

[18] The difficulties arising from the grants of exemption from administrative duties are among the reasons for the practice of distraint of knighthood which developed in the thirteenth century. Gaillard Lapsley, 'Buzones', E.H.R. xlvii (1932), 177–93, 545–67; M. R. Powicke, 'Distraint of Knighthood under Henry III', Speculum, xxv (1950), 457–70; R. F. Treharne, 'The Knights in

merchants and of all men of the city, and also to the great loss of the lord king, since, when the lord king tallages the said city, they bear no share along with the citizens, and refuse to bear any share, in tallages and in doing other services to the lord king.

27. Further, they seek a remedy concerning alienated marriage portions, as in cases of this kind: if anyone has given to another a carucate of land as a dowry along with a daughter or a sister, to have or to hold to them and their heirs issuing from the daughter or sister, provided that if the daughter or sister shall die without any heir of her body, the land and all appurtenances shall revert entirely to him who gave the land as a dowry, or to his heirs; and whereas the gift is not absolute but conditional, nevertheless, women, after the deaths of their husbands, in their widowhood, give or sell the dowries, and enfeoff them as they choose, although they have no heirs of their bodies, and so far enfeoffments of this kind have not been annulled. Therefore they ask, that as a matter of equity in right, on grounds of this condition, a remedy shall be provided to annul this kind of enfeoffment, either by writ of entry or by some other competent means, and that in such cases the courts shall be empowered to proceed to judgement in favour of the petitioner.[17]

28. Further, they ask a remedy in this: that the lord king freely grants to the knights of his realm acquittances, so that they shall not be put on assizes, juries, or recognitions, with the result that, in many counties, for lack of knights it is not possible to hold any grand assize, so that pleas of this kind remain unfinished, and petitioners never obtain justice.[18]

29. Further, in many counties it is customary that if anyone brings a writ of right directed to the next chief lord of the fee, and the petitioner, according to the custom of the realm, has proved default of the court of his chief lord, and then goes to the county court and asks that his adversary shall be summoned to appear at the next county court, if the next highest chief lord of the said fee appears, and demands his jurisdiction in the matter, he will get it;

the period of Reform and Rebellion', *B.I.H.R.* xxi (1946), 1–12; N. Denholm-Young, 'Feudal Society in the Thirteenth Century, the Knights', *History*, xxix (1944), 107–19, also in *Collected Papers*, pp. 56–67; A. B. White, *Self-Government at the King's Command, a Study in the Beginnings of English Democracy* (1933).

curiam inde et habebit: et, probata defalta curie, ueniet adhuc alter superior dominus feodi illius et petit similiter et habebit: et sic de singulis capitalibus dominis quotquot fuerint superiores. Quod est aperte contra iusticiam, cum in breui contineatur quod capitalis dominus feodi cui breue dirigitur plenum rectum teneat quod uicecomes faciat, etc.[19]

4

c. 18 JULY 1258[1]

*Litera cuiusdam de curia regis de parliamento Oxonie.**

Salutem. Sciatis quod in parliamento Oxonie factus fuit iusticiarius Anglie[2] dominus Hugo le Bigot, qui iurauit se exhibiturum iustitiam omnibus querelantibus, et quod hoc non dimitteret pro domino rege uel regina, seu pro filiis eorum, siue pro aliquo uiuente, uel re aliqua; nec odio uel amore, nec prece nec precio.

f. 83 Nec quicquam ab aliquo recipiet, | nisi esculenta et poculenta que ad mensam diuitis deferri solent. Postea ibidem commissa fuerunt omnia castra domini regis certis personis Anglicis, que fere omnia prius erant in manibus alienigenarum.[3] Postea autem expositis articulis prenotatis[4] inter xxiiii.[a] iuratos contentum erat, quod quia dominus rex pauper erat, ita quod si esset persecutus ipse uel regnum suum per aliquem principem uicinum, immineret ei

---

[a] *Anglicarum Scriptores*, i. 410 prints xxiv. This is copied in *Ann. Mon.* i. 444 perhaps because the editor only used a text of the *Anglicarum Scriptores* or because he failed to notice the point when collating the *Anglicarum Scriptores* text with the MS.

---

* *Text*: British Museum, Cotton MS. Vespasian E. iii, ff. 82^v–83^v (old ff. 79^v–80^v (V)). *Printed*: *Ann. Mon.* i. 443–5; *Anglicarum Scriptores*, i. 410–11; partly translated, Hennings, pp. 161–3. *See*: *Baronial Plan*, pp. 70–1, 175–8, 388–9. The title, in the MS., is in red. There are no paragraphs.

---

[19] The practice described in this clause is evidence of the efforts of the nobles to protect their courts from the results arising from the writ of right and the writ *praecipe*. The clause also shows both that the nobles were not following their own interests when they made the petition and the popularity of the county court which dispensed the king's justice.

and when default of court has been proved, yet the next highest
lord of the fee appears, and he similarly demands his court, and
will get it: and so with all the chief lords, as many as there may be
higher. And this is manifestly contrary to justice, since in the writ
it is stated that the chief lord of the fee to whom the writ is directed
shall do full right, otherwise let the sheriff do it.[19]

4

c. 18 JULY 1258[1]

A Letter from a Member of the King's Court about the Parliament at Oxford

Greetings. Know that in the Parliament of Oxford Lord Hugh
Bigod was made justiciar of England,[2] and that he took oath that
he would show justice to all making complaint, and that he would
not falter in this for the lord king or the queen, or for their sons,
or for any living person or for any thing, nor from hate nor love,
nor prayer nor payment; and that he would accept nothing from
anyone except such food and drink as are usually brought to the
table of a well-to-do man. Then, all the castles of the lord king
were entrusted there to certain Englishmen, nearly all of them
having previously been in the hands of foreigners.[3] Then, after
the articles noted[4] above had been brought forward, it was agreed
among the twenty-four sworn men that the lord king was impoverished, to such an extent that if he or his kingdom were
attacked by any neighbouring prince grave peril would threaten

---

[1] This date is suggested by the fact that the letter mentions the crossing of
the Lusignans from Dover on 14 July and by the statement in the *Lib. de Ant.
Leg.*, p. 38, that some of the baronial twelve were in London on 23 July, a situation forecast at the end of this letter. There is no evidence to support the date
suggested in *Baronial Plan*, p. 80, n. 1.

[2] See doc. 3, n. 10; *Lib. de Ant. Leg.*, p. 38.

[3] See doc. 5, n. 23 where the appointment of castle constables is considered.
The events described in this letter show the extent to which the petition of the
barons was being answered and the fulfilment of the aims expressed in the Provisions of Oxford (doc. 5).

[4] The 'articles noted above' are those of the petition of the barons. The letter
follows immediately after the petition in the MS.

et regno suo graue periculum, et forsitan subuersio totius regni;
unde prouisum fuit ut restituerentur ei omnes terre, et omnia
tenementa et castra per ipsum de corona alienata.[5] Cui articulo
fratres sui Pictauienses et quidam Anglici eorum fautores, uidelicet
Henricus filius regis Alemannie et Iohannes de Warenne,[6] con-
tradixerunt, et uersus Wintoniam[7] recesserunt omnes, excepto
filio regis Alemannie, licentia non petita. Set ipse, cum barones
suum requirerent iuramentum de stando prouisionibus eorum,
respondit quod terram non habuit nisi ad uoluntatem patris sui,
et ideo eo inconsulto noluit, sicut nec debuit aliquod prestare
iuramentum, desicut eorum par non fuit. Et habuit tunc diem
deliberandi ad consulendum patrem suum, uidelicet xl. dies.[8]

Postea autem accesserunt omnes barones cum equis et armis
una cum domino rege apud Wintoniam, parati obsidere castrum
electi Wintoniensis, de Wluesh', et postea alia castra sua, et castra
W. de Valentia, et persequi eos usque ad ultimum exterminium,
nisi resilirent ab errore incepto contra communitatem regni super
prouisionibus baronum. Postea reconciliatus fuit Iohannes de
Warenn' cum difficultate, et prestitit iuramentum pro uoluntate
ipsorum. Postea uero fratres regis apud Wluesh' existentes miserunt
ad barones nuncios suos, uolentes reconciliari, dicentes quod
parati erant in omnibus stare ipsorum prouisionibus. Quibus fuit
responsum, quod cum iurassent a principio prouidere una cum
eis reformacioni et utilitaci domini regis et regni, et sic de Oxonia
recessissent tamquam domini regis et communitatis seductores
et tamquam fide mentiti, articulis et prouisionibus ipsorum
contradicendo, de eis minime poterat aliqua haberi confidentia,
propter quod necesse fuit quod omnes exirent a regno cum tota
sequela sua, usque dum status regni reformaretur; et postea
dominus rex secundum quod haberet consilium, pro eis mandaret.
Et cum dominus rex offerret dare caucionem securitatis pro eis,
quod nullum pararent baronibus impedimentum uel grauamen,
nec quod uenirent contra prouisionem ipsorum, concessum fuit

[5] The steps taken by the nobles to control wardships, escheats, and royal
grants were a cause of complaint by the king. See docs. 12, 29–31.

[6] John de Warenne, earl of Surrey, had married Alice, uterine sister of King
Henry and sister of the Lusignan brothers. See doc. 1, n. 2.

[7] The Lusignans fled from Oxford, on or before 28 June, to Wolvesey castle,
in Winchester, of which Aymer de Lusignan was lord. The nobles at Oxford
moved to Winchester where they stayed until 12 July. On 14 July the Lusignans
left Dover—not 18 July as in *Baronial Plan*, p. 78 (Richardson and Sayles,
B.J.R.L. xvii (1933), 295).

him and his realm, and perhaps even the overthrow of the entire kingdom; and so provision was made to restore to him all the lands, holdings and castles alienated from the crown by him.[5] This article his Poitevin brothers and certain English supporters of theirs, namely Henry the son of the king of Germany and John de Warenne,[6] opposed; and they all, except the son of the king of Germany, left for Winchester[7] without asking permission. As for Henry, when the barons demanded his oath of standing by their provisions he replied that he held no land save at the goodwill of his father, and that therefore, without consulting him, he was unwilling to take any oath, and that he ought not to do so, since he was not their peer. And he was then given a respite of forty days for consulting his father.[8]

After that all the barons, together with the lord king, came with horses and arms to Winchester, ready to besiege the bishop-elect of Winchester's castle, Wolvesey, and after that his other castles, and the castles of William de Valence, and to pursue them to farthest limits unless they abandoned the error which they had conceived against the community of the realm on the provisions of the barons. Then John de Warenne was, with difficulty, reconciled, and he took the oath as they required. Then the king's brothers at Wolvesey sent envoys to the barons, proposing reconciliation, and saying that they were ready to stand by their provisions at all points. Answer was given them that since at the beginning they had sworn to provide, together with the others, for the reformation and good of the lord king and the realm, and nevertheless had fled from Oxford like traitors to the lord king and the community, and as men forsworn, opposing the barons' articles and provisions, no confidence whatsoever could be placed in them; and that therefore it was necessary that they should all leave the kingdom, with all their followers, until the state of the realm should have been reformed, and after that the lord king would make orders for them according to the advice which would be given him. And when the lord king offered to give a pledge of guarantee for them that they would not plot any hindrance or harm to the barons, and that they would not act against their provisions,

---

[8] Henry's father, Richard of Cornwall, who had been elected emperor, was in Germany, May 1257 to Jan. 1259.

et prouisum quod unum e duobus eligerent et facerent, uel quod exirent a regno sicut predictum est, uel quod duo ex ipsis, Gwido uidelicet et Galfridus de Lysingam, exirent a regno finaliter, et electus Wint' et Willelmus de Valencia, qui terras habent in Anglia, morarentur in Anglia sub salua et decenti custodia per barones prouidenda, donec status regni reformaretur. Tandem elegerunt omnes exire a regno dum tamen possent habere exitus terrarum suarum: quod utique non fuit eis de plano concessum; set ut congruam suam haberent sustentacionem de terrarum suarum exitibus, per prouisionem baronum, et residuum in terra moraretur ad opus ipsorum custodiendum, et processu temporis, si uideretur expedire, eis liberandum; quod non creditur euenire. Et cum postea peterent ut possent habere thesaurum suum secum; concessa fuerunt eis tantum sex milia marcarum, et residuum morabitur in terra, ad satisfaciendum inde omnibus de eis conquerentibus et balliuis suis; et quod superfuerit custodietur ad opus ipsorum. Postea autem petito et obtento saluo conductu, recesserunt omnes cum predictis sex milibus marcis tantum, et die Dominica proxima post Translacionem beati Thome martyris apud Doroberniam transfretauerunt. Et missi sunt milites ad f. 83ᵛ arrestandum et con|signandum thesauros suos in locis diuersis religiosis.[9]

Postea[10] autem dominus Edwardus, cum maxima difficultate ad hoc inductus, se supposuit baronum ordinacioni et prouisioni. Qui etiam commiserunt ei certos quatuor consiliarios, scilicet dominos Iohannem de Bailol, Iohannem de Gray, Stephanum Lungespeye et Rogerum de Monte Alto.[11] In breui uero prouidebunt de statu hospicii ipsius et hospicii domini regis.[12] Sepius autem rogauit eos dominus rex, quod nullus moraretur cum eo nisi Anglicus; et ita erit. Magna et ardua habent ipsi barones prouidenda, que non possunt cito uel de facili consummari et effectui mancipari. Prouidebunt etiam in breui una cum domino rege apud Lond' plura tangencia alienigenas, tam Romanos, quam

---

[9] The negotiations with the Lusignans show the determination of the nobles to reach a fair solution of the problem. The absence of hatred and vindictiveness is worthy of note. See *Baronial Plan*, pp. 76–81.

[10] The word 'afterwards' has led many scholars to suggest that Edward submitted after the Poitevins left England. (J. H. Ramsay, *The Dawn of the Constitution* (1908), p. 175; T. F. Tout, *Political History of England, 1216–1377* (1920), pp. 102–3; 'Baronial Council', pp. 122–3). Clause 26 of the Petyt MS. gives definite evidence of Edward submitting on 10 July; on 12 July he cancelled, 'by mandate of the king and the council', the appointment of Geoffrey de

it was provided and granted that they should choose and do one of two things: either that they should all leave the kingdom as has been said, or that two of them, Guy and Geoffrey de Lusignan, should leave the land for ever, and that the bishop-elect of Winchester and William de Valence, who held lands in England, should stay in England under suitable safe-custody provided by the barons until the state of the realm should have been reformed. Finally they chose that all should leave the kingdom provided they might have the profits of their lands: but this was not granted to them unconditionally, but only that they might have fitting maintenance, by the provision of the barons, out of the profits of their lands, the balance remaining in England to be kept for their use, and in due course to be restored to them if it were judged fitting; which is not thought likely to happen. And when they then asked that they might take their treasure with them, they were allowed only 6,000 marks, and the balance will stay in England to satisfy all who complain against them and their bailiffs, and anything left over will be kept for their use. Afterwards, having requested and obtained safe conduct, they all left with the stated 6,000 marks only, and on the Sunday next after the Translation of St. Thomas the Martyr (14 July) they crossed at Dover. And knights were sent to seize and take charge of their treasure in various monasteries.[9]

Afterwards,[10] the Lord Edward, persuaded only with the greatest difficulty, submitted himself to the ordinance and provision of the barons, who appointed for him four counsellors, lords John de Balliol, John de Grey, Stephen de Longespée and Roger de Mold.[11] Soon they will make arrangements for the state of his household and of the household of the lord king.[12] The lord king has often begged them that none but Englishmen shall stay around him, and so it will be. The barons have to make great and difficult arrangements, which cannot be quickly or easily consummated and brought to effect. Soon they will make provision at London, together with the lord king, on many matters touching aliens, both

Lusignan as seneschal of Gascony (*C.P.R. 1247–58*, p. 664; *B.J.R.L.* xvii (1933), 320).

[11] This is the only mention of the four councillors. Stephen de Longespée was third son of William de Longespée, illegitimate son of Henry II. Thus Stephen was cousin of Henry III. In Oct. 1258 he became Chief Justiciar of Ireland. See doc. 16, n. 1.

[12] Cl. 30 of the Petyt MS. (see below, p. 96, Additional Texts, iii), gives details of the plan to control the household of the Lord Edward. See *B.J.R.L.* xvii (1933), 299–300, 321; *Baronial Plan, passim*.

96 DOCUMENTS OF THE

mercatores, Camsores, et alios.[13] Ad deposicionem eciam et priuacionem electi Winton' innici proponunt barones precise, et iam confederati sunt cum monachis sancti Swithuni.[14] Ferociter procedunt barones in agendis suis; utinam bonum finem sorciantur.

5

JUNE–JULY 1258

Provisiones Oxonie*[1]

Fuerunt etiam in eodem parliamento apud Oxon xxiiii. electi, uidelicet xii. ex parte domini regis, et totidem ex parte communitatis,[2] quorum ordinacionibus et prouisionibus dominus rex

* *Text*: British Museum, Cotton MS. Vespasian E. iii, ff. 83ᵛ–85ᵛ (old ff. 80ᵛ–82ᵛ) (V). Follows doc. 4 after paragraph which precedes the heading, *Provisio facta apud Oxon. Printed: Ann. Mon.* i. 446–53; *Anglicarum Scriptores,* i. 412–16; Stubbs, pp. 378–84. *Additional Texts*: i. British Museum, Cotton MS. Tiberius, B. iv, ff. 213–214ᵛ (T); ii. British Museum, Stowe MS. no. 1029, ff. 170ᵛ–176 (extracts); iii. Inner Temple, Petyt MS. no. 533/6, ff. 53–6 (abstract); printed *B.J.R.L.* xvii (1933), 317–21; iv. *Flores Historiarium,* ii, 473–4 mentions a document *quarum tenor in fine huius libri, una cum prouisionibus Oxonie apponetur.* This text is lost. *See: Baronial Plan,* pp. 82–101; *Reform and Rebellion,* p. 71; *Baronial Council,* p. 121; E. F. Jacob, *History,* ix (1924–5), 191, and *E.H.R.* xli (1926), 559; H. G. Richardson and G. O. Sayles, 'The Provisions of Oxford', *B.J.R.L.* xvii (1933), 291–321.

Texts vary in spelling, order of arrangement, and details of information. These differences result from the attempts of those who were in charge of the MSS. to keep them up to date. See *B.J.R.L.* xvii for full discussion. None of the texts was enrolled or circulated. All are in French, except for clause 1 which was to be the basis of action by the administrative machinery of the realm (docs. 6–8). It is assumed that clauses written in Latin were for publication while those in French were memoranda not for publication. It has been suggested that this principle explains why document 11, the legal reforms of the Provisions of Westminster, was written in Latin, and why document 12, the administrative resolutions, was written in French. However, the words in Trevet, *Annales* (1845), p. 248, suggest that the rules for administrative action, detailed in cl. 5 of document 12, were published in the county of Hereford. Thus it may be suggested that the chancery clerks enrolled in Latin what was needed for the central administration; but information, such as was in document 12, would be sent in French to the sheriffs and knights in the county courts. Documents 30 and 31 illustrate another possible distinction between Latin and French documents, the former being the king's official complaints against the Council, the latter being memoranda recording the work of the arbitrators. See docs. 30 and 31 below.

In V the first word 'Prouisum' has the initial letter in blue; the titles to clauses 2–21 are in red; initial letters of titles to clauses 22, 23 in red; title of

Romans and merchants, money-changers, and others.[13] The barons propose nothing less than to embark upon the deposition and deprivation of the bishop-elect of Winchester, and they have already made an understanding with the monks of St. Swithun's.[14] The barons are going ahead fiercely in what they are doing: please God that they obtain a happy ending!

5

JUNE–JULY 1258

The Provisions of Oxford[1]

In the same parliament at Oxford twenty-four men were elected, twelve from the king's side and as many from the community's side,[2] to whose ordinances and provisions the lord king and the

clause 24 in red. The clauses have been numbered for ease of reference. Cotton MS. Tiberius B. iv contains clauses 1–12, omits clauses 13–23 and ends with clause 24. There are no paragraphs in the text, which is divided by a touch of red on the initial letter of each clause. Stowe MS. no. 1029 heads the extracts with the words *Rot. Parl. 42 Hen. III*. The clauses about the royal household, parliament, the oath of the councillors, and the names of the councillors appear.

---

[13] *Lib. de Ant. Leg.*, p. 39 mentions the activity of the nobles in London. Among the questions to be asked by the knights visiting the shires (doc. 5, cl. 1) was one about usurers, forgers, and money clippers (*Chron. Majora*, vi. 397–400; *Reform and Rebellion*, p. 33). *Camsores* were natives of Cahors. See doc. 3, cl. 26.

[14] The nobles assumed that Aymer de Lusignan had lost his claims on Winchester as soon as the Lusignans left England. Late in 1258, they tried to get the king to appoint Henry de Wingham, the chancellor, to the see. King Henry refused to act until the pope had deposed Aymer, but in Aug. 1259 a papal envoy ordered that Aymer be restored to Winchester. Aymer did not return to England: he died in Paris on 4 Dec. 1260. The pope's support for Aymer was also support for the king, a factor of the greatest importance in restoring Henry's power in 1261.

[1] The term Provisions of Oxford seems to have been used, in the latter half of the thirteenth century, to refer to all the enactments made by the Baronial Council up to, and including, those in Oct. 1259. In addition the term was used, like the appeal to Magna Carta, as a cure for all ills by those who had complaints but little knowledge of the available remedy. See doc. 11; E. F. Jacob, *History*, ix (1924), 188–200. See cl. 18.

[2] The statement that the twenty-four were elected at Oxford, sometime after 9 June, is not correct. The royal twelve seem to have been chosen by 2 May. Doc. 2, n. 1.

et dominus Edwardus filius eius, sicut superius prenotatur, se supposuerunt, super status eorundem et totius Anglie correctione, et in melius reformatione. Plura etiam fuerunt ibidem et alibi pertusa, que inferius continentur.

Prouisio facta apud Oxon

1. Prouisum est quod de quolibet comitatu eligantur quatuor discreti et legales milites qui, quolibet die ubi tenetur comitatus, conueniant ad audiendum omnes querelas de quibuscumque transgressionibus et iniuriis quibuscumque personis illatis per uicecomites, balliuos, seu quoscumque[a] alios,[3] et ad faciendum tachiamenta que ad dictas querelas pertinent usque ad primum aduentum capitalis iusticiarii in partes illas. Ita quod sufficientes capiant plegios a conquerente de prosequendo, et similiter ab eo de quo[b] queritur, ueniendo et iuri parendo coram prefato iusticiario in primo aduentu suo. Et quod predicti quatuor milites inrotulari faciant omnes predictas querelas cum suis attachiamentis ordinate et serie, scilicet de quolibet hundredo separatim et per se. Ita quod prefatus iusticiarius in primo aduentu suo possit audire et terminare prefatas querelas sigillatim de quolibet hundredo.[4] Et scire faciant uicecomiti quod uenire faciat coram prefato iusticiario in proximo aduentu suo, ad dies et loca que eis scire faciet, omnes hundredarios et balliuos suos. Ita quod quilibet hundredarius uenire faciat omnes conquerentes et defendentes de balliua sua, successiue, secundum quod prefatus iusticiarius duxerit de predicto hundredo placitare. Et tot et tales tam milites quam alios liberos et legales homines de balliua sua per quos rei ueritas melius conuinci poterit; ita quod omnes simul et semel non uexentur, set tot ueniant quot possunt una die placitari et terminari.

Idem prouisum est quod nullus miles de predictis comitatibus, occasione acquietantie quod non ponatur in iuratis uel assisis, per cartam domini regis deferatur,[5] nec quietus sit quo ad prouisionem istam sic factam pro communi utilitate tocius regni.

[a] V *adds* ad.   [b] Stubbs, p. 378, *prints* et de eo de quo *instead of* et similiter ab eo de quo.

---

[3] The threat to inquire into the actions of 'any other persons' laid the actions of non-royal officials open to scrutiny. This proved to be one of the factors dividing the less advanced reformers from those who were more radical. The

Lord Edward his son, as has been said, submitted themselves, for the correction and reform both of their own affairs and of the state of the realm. Many other things were discussed there and elsewhere, which are given below.

The Provision made at Oxford

1. It is provided that from each county four prudent and law-worthy knights shall be chosen, who, on every day when the county court meets, shall attend to hear all complaints of any trespasses and injuries whatsoever, done to any persons whatsoever by sheriffs, bailiffs, or any other persons,[3] and to make the attachments arising from these complaints, until the first visit of the chief justiciar to those parts. This they shall do in such fashion that they shall take sufficient pledges from the plaintiff that he will prosecute, and from the defendant that he will come to stand to right before the said justiciar on his first visit; and that the four knights shall have all the complaints, with their attachments, enrolled in order and sequence, separately and severally for each hundred, so that on his first visit the justiciar shall be able to hear and determine the complaints separately for each hundred.[4] And the knights shall inform the sheriff that he shall summon all the hundredmen and their bailiffs to appear before the said justiciar on his first visit, at the day and place of which he will notify them, so that every hundredman may summon all the plaintiffs and defendants in his bailiwick in turn, accordingly as the justiciar may decide to take the pleas of the hundred, together with so many and such knights and other free and law-worthy men of his bailiwick as may be needed for deciding the truth in these matters, and so that all shall not be put to inconvenience at one and the same time, but only so many shall come as can be heard and dealt with in one day.

It is also provided that no knight of any of these counties shall be excused on grounds of any quittance by royal charter saying that he is not to be placed on juries or assizes,[5] nor shall he be quit from this provision which has been made for the common good of the whole realm.

threatened split was momentarily healed in the spring of 1259 (doc. 10), but although a semblance of unity was maintained for the rest of 1259 the threatened split was always present (doc. 12, cl. 6). See doc. 31, cl. 3.

[4] Doc. 13; *Baronial Plan, passim*; *Reform and Rebellion*, pp. 42–65.

[5] Doc. 3, cl. 28.

2. Electi ex parte domini regis[6]

Dominus Londoniensis episcopus, dominus Wintoniensis electus, dominus H. filius regis Alemannie, dominus I. comes Warenne, dominus Guido de Lysinan, dominus W. de Valencia, dominus I. comes Warewic, dominus Iohannes Mansel, frater I. de Derlingt, abbas Westmonasterii, dominus H. de Wengham.

3. Electi ex parte comitum et baronum[7]

Dominus Wigornensis episcopus, dominus Symon comes Leycestrensis, dominus Ricardus comes Glouernie, dominus Humfridus comes Herefordie, dominus Rogerus Marescallus, dominus Rogerus de Mortuomari, dominus I. filius Galfridi, dominus Hugo le Bigot, dominus Ricardus de Gray, dominus W. Bardulf, dominus P. de Monteforti, dominus Hugo Dispensarius.

Et si contingat aliquem istorum necessitate interesse non posse, reliqui istorum eligant quem uoluerint, scilicet alium necessarium loco absentis ad istud negotium prosequendum.

4. Ceo iura le commun de Engletere a Oxneford

Nus, tels et tels, fesum a sauer a tute genz, ke nus auum iure sur seintes Euangeles, e sumus tenuz ensemble par tel serment, e premettuns en bone fei, ke chescun de nus a tuz ensemble nus entre eiderums, e nus e les nos cuntre tute genz, dreit fesant, e rens pernant ke nus ne purrum sanz mes fere, salue la fei le rei e de la corune. E premettuns sur meime le serment, ke nul de nus ia ren ne prendra de tere ne de moeble, par que cest serment purra estre desturbe, u en nule ren empeyre. E si nul fet encontre ceo, nus le tendrums a enemi mortel.

5. Ceo est le serment a uint e quatre

Chescun iura sur seintes Euangeles, ke il al honur de Deu, e a la fei le rei, e al profit del reaume, ordenera e tretera ouekes les auant dit iures sur les refurmement e le amendement del estat del

---

[6] Only eleven people are named here. The twelfth was Boniface of Savoy. Henry of Almain was son of Richard of Cornwall. John de Darlington, a Dominican, was the king's confessor; Richard de Crokesley, abbot of Westminster was a close friend of Henry III. Fulk Basset, bishop of London, was the only reformer in this group. His importance in the Church is the only reason which may be suggested for his inclusion in this group.

2. Elected on the king's side[6]

The lord bishop of London; the lord bishop-elect of Winchester; the lord Henry, son of the king of Germany; the lord John, Earl Warenne; the lord Guy de Lusignan; the lord William de Valence; the lord John, earl of Warwick; lord John Mansel; brother John of Darlington; the abbot of Westminster; the lord Henry de Wingham.

3. Elected on the earls' and barons' side[7]

The lord bishop of Worcester; the lord Simon, earl of Leicester; the lord Richard, earl of Gloucester; the lord Humphrey, earl of Hereford; the lord Roger, the marshal; the lord Roger de Mortimer; the lord John fitz Geoffrey; the lord Hugh Bigod; the lord Richard de Grey; the lord William Bardolf; the lord Peter de Montfort; the lord Hugh Despenser. And if it should happen that any of these, by necessity, cannot be present the rest of them shall choose anyone whom they will to be the substitute necessary, in place of the absentee, for carrying out this business.

4. This is the oath of the community of England at Oxford

We, so and so, cause all people to know that we have sworn on the Holy Gospels, and by that oath are bound together, and promise in good faith, that each of us and all together will help each other and our people, against all men, that we will do justice and take nothing that we cannot take without doing wrong, saving our fealty to the king and to the crown. And on the same oath we promise that henceforth none of us will take any thing, in land or in goods, whereby this oath can be disturbed or in any way impaired. And if anyone opposes this, we will treat him as a mortal foe.

5. This is the oath of the twenty-four

Each swore on the Holy Gospels, that, to the honour of God, his fealty to the king, and to the profit of the realm, he would negotiate and decree, along with the said sworn men, for the reform and redress of the state of the realm; and that he would not falter for

---

[7] Hugh Bigod was brother of Roger Bigod, earl of Norfolk and marshal of England. Peter de Montfort of Beaudesert, co. Warwick, was not related to the earl of Leicester. See *Baronial Plan* and *G.E.C.* for biographical details of those here named. *C.P.R. 1247–58*, p. 637 is incorrect in calling the earl of Gloucester one of the twelve of the king's council.

reaume. E ke ne lerra pur dun, ne pur promesse, pur amur, ne pur hange, ne pur pour de nulli, ne pur gain, ne pur perte, ke leaument ne face solum la tenur de la lettre, ke le rei ad sur ceo done et sun fez ensement.

6. Ceo iura le haute iustice de Engletere[8]

Il iure ke ben et leaument a sun poer fra ceo ke apent a la iusticerie de dreiture tenir, a tute genz al prou le rei e del reaume, solum la purueaunce fete et a fere par les uint et quatre, et par le cunseil le rei e les hauz humes de la tere, ki li iurrunt en cestes choses a aider e a meintenir.[c]

7. Ceo iura le chanceler de Engletere

Ke il ne enselera nul bref fors bref de curs sanz le comandement le rei e de sun cunseil ke serra present.[9] Ne enselera dun de grant garde, ne de grant [deneres],[d] ne de eschaetes, sanz le assentement del grant cunseil u de la greinure partie. Ne ke il ne enselera ren ke seit encontre le ordinement, ke est fet et serra a fere par les uint et quatre, u par la greinure partie. Ne ke il ne prendra nul loer autrement ke il nest diuise as autres. E lem li baudra un companium en la furme ke le cunseil puruerra.

8. Ceo est le serment ke les gardens des chastels firent[10]

Ke il les chastels le rei leaument e en bone fei garderunt al oes le rei e de ses heyres. E ke les rendrunt al rei u a ses heyrs et a nul autre, e par sun cunseil et en nule autre manere; ceo est a sauer, par prodes homes de la tere esluz a sun cunseil, u par la greinure partie. E ceste furme par escrit dure deske a duze ans. E de ilokes en auant par cest establement et cest serment ne seint constreint, ke franchement ne les pussent rendre al rei u a ses heirs.

[c] meitenir V.　　[d] *blank* V.

---

[8] Doc. 3, n. 10.
[9] Doc. 31, n. 11. During the king's absence in France, Nov. 1259–Apr. 1260, the great seal was kept by the chancellor, who accompanied Henry III, while the exchequer seal was used in England (*Baronial Plan*, p. 195).

gifts, promise, love, hate, nor fear of anyone, nor for gain nor for loss, in loyally acting in accordance with the tenor of the letter which the king has given him for this matter, and in accordance with his fealty.

6. This is the oath of the chief justiciar of England[8]

He swears that he will do well and loyally, to the best of his power, that which is proper to the justiciarship in upholding right, to all persons, to the profit of the king and of the realm, according to the provisions made and to be made by the twenty-four and by the king's council and the great men of the land, who swear to help and to support him in these things.

7. This is the oath of the chancellor of England

That he will seal no writ, except routine writs, without orders from the king and those of his council who shall be in attendance;[9] nor will he seal any grant of a greater wardship, or of a large sum of money, or of escheats, without the consent of the great council or of the majority thereof; nor will he seal anything that is contrary to the ordinances made and to be made by the twenty-four, or by the majority thereof. And that he will take no payment beyond what is arranged by the others. And a colleague will be provided for him in the manner which the council shall decide.

8. This is the oath of the castellans[10]

That they will keep the king's castles loyally and faithfully to the use of the king and of his heirs, and that they will restore them to the king and his heirs and to no one else, and by his council and in no other way—that is to say, by the good men of the land elected to his council, or by the majority thereof. And this written commission shall be valid up to twelve years, and from that time onwards they shall no longer be bound by this decree and this oath, but may freely restore them to the king and his heirs.

---

[10] *C.P.R. 1247–58*, p. 637. In May 1261 Hugh Bigod refused to surrender Scarborough and Pickering castles to the king. He claimed that the decision of the majority of the council was necessary (*Foedera*, 1. i. 408). The reason for the twelve-year period is discussed in *Baronial Plan*, p. 99.

9. Ceo sunt ceus ke sunt iurez del cunseil le rei[11]

Archiepiscopus Cant', episcopus Wigorn', comes Leycestr', comes Glouern', comes Marescallus,[e] Petrus de Sabaudia, comes Albemarlie, comes Warewik', comes Hereford, Iohannes Mansel, Iohannes filius Galfridi, Petrus de Monteforti, Ricardus de Gray, Rogerus de Mortuomari, Iacobus de Aldithelege.

Les duze de par le rei unt eslu ⎫ Le cunte Roger le Marescall',[e]
des duze de par le commun   ⎭   Hugo de Bigot.
E la partie uer le commun ad ⎫ Le cunte de Warewik',
eslu des xii. ke sunt de par le rei ⎭ Johannes Mansel.

f. 84ᵛ | E ces quatre unt poer a eslire le cunseil le rei, et quant il unt eslu, il les mustrunt as uint et quatre; et la u la greinure partie de ces asente, seit tenu.

10. Ces sunt les duze ke sunt eslu per les baruns a treter a treis parlemenz per an oueke le cunseil le rei pur tut le commun de la tere de commun bosoine[12]

Episcopus Lond', comes Wint', comes Hereford', Ph. Basset, Iohannes de Bailol', Iohannes de Verdun, Johannes de Gray, Rogerus de Sumer', Rogerus de Montealto, Hugo Dispensarius, Thomas de Gresley, Egidius de Argenten.

11. Ces sunt les uint et quatre ke sunt mis per le commun a treter de aide le rei[13]

Episcopus Wigorn', episcopus Lond', episcopus Sar', comes Leycestr', comes Glouern', comes Marescallus, Petrus de Sabaudia, comes Hereford', comes Aubemar', comes Winton', comes Oxon',

[e] Marscall V.

[11] Biographical details can be seen in *Baronial Plan* and *G.E.C.* The machinery adopted for choosing the council is worthy of note, as is the final decision of the twenty-four. See below, cl. 23. Those who formed the Council of Fifteen consisted of nine of the baronial twelve. The remaining six were three of the royal twelve (the archbishop of Canterbury, the earl of Warwick, and John Mansel), together with three royalists who had not previously been named: Peter of Savoy; the earl of Aumale, a Norman who had married the heiress of the earldom; and James de Audley, connected by marriage with the Longespée family. See doc. 4, n. 11. Hugh Bigod, another of the baronial twelve, as justiciar, was *ex officio* a member of the council. The two remaining baronial twelve, Despenser and Bardolf were members of the twelve representing the *commun* (cl. 10; *Baronial Plan*). The words 'sworn to the king's council' suggests that the councillors took an oath, but the wording is not known. Possibly the oath may have been similar

9. These are the persons who are sworn to the king's council[11]

The archbishop of Canterbury; the bishop of Worcester; the earl of Leicester; the earl of Gloucester; the earl Marshal; Peter of Savoy; the earl of Albemarle; the earl of Warwick; the earl of Hereford; John Mansel; John fitz Geoffrey, Peter de Montfort; Richard de Grey; Roger de Mortimer; James de Audley. The twelve on the king's side have chosen, from the twelve on the community's side—the earl Roger the marshal, Hugh Bigod. And the community's side has chosen from the twelve on the king's side—the earl of Warwick, John Mansel. And these four have power to choose the king's council, and when they have chosen them, they shall report to the twenty-four; and whatever names receive the assent of the majority of the twenty-four shall stand.

10. These are the twelve who are chosen by the barons to negotiate, at the three parliaments each year, with the king's council on behalf of the whole community of the land in the common business[12]

The bishop of London; the earl of Winchester; the earl of Hereford; Philip Basset; John de Balliol; John de Verdun; John de Grey; Roger de Somery; Roger de Mold; Hugh Despenser; Thomas de Grelley; Giles de Argentin.

11. These are the twenty-four who are appointed by the community to negotiate for the aid for the king[13]

The bishop of Worcester; the bishop of London; the bishop of Salisbury; the earl of Leicester; the earl of Gloucester; the earl Marshal; Peter of Savoy; the earl of Hereford; the earl of

to that taken by the twenty-four (cl. 5). In the evidence submitted to Louis IX for his consideration at Amiens in Jan. 1264 mention is made of the obligations involved in the councillors' oath. The Annals of Burton gives, in full, the oath taken by the king's councillors in 1257 (*Ann. Mon.* i. 395–7; doc. 37B, cl. 12).

[12] See *Baronial Plan* and *G.E.C.* for biographical details. Both T and V name the earl of Hereford among those who represent the *commun*, but as the earl was one of the Council of Fifteen his son must have been intended. As both T and V make the same mistake the error was probably in the official memoranda. Members of the twelve representing the *commun* are mentioned in the spring and autumn of 1259, and they may have been acting with the council in the spring of 1261 (docs. 10, 12, 13, 31, n. 20). See *Baronial Plan*, pp. 86–7 for discussion of the relationship between the council and the twelve.

[13] See *Baronial Plan* and *G.E.C.* for biographical details. The Apr. 1258 parliament promised an aid on conditions (doc. 1). There is no evidence of these twenty-four meeting or of an aid being granted.

Iohannes filius Galfridi, Johannes de Gray, Johannes de Bailol, Rogerus de Mortuomari, Rogerus de Montealto, Rogerus de Sumer', Petrus de Monteforti, Thomas de Greley, Fulco de Kerdiston', Egidius de Argenton', Iohannes Kyriel, Philippus Basset, Egidius de Erdinton'.

E si aukun de ces ne i pusse estre u ne voile, a ces ke i serrunt apent poer de autre eslire en sun liu.

12. Del estat de seint eglise

A remembrer fet ke le estat le seint Eglise sei amende par les uint et quatre esluz a refurmer le estat del reaume de Engletere, kant il uerrunt liu et tens, solum le poer ke il en unt par la lettre le rei de Engletere.[14]

13. De la haute iustice

Derichef ke iustice seit mis un u deus,[15] et quel poer il auera, et ke il ne seit fors un an. Issi ke al chef del an respoine deuant le rei et sun cunseil de sun tens et deuant celui ke serra apres lui.

14. Del tresorer, e de la eschecker

Autel del tresorer. Mes ke il rende acunte al chef del an. E bone genz autres seient mis al escheker solum le ordenement les avant dit uint et quatre. E la uengent totes les issues de la tere, et en nule part ailurs.[16] E ceo ke lem uerra amender seit amende.

15. Del chanceler

Autel del chanceler. Issi ke al chef del an respoinse de sun tens. E ke il ne ensele hors de curs par la sule uolunte del rei; mes le face par le cunseil ke serra entur le rei.

16. Del poer la iustice e de bailiuis

La haute iustice a poer de amender les tors fez de tutes autres iustices, et de ballifs, e de cuntes, et de baruns, et de tutes autres genz, solum lei et dreit de la tere. E les brefs seient[f] pledez solum lei de la tere, e en leus deues. E ke la iustice ne prenge ren si ne seit present de pain et de uin et de teles choses, ceo est a

seint V.

---

[14] This presumably alludes to document 2.

Albemarle;the earl of Winchester; the earl of Oxford; John fitz
Geoffrey; John de Grey; John de Balliol; Roger de Mortimer;
Roger de Mold; Roger de Somery; Peter de Montfort; Thomas de
Grelley; Fulk de Kerdiston; Giles de Argentin; John Criol; Philip
Basset; Giles de Erdinton. And if any of these cannot or will not
attend, those who are present have power to choose someone else
in his place.

12. Concerning the state of holy Church

Be it noted that the state of the holy Church should be amended
by the twenty-four chosen to reform the state of the realm of
England, as soon as they can find time and occasion, according to
the power given them by the letter of the king of England.[14]

13. Concerning the chief justiciar

Further, let one or two justiciars[15] be appointed, and whatever
power he has, he shall hold for one year only: provided that at the
end of the year he shall answer before the king and his council for
his period of office, and in the presence of his successor.

14. Concerning the treasurer and the exchequer

The same as to the treasurer; but he must render account at the
end of the year. And other good men shall be appointed at the
exchequer according to the ordinances of the twenty-four. And
all the revenues of the land shall come there, and nowhere else.[16]
And whatever seems to require reform shall be reformed.

15. Concerning the chancellor

The same as to the chancellor, so that at the end of the year he
shall answer for his term. And he shall seal no writs, other than
routine writs, on the sole command of the king, but he shall do it
by order of the council attending the king.

16. Concerning the power of the justiciar and the officials

The chief justiciar has power to put right the wrongs done by
all other justices, and by officials, by earls, barons and all other
persons, according to the law and justice of the land. And writs
shall be pleaded according to the law of the land and in the proper
places. And the justiciar shall accept nothing except presents of

[15] There is no evidence of two justiciars working together. Note the council's
intention of exerting control of this and other offices.
[16] Henry III had used the wardrobe to bypass the exchequer, this the
reformers planned to stop.

sauer, uiandes et beifres, sicum lem ad este acustume a porter as tables de prodes homes a la iornee. E ceste meime chose seit entendue de tuz les cunseilers le rei et de tuz ses ballifs. E ke nul ballif par achesun de plai u de sun office ne prenge nul loer par sa main, ne par autru en nule manere. E si il est ateint, ke il seit reint, et cil ke done autresi. E si couent ke le rei done a sa iustice et a sa gent ke le seruent, ke il ne eient mester ke il ren prengent de autrui.

17. De uescuntes[17]

Les uescuntes seient purueus, leus genz et prodes homes et tere tenanz; issi ke en chescun cunte seit un uauasur del cunte memes f. 85 | uescunte, ke ben et leuement trete la gent del cunte et dreitement. E ke il ne prenge loer, e ke il ne seit uescunte fors un an ensemble. E ke en le an rende ses acuntes al echeker, e respoine de sun tens. E ke le rei lui face del soen, solum sun afferant coment il pusse garder le cunte dreitement. Ee ke il ne prenge nul loer, ne li ne ses ballifs. E si il seient ateint, seient reinz.

A remembrer fet ke lem mette tel amendement a la Gyuerie et as gardeins de la Gyuerie, ke lem i sauue le serement.[18]

18. De eschaeturs[19]

Bons eschaeturs seient mis. E ke il ne prengent rens des bens as morz, de queles teres deiuent estre en la main le rei. Mes ke les executours[g] eient franche administraciun des bens, deske il auerunt fet le gre le rei si dette lui deiuent. E ceo solum la furme de la chartre de franchise. E ke lem enquerge des tors fez ke eschaeturs unt fet ca en arere, et seit amende de cel et de tel.[h] Ne tailage ne autre chose ne prenge, fors si come il deuera solum la chartre de franchise.

La chartre de franchise seit garde fermement.

---

[g] executours T; eschaeturs V.   [h] lel V.

---

[17] Control of the sheriff was a key point in the plans of the reformers. See *Baronial Plan, passim.*

[18] Doc. 3, n. 15.

[19] *Baronial Plan, passim; Magna Carta,* pp. 195, 221, 233, 257, 309, 321. See [g] above.

bread, wine, and such like, that is of food and drink such as is customarily brought to the tables of well-to-do men in the course of the day. And this same thing shall apply to all the king's councillors and to all his officials. And let no official, by reason of a plea, or of his official duties, take any reward, whether by his own hand or by the agency of anyone else in any way. And if he be found guilty, let him be punished, and the giver with him; for it is right that the king should pay his justices, and all those who serve him, sufficiently that they shall have no need to accept anything from anyone else.

17. Concerning the sheriffs[17]

Sheriffs shall be appointed who are loyal men and sound landholders, so that in each county there shall be as sheriff a vavasour of that same county, who will deal well, loyally, and uprightly with the people of the county. And let him take no payment, and let him not be sheriff for more than one year at a time. And during the year let him render his accounts at the exchequer, and answer for his term. And let the king pay him out of his own revenues, according to his proffer, sufficiently to enable him to administer the county justly. And let him take no bribes neither himself nor his officials. And if they be found guilty, let them be punished.

Be it noted to provide such reforms in the Jewry and concerning the keepers of the Jewry as to redeem the oath thereby.[18]

18. Concerning escheators[19]

Let good escheators be appointed, and let them take nothing from the property of the dead whose lands ought to come into the king's hands, but let the escheators have free administration of these goods as soon as they have satisfied the king if they owe him any debt: and this, in accordance with the charter of liberties. And let inquiry be made concerning the wrongs done by escheators in times past, and let redress be made accordingly. And they shall take no tallage or any other thing save what they ought according to the charter of liberties.

The charter of liberties shall be firmly observed.

19. Del eschange de Lundres[20]

A remembrer fet del exchange de Lundres amender, et de la cite de Lundres, et de totes les autres citez le rei, ke a hunte et a destructiuns sunt alez per tailages et autres oppresions.

20. De hospicio regis et regine[21]

A remembrer fet del hostel le rei et la regine amender.

21. Des parlemenz, quanz serrunt tenuz per an et coment.[22]

Il fet a remembrer ke les xxiiii. unt ordene ke treis parlemenz seient par an. Le premerein as utaves de Sein Michel: le secund de demein de la Chandelur: le terz le premer ior de June, ceo est a sauer, treis semeines deuant le Seint John. A ces treis parlemenz uendrunt les cunseilers le rei esluz, tut ne seient il pas mandez pur uer le estat del reaume, et pur treter les cummuns bosoingnes del reaume et del rei ensement. E autre fez ensement quant mester serra per le mandement le rei.

22. Si fet a remembre ke le commun eslise xii. prodes homes, ke uendrunt as parlemenz et autre fez quant mester serra, quant le rei u sun cunseil les mandera pur treter de bosoingnes le rei et del reaume. E ke le commun tendra pur estable ceo ke ces xii. frunt. E ceo serra fet pur esparnier le cust del commun.

23. Quinze serrunt nomez par ces quatre, ceo est a sauer, per le cunte le Marechall', le cunte de Warewik', Hugo le Bigot et John Mansel, ki sunt esluz par les xxiiii. pur nomer les deuant dit quinze, les queus serrunt de cunseil le rei. E serrunt cunfermez par les auant dit xxiiii. u par la greinore partie de els. E auerunt poer del rei conseiler en bone fei del gouernement del reaume, et de totes choses ke al rei u al reaume pertenent. E pur amender et adrescer totes les choses ke il uerrunt ke facent a adrescer et amender. E su le haute iustice, et sur totes autres genz. E si il ne poent tuz estre, ceo ke la greinure partie fra, serra ferm et estable.

[20] *Magna Carta*, pp. 309, 321; *Baronial Plan*, pp. 97, 246; G. A. Williams, *Medieval London, from commune to capital* (1963), and 'London, 1216–1337' (1961).
[21] Doc. 4, n. 12. The king complained bitterly of interference in his household, docs. 31, 37A, 38.

19. Concerning the mint of London[20]

Be it noted to reform the mint of London; and also to reform the state of the city of London, and of all the other cities of the king, which have gone to poverty and ruin on account of tallages and other oppressions.

20. Concerning the household of the king and queen[21]

Be it noted to reform the household of the king and queen.

21. Concerning parliaments: when they shall be held every year and how[22]

Be it noted that the twenty-four have decreed that there shall be three parliaments every year: the first at the octaves of Michaelmas [6 October], the second on the morrow of Candlemas [3 February], and the third on the first day of June, that is, three weeks before St. John. To these three parliaments shall come the elected councillors of the king, even if they be not summoned, to review the state of the realm and to deal with the common business of the realm and of the king together; and at other times by the king's summons when need shall be.

22. Be it also noted that the community should choose twelve sound men who shall come to the parliaments, and at other times when need shall be, when the king and council shall summon them, to deal with the business of the king and of the realm: and that the community will accept as settled whatever these twelve shall do. And this shall be done to spare the cost to the community.

23. Fifteen shall be nominated by these four: the earl Marshal, the earl of Warwick, Hugh Bigod and John Mansel, who have been chosen by the twenty-four to nominate the fifteen who are to be the king's council. And they shall be confirmed by the twenty-four or by the majority of them. And they shall have power to advise the king in good faith on the government of the kingdom and on all things touching the king and the kingdom; and to amend and redress everything that they shall consider to need redress and amendment; and over the chief justiciar and all other persons. And if they cannot all attend, whatever the majority shall decide shall be firm and settled.

[22] The composition of parliaments during the period of baronial administration has been the subject of much discussion. See *Baronial Plan*, *passim*; R. F. Treharne, 'The Nature of Parliament in the Reign of Henry III', *E.H.R.* lxxiv (1959), 590–610; introduction, pp. 11, 29, 51–2.

24. Ceo sunt les nums des cheueteins chasteaus le rei, et de ceus ke les unt engarde

Robertus de Neville—Bamburg, Nouumcastrum super Tyne; Gilbertus de Gant—Scardeburg; Willelmus Bardulf—Notingh'; Radulfus Basset de Sapercot—Norhamton'; Hugo Bigot—Turris Londoniarum; Ricardus de Gray—Douer; Nicolaus de Moules—Rou'et Cant';———Wintonia;[23] Rogerus de Samford'—Porecestria;

f. 85ᵛ | Stephenus Longeespe—Corfe; Matheus de Besill'—Gloucestria; Henricus de Tracy—Exonia; Ricardus de Rochele—Haldesham; Johannes de Gray—Herefordia; Robertus Walrant—Sar'; Hugo Dispensarius—Horestan; Petrus de Monteforti—Bruge Walt;ⁱ Comes Warewik—Diuises; Johannes filius Bernardi—Oxonia.

6

4 AUGUST 1258

*Pro inquisitionibus faciendis per singulos comitatus Angli."**

Rex Aluredo de Lincolnia, Iuoni de Rocheford, Iohanni de Stroda et Willelmi de Kaynnes de comitatu nostro de Dorset,¹ salutem.

Cum nuper in parliamento nostro Oxonie communiter fuerit ordinatum, quod omnes excessus, transgressiones, et iniurie facte in regno nostro, inquirantur per quatuor milites singulorum comitatuum, ut cognita inde ueritate facilius corrigantur; qui quidem quatuor milites ad predictam inquisitionem fideliter

ⁱ *For* Bruges (*Bridgnorth*) *see C.P.R. 1247–58, p. 638.*

ᵃ *Written in left-hand margin of patent roll.*

---

* *Text:* Rot. Pat. 42 Hen. III, m. 3. *Printed:* C.P.R. *1247–58,* p. 645 (abstract). *Additional Texts:* i. British Museum, Cotton MS. Nero D. i, f. 119ᵛ (N; see doc. 9, note). *Printed:* Chron. Majora, vi. 396–7. ii. British Museum, Cotton MS. Vespasian, E. iii, f. 86ʳ⁻ᵛ (old f. 83ʳ⁻ᵛ) (V). *Printed:* Ann. Mon. i. 456–7; Foedera, I. i. 375. *See:* Baronial Plan, pp. 108–9; Reform and Rebellion, pp. 19–39.

---

²³ The absence of the name of the guardian of Winchester castle, and the non-appearance of Stephen de Longespée as constable of Sherborne castle, Dorset, suggests that this list dates from the first week of July. William de Clare, brother of the earl of Gloucester, who had been appointed to Winchester, died early in July while Stephen de Longespée became constable of Sherborne on 11 July (*C.P.R. 1247–58,* pp. 638, 639). William de Clare appears as constable

24. These are the names of the chief royal castles and of those who hold them in custody

Robert de Neville—Bamborough, Newcastle upon Tyne; Gilbert de Ghent—Scarborough; William Bardolf—Nottingham; Ralph Basset of Sapcote—Northampton; Hugh Bigod—The Tower of London; Richard de Grey—Dover; Nicholas de Moules—Rochester and Canterbury; ————Winchester;[23] Roger de Samford—Porchester; Stephen de Longespée—Corfe; Matthew de Besill—Gloucester; Henry de Tracy—Exeter; Richard de Rochele—Hadleigh; John de Grey—Hereford; Robert Walerand —Salisbury; Hugh Despenser—Hoarstone; Peter de Montfort— Bridgnorth; the earl of Warwick—Devizes; John fitz Bernard— Oxford.

6

4 AUGUST 1258

Order to hold inquiries in all the counties of England

The king to Alured de Lincoln, Ivo de Rocheford, John de Strode and William de Kaynes of our county of Dorset, greeting.[1]

Whereas it was recently ordered by common agreement in our parliament of Oxford that inquiry should be made by four knights in each county into all excesses, trespasses, and acts of injustice committed in our realm, so that once the truth was known about them they might be the more easily corrected; and that in the full

of Winchester in Cotton MS. Tiberius, B. iv, f. 214ᵛ. This is an example of the variation between the different MSS. of the Provisions of Oxford. See *Baronial Plan*, pp. 74–5. *C.P.R. 1247–58*, pp. 637–9 lists those castles which changed hands and names the constables who were replaced. The fulfilment of the reformers' aim in replacing alien constables may be seen in some cases; Elias de Rabayne lost Corfe castle, but Mathias de Besill, a Burgundian who had been appointed to Gloucester in 1251 and 1256, remained in command of that castle. Furthermore, royalists were not excluded. Robert Walerand was steward of the household (doc. 1, n. 9), the earl of Warwick was a royal favourite (ibid., n. 4), Nicholas de Molis had been seneschal of Gascony 1243–5, Stephen de Longespée was related to Henry III (doc. 4, n. 11). Thus the reformers were not influenced by violent opposition to the crown when they appointed new constables.

¹ N and *Chron. Majora*, vi. 396–7 name the knights for Hertfordshire. *C.P.R. 1247–58*, p. 648 prints, in error, Herefordshire. The text in V is wrongly addressed to a sheriff; no county is named.

faciendam corporale prestiterunt sacramentum in pleno comitatu, uel coram uicecomitibus et coronatoribus, si comitatus ille in proximo non teneatur, sicut singulis uicecomitibus nostris iniunximus: mandamus uobis in fide qua nobis tenemini, quod prestito huiusmodi sacramento sicut predictum est, per sacramentum proborum et legalium hominum de comitatu predicto, per quos rei ueritas inde melius sciri poterit, diligenter inquiratis per comitatum predictum de omnimodis excessibus, transgressionibus, et iniuriis in eodem comitatu a temporibus retroactis, per quascumque personas, uel quibuscumque illatis, et hoc tam de iusticiariis, uicecomitibus, quam de aliis balliuis nostris, et ceteris quibuscumque personis: et inquisitionem inde factam sub sigillis uestris et sigillis eorum per quos facta fuerit, deferatis apud Westmonasterium in octauis sancti Michaelis, in propriis personis uestris liberandam consilio nostro ibidem. Mandamus etiam uicecomiti nostro comitatus predicti quod accepto a uobis corporali sacramento in forma predicta, tot et tales milites et alios eiusdem comitatus, per quos dicta inquisitio melius fieri poterit, uenire faciat coram uobis ad dies et loca que ei assignaueritis. Nolumus tamen uicecomitem nostrum eiusdem comitatus nunc presentem, sub huiusmodi inquisitione comprehendi; nisi ipse forsan prius uicecomes extiterit in comitatu predicto; quia de illo tempore uolumus quod de ipso sicut de aliis inquiratur. Nec eciam uolumus in predicta inquisitione reuolui transgressiones aut iniurias que alias coram iusticiariis nostris per iustum iudicium curiae nostre et secundum legem terre nostre terminate sunt, aut per breuia nostra attachiate. In cuius rei testimonium has litteras nostras uobis mittimus patentes. Teste rege apud Westmonasterium iiii die Augusti[2] per consilium regis, anno regni nostri xlii.

[2] N and V are dated 28 July. The letters patent, directed to thirty-eight counties, are dated 4 Aug. (*C.P.R. 1247–58*, pp. 645–9). The problem of the extent to which the date given to a document, when it was recorded by the chancery, may be accepted as the true date of that instrument is discussed by Sir H. C. Maxwell-Lyte, *Historical Notes on the use of the Great Seal of England* (London, 1926), pp. 241 ff.

county court, or before the sheriffs and the coroners, if the county court was not to meet very shortly, these four knights should take their personal oaths to make the inquisition faithfully, as we have ordered all of our sheriffs to arrange; we now order you, in the fealty in which you are bound to us, that, after taking this oath in the manner stated above, you should carefully inquire, throughout your county, by the oaths of trusted and law-worthy men of the county, by whom the facts of the matter can best be elicited, into all excesses, trespasses, and acts of injustice committed in the said county from past times, by no matter what persons, done to anyone whatsoever, and this should cover our justices, sheriffs, and our other bailiffs, and all other persons whatsoever. The record of the inquisition thus made, under your seals and the seals of those by whom this was done you must bring to Westminster on the octave of Michaelmas (6 October) to be there delivered by you personally to our council. And we order our sheriff of the said county, having received your personal oath in the manner described, to summon before you on the days and at the places which you will appoint for him, so many and such knights and others of the same county as will enable the said inquiry best to be carried out. We do not wish our present sheriff of the county to be included in this inquiry now, unless perhaps he was sheriff of the county on an earlier occasion, in which case we wish the inquiry to cover him for that earlier term of office, as with any others. Nor do we wish trespasses and injustices which have been settled elsewhere, before our justices by the just judgement of the court and in accordance with the law of our land, or which have been given a date elsewhere by our writ, to be considered in the present inquiry. We send these letters patent in testimony of this matter. Witness the king at Westminster, by the king's council, 4 August in the 42nd year of our reign.[2]

7

18 OCTOBER 1258

Henri, a tuz ses feaus[a] . . .*

Henri, par la grace deu rey de Engleterre, seignur de Irlaunde, duc de Normandie et de Aquienne, et cunte de Anjou[1] a tuz ses feaus, clers et lays, saluz.

Sachez ke nus uoluns et otriuns ke co ke nostre cunseil u la greignure partie de eus, ki est eslu par nus ou par la commune de nostre reaume, a fet et fera al honur de Deu et de nostre fei et pur profit de nostre reaume, si come il ordenera, seit ferm et estable en tuttes choses a tuz iurs. Et comandons et enioinons a tuz feaus et leaus en la fei kil nus deiuent, kil fermement teignent et iurgent a tenir et a maintenir, les establissemens ke sunt fet u sunt a fere par lauant dit cunseil u la greignure partie de eus, en la maniere kil est dit desus.[2] Et kil sentre eident a ce fere par meismes tel serment cuntre tutte genz dreit fesant et prenant. Et ke nul ne preigne de terre ne de moeble par quei ceste purueaunce puisse estre desturbee u empiree en nule manere. Et se nul u nus uiegnent encuntre ceste chose, nus uolons et comandons ke tuz feaus et leaus kes teignent a enemi mortel.[3] Et pur ce ke nus uolons ke ceste chose seit ferme et estable, nos enueons nos lettres ouertes seeles de nostre seel en chescun cunte a demorer la en tresor. Tesmoin meimeismes a Londres le disutime iur de Octobre, lan de nostre regne quaraunte secund.

[a] *In left-hand margin of patent roll.*

---

* *Text*: Rot. Pat. 42 Hen. III, m. 1. *Printed*: *C.P.R. 1247–58*, p. 656 (abstract); *Foedera*, I. i. 377–8. *Additional Text*: British Museum, Cotton MS. Vespasian, E. iii. f. 86 (old f. 83) (V). *Printed*: *Ann. Mon.* i. 455–6 (this text has many errors); *Anglicarum Scriptores*, i. 417–18. *English Text*: Rot. Pat. 43 Hen. III, m. 15. *Printed*: *C.P.R. 1258–66*, p. 3 (abstract); *Foedera*, I. i. 378; Stubbs, pp. 387–9 gives translation into modern English. *See*: *Baronial Plan*, p. 119.

The English text on the patent roll was addressed to the people of Huntingdonshire; the one sent to Oxfordshire, which is in the municipal archives at Oxford, was published with a facsimile in *Royal Letters addressed to Oxford*, ed. O. Ogle (1892), p. 12. The texts and facsimiles of the English and French letters, together with a discussion of the handwriting of the English text, appear in *New Palaeographical Society*, 1st series (1905–6), pl. 73.

See A. J. Ellis, 'On the only English proclamation of Henry III', *Trans. of the Philological Society*, 1868, pp. 1–135; W. W. Skeat, 'On the only English

7

18 OCTOBER 1258

Henry, to all his faithful [subjects] . . .

Henry, by grace of God king of England, lord of Ireland, duke of Normandy and of Aquitaine, and count of Anjou,[1] to all his faithful subjects, clergy and laity, greeting.

Know that we will and grant that whatever our council, which has been elected by us and by the community of the realm, or the majority thereof, has done and shall do for the honour of God, our own faith, and the prosperity of our realm, in the form in which they shall decree it, shall be confirmed and established in all things for ever. And we command and admonish all faithful and loyal men, by the fealty that they owe us, firmly to hold, and to swear to observe and maintain these statutes which have been made or shall in future be made by the council or by the majority thereof in the manner stated;[2] and that all men aid each other in doing this, by the same oath, against all men who either give or receive a bribe. And that none shall take land nor goods in any way which would infringe or impair this provision in any way. And if any should oppose this decree, we will and command our faithful subjects to treat them as our mortal enemies.[3] And since we wish this act to be firm and enduring, we are sending our letters patent, sealed with our seal, to every county to remain there in its archives. Witness ourselves at London, 18th day of October, in the 42nd year of our reign.

Proclamation of Henry III, 18 October 1259', ibid., 1880–1, App. vi, p. 169. This is one of two documents (the other is document 8) which the Burton annalist says were written in Latin, French, and English (*Ann. Mon.* i. 453). The Latin text has not survived.

---

[1] King Henry III used the titles of duke of Normandy and count of Anjou until 3 Dec. 1259 when the Peace of Paris was finally ratified (docs. 38, 41A).

[2] The papal bulls issued in Apr. and May, 1261, released the king's subjects from these oaths (docs. 33, 34).

[3] Several clauses of the Provisions of Oxford had enjoined upright behaviour doc. 5, cls. 8, 16–18).

Et ceste chose fu fete deuant Boneface, archeueske de Cantrebure, Gautier de Cantelou, eueske de Wyrecestre, Simon de Montfort, cunte de Leycestre, Richard de Clare, cunte de Gloucestre et de Hertforde, Roger le Bigod, cunte de Norf' et mareschal de Engleterre, Humfrey de Bohun, cunte de Hereforde, Piere de Sauoye, Guilame de Forz, cunte de Aubemarle, Iohan de Plesseiz, cunte de Warrewyk, Roger de Quency, cunte de Wyncestre, Iohan le fiz Geffrey, Piere de Muntfort, Ricard de Gray, Roger de Mortemer, James de Audithele, Hugues le Despenser.[4]

8

20 OCTOBER 1258

Ordinatio Vicecomitum[1]*

Henri, par la grace deu rey de Engleterre, seignur de Irlaunde, duc de Normandie et de Aquienne, et cunte de Anjou, a tutte gent del cunte de Rotelaunde ke cestes lettres uerrunt, saluz.

Pur ce ke nus desirons et uolons ke hastiue dreiture seit fete par tut nostre reaume, ausi al poure cum al riche, nus uoloms et comandoms ke les torz kunt este fet de nostre tens en uostre cunte, ki kunkes les eit fet, seent mustre a quatre cheualers ke nus auums a ce aturne, si einz ne lur eent este mustre, et nus al plus hastiuement ke nus purrons les ferrons amender et adrescer. Mes si nus ne poons si hastiuement ceste chose fere cum nus uodrions, et cum mester serreit et a nus et a uus, ne uus deuez pas merueiller ke la chose est si lungement mal alee, a nostre damage et a uostre,

---

* *Text*: Rot. Pat. 42 Hen. III, m. 1. *Printed*: *C.P.R. 1247–58*, pp. 655–6 (abstract); *Royal Letters*, ii. 130–2. *Additional Text*: British Museum, Cotton MS. Vespasian, E. iii, ff. 85ᵛ–86 (old ff. 82ᵛ–83) (V). *Printed*: *Ann. Mon.* i. 453–5. This differs in wording and spelling from the enrolled text. The translation in *Ann. Mon.* i. 505–7 is faulty. *See*: *Baronial Plan*, pp. 119–20.

There were no paragraphs in the enrolled text. This is the second letter (the other is document 7), which the Burton annalist says was written in Latin, French, and English to be read by the sheriffs in the county court (*Ann. Mon.* i. 453). The Latin and English texts have not survived. The familiarity of Matthew Paris, together with the Dunstable and Burton annalists, with this ordinance is proof of its publication (*Chron. Majora*, v. 720; *Ann. Mon.* ii. 210).

And this act was done in the presence of Boniface, archbishop of Canterbury, Walter de Cantilupe, bishop of Worcester, Simon de Montfort, earl of Leicester, Richard de Clare, earl of Gloucester and Hertford, Roger Bigod, earl of Norfolk and marshal of England, Humphrey de Bohun, earl of Hereford, Peter of Savoy, William de Forz, earl of Albemarle, John de Plessis, earl of Warwick, Roger de Quency, earl of Winchester, John fitz Geoffrey, Peter de Montfort, Richard de Grey, Roger de Mortimer, James de Audley, Hugh Despenser.[4]

8

20 OCTOBER 1258

The Ordinance of Sheriffs

Henry, by God's grace king of England, lord of Ireland, duke of Normandy and of Aquitaine, and count of Anjou, to all people of the county of Rutland who shall see these letters, greeting.[1]

Since we wish and will that speedy justice be done throughout our realm, no less to the poor than to the rich, we will and command that the wrongs which have been done in our time in your county, no matter who has done them, be reported to the four knights whom we have appointed for this purpose, if they have not already been so reported, and we will have them amended and redressed as fast as we can. But if we cannot accomplish this as fast as we would like and as need may be, both for our sake and for yours, you must not be surprised, for these things have gone amiss for so long, to our loss as well as to yours, that it can by no

On 7 Nov. 1258 Robert of Fulham, an exchequer clerk, was paid 50s. for his work writing charters in French and English to be sent, by order of the council, to the counties of England (*C. Lib. R. 1251–60*, p. 440).

---

[4] These witnesses are the Council of Fifteen, minus John Mansel, together with Hugh Despenser and Roger de Quency who were among the twelve to represent the *commun*. The witnesses are named in the same order in V, but the earls of Norfolk and Hereford are omitted. The English text omits the earl of Hereford, Roger de Quency, and Hugh Despenser but ends with the phrase 'and others after them'.

[1] This document is fully considered in introduction pp. 14–15. See doc. 7, n. 1.

kele ne puet mie si tost estre amendee; mes par les premereins
amemdemenz ke serrunt fez es premers cuntez u nus enuerruns
nostre iustise et de nos autres prodeshommes pur ce fere, purrez
auer certeine esperance kausi fra lem a uus al plus tost ke lem
purra.

Et sachez ke nus auuns fet iurer chescun de noz uiscuntes icel
serrement, kil nus seruira leaument et tendra a sun poer ce kest
desuz escrit; cest a sauer kil fra dreiture communaument a tutte
gent selonc le poer kil a de sun office, et ce ne lerra pur amur ne
pur haine, ne pur pour de nuli, ne pur nule coueitise, kil ausi ben
et ausi tost ne face hastiue dreiture al poure cum al riche, ne de
nul ren ne prendra, ne par li ne par autri, ne par nule maniere dart
ne dengin par achesun de sa baillie, fors solement mangers et
beuires ke lem acostome de porter as tables ausi cum a une iurnee
al plus, ne kil naura ke cint[a] cheuaus en leu u il herberge oueke
autre par acheisun de sa baillie, noueke nuli ne herbergera keit
meins de quarante liuree de terre, nen nule meisun de religion ke
meins eit de la ualue de cent mars chescun an de terres u de rentes,
noueke les desusdit ne herbergera kune feiz denz lan u deu feiz al
plus et ke ce ne fra for par lur preere u par lur uolente, et ke ce a
custume ne trerra, et sil couient kil i herberge plus, kil ne prendra
de presenz ne dautre chose ke plus uaille de duzze deners, et ke
de serianz naura fors tant cum il couendra besoinablement pur
garder sa baillie, e ke serianz prendra de quels il seit si seur kil
puisse respondre de lur fez, e kele pais ne seit trop greue par lur
manger ne par lur beuire, et ceus tant cum il sunt en baillie de
nul humme, clerc ne lay, franc ne uilein, de meisun de religiun,
ne de uilee ne demandront ne prendront aignel, garbe ne ble, ne
ne laine, nautre manere de moeble, ne dener, ne ke le uaille,
sicum plusurs unt acustomee za en ariere. Ce lur face iurer le
uiscunte quant il les mettra en baillie. Et ke cuntez, hundrez,
wapentaks, ne nule autre baillie de nostre reaume ne baudra a
ferme a nuli.

Et seent certeins uiscuntes et tutte autre maniere de bailliz,
ke si nul est ateint de nule manere dautre prise ke desus est escrit
par achesun de sa baillie, kil serra renit, et ausi le donur cum le
pernur, kar nus auums purueu par le cunseil de nos hauz hummes

---

[a] V *records* cync (*printed* eyne) cheuaus *which is wrongly translated as 'his
own horse'. Many other mistakes are made in translation* (Ann. Mon. i. 506).

means be so speedily put right; but, from the first corrections which will be made in the first counties into which we shall send our justiciar and other good men of ours for this purpose, you can take sure hope that we shall do the same for you as early as we can.

And know that we have made each of our sheriffs swear this oath: that he will serve us loyally and will observe, to the best of his ability, what follows: that is, that he will do justice in common to all people, according to the power which his office gives him, and that he will not waver in this for love nor for hate, nor for fear of anyone, nor for any greed, but that he will do speedy justice as well and as quickly to the poor as to the rich; nor will he take anything from anyone, either himself or by the hand of anyone else, nor by any kind of trick or device, by pretext of his office, save only food and drink such as is usually served at table in one day at most; and that he will not have more than five horses in any place where he stays with someone else in the exercise of his office; and that he will not stay with anyone who has less than £40 yearly of land, nor in any religious house which has less than the value of 100 marks a year in lands and rents; nor will he stay with any of these more than once a year, or twice at most; and that he will not do this save at their request or by their wish, and that he will not make a precedent of it; and that if it is agreed that he should stay there, he shall not take, by way of present or any other thing, anything worth more than twelve pence; and that he will not keep more sergeants than he really needs to keep his bailiwick; and that for sergeants he will take only men of whom he is so sure that he can answer for their actions; and that the district shall not be too burdened by their food and drink; and these men, as long as they remain in office, shall not ask for nor take from any man, clerk or lay, free or villein, nor from any house of religion nor township, lamb, sheaf, corn, wool, nor any other kind of goods, nor money, nor anything that has money value, as many have been accustomed to do in past times. This the sheriff shall make them swear when he places them in office. And that he will not let out at farm to any-one counties, hundreds, wapentakes, nor any other bailiwick of our realm.

And let sheriffs and all other kinds of officials be sure that if anyone is attainted of taking anything, by reason of his office, other than that which is prescribed above, he will be punished, and the giver as well as the receiver, for we have provided, by

ke tuz iurz mes seit fete plenere et hastiue dreiture a tuz, sanz
nule maniere de luer. E pur ce nus comandons et defendons a tuz
et a tuttes, ka nuls de noz bailliz ren noffrent ne promettent ne
donient, sur peine destre renit. Kar quant le uiscunte uend al
chef del an, sur sun acunte lem li aluera ses couenables despens
kil aura fet pur sa baillie garder, et pur li et pur le luer de ses
serianz. Et pur ce lur donuns le nostre, ke nus ne uolons kil eent
achesun de ren prendre dautri; et nus uolons ke nul de noz
bailliz ke nus mettons en nostre terre, ne uiscunte nautre, ne
demuerge en sa baillie plus dune anee. Et pur ce uus fesuns a
sauer ke si dureces u torz uus seent fet par les auant dit bailliz, ke
uus meains le dotez et plus seurement lor torz mustrez.

Tesmoin mei meimes a Westmostier, le uintime iur de Octobre,
lan de nostre regne quaraunte secund.

9

AUTUMN 1258

*Prouidencia Baronum Anglie**

Prouidencia baronum Anglie anno regni regis Henrici xl secundo.
De sectis curiarum.[a]

1. Sic iustum et conueniens esse uidetur,[1] ut scilicet tenens
quando ex forma sui feofamenti tenetur ad sectam per uerba in
carta sua contenta, eam faciat in forma feofamenti sui.

---

[a] *The close link with document 11 is shown by the words* De sectis curiarum;
see p. 137. N *has a long rubric in red*: Hic est noua prouisio magnatum Anglie
publicata apud nouum Templum mense Marcio anno regni regis Henrici III
xliii propter communem utilitatem tocius regni et ipsius regis de cuius consensu
et uoluntate processit ipse (*sic*) prouisio et publicacio.

---

* *Text*: Cambridge University Library MS. Mm. i. 27, ff. 73ᵛ–74 (M).
Printed: *Reform and Rebellion*, pp. 366–9. *Additional Text*: British Museum,
Cotton MS. Nero D. i, f. 82 (N). This MS. contains the *Additamenta* of Matthew
Paris' *Chronica Majora*, vi (ed. H. R. Luard, London, 1882). The document is
mentioned in *Chronica Majora*, vi. 496, but the text is not printed. *Reform and
Rebellion*, pp. 366–9 compares the two texts which may both have been copied
from the same original. *See*: *Baronial Plan*, pp. 133–7; *Reform and Rebellion*,
pp. 78–83.

counsel of our magnates, that henceforth full and swift justice shall always be done to all, without any kind of reward. And therefore we command and forbid to all that they shall offer, promise, or give nothing to any of our officers, under penalty of punishment. For when the sheriff comes at the end of his year, he will be allowed on his account the reasonable expenses which he will have incurred in keeping his bailiwick, both for himself and for the hire of his sergeants, and for this we give him of our own revenues, since we wish that he shall have no reason to take anything from someone else. And we will that none of our bailiffs whom we appoint in our lands, neither sheriff nor any other, shall remain in his office for more than one year, and this we wish you to know so that if hardships or wrongs are committed against you by the said bailiffs, you shall fear them all the less, and more boldly reveal their wrongdoing.

Witness myself at Westminster, the twentieth day of October in the forty-second year of our reign.

9

AUTUMN 1258

Provisions of the English barons

Provisions of the English barons in the forty-second year of the reign of King Henry concerning suit of court.

1. It is considered just and fitting,[1] when a tenant is bound to do suit of court by the terms of his charter of enfeoffment, that he do it in the form of his enfeoffment.

The phraseology of this document suggests that it records a debate in council, the royalists making a proposal, the reformers, on their side (*contra*), confirming, adding to or qualifying it. See below, n. 3. The Cambridge MS. is divided by paragraph signs; these sections have been reproduced as separate paragraphs which are numbered for ease of reference. This document is closely linked in content with document 11; only three clauses (nos. 21-3) do not form the basis of clauses in the later document. See appendix 1 and introduction, pp. 15-17, for comment on this document.

---

[1] An example of phraseology suggesting discussion in council. See cls. 7, 17, 18, 21.

2. Illi autem qui feofati sunt per cartas continentes seruicium certum, pro omni seruicio et consuetudine et per specialia uerba in carta contenta non tenentur ad ipsam sectam faciendam de cetero.

3. Illi autem qui tempore conquestus, uel a tempore ultra quod accio non conceditur sectam continue fecerunt pro tenementis suis, eam faciant sicut antiquitus facere consueuerunt nisi quietam clamanciam postmodo habuerint.

4. Illi autem qui nec sectam facere consueuerunt,[b] nisi quidem nouiter per districcionem et uoluntatem magnatum aut aliorum ad ipsam sectam faciendam sunt coacti, de cetero facere[c] non teneantur, nec[d] aliquo tempore ualeat dominus curiarum huius habere seisinam ut per eam accionem aliquam contra tenentes de cetero instituere possint.

5. Prouisum est insuper ut si hereditas de qua una secta tantummodo debetur et ad[e] participes plures eiusdem hereditatis deuoluatur, aut forte ad plures manus hereditas illa per feofamentum deueniat, unica inde fiat secta prout dum hereditas fuit integra fieri debuit et consueuit, et participes huius hereditatis contribuant ad sustentacionem secte predicte.

6. Simili eciam modo contribuere teneantur qui ex feofamento tenent huiusmodi hereditatem nisi feofator eorum eos inde debeat et possit acquietare.

7. Videtur autem conueniens, quod si domini curiarum aliquos contra hanc prouisionem ad sectam faciendam distringant, tunc ad querelam tenentis domini attachiantur quod ad diem breuem sibi prefigendum uenient ad curiam domini regis, inde responsuri, dum tamen unicum precedat essonium si fuerint infra regnum, et interim deliberentur aueria si capta fuerint occasione predicta, et deliberata remaneant quousque placitum inter ipsos fuerit terminatum.

8. Et si illi, de quibus querela facta fuit, ad diem sibi per essoniatorem suum datum uenire contempsit, tunc procedatur ad districcionem per terras et catalla quod ueniant ad alium diem sibi prefigendum.

9. Et si tunc ad diem illum non uenerint, tunc ille dominus curie seisinam amittat illius secte et tenens inde quietus recedat, donec ipse qui sectam illam[f] exigit sibi perquisierit per breue de recto si sectam illam ulterius exigere uelit.[g]

---

[b] *This text is very corrupt,* N *makes better sense*: Illi autem qui nec per formam cartarum suarum ad sectam tenentur nec ab antiquo sectam facere consueuerunt.
[c] ad ipsam faciendam N.   [d] ob N.   [e] ad *ins.* MN.   [f] ipsam N.

2. However, those whose charters of enfeoffment mention in detail a fixed service, in lieu of all kind of service and due, set out clearly in the words of the charter, shall not be held to suit of court in future.

3. Those who, at the time of the conquest or before the time of legal memory, did suit of court for their holdings, shall continue to act as they did formerly, unless they have a later quittance.

4. Those who were not accustomed to do suit of court, unless they have recently been forced to do such suit by distraint and power of great nobles and others, shall not in future be coerced to do suit of court, nor at any time shall it be possible for the lord of such courts to have such seisin of suit of court so that, by this power, they can bring action against their tenants in any other matter.

5. It is provided, moreover, that if an inheritance from which only one suit of court is due, be divided into many parts, or the inheritance, by chance, fall into many parts by enfeoffment, only one suit of court shall be performed as was due and customary when the inheritance was whole. Those who have divided the inheritance shall co-operate to continue the suit of court.

6. Similarly, those who are enfeoffed to hold an inheritance of this kind must perform suit of court unless he who enfeoffed them should, and can, grant quittance.

7. It seems to be acceptable that if the lords of courts distrain anyone to perform suit of court against this provision, such lords shall be attached, on the plea of the tenant, to appear in the court of the lord king, at an early date, to answer there, provided that one essoin be allowed if they be within the realm. Meanwhile let the beasts of the complainant be freed if they have been seized for this reason and let them remain free until the plea between the suitors be ended.

8. If those against whom the plea was made scorn to appear on the day allowed them by essoin, process of distraint, by land and chattels, shall be enforced to cause them to appear on another day granted to them.

9. If they do not appear on that day, the lord of the court against whom the complaint is made shall lose seisin of the suit of court and the tenant may withdraw in peace until he who claims the suit of court shall demand it from the tenant by writ of right if he wishes further to claim the suit of court.

---

[g] *Reform and Rebellion*, p. 367, n. 12 *is correct in comment on* N *which differs only in using the verb* uoluerit.

10. Si vero illi, qui sectam exigunt, uenerint et ostendere non possint quod secta illa ad ipsos pertineat conquerentibus dampna sua restituant que per huiusmodi districcionem a tempore huius constitucionis sustinuerunt, et conquerentes de secta illa quieti remaneant ut predictum est.

11. Similiter autem tenentes, si sectam illam subtrahant ad quam per hanc constitucionem tenentur et quam hucusque fecerunt, domini curie sub eadem sceleritate[h] suam consequantur iusticiam[h] ita quod si tenentes post districcionem factam per terras et catalla ad curiam domini regis uenire contempserint. Domini curie per defaltam tenentium seisinam suam recuperent de secta predicta donec tenentes per legem terre sibi inde perquisierint, si forte prius ad huiusmodi sectam de iure non tenebantur.

12. Et subtrahentes sectam illam debitam et consuetam ad dampna dominis suis refundenda que per hanc subtraccionem a tempore huius constitucionis sustinuerint compellantur.

13. De hiis autem sectis que ante constitucionem istam subtracte fuerant de quibus accio dominis curiarum competebat, currat accio, secundum easdem leges et constituciones secundum quas prius currere consueuit.

14. De turnis uicecomitis[2] qui pro pace domini regis conseruanda fuit prouisum, et ubi essonium non habet locum nec admittitur attornatus, sic prouisum est ut nec episcopi nec abbates nec priores nec comites aut barones ibi necesse habeant uenire.

15. Similiter autem nec alii ampla feoda tenentes per que ad pacis et legis obseruanciam satis sunt astricti, nisi specialiter et ob specialem causam ibi fuerint uocati unde eciam contradictum

f. 74 est ut qui[i] feoda habent per que satis astringuntur | ad pacem et legem obseruandam non puniantur, si ad turnum non uenerint, dum tamen eodem tempore infra balliam illam non fuerint ubi turnus tenetur, aut egritudine, aut alia impotencia que per liberos et legales homines testificata fuerit non puniantur si ad turnum non uenerint.

16. Quicunque autem ibi uenire tenentur, et defaltam fecerint, non amercientur nisi secundum formam amerciamentorum que in magna carta continentur, nec compellantur ad eum turnum uenire

<hr/>

[h] celeritate iusticiam suam consequantur N. Sceleritate *probably a play on words.*   [i] N *ends here. In the margin, in later hand, is* 'v Annales Burton', *alluding to the resemblance between this text and document 11 in the Burton annals.*

10. If those who claim suit of court appear in court, and cannot show that the suit of court is due to them, they shall restore to the plaintiffs the damages which the plaintiffs have sustained arising from the said distraint from the time of this constitution, and the plaintiffs in this suit shall remain quit as aforesaid.

11. Similarly, if tenants withdraw a suit of court to which, by this constitution, they are bound and which hitherto they have performed, the lords of the courts claiming suit of court shall obtain justice with the same speed as if the tenants, after distraint by land and chattels, scorned appearing in the court of the lord king. The lord of the court shall recover seisin of the suit of court by default of the tenant until the tenants shall sue the lord, by the law of the land, if by chance they had not previously been bound to such suit of court.

12. Those who withdraw due and customary suit of court shall be compelled to refund to their lords the damages which the lords have suffered by such withdrawal from the time of this constitution.

13. Concerning those suits of court which were withdrawn before this constitution and for which action was begun by the lords of the courts to which suit was due. In such cases the action will proceed according to those laws and customs which formerly decided these matters.

14. Concerning the sheriff's tourn,[2] which was provided to conserve the peace of the lord king, where essoin is not allowed nor attorneys accepted. It is provided that neither bishops, abbots and priors, nor earls nor barons need attend.

15. Similarly those holding wide lands, where peace and the law are satisfactorily preserved, need not attend unless they shall have been summoned for a special reason, whence it is also argued that those who have fees, in which they satisfactorily observe peace and the law, are not to be punished if they do not come to the tourn, provided that they were not in the district where the tourn was held, if they were hindered by sickness or by other impediment, proof of which can be sworn by free and law-abiding men.

16. Whoever is forced to appear at the sheriff's tourn and defaults shall only be amerced according to the form of amercement mentioned in Magna Carta, nor shall any be compelled to

No reason is known why N ends here as f. 82ᵛ is blank.

---

[2] Doc. 3, n. 11.

nisi illi qui de singulis uillis ad inquisitionem faciendam fuerint necessarii, prout continetur in carta predicta.

17. Illud autem communiter concessum est et contradictum[3] ut fines pro pulcro placitando[4] uel per sic[j] quod non occasionentur de cetero non capiantur.

18. Prouisum est insuper a domino rege, nec non a proceribus contradictum, ut in accione dotis, que dicitur unde nichil habet, dies de cetero a tribus septimanis in tres septimanas[5] semper prefigatur.

19. Similiter in assisis ultime presentacionis et in placito quod dicitur quare impedit ne contra iusticiam fraus fiat ecclesiarum patronis.

20. De cartis autem excepcionum, scilicet ne in assisis iuratis inquisicionibus seu recognicionibus ponantur impetrantes, sic a proceribus contradictum[3] est ut si necessarium sit eorum iuramentum ueluti propter magnam assisam aut alias assisas, ubi sine ipsorum iuramento iusticia fieri non possit, iurare compellantur salua tamen eis extra causas consimiles indulgencia a principe sibi concessa.

21. Prouisum[6] est eciam de consilio et consensu magnatum et procerum ut accio siue breue de ingressu[k7] ad gradus de cetero non artetur, sed locum habeat ad quantumcunque gradum res perueniat deforciata dumtamen huius accionis prescriptam uiam non precludat petenti.

22. Fit autem huius accionis prescriptio, sicut et mortis antecessorum.[8]

23. Forma autem breuis talis in huiusmodi causis competenter esse potest. Rex uicecomiti salutem. Precipe Roger de Mortuo Mari quod iuste et sine dilacione reddat Petro de Monte Forti

---

[j] *Sense would be improved if* pro eo *were read instead of* per sic.   [k] Breue de ingressu *in left-hand margin.*

---

[3] This word does not always mean 'contradict'.

[4] Doc. 3, n. 9.

[5] The hundred court met at intervals of three weeks. See H. M. Cam, *The Hundred and the Hundred Rolls* (1930); also, 'Studies in the Hundred Rolls', in *Oxford Studies in Social and Legal History*, vi (1921).

[6] Clauses 21–3, 25 appear, with variations of wording, at the end of a text of document 11 in N ff. 139–140ᵛ, printed in *Reform and Rebellion*, pp. 375–6 (doc. 11, n. *i*). This is additional evidence of the link between this document and document 11.

come to the tourn unless they be among those from different vills whose presence is necessary to hold an inquisition, as is mentioned in the charter.

17. It is generally discussed and decreed[3] that fines for *beau plaider*,[4] or for not being troubled on that account, shall not be levied in future.

18. Furthermore, it is provided by the king, and not opposed[4] by the nobles, that, henceforward, in actions of dower called *unde nihil habet*, sessions will be held each three weeks.[5]

19. Similarly in assizes of *darrein presentment* and in pleas called *quare impedit*, lest injustice be caused against the rights of patrons of churches.

20. Concerning charters of exemption, that those who have obtained them shall not be placed on juries, inquisitions, or recognitions, it is argued[3] by the nobles that if their oath is necessary for a grand assize or for other assizes, whereby without their oath justice cannot be done, such men must give their oath saving that they be not summoned for other cases from which they are excused by the liberty granted to them by the ruler.

21. It is also provided,[6] by counsel and consent of the great nobles and chief men, that henceforward the action or writ of entry[7] shall not be confined to the degrees but that it may be brought at whatever degree the disseised land is transferred, provided that this does not debar the set procedure of this action to the petitioner.

22. Limitation of time similarly influences both this action and actions of *mort d'ancestor*.[8]

23. A suitable form of writ in cases of this kind is: The king to the sheriff, greeting. Order Roger de Mortimer that he restore, duly and without delay, to Peter de Montfort the manor of *Stoke*

[7] Writs of entry, which were limited by time, were also distinguished in four degrees, covering the extent of the writ, against whom, and for whom it might act. Five conditions were accepted which could free the writ from the restrictions imposed by the degrees, which Bracton wished to abolish. (G. Jacob, *A New Law Dictionary* (1772), s.v. Entry; *De Legibus et Consuetudinibus Angliae*, ed. G. E. Woodbine (Yale U.P. 1940), iii. 156-60.) This clause does not appear in the Provisions of Westminster issued in the autumn of 1259, but it is found in the reissue of 1263 and so passed into the statute of Marlborough (*King Henry III*, p. 400, n. 3; *Reform and Rebellion*, pp. 81-2, 124; *S. of Realm*, i. 23).

[8] Writs of *mort d'ancestor* were controlled by limits of time and person (Jacob, op. cit., s.v. Assise of *mort d'ancestor* and s.v. Limitation). Legislation changing limitation may be seen in *S. of Realm*, i. 3, cl. 8; 8, cl. 1; 21, cl. 9; 36, cl. 39; 72, cl. 2; 107, Statute of Quo Warranto; iii. 747, cl. 2.

manerium de Stoke cum pertinenciis, quod idem dimisit Rogero de Sancto Iohanne ad terminum qui preteriit, et quod ad ipsum Petrum reuerti debet ut dicitur, et nisi fecerit etc.

24.[9] Iterum de essoniis[10] conueniens est uidelicet, ex quo de iuris beneficio conceduntur essonia, nullus cogatur iurare de impotencia ueniendi, set fidelitati ipsius credatur, qui se fecit essoniare secundum iuris beneficium; non enim uidetur necessitas que ex infirmitate proueniet eam esse quare concessum fuit essoniari, cum per attornatum possit uentilari, sed magis ex iuris beneficio et equitatis et pro possidente quodammodo prebuntur. Conceditur namque ipsis attornatus idem beneficium cum ipsi ad prosecucionem seu defensionem causarum fuerint assignati. Exemplum huius est essonium de malo lecti ubi adiudicatur languor secundum statum quod asserit et pretendit.

25. Contradictum est eciam ut accio de morte antecessorum, sicut contra custodes concedatur, sic eciam contra omnes ingressum per ipsum habentes concedatur, nec obesse debet quod breue de ingressu in quibusdam casibus haberi possit, cum aliud breue sic originale uniuersaliter locum non habeat et eciam quia ubi in eodem casu acciones diuerse haberi possunt, nullam alteram tollit ueritatem simul et semel institui diuerse non possunt.

10

22 FEBRUARY, 28 MARCH 1259

Ordinationes Magnatum*

Henri par la grace deu, rei de Engleterre, seignur de Irlande, duc de Normandie, de Aquitaine et cunte de Aniou, a tuz ses feaus clers et lais, del cunte de Eurewik', saluz.

Sachez ke noz hummes qui sunt de nostre cunseil, par commun assent, pur lamendement et le releuement del estat de nostre

---

* *Text*: Rot. Pat. 43 Hen. III, m. 10. *Printed*: *C.P.R. 1258–66*, p. 19 (abstract); *Foedera*, I. i. 381. *See*: *Baronial Plan*, pp. 137–41; *Reform and Rebellion*, pp. 72, 83–6. See introduction, pp. 17–18, for comment on this document.

---

[9] This clause is not in document 11 but it appears, in different wording, in Bodley MS. 91 and in the patent roll text dating from 1263. See document 11, n. *e* and *S. of Realm*, i. 9, n. 13.

with its appurtenances which he demised to Roger de St. John for a period which has just ended, and which, it is said, should be restored to the said Peter, and unless he do this, etc.

24. Concerning[9] essoins,[10] it is befitting that, when essoins are granted by favour of law, no person be forced to swear to his inability to attend court but confidence be placed in the word of him who is essoined according to the favour of law. Nor does it seem to be necessary that such person should come from a sick-bed because he was granted an essoin, as he can be examined by an attorney, but rather essoins are provided for the benefit of law and equity and in a certain way on behalf of the possessor. The same 'benefit of attorney' is allowed whether they have been assigned to the prosecution or the defence of actions. An example is an essoin for illness in bed where the illness is judged according to the state that is claimed and asserted.

25. The action of the writ of *mort d'ancestor* is different, as it is granted against the guardians and against all having entry by right of such writ. But it should not stop a writ of entry being obtained in such cases, as such an original writ has no sweeping power and also because where, in such a matter, diverse actions may be held, it brings no additional truth, and differing actions may not be instituted at one and the same time.

10

22 FEBRUARY, 28 MARCH 1259

The Ordinances of the Magnates

Henry, by God's grace king of England, lord of Ireland, duke of Normandy and of Aquitaine, and count of Anjou, to all his faithful subjects, clergy and laymen, of the county of York, greeting.

This is to make it known that our councillors, by common consent, and for the betterment and relief of the state of our realm,

---

[10] Essoins varied in the length of time for which they allowed absence. An essoin *de terra sancta* granted absence for a year and a day, while the essoin *de malo lecti* ordered that the recipient be viewed by four knights (Jacob, op. cit., s.v. Essoin).

regne, unt grante pur sei et pur lur eirs, kil alur sugez et a lur hommes tendrunt a tuz iurz tuttes les bones leis, et les bones custumes, les queles nuz auons a noz grantez pur nus et pur noz eirs; et de ce unt lur escit fet, le quel nus auons ueu en icest furme.

'Le cunseil le rei et les duze esluz par le commun d'Engleterre,[1] saluent tutte gent. Pur ce ke nostre seignur le rei ueut et desire, ke hastiue dreiture seit tenue et faite a tuz communaument par tut sun reaume; et ueut ensement, ke les torz kunt este fet par ses baillifs et par autres en za seent amendez; nus uoloms, grantons et otrions, de la nostre part, ke les torz ke nus et noz baillifs auom fet a noz suzgez u a noz ueisins,[2] seent amendez par le rei et par sa iustise, ut par caus kil i aturnera, sanz delai et sanz cuntredit de nus u de noz; ce kil trouerunt par pleintes, en tel manere, ke ce ke couent estre pleide par brief solonc lei de terre, par bref seit pleide sicum il deit, sicum franc tenement et ce kapent a franc tenement, et en leu ou il deit.[3] Ne nus nel destourberons par menaces, ne par poer, nen autre manere nuli kil ne puisse franchement pleindre sei de nus et de noz, et suire sa querele; ne maugre ne li sauerons, ne mal ne li querrons, pur ses pleintes ne pur ses suites.

Dautre part nus uolons et auons grante pur nus et pur noz eirs, ke les pointz des charters de franchises, ke le rei ad grante endreit sei et ses baillifs, et ceus qui tenent en chef de lui, ke nus tendrons endreit nus, et endreit de noz tenanz et de noz ueisins, ausi ben en noz demeines cum en noz franchises. Derechief ce ke le cunseil le rei ad establi et establira, entre ci et la tuz seinz prochein auenir, endreit del rei et ses sugez, quant a suite de curz, et amerciementz, et gardes, socages, et ses fermes et autre manere de franchises, et dordeinemenz ke sunt a releuement del estat del regne, nus garderons endreit nus et de noz suzgez, pur nus et pur noz eirs.[4] Dautre part, tel serment cum le rei fet fere a ses uiscuntes et a ses autres baillifs, nus frons fere a noz baillifs, ausi ben de noz demeines cum de nos franchises, par deuant les quatre cheualers esleuz en chescun cunte, u autres ki serrunt a ce fere par le cunseil ordene, en noz pleneres curz. Issi ke nos franchisez ne franche custumes ne seent blesmies, ne ne puisse

[1] Doc. 5, n. 12.   [2] Ibid., n. 3.

[3] *Reform and Rebellion*, p. 83 and *Baronial Plan*, p. 137, n. 3, differ in the translation of this sentence. The latter translation has been accepted. See *Baronial Plan*, loc. cit. for reasons.

[4] An allusion to document 9 and anticipation of document 11.

have granted, for themselves and their heirs, that they will always observe towards their subjects and their men the good laws and the good customs which we, for ourselves and our heirs, have granted to our subjects: and they have drawn up their charter to this effect, which we have seen, in the following form.

'The king's council and the twelve elected by the community of England[1] greet all men. Since our lord the king wishes and desires that swift justice be observed and done to all in common throughout his realm, and also wishes that whatever wrongs have been committed by his officers and by others in former times should be redressed, we will, grant, and offer, on our part, that all wrongs which we and our bailiffs have done to our subjects or to our neighbours[2] shall be corrected by the king and by his justiciar, or by those whom he shall appoint for this purpose, without hindrance or opposition from us and ours. If what is found by complaint can properly be pleaded by writ according to the law of the land, such as freehold and anything pertaining to freehold, it shall be pleaded by writ as it should be, and in the customary place.[3] And we will hinder no one by threats, nor by power, nor in any other manner, from freely making complaint of us and of our men, and from prosecuting his complaint, nor will we remember it against him, nor attempt any reprisal against him by reason of his complaints and prosecutions.

Moreover we will and have granted, for us and for our heirs, that the articles in the charter of liberties which the king has granted regarding himself and his officers, and to those who hold of him in chief, we will observe as regards ourselves towards our tenants and our neighbours, both in our demesnes and in our liberties. Moreover, whatever the king's council has established or shall establish between now and All Saints' next [November 1], regarding the king and his subjects, with respect to suit of courts, amercements, wardships, socage, and his farms and other sorts of liberties, and anything else thereafter which shall be for the reform of the state of the realm, we will uphold it as between ourselves and our subjects, both we ourselves and our heirs.[4] Moreover, that same oath which the king caused his sheriffs and his other officers to take, we will make our officers swear, both those of our demesnes and those of our liberties, in our full courts before the four knights elected in each county or any other persons appointed by the council to act as knights, on condition that our franchises and free

turner a deseritement de nus u de noz eirs; et ce a chescun remue-
ment de baillifs; cest asauer, kil leaument seruirent al rei en ce
kafert alui et ses franchises, et a nuz et ce kafert a noz franchises
et a noz demeines; et kil feront dreiture communaument a tutte
gent, solonc le poer de lur office; et ce ne lerrunt pur pour, ne
pur amur, ne pur haine, ne pur coueitise; et ke de nul ne de nule
rien ne prendront, par eus ne par autre, ne par nule manere dart u
dengin, par achesun de luy baillie, par unt dreit soit delae, u tort
fet; fors sulement beiures et mangers, ke lem ad acustume deporter
as tables, ausi cum a un iur al plus.

Et ceus qui gardent franchises iurrunt, kil serianz nauront
fors tant cum il couendra bosoignablement pur garder lur baillie,
et kil teus seriantz prendrunt pur ki fez il uolent respundre; et
ceus, tant cum il sunt en baillie, de nul humme, clerc ne lai,
franc ne uilein, de meisun de religion, ne de uilee, ne demanderont
ne prendront aignel, ne garbe, ne ble, ne toison, ne dener, ne ke
le uaille, ne scothales ne festales ne frunt. Et seent certeins tote
manere de baillifs, ke sil sunt ateint de nule manere dautre prise,
ke desus est nome, par acheisun de sa baille, kil serrunt reinz;
et ausi ben le donur cum le pernur, si le donur le ceilt par quoi
il seit ateint par autre ke par li. Et le seignur aura la merci u la
raunzun, sil fet le trespas amender en sa curt.[5] Nus promettons
ensement sur noz sermenz, ke nul de nus, pur don ne pur rente,
ne prendra en mein dauouer nul humme ke nostre humme ne seit
par reisun, cuntre ses seignurages, ne cuntre ses ueisins, ne cuntre
null autre. Et tuttes ces choses desus dite uolons nus, otrions et
ordeinons, ke seent fermement tenues, et de nus et de tutte
la gent de ce reaume.' Et cest escrit fu fet et ordeine par les desus
diz, le iur sein pere, el meis de Fevrer, lan nostre seignur milime
ducentime cinquante et utime.[6] Et en testmoine de ceste chose nus
auons mis noz seauz a cest escrit.

Et pur ce ce ke nus uolons ke cest ordeinement seit fermement
tenu desore en auant, auons mande a tuz noz uiscuntes keus le
facent tenir communaument en lur baillies sicum il est purueu.
Et en testmoin de ce auons fet mettre nostre seel a ceste lettres
ouertes.

Testmoine meimeimes a Westmoster, le uint et utime iur de
Marz, lan de nostre regne quarante et tierz.

[5] Note resemblance to document 8. The four knights are presumably those
mentioned in document 5, cl. 1.

customs shall in no wise be infringed, and that this cannot disinherit us or our heirs. And we will do this at every change of
officials; that is to say, they shall swear that they will loyally serve
the king in what pertains to him and to his liberties, and us in
what pertains to our franchises and demesnes; and that they will
do right commonly to all people, according to the powers vested
in their offices; and that they will not falter in this for fear, nor
for affection, nor for hatred, nor for greed; and that from no one
will they take anything, either directly or indirectly, or by any kind
of trick or device, by reason of their office, whereby justice is delayed or wrong done, saving only such food and drink as is
customarily brought to table in a single day at most.

And those who administer the liberties shall swear that they will
have no more sergeants than are necessary for keeping their
charges, and that they will employ as sergeants only those men
for whose actions they are willing to be responsible; and these men,
as long as they are in office, shall not demand from anyone, cleric
or layman, freeman or villein, house of religion or township any
lamb, sheaf, corn, fleece, money, or anything else of value, and
that they will not make scot-ales nor feast-ales. And let every sort
of bailiff be certain that if they are attainted of any manner of
imposition named above, by reason of their office, they will be
punished, and the giver as well as the receiver, if the giver con-
ceals the payment and is attainted by any other person. And the
lord shall have the amercement and the penalty if he causes the
trespass to be put right in his own court.[5] We also promise, on
our oaths, that none of us, neither for gift nor for future payment,
will undertake to avow any man who is not rightly one of ours,
against his lords, nor against his neighbours nor against anyone
else. And all these things we will, offer, and decree shall be firmly
maintained by us and by all the people of this kingdom.' And this
charter was made and decreed by the aforesaid on St. Peter's day
[22 February] in the month of February, in the year of our Lord
1258[6] [1259, modern style]. And in testimony of this we have
set our seals to this document.

And since we wish that this ordinance be firmly kept henceforth, we have ordered all our sheriffs to cause it to be kept everywhere throughout their bailiwicks as is provided. And in testimony
of this we have caused our seal to be set to these letters patent.
Witness myself at Westminster, 28 March, the 43rd year of our
reign [1259].

[6] Chancery clerks dated their year from 25 Mar.

Consimilis littera in gallico[7] dirigitur singulis comitatibus
Anglie. Et mandatum est singulis uicecomitibus Anglie, quod
predictas litteras pro communi comodo regni confectas in plenis
comitatibus suis, et in singulis hundredis eorumdem comitatuum
et alibi per balliuam suam publice legi et tenorem earumdem de
omnibus firmiter faciant obseruari.
Teste rege apud Westmonasterium xxviii die Martii.

11

OCTOBER 1259

*Prouisiones Westmonasterii**[1]

De prouisionibus factis per regem et consilium suum.—Anno ab
incarnacione domini Mᵒ.CCᵒ.Lᵒ. nono[a] regni autem H. regis

[a] xcclix M.

---

* *Text*: (a) Rot. Claus. 44 Hen. III, m. 17d. *Printed*: *C.R. 1259–61*, pp. 146–
50; *S. of Realm*, i. 8–11 (compares B and text b with text a); *Stubbs*, pp. 390–4.
(b) Rot. Pat. 47 Hen. III, pt. 1, m. 13 schedule. A reissue in Jan. 1263, of (a)
with some alterations. *Printed*: *C.P.R. 1258–66*, p. 253 (abstract); *S. of Realm*,
i. 8–11 compared with (a). Mistakenly called m. 14 schedule. (c) British Museum,
Cotton MS. Claudius D. ii, ff. 128ᵛ–131 (old 126ᵛ–129) (C). Dated Worcester,
13 Dec. 1264, reissue of (b). *Printed*: *Registrum Malmesburiense*, i. 42–50. Dated
Worcester, 14 Dec. 1264. *Additional Texts*: (i) Bodleian Library, Bodley MS. 91,
ff. 133–5 (B). A copy of (b). (ii) Cambridge U.L., MS. Mm. i. 27, ff. 75–6 (M).
(iii) British Museum, Cotton MS. Vespasian E. iii, ff. 91–92ᵛ, 94–95ᵛ (old
88–89ᵛ, 91–92ᵛ) (V). *Printed*: *Ann. Mon.* i. 471–6, 480–4; *Anglicarum Scriptores*,
i. 428–31, 434–6. (iv) British Museum, Cotton MS. Nero D. i, ff. 139–140ᵛ (N).
Mentioned *Chron. Majora*, vi. 512. *Printed*: *Reform and Rebellion*, pp. 375–6.
See: *Baronial Plan*, pp. 164–9, 295–6, 390–1; *Reform and Rebellion*, pp. 76–7,
87–8, 124–5, 370–6; *Baronial Council*, pp. 120, 127–8; N. Denholm-Young, 'The
Winchester–Hyde Chronicle', *E.H.R.* xlix (1934), 85–93 (mistake on p. 92,
c. 1: f. 133 not f. 135); 'Robert Carpenter and the Provisions of Westminster',
ibid., l (1935), 22–35; *Collected Papers*, pp. 86–110.
V has Latin and French copies of the texts, but the order of the clauses is not
the same. The Latin text ends with a clause which is the same as cl. 24 of the
text here printed. This clause does not appear in the French text until cl. 21 of
the administrative and political section of the text (doc. 12). Both Latin and
French texts contain two clauses which are not in the close roll.
N, a French text, is the same as the French text in V but, in addition, it has
the clause which appears as cl. 24 of the text here printed and at the end of the
Latin text in V. *Baronial Plan*, pp. 370–1 analyses the close roll, V, N, and
M texts.
M is a collection of law tracts and statutes. It is quarto, on parchment, in law
French and Latin and by an early fourteenth-century hand. The text of this

Identical letters in French[7] are sent to all the counties of England, and all the sheriffs of England are ordered to have these letters, thus made for the common good of the realm, publicly read in their full county courts and in each of the hundreds of their counties, and elsewhere throughout their bailiwicks, and to cause the substance of these letters to be observed firmly by all men.

Witnessed the king at Westminster, 28 March.

11

OCTOBER 1259

The Provisions of Westminster (Legal Resolutions)[1]

Concerning provisions made by the king and his council. In the year of the Incarnation of our Lord, 1259, and in the forty-third

document is headed *Prouidencie legum facte apud Oxoniam per dominum H. regem, filium regis Johannis, et barones Anglie, anno regni regis H. xl tercio. De sectis cur.* See doc. 9, n. *a.* Among the documents are copies of the letters exchanged between Simon de Montfort, King Henry, and Richard of Cornwall on the eve of the battle of Lewes (ff. 66ᵛ, 67). *Printed: Foedera* I. i. 440 from *Flores Historiarum* l. ii. 492–4. King's letter, in the chronicle, dated 12 May, M text dated 13 May. M possibly more accurate, battle on 14 May 1264. M has accounts of the battles of Lewes and Evesham (ff. 67, 67ᵛ), and letter announcing peace on 25 May 1264. *Printed: Foedera* I. i. 441 from Rot. Pat. 48 Hen. III, pt. i, m. 13ᵛ, *C.P.R. 1258–66,* p. 359.

B is a copy of the Hyde Chronicle containing, towards the end, a corpus of documents, one of which is a copy of the 1263 reissue of the Provisions of Westminster. B is compared with M, close, and patent roll texts in appendix II.

Significant variations in the wording of the texts are mentioned in footnotes. See appendix I for links between this document and documents 3, 9, 12.

---

[7] Docs. 7, 8, introduction.

[1] The distinction between the legal, political, and administrative clauses was made by Sir F. M. Powicke, *Baronial Council,* p. 130. These enactments were never called Provisions of Westminster in the thirteenth century. The text in the Matthew Paris is headed *Prouisiones noue baronum (Reform and Rebellion,* p. 370) while the heading of the close roll text is printed with this document. On some occasions enactments made on this document were said to be the result of the Provisions of Oxford. Thus *C.P.R. 1266–72,* p. 630 speaks in this way of cl. 11 while Trevet, *Annales,* Eng. Hist. Soc. 1845, p. 248, speaks of the eyre being held *contra formam prouisionum Oxonie* whereas the rule being broken was cl. 5 of document 12. The Dunstable and London annalists say that the Provisions of Oxford were reissued in 1263 when speaking of the re-publication of document 11 *(Ann. Mon.* iii. 221; *Lib. de Ant. Leg.,* p. 52).

filii regis Iohannis xliij⁰.,^b conuenientibus apud Westmonasterium² in quindena Sancti Michaelis ipso domino rege et magnatibus suis, de comuni consilio et consensu dictorum regis et magnatum facte sunt prouisiones subscripte per ipsos regem et magnates et publicate in hunc modum.

1. De sectis faciendis ad curias magnatum et aliorum dominorum ipsarum curiarum prouisum est et concorditer statutum quod nullus qui per cartam feofatus est distringatur decetero ad sectam faciendam ad curiam domini sui, nisi per formam carte sue specialiter teneatur ad sectam faciendam; hiis tantum exceptis quorum antecessores uel ipsimet huiusmodi sectam facere consueuerunt ante primam transfretacionem dicti domini regis in Britanniam a tempore cuius transfretacionis elapsi fuerunt xx^{ti}. et nouem anni et dimidius tempore quo hec constitutio facta fuit; et similiter nullus feofatus sine carta a tempore conquestus uel alio antiquo feofamento distringatur ad huiusmodi sectam faciendam, nisi ipse uel antecessores sui eam facere consueuerunt ante primam transfretacionem dicti domini regis in Britanniam.

2. Et, si hereditas aliqua de qua tantum una secta debebatur ad plures heredes participes eiusdem deuoluatur, ille qui habet einesciam hereditatis illius unicam faciat sectam pro se et participibus suis, et participes sui pro portione sua contribuant ad sectam illam faciendam; similiter eciam, si plures feofati fuerint de hereditate aliqua, de qua unica secta debebatur, dominus illius feodi unicam habeat inde sectam nec possit de predicta hereditate nisi unicam sectam exigere sicut fieri prius consueuit. Et si feofati illi warantum uel medium non habeant qui inde eos acquietare debeat, tunc omnes feofati contribuant pro portione sua ad sectam illam faciendam.

3. Si autem contingat quod domini curiarum tenentes suos contra hanc prouisionem pro huiusmodi secta distringant, tunc ad querimoniam tenentium illorum attachientur quod ad curiam regis ueniant ad breuem diem inde responsuri et unicum habeant essonium si fuerint in regno, et incontinenti deliberentur conquerenti aueria siue districciones alie hac occasione facte, et

^b xliiii M. B *dated* mcclx secundo, *text b dated* mcc sexagesimo secundo. *See doc. 10, n. 6 for explanation of this date. Text b dated* xii die Junii *for* xii die Januarii. *Baronial Plan*, pp. 295–6, n. 6.

² *facta apud Oxoniam* M. See E. F. Jacob, 'What were the "Provisions of Oxford"?', *History*, ix (1924), 188–200 for a discussion of the general use of this term.

year of the reign of King Henry son of King John, the king and his magnates having met at Westminster[2] in the quinzaine of Michaelmas [13 October], by the common counsel and consent of the king and his magnates the provisions written below were made by the king and the magnates, and were published in this manner.

1. In the matter of performance of suit at the courts of magnates and of other lords of such courts, it is provided and commonly agreed that no one enfeoffed by charter shall henceforth be distrained to do suit at the court of his lord unless he is specially required by the words of the charter to do suit, with the exception of those whose ancestors, or who themselves, customarily did such suit before the first crossing of the lord king to Brittany, from which time twenty-nine and a half years have elapsed down to the time when this rule was framed: and similarly, no one enfeoffed without a charter from the time of the Norman conquest or by any other ancient enfeoffment shall be distrained to do such suit, unless he or his ancestors customarily performed it before the first crossing of the said lord king to Brittany.

2. And, if any inheritance from which only one suit is due devolves on several heirs as sharers of the inheritance, he who has the first-born's share of the inheritance shall perform one suit for himself and his coparceners, and his coparceners shall contribute to the performance of that suit according to their own shares; and similarly, if several persons were enfeoffed with any inheritance from which only one suit is due, the lord of that fee shall have one suit only from it, nor can he require more than one suit from the inheritance, just as he was accustomed to do previously. And if those who are enfeoffed have no warrant or agent whose duty it is to acquit them for it, then all of the enfeoffed shall contribute, according to their portions, to doing this suit.

3. If, however, it should happen that lords of courts, contrary to this provision, distrain their tenants for this kind of suit, then, on their tenants' complaint, let them be attached to come to the king's court at an early date to answer this charge, and they shall have only one single essoin if they are within the kingdom, and immediately the beasts or other pledges seized for this occasion shall be restored to the complainant and shall remain so restored

deliberata remaneant donec placitum inter eos terminetur. Et, si domini curiarum, qui districciones huiusmodi fecerint, ad diem ad quem attachiati fuerint non uenerint, uel diem per essonium sibi datum non obseruauerint, tunc mandetur uicecomiti quod eos ad diem illum uenire faciat, ad quem diem si non uenerint, mandetur uicecomiti quod distringat eos per omnia que habent in balliua sua, ita quod regi respondeat de exitibus; et quod habeat eorum corpora ad certum diem prefigendum, ita quod, si die illo non uenerint, pars conquerens eat inde sine die et aueria siue alie districciones deliberata remaneant donec ipsi domini sectam illam recuperauerint per consideracionem curie domini regis; et cessent interim districtiones huiusmodi, saluo dominis curiarum iure suo de sectis illis perquirendis in forma iuris cum inde loqui uoluerint. Et cum domini curiarum uenerint responsuri conquerentibus de huiusmodi districcionibus, si super hoc conuincantur, tunc per consideracionem curie[c] recuperent conquerentes uersus eos dampna sua que sustinuerunt occasione predicte districcionis. Simili autem modo, si tenentes post hanc constitutionem subtrahant dominis suis sectas quas facere debent et quas ante tempus supradicte transfretacionis et hactenus facere consueuerunt, per eandem iusticiam et celeritatem quoad dies prefigendos et districciones adiudicandas consequantur domini curiarum iusticiam de sectis illis una cum dampnis suis quemadmodum tenentes sua dampna recuperant. Et hoc scilicet de dampnis recuperandis intelligatur de subtraccionibus sibi factis et non de subtraccionibus factis predecessoribus ipsorum, uerumptamen domini curiarum uersus tenentes suos seisinam de sectis huiusmodi recuperare non poterunt per defaltam[3] sicut nec hactenus fieri consueuit. De sectis autem que ante tempus supradicte transfretacionis subtracte fuerint currat lex comunis sicut prius currere consueuit.

4. De turno uicecomitis prouisum est ut necesse non habeant ibi uenire archiepiscopi, episcopi, abbates, priores, comites, barones, nec aliqui religiosi seu mulieres nisi specialiter eorum presencia exigatur; set teneatur turnus sicut temporibus predecessorum domini regis teneri consueuit. Et, si qui in hundredis diuersis habeant tenementa, non habeant necesse ad huiusmodi

---

[c] M reads curie domini. *Continues, after two solidi, with cls. 9 and 10 of text a. Two solidi at end of cl. 10 are followed by cl. 12 of text a, of which cls. 11 and 14 are omitted.*

until the plea between them has been determined. And if lords of courts who have committed such distraints do not appear on the day for which they were attached, or do not observe the day allowed them for essoin, then the sheriff shall be ordered to make them come on another day: and if on that day they fail to appear, the sheriff shall be ordered to distrain them by all that they hold in his bailiwick, provided that he answer to the king for the proceeds, and that he shall produce their persons on a certain day, to be fixed; so that, if on that day they do not come, the plaintiff shall depart *sine die*, and the beasts or other pledges shall remain released until the lords shall have recovered the suit by the judgement of the court of the lord king; and meanwhile let all such distraints cease, saving to the lords of courts their right to recover such suits by due legal process when they shall be willing to come and sue for it. And when lords of courts come to answer plaintiffs on such distraints, if they are convicted of them, then by the judgement of the court the plaintiffs shall recover from them the damages which they have suffered by reason of these distraints. And in like manner, if, after this constitution, tenants withdraw from their lords the suits which they ought to perform, and which they customarily did perform before the time of the crossing and up till now, the lords of courts shall obtain justice in those suits, together with their damages, by the same process and speed, with regard to the fixing of dates and adjudicating distraints as those by which the tenants recover their damages. And this shall be understood to apply, for the recovery of damages, to withdrawals made from them, but not from their predecessors. However, lords of courts cannot recover seisin of such suits against their tenants' default,[3] for such has never yet been the practice. As for suits which were withdrawn before this crossing, let the common law operate as it has customarily done hitherto.

4. Concerning the sheriff's tourn, it is provided that archbishops, bishops, abbots, priors, earls, barons, monks, and women need not attend unless their presence is specially required; but let the tourn be held as it was customarily held in the times of the predecessors of the lord king. And any who have holdings in different hundreds need not attend these tourns except in hundreds

[3] Faced with the rivalry of the royal courts the nobles were going to extreme lengths to maintain their own courts. Demands for suit of court were enforced by distraint and lords were claiming, unjustifiably, that default by tenants allowed the lord to recover suit of court.

turnum uenire nisi in balliuis ubi fuerint conuersantes; et teneantur turni secundum formam Magne Carte regis et sicut temporibus regum Iohannis et Ricardi teneri consueuerunt.

5. Prouisum est eciam quod nec in itinere iusticiariorum nec in comitatibus nec in curiis baronum decetero ab aliquibus recipiantur fines pro pulcre placitando neque per sic quod non occasionentur.

6. In placito uero dotis quod dicitur 'unde nichil habet' dentur decetero quatuor dies per annum ad minus et plures ei comode fieri posset.[4]

7. In assisis[d] Vltime presentacionis, et in placito Quare impedit de ecclesiis uacantibus detur dies de quindena in quindenam uel de tribus septimanis in tres septimanas prout locus propinquus fuerit uel remotus. Et in placito Quare impedit, si ad primum diem ad quem summonitus fuerit non ueniat nec essonium mittat impeditor, tunc attachietur ad diem alium, quo die si non uenerit nec essonium mittat, distringatur per magnam districcionem superius dictam. Et, si tunc non uenerit, per eius defaltam scribatur episcopo quod reclamacio impeditoris illa uice conquerenti non obsistat saluo impeditori alias iure suo cum inde loqui uoluerit.[e]

8. De cartis uero exempcionis et libertatis ne ponantur impetrantes in assisis, iuratis uel recognicionibus, prouisum est ut, si adeo necessarium sit eorum iuramentum quod sine eo iustitia exhiberi non possit ueluti in magna assisa et perambulacionibus, et ubi in cartis uel scripturis conuencionum fuerint testes nominati, aut in attinctis uel casibus aliis consimilibus, iurare cogantur, salua sibi alias libertate et exempcione sua predicta.

9. Si heres aliquis post mortem sui antecessoris infra etatem extiterit et dominus suus custodiam terrarum suarum habuerit, si dominus ille dicto heredi, cum ad legitimam etatem peruenerit, terram suam sine placito reddere noluerit, heres ille terram suam ut de morte sui antecessoris recuperabit una cum dampnis que sustinuerit per illam detencionem a tempore quo legittime fuerit

---

[d] *Ann. Mon.* i. 473 *reads* essiones *but ibid.*, p. 481 *and* N *read* assisis *and* assises.   [e] B *and text b follow the text printed above to this point but add a new clause (S. of Realm, i. 9, n. 13). Both continue to follow the above text until the end of clause 13 but omit clause 14 of the above text. Henceforward* B *is the same as the above text except that clause 23 of* B *reproduces clause 18 of the above text. The additional clauses in text b are the same as those in* B. *See appendix* 11 *for comparisons of the text printed above with* B, M, *and text b. Text b was reissued in Dec. 1264. See document* 9, n. 9.

where they have residences; and let the tourns be held according to the form of the Great Charter of the king, and as it was customarily held in the times of King John and King Richard.

5. It is provided that in future neither in the eyres of justices nor in shire courts nor in courts baron shall fines be taken from anyone for 'fair pleading', nor in order that they shall not be amerced for this.

6. In pleas of dower known as *unde nihil habet* in future at least four days a year shall be allowed, and more if it can conveniently be done.[4]

7. In assizes of *darrein presentment* and in pleas of *quare impedit* concerning vacant churches, let days be given from fortnight to fortnight or from three weeks to three weeks, accordingly as the place is near or far. And in pleas of *quare impedit*, if the defendant does not appear or send an essoin on the first day for which he was summoned, let him be attached for another day, and if on that day he does not appear or send an essoin, then let him be distrained by the great distraint mentioned above. And if he does not appear then, then by reason of his default let the bishop be notified that the defendant's claim shall not obstruct the plaintiff in this case, saving to the defendant otherwise his right when he shall be willing to sue for it.

8. Concerning charters of exemption and of liberty granting that those who have obtained them shall not be placed on assizes, juries, or recognitions, it is provided that, if their oath is so necessary that justice cannot be done without it, as in a grand assize or in a perambulation, or in cases where they are named as witnesses in charters or in written agreements, or in attaints or similar cases, they shall be compelled to take oath, saving to them on other occasions their liberty and exemption.

9. If after the death of his ancestor any heir was under age, and his lord had the custody of his lands, and when the heir has come of age, the lord refuses to restore his land to him without a lawsuit, the heir shall recover his land as from the death of his ancestor together with the damages which he has suffered by such detention, from the time when he came of lawful age: but if, at the death of his ancestor the heir was already of full age, and is found to be

---

[4] This is one day in each of the four law terms of the Court of Common Pleas at Westminster.

etatis; quod si heres in morte sui antecessoris plene fuerit etatis et heres ille apparens et pro herede cognitus inuentus sit in hereditate illa, capitalis dominus eius eum non eiciat nec aliquid ibi capiat uel amoueat, set tantum simplicem seisinam faciat pro recognicione dominii sui.

10. Et, si capitalis dominus heredem huiusmodi extra seisinam maliciose teneat, per quod per actionem mortis antecessoris uel consanguinitatis oporteat ipsum placitare, tunc dampna sua recuperet sicut in actione noue disseisine.

11. Nulli decetero liceat ex quacunque causa districciones facere extra feodum suum neque in regia aut communi strata nisi domino regi et ministris suis.

12. Prouisum est eciam quod, si terra que tenetur in socagium[5] sit in custodia parentum heredis eo quod heredes infra etatem fuerint, custodes illi uastum facere non possunt neque uendicionem nec aliquam destruccionem de hereditate illa, set saluo eam custodiant ad opus dicti heredis, ita quod, cum ad etatem peruenerit, sibi respondeant per legitimam computacionem de exitibus dicte hereditatis, saluis ipsis custodibus racionabilibus misis suis, nec eciam possunt dicti custodes maritagium dicti heredis dare uel uendere, nisi ad comodum ipsius heredis.

13. Nullus escaetor aut inquisitor uel justiciarius ad assisas aliquas capiendas specialiter assignatus, uel ad querelas aliquas audiendas et terminandas, de cetero potestatem habeant[f] amerciandi pro defalta comunis summonicionis nisi capitalis iusticiarius uel iusticiarii itinerantes in itineribus suis.

14. Viris autem religiosis non liceat ingredi feodum alicuius sine licencia capitalis domini, de quo, scilicet, res ipsa immediate tenetur.[g]

15. De essoniis autem prouisum est quod in comitatibus, hundredis, aut curiis baronum uel alibi nullus habeat necesse iurare pro essonio suo warantizando.

16. Nullus[h] decetero, excepto rege, placitum teneat in curia sua de falso iudicio facto in curia tenentium suorum, quia huiusmodi placita ad coronam specialiter pertinent et dignitatem regis.[6]

---

[f] habeat text b.   [g] This clause does not reappear in any of the other texts.
[h] This clause, in the close roll, appears at the end of clause 18 but is marked for transfer to the place which it occupies in the text printed above.

---

[5] Socage tenure, Anglo-Saxon in origin, was for non-military service, rent being in labour or in kind. The overlord of socage tenants possessed no rights of wardship or marriage.

the heir apparent and is known to be the heir of that inheritance, the chief lord shall not eject him nor take nor remove anything from the inheritance, but may make only formal seisin as recognition of his overlordship.

10. And if the chief lord maliciously keeps such an heir out of his inheritance, so that he is forced to institute proceedings by an action of *mort d'ancestor* or cousinage [kinship], then he shall recover damages as if in an action of *novel disseisin*.

11. No one in future shall be allowed for any reason to make distraints outside his own fee nor in the king's highway nor in the common street, except the lord king and his officers.

12. It is also provided that, if land which is held in socage[5] is in the custody of the relatives of the heir because the heir is under age, the guardians cannot make any waste, sale, or any other diminution of the inheritance, but shall keep it safely for the use of the heir, so that, when he shall come of age, they may answer to him by lawful computation for the proceeds of the said inheritance, allowing their reasonable expenses to the guardians, nor can the guardians give or sell the marriage of the heir, save for the good of the heir himself.

13. No escheator, inquisitor, or justice specially assigned to take any assizes or to hear and determine any complaints shall in future have power to amerce for default of common summons, except the chief justiciar, and the itinerant justices on their eyres.

14. Monks shall not be allowed to enter the fee of anyone without the permission of the chief lord, from whom that property is held.

15. Concerning essoins, it is provided that in county courts, hundreds, and courts baron, or elsewhere, no one shall need to take oath to warrant his essoin.

16. No one in future save the king shall hold in his court any plea of false judgement made in a court of one of his tenants, since such pleas specially belong to the royal crown and dignity.[6]

[6] Faulty justice was a crown plea in the *Leges Henrici* (Stubbs, p. 124, cl. x. 1). Document 3, cl. 29 petitions against the interference, shown by the owners of private courts, against cases going to the royal courts.

17. Prouisum est eciam quod, si aueria alicuius capiantur et
iniuste detineantur, uicecomes post querimoniam inde sibi factam
ea sine impedimento uel contradiccione eius qui dicta aueria cepit
deliberare possit, si extra libertates capta fuerint, et, si infra
libertates huiusmodi capiantur aueria et balliui libertatum ea
deliberare noluerint, tunc uicecomes per defectum dictorum
balliuorum ea faciat deliberari.

18. Nullus decetero distringere possit libere tenentes suos ad
respondendum de libero tenemento suo neque de aliquibus ad
liberum tenementum suum spectantibus sine breui regis,[7] nec
iurare faciat libere tenentes suos contra uoluntatem suam, desicut
nullus hoc facere potest sine precepto regis.

19. Prouisum est eciam quod, si balliui qui compotum dominis
suis reddere tenentur se subtraxerint et terras uel tenementa non
habuerint per que distringi possint, tunc per eorum corpora
attachientur, ita quod uicecomites, in quorum balliuis inuenientur,
eos uenire faciant ad compotum suum reddendum.

20. Item firmarii tempore suarum firmarum uastum uel uendicionem uel exilium non faciant de boscis, domibus, hominibus,
nec de aliis aliquibus ad tenementa que ad firmam habuerint
spectantibus, nisi specialem habeant concessionem per scripturam
sue conuencionis mencionem habentis quod hoc facere possint.
Et, si fecerint et de hoc conuincantur, dampna plene refundant.

21. Iusticiarii itinerantes decetero non amerciant uillatas in
itinere suo pro eo quod singuli xij. annorum non uenerint coram
uicecomite et coronatoribus ad inquisiciones de morte hominis
aut aliis ad coronam pertinentibus, dum tamen de uillis illis
ueniant sufficienter per quos inquisiciones huiusmodi plene fieri
possint.

22. Murdrum decetero non adiudicetur coram iusticiariis ubi
infortunium tantummodo adiudicatum est, set locum habeat
murdrum in interfectis per feloniam et non aliter.

23. Prouisum est insuper quod nullus, qui coram iusticiariis
itinerantibus uocatur ad warantum de placito terre uel tenementi,
amercietur decetero pro eo quod presens non fuerit, excepto primo
die aduentus ipsorum iusticiariorum, set, si warantus ille sit infra
comitatum, tunc iniungatur uicecomiti quod ipsum infra diem

---

[7] If a tenant's complaint referred to freehold he had to act through a royal
writ rather than being allowed to use the proceedings of the *querula* which
involved no writ.

17. It is also provided that, if anyone's beasts are seized and unjustly detained, the sheriff, upon complaint made to him about the matter, shall have power to release them without hinderance or opposition from him who seized the beasts, if they were taken outside the liberty; and if the beasts were taken within such liberties, and the bailiffs of the liberties refuse to release them, then the sheriff, on account of the default of the bailiffs, shall cause them to be released.

18. No one henceforth shall be able to distrain his free tenants to make answer concerning their freeholds, nor concerning anything pertaining to the freeholds, without the king's writ,[7] nor may he force his free tenants to take oath against their wills, since no one can do this save by the king's precept.

19. It is also provided that if bailiffs who ought to render account to their lords shall abscond, and have no lands or property whereby they can be distrained, then they shall be attached by their persons, so that the sheriffs in whose bailiwicks they are found, shall compel them to come to render their accounts.

20. Further, farmers, during the period of their farms, shall make no waste, sale, or alienation of woods, houses, men, or any other things pertaining to the tenements which they have at farm, unless they have special concession in their written agreements stating that they may do these things: and, if they have done them, and are convicted of them, they shall refund full damages.

21. Itinerant justices in future shall not amerce townships in their eyres because not all men of the age of twelve years have come before the sheriff and coroners for inquests upon dead men or other crown pleas, provided that enough men come to enable such inquests to be made properly.

22. Henceforth *murdrum* shall not be adjudged before the justices where the verdict is one of accident only; and *murdrum* shall be incurred only in felonious slayings, and not otherwise.

23. It is also provided that no one who is vouched to warranty before the itinerant justices in a plea of lands or tenements shall in future only be amerced because he was not in attendance on the first day of arrival of the justices: but, if the warrantor is within the county, then the sheriff shall be instructed to cause him to appear

tercium uel quartum secundum locorum distanciam faciat uenire sicut in itinere iusticiariorum fieri consueuit. Et, si extra comitatum maneat, tunc racionabilem habeat summonicionem xv. dierum ad minus secundum discrecionem iusticiariorum et legem comunem.

24. Si^i clericus aliquis pro crimine aliquo uel recto quod ad coronam pertineat, arestatus fuerit et postmodum de precepto regis in ballium traditus uel replegiatus extiterit, ita quod hii quibus traditur in ballium eum habeant coram iusticiariis, non amercientur decetero illi quibus traditus fuit in ballium uel alii plegii sui, si corpus suum habeant coram iusticiariis, licet coram eis propter priuilegium clericale respondere nolit uel non possit.^{j}

12

OCTOBER 1259

Prouisiones Westmonasterii$*^1$

1. Derichef,^{a} ke iustices seient purueuz de aler par la tere. E seit un des duze ou des autres del commun pur ueer ke dreiture seit fete al pleinanz et a tuz autres. E si il ueient ke les establissimenz ke sunt fetz al pru del reaume ke sunt e serrunt, seit mande as cuntez ke il seient tenuz.

2. Ensement ke les purueances ke sunt fetes pus le commencement de ces establisemenz seient leuez et maintenuz.

^{i} *This clause appears at the end of both the French text in* N *and in the Latin text* V. *In the French text* V *it is among the administrative clauses (doc. 12, cl. 21; Reform and Rebellion, p. 376).* N, *having variations in wording, continues in Latin with clauses 21–3, 25 of document 9. This suggests that the scribe believed that document 11 should include all the clauses of document 9; when he found this was not so he made the additions (doc. 9, n. 6).* ^{j} B *continues with the extra clauses as in text* b (S. *of Realm, i. 11, n. 11).* M *continues with clauses beginning* Prouisum est *and* Similem insuper, *as at the end of letter patent, but omits the last clause. The MS. continues with examples of writs, probably the* Examen Cartarum *printed in Sir William Dugdale's* Origines Juridicales (1666), *p. 57.*

^{a} *See text comments of documents 5 and 30 for consideration of the use of Latin or French.*

---

* *Text*: British Museum, Cotton MS. Vespasian, E. iii, ff. 92^v–93^v (old

on the third or the fourth day, according to the distance of the place, as is customarily done before the justices in eyre: and if he dwells outside the county, then let him have reasonable summons of fifteen days at least, according to the discretion of the justices and the common law.

24. If a clerk is arrested for any crime or offence pertaining to the crown, and then by precept of the lord king he is given in bail or replevied, so that those to whom he is given in bail shall produce him before the justices, in future his manucaptors or other sureties shall not be amerced, provided they produce him in person before the justices, even if, when he appears before them, he either will not or cannot answer, on account of clerical privilege.

12

OCTOBER 1259

The Provisions of Westminster [Administrative and Political Resolutions][1]

1. Further, that justices be appointed to go throughout the land. And there shall be with them one of the twelve or of the rest of the community to see that justice is done to the plaintiffs and to all others. And they shall also see that the establishments which are made for the good of the realm, both those already made and those still to be made, are enjoined upon the counties for observance.

2. Also that the provisions which are made since the beginning of the present establishments shall be declared and upheld.

ff. 89ᵛ–90ᵛ) (V). *Printed*: *Ann. Mon.* i. 476–9 (translation 507–10); *Anglicarum Scriptores*, i. 431–3. *Additional Text*: British Museum, Cotton MS. Nero, D. i, ff. 138ᵛ–139 (N), mentioned *Chron. Majora*, vi. 512. *Printed*: *Reform and Rebellion*, pp. 372–4, 376; collated with (V). *See*: *Baronial Plan*, pp. 165–9, 178–91; *Reform and Rebellion*, pp. 87–8, 90–6, 370–6; 'Baronial Council', p. 130.

The early clauses in N, which omits clauses 10, 11, 13, and 14 of V, are shorter and differ from those in V. V is divided into paragraphs, the initial letters of which alternate in red and blue. Numbering has been added for convenience of reference.

---

[1] Doc. 11, n. 1. It is of interest to note that this document was known at St. Albans as well as at Burton, but the contents do not suggest that it was distributed to be read in the county court.

3. Derichef les roules de ces establissimenz seient luz et fermez. E les chartres de franchise et de la forest seient tenues et maintenues.

4. Purueu est ensement ke nul ne uenge al parlementer a cheuaus, ne a armes ne arme, si il ne seit mande especialment par le rei ou par sun conseil, ou par bref pur communes bossoines de la terre.[2]

5. La ou iustices erranz errerent dereinement, seient aturnez prodes homes et sages de oir et demander totes les plaintes ke poeient estre terminez sanz bref de set anz en ca; einsi ke si nul ne se seint pleint deuant les set anz, et ne eit pas eu dreiture, ke il recouere a dreiture auer. E il eient poer de enquere des uescuntes et de lur baillifs coment il se sunt portez uer le pais pus les establissemenz.

6. Ausi enquergent des baillifs as riches homes de la terre, e des riches homes memes.

7. Iustices erranz eient memes le poer ke uescuntes en lur eire; ensement en lur poer demeine par lur eire. E seient purueuz ke mesne gent del conseil deus ou treis seient adesseement entur le rei de parlement en parlement.[3] E a chescun des parlemenz seient f. 93 changez e mis autres. | E seit lur fet ueu a chescun parlement. E seit amende si rens i seit a amender par ces del cunseil. E si nule grant bossoine surde entre les parlemenz ke ne porra estre termine par les deuant dit deus ou treis, ou ke ne purra estre delae en bone manere deskes al procein parlement, tuz ces del conseil seint mandez par bref pur cele bosoine terminer. E seit mis en le bref le achesun del mandement, si ceo ne seit secre. E si nuls des autres del conseil, ou des auant dit deus ou treis, uengent a curt par le mandement le rei ou pur sa bosoine demeine, ke il seient al conseil le rei tant come les bossoines durent, oue les lur propres et oue les bossoines le rei pur quei il sunt mandez.

8. Il fet a remembrer ke deus prodes homes seient purueuz a uendre les gardes ke ore en dreit sunt en la main le rei.

9. Derichef ke deus prodes homes seient purueuz a ordener ensement oueke le conseil del escheker de uescuntes et de cuntez.[4]

---

[2] Doc. 29, cls. 32, 36. This clause may have been occasioned by the enmity between Gloucester, Leicester, and the Lord Edward.

[3] This clause seems to be directed against the practical control of policy falling into the hands of a small group of individuals—the leading earls.

[4] See cl. 22 below. As the appointment of sheriffs was overdue (doc. 5, cl. 17) it was planned that those who should hold office in the year 1259–60 would be

3. Further, the documents recording these establishments shall be read and confirmed, and the charters of liberties and of the forest shall be kept and enforced.

4. It is also provided that no one shall come to parliament with horses and arms, or in armour, unless this be specially ordered by the king or by his council, or by writ, for the common business of the land.[2]

5. Where the itinerant justices have lately been on eyre, let sound and wise men be appointed to receive and to ask for all complaints which can be determined without a writ, for seven years from that time, provided that if anyone has not made complaint before these seven years are ended, and has not had justice, he may recover and secure justice. And they shall have power to inquire about the sheriffs and their bailiffs to see how they have behaved towards the neighbourhood since these establishments were issued.

6. Let them also inquire about the bailiffs of the great men in the land, and about the great men themselves.

7. Itinerant justices shall have the same power as sheriffs during their eyre, and their power shall remain throughout their eyre. And let it be arranged that two or three councillors of middle rank shall be in constant attendance on the king from one parliament to the next, and let them be changed and others replace them at each parliament.[3] And let their actions be reviewed at each parliament, and if there is anything that requires amendment, let it be amended by the councillors. And if any important matter arises in between parliaments, which cannot be settled by the two or three, or cannot satisfactorily be delayed to the next parliament, all the councillors shall be summoned by writ to settle the business, and the reason of the summons shall be stated in the writ unless it is secret. And if any others of the council, or of the said two or three, come to the court by the king's command, or for his own affairs, let them be present at the king's council as long as their business lasts, whether their own or the king's, for which they were summoned.

8. Let it be noted that two good men be appointed to sell the wardships which shall henceforth be in the king's hand.

9. Moreover, let two good men be appointed to decide, along with the advice of the exchequer, about sheriffs and counties.[4]

---

chosen by the justiciar and those named. There is no evidence to indicate whether the exchequer barons chose one of the four men or accepted one of the four. It is possible that the four knights who were to enquire about mal-administration in the counties in 1258 (doc. 5, cl. 1), chose the sheriffs in the autumn of 1258, and the method suggested in this document may have been used in the spring of 1259 (*Baronial Plan*, pp. 182-3, 205-6; doc. 31, cl. 6).

10. Derichef seient purueu genz de aler oueke le rei en France. E queus demorrunt en la tere pres de la iustice.[5]

11. E ke as messagers de Wales seit respundu.

12. E purveu seit coment les brefs de purueances et des establissemenz hors de la chancelerie iscerunt sanz delay.

13. Ensement et de messagers ke irrunt a Rome.[6]

14. As gardes uendre meintenant seient mis la iustice, le tresorer, mestre Thomas de Wimundeham, sire Roger de Torkeby, sire Henry de Baa. E ke ces memes ordeinent et purueient en queus articles la reine deit auer or.

15. Purueu est ke memes ces uengent al escheker, et ueient les sumes de totes maneres de tailages ke unt este mises pus le tens cest rei. E ke il esment cum ben chescun poet amonter.

16. E [b]ces memes purueient coment lem deit aler auant en pleez de costumes et de seruices.[7]

17. Ensement purueient coment lem deit aler auant en eschaetes et en gardes.

18. Purveu seit quels genz deiuent aler a amender les trespas et les torz fetz, ke poent estre terminez sanz bref.

19. La iustice le purueie oueke les autres. E quels serrunt al Banc[8] oueke le iustices, e quels al eschecker.

20. Purueu est ke quatre cheualers seient mis en chescun cunte pur uer le torz ke uescuntes funt. Si il auent ke torz facent, ke ces quatre amonestent les uescuntes ke il les facent amender. E si il nel uolent amender, mettent les torz fez en un roule, e les mostrent a la haute iustice al chef de an, kant il les demandera; ou auant, si il les demande, si einsi est ke les pleintifs as quels

---

[b] *The following two clauses in* N *replace clauses 16–19 of* V: Et ceus memes purueient cument lem deit aler auant en plaiz de wardes, e de eschetes, e en plez de custumes e de seruises e en plez de warantye de chartre e de couenant et de bref de trespas. Coment lem pot abreger sulun dreit le delay e des autres semblabes plez.

Purueu est ke la iustice oue le consel des autres e del escheser purueient quele gent irrunt entuz les cuntez de Engletere pur amender les forfez e les trespas ke poent estre termine sant bref. E queus deus prudes homes sages seient ouek la iustices au banc, e autres deus [ou]e ceus al eschecer puruer ke draitur sait fet e tenu. *See n. 7.*

---

[5] Doc. 15, n. 1. The king was absent from England 14 Nov. 1259–23 Apr. 1260.

[6] *Baronial Plan, passim* for negotiations with Rome and Wales.

[7] The two clauses in N which replace clauses 16–19 of V read 'And these same shall provide how one should proceed in pleas of wardships and of escheats

10. Further, let it be provided who shall go with the king to France and who shall stay in this country with the justiciar.[5]

11. And let a reply be made to the messengers from Wales.

12. And let arrangements be made for issuing the writs of these provisions and establishments from the chancery without delay.

13. And also for sending messengers to Rome.[6]

14. To sell the wardships now, the justiciar, the treasurer, Master Thomas de Wymondham, Sir Roger de Thurkelby, and Sir Henry de Bath shall be appointed. And these same men shall determine and decree in what matters queen's gold shall be paid.

15. It is also provided that these same men shall come to the exchequer, to discover the amounts of all kinds of tallages imposed during the present reign, and they shall estimate how much each of them amounted to.

16. And these same men shall provide how one should proceed in pleas of customs and service.[7]

17. Also they shall provide how one should proceed in escheats and wardships.

18. Be it provided who should go to amend injuries and wrongs done which can be terminated without writ.

19. Let the justiciar provide this with the others: what persons shall be at the court of common pleas[8] with the judges and what persons at the exchequer.

20. It is provided that four knights shall be appointed in each county to review the wrongs committed by the sheriffs. And if it happen that the sheriffs do wrong, let these four warn the sheriffs to put things right; and if they will not put them right, let them record in writing the wrongs done and report them to the chief justiciar at the end of the year, or earlier if he should ask for them, always provided the plaintiffs, to whom the wrongs were done, are

---

and in pleas of customs and in pleas of warranty of charter, covenant, and writs of trespass. How delays may be shortened while still preserving right, and in other similar pleas.'

'It is provided that the justiciar, with the counsel of others and of the exchequer, shall arrange who shall visit the counties of England to redress the wrongs and injuries which can be dealt with without a writ. And that two good and wise men shall be with the justices at the bench and two others at the exchequer, to see that right be done and maintained.'

[8] *Ann. Mon.* i. 509 n. mistakenly calls this the king's bench.

les torz sunt fez uoillent suire. E ke ces auant dit quatre cheuellers
ne eient nul poer a desturber les uescuntes de lur office fere.[c9]

21. Si clerc seit rette de mort de home, de roberie, ou de larecin,
ou de autre crime ke apende a la corune, e pus seit liuere en bail
par comandement le rei a duze prodes homes ke il le eient pardeuant iustices, ou lesse par pleges par commandement le rei;
si les auant dit duze ou les pleges eient sun cors al premer ior
pardeuant iustices, ne seient pas deshoremes amerciez, tut ne
uoile le clerc respondre, ne a dreit ester, en la curt le rei, de si
cume il ne furent de autre chose pleges ou main pernant, fors de
auer le cors le clerc auant.[d]

22. La haute iustice, le tresorer, sire Henry de Baa, sire Roger
f. 93ᵛ de Turkeby, et les baruns | del escheker purueient cest an mein-
tenant queus prodes homes e leaus e sages seient uescuntes cest an.
E seient uauasurs de memes les cuntez. E encuntre le prochein
an al prochein cunte deuant la Saint Michel seient esluz en plein
cunte quatre prodes homes e leaus, e ke seint profitables al rei e al
cunte en cel office. E seient a la Seint Michel al escheker. E les
baruns prengent les plus suffisanz a lur esgart.

23. Derichef seient esluz par la haute iustice et par le tresorer
prodes homes en cest Aduent, e en ces iurs de festes encuntre le
procein parlement, ceo ke serra a amender al grant escheker e al
escheker as Gyus. E par ces meymes seit purueu resonable sus-
tenement a ces ke serrunt al un escheker et al autre.

24. Purueu est ke sire Thomas de Gresly, iustice de la forest,
prenge Nicholas de Ramesey e treis cheualers de chescun cunte,
et enquergent le estat des forestz, de uert et de ueneyson, et de
uentes et de destructions; e par ki eles sunt fetes. E enquergent
de malueises usages de pleez de la forest, et par queus eles sunt
aleuez, e de quel tens; e quant ceo auera feit, face le a sauer al
rei et a sun cunseil.

25. Memes ceste manere seit feit des forestz de la Trente. Ke la
haute iustice purueie quatre cheualers et enquerge de totes les
forest de la Trente en la manere ke est desus dit.

---

[c] N *inserts, at this point,* Purueu est ke la haute iustice, le chanceler, e le
tresorer demorent en lur baillies tekes al prochein perlement.   [d] *Although
the wording is very different this clause means the same as cl. 24 of document 11.*

---

[9] The clause inserted by N at this point reads 'It is provided that the chief
justiciar, the chancellor and the treasurer shall remain in their offices until the
next parliament'. See *Baronial Plan,* p. 179; *British Chronology,* pp. 70–1, 83, 100.

willing to prosecute. And these four knights shall have no power to hinder the sheriffs in the performance of their duties.[9]

21. If a clerk be accused of murder, robbery, or of larceny or of another crime which is a crown plea, and is then freed on bail, by order of the king, to twelve worthy men to have him before the judges, or released through pledges by command of the king: if the twelve, or the pledges, have him before the judges on the first day, they shall not henceforth be fined if the clerk be not willing to answer, or to do right, in the king's court, in as much as they were not pledges or guarantors for any other thing except that they produced the clerk before the court.

22. The chief justiciar, the treasurer, Sir Henry de Bath, Sir Roger de Thurkelby, and the barons of the exchequer shall decide now, this year, which sound loyal and wise men shall be sheriffs for the present year. And they shall be vavassors of the same counties. And in preparation for the next year, at the last county court before Michaelmas [29 September], let four sound and loyal men, who will be useful in that office both to the king and to the county, be elected in full county court, and let them present themselves to the exchequer at Michaelmas; and the barons will select the best men in their opinion.

23. Further, let sound and wise men be appointed by the justiciar and the treasurer, to decide, during Advent and the first days before the next parliament, what reforms are needed at the great exchequer and at the exchequer of the Jews. And let these same men provide reasonable maintenance for those who shall be at either exchequer.

24. It is provided that Sir Thomas de Grelley, justiciar of the forest, shall take Nicholas de Ramsey and three knights from every shire, and they shall investigate the state of the forests, vert and venison, sales and damage, and by whom these things have been done. And let them investigate abuses of forest pleas, and by whom these were begun, and when; and when they have done this let them report to the king and his council.

25. In the same way let the forests beyond Trent be investigated by the chief justiciar, who shall choose four knights in each county and investigate all the forests beyond Trent, in the manner stated above.

26. Le erceueskes et le eueske de Wirecestre, le cunte le Mareschal, le cunte de Warewik, seient oueke la iustice as granz bossoinz del regne treter, tant come le reis est hors de Engletere. E tuz cels de cunseil e les xii. de par le commun ke en Engletere demorent, si mester seit, seient mandez. Sire Phelippe Basset et sire Roger de Mortem⟨er⟩ seient adesseement oueke la iustice.[10]

27. Purueu est ke la iustice purueie ke les chasteleins eint resnable sustenance as chasteaus le rei garder et a sustenir les.[11]

28. Purueu est de mettre deus prodes homes del commun ou des xii. ke sunt par le commun ou des autres, oueke les iustices al Banc. E ke il ueient ke dreiture seit fete. E en meime la manere seient mis deus prodes homes del commun[12] ou des xii. ke sunt par le cummun ou des autre al escheker.[e]

29. Ces sunt les purueances et les establissimenz fetz a West-moster al parlement a la Seint Michel par le rei et sun conseil et les xii. par le commun conseil esluz par devant le communance de Engletere,[13] ke dunke fu a Westmuster le an del regne Henri le fiz le rei Iohan quarantime terz.

---

[e] N *omits this clause but records the circuits for the eyre. See document 13.*

---

[10] Basset was justiciar 14 June 1261–18 July 1263 when the king was re-asserting his power. Mortimer was the leading Marcher to whom the Lord Edward escaped in May 1265.

[11] N follows V, with variations, to this point when N continues with the names of the judges and the circuits for the special eyre. This information has been printed with document 13 which records the arrangements for the eyre. See doc. 13, n. 10.

26. The archbishop, the bishop of Worcester, the earl marshal, and the earl of Warwick shall stay with the justiciar to deal with the important matters of state business as long as the king shall be out of England. And all members of the council and of the twelve chosen by the community who stay in England, shall be summoned if need arise. Sir Philip Basset and Sir Roger Mortimer shall be in attendance on the justiciar.[10]

27. It is provided that the justiciar shall arrange for the castellans to have reasonable allowances for keeping the king's castles and for maintaining them.[11]

28. It is resolved to place two worthy men of the community[12] or of the twelve who are elected by the community or of the others to sit with the justices at the bench, so that they may see that justice be done. And in the same way let two good men of the community or of the twelve elected by the community or of the others be placed at the exchequer.

29. These are the provisions and establishments made at Westminster at the Michaelmas parliament by the king and his council and the twelve elected by the common counsel, in the presence of the community of England, which was then at Westminster, in the 43rd year of the reign of Henry, the son of King John.[13]

[12] This may be a clerical error for *conseil* (council).
[13] This clause has been used by E. F. Jacob as evidence to prove that parliament consisted only of the Council of Fifteen and of the twelve nominated to represent the *commun* (*Simon de Montfort*, p. 170). This has been shown to be incorrect. See introduction, p. 11.

13

NOVEMBER 1259

*Prouisiones facte de illis qui de consilio una cum iusticiariis itinerabunt per diuersa loca ad inquisiciones faciendas et transgressiones emendandas uel corrigendas ante Pascha anno xliiii**

1. Prouisio^{a1} de illis qui de consilio una cum iusticiariis itinerabunt per diuersa loca ad inquisiciones faciendas et transgressiones corigendas, uidelicet, quod sex de consilio regis eligantur, quorum quilibet una cum aliquo de duodecim et aliquo de iusticiariis ad hoc eligendis^2 in uno sex locorum per Angliam, que debent diuidi per comitatus, eat et inquirat de transgressionibus factis secundum articulos quos habebunt ordinatos per consilium et placitent breuia de dote unde nichil habet, scilicet de tenementis unde uir mulieris obiit seisitus, de ultima presentacione, de morte antecessoris, de noua disseisina, et de attinctis, ita quod, si eadem

---

^{a} N *f. 138 has rubric*: Prouisiones noue baronum subscribuntur hic tam de iusticiariis itinerantibus quam de singulis articulis iusticie et pacis. Que et Latine scribuntur et Gallice. *Both* N *and* M *continue, having unimportant detailed differences in wording, with an introduction*: Prouisio de illis qui de consilio una cum iusticiariis itinerabunt per diuersa loca ad inquisiciones faciendas et transgressiones emendandas uel corrigendas ante pascha anno xliiii°. *The close roll has no heading.*

---

* *Text*: Rot. Claus. 44 Hen. III, m. 18d. *Printed*: *C.R. 1259–61*, pp. 144–5. *Additional Texts*: i. British Museum, Cotton MS. Nero, D. i, ff. 138^v–139 (N); mentioned *Chron. Majora*, vi. 512. *Printed*: *Reform and Rebellion*, pp. 370–2. ii. Cambridge U.L., MS. Mm. i. 27, ff. 74–74^v (M). *Printed*: *Reform and Rebellion*, pp. 370–2—collated with (i). Cambridge U.L., MS. Catalogue iv. 119 mentions a document *Prouisiones facte de illis qui de consilio una cum iusticiariis itinerabunt per diuersa loca ad inquisiciones faciendas et transgressiones corrigendas, anno regni regis Johannis xliiii* (*sic*). The author of the catalogue does not try to identify this MS. which bears an introduction similar to M and N. *See*: *Baronial Plan*, pp. 196–204; *Reform and Rebellion*, pp. 96–101, 370–2. See introduction, pp. 26–7 for comment on this eyre.

The text here printed follows the paragraphs in the close roll. The dorse of m. 18 of the close roll for 44 Henry III (*C.R. 1259–61*, pp. 141–5) is entirely occupied by the above memorandum and by the letters necessary for commencing the special eyre: commissions and instructions to the justices on seven circuits, 28 Nov. 1259 (ibid., pp. 142–3); instructions to the sheriff of Hunt-

13

NOVEMBER 1259

*Provisions made concerning those of the council who will go
on circuit, in divers places with the judges, before Easter in
the forty-fourth year [of the reign of Henry III, 1260] to
hold inquisitions, correct and amend transgressions*

1. The provision[1] concerning those members of the council who
will go on eyre throughout the different districts to hold inquiries
and to correct trespasses: namely, that six of the king's council
shall be chosen, each of whom, together with one of the twelve and
one of the justices, chosen for this purpose,[2] shall go into one of
six circuits in England, which shall be divided by counties, and
shall inquire about trespasses committed, according to the articles
which they will have, ordained by the council; and they shall also
plead writs of dower *unde nichil habet* (that is, of holdings of which
the husband of a woman has died seized), of *darrein presentment*, of
mort d'ancestor, of *novel disseisin* and of attaints, provided that, if

---

ingdonshire, and those of all other counties south of the Trent, to proclaim the
special eyre and to make the necessary advance arrangements, 28 Nov. 1259
(ibid., pp. 141–2; *Royal Letters*, ii. 141–2); instructions to Hugh Despenser to
proceed to Oxford in order to commence the hearings on the morning of the
Epiphany (7 Jan. 1260), after preliminary arrangements had been made by one
of his clerks and his colleague Nicholas de Turri, 4 Dec. 1259 (*C.R. 1259–61*,
pp. 143–4). Presumably similar instructions were sent to the members of the
other five commissions—Hugh Bigod's circuit being excluded.

The N text of the administrative and political clauses (doc. 12) follows V,
with variations, to the end of cl. 27. At this point N names the judges and the
circuits. See n. 10.

---

[1] N begins: 'The new provisions of the barons are written below, both concerning itinerant justices and concerning justice and peace. These articles will
be written in Latin and French.' No copy of the French text, for distribution to
the counties to be visited, has survived. N continues, and M begins: 'Provision
concerning those of the council who will travel with the judges to divers places
to hold inquisitions and right transgressions before Easter in the 44th year' [of
the reign of the king].

[2] Doc. 12, cl. 1 states that 'one of the twelve or of the rest of the community'
shall accompany each of the circuits planned; these regulations add a member
of the council. See nn. 4, 6 below.

placita infra tam breue tempus terminari non possint, ea atterminent *b*coram[3] iusticiariis de Banco preter placita noue disseisine.

2. Item quod per breuia regis*b* mandetur uicecomitibus quod puplice clamari faciant in ciuitatibus, burgis, et mercatis quod omnes qui conqueri uoluerint de transgressionibus factis a septennio et citra, que coram iusticiariis antea non fuerint terminate et que terminari possunt sine breue, exceptis placitis de corona, nisi ille qui appellatus uel rettatus fuerit sit in gaola, ueniant ⟨coram⟩ predictis iusticiariis ad dies et loca que in predictis litteris regis continentur.

3. Item uenire faciant coram eis dictis diebus et locis xij. tam milites quam alios liberos et legales homines de quolibet hundredo, quibus dicti iusticiarii liberent*c*[4] primo die articulos de quibus est inquirendum et assignent eis alium diem racionabilem scilicet in crastino Epiphanie,*d* quo rediant coram eis et reddant suum ueredictum cum predictis articulis.

4. Item quod secundum querelas factas et racionem earum summoniantur uel attachientur transgressores quod sint coram eis diebus et locis quibus predicti xij. cum suo ueredicto redibunt, ita quod uenient sine essonia nisi racionabilis causa subsit quare debeant essoniari que possit inquiri per uicinos.

5. Item quod puplice clametur sicut predictum est quod omnes qui post ultimum parliamentum Oxonie aliquid dederint cuiuscunque balliuis regis uel aliis pro iusticia habenda, facienda, uel differenda, illud statim exponant predictis iusticiariis alioquin, si per alios inde conuincantur, grauiter puniantur secundum quod continentur in prouidencia facta per consilium.[5]

6. Item quod puplice clametur sicut predictum est quod omnes qui fuerunt balliui regis uel balliui magnatum a septennio et citra sint coram predictis*e*[6] iusticiariis in*f*[7] crastino Epiphanie.

---

b–b Coram banco preter placitum noue dissesine et placitent de omnibus querelis exceptis libero tenemento pertinentibus quod per breuia domini regis M. *c* illi de consilio liberent M. *This difference between the texts suggests an alteration in plan for the administration of the eyre.* *d* *This date is not in* M. *e* de consilio in eorum aduentu N. *See n. c.* *f* in eorum adventu in crastino Epiphanie M.

---

[3] M reads: 'before the bench except pleas of *novel disseisin* and they may consider cases of all complaint except those pertaining to freehold which must be heard by royal writ'. See doc. 11, n. 7. For information on these assizes, see *Taswell Langmead's English Constitutional History*, ed. T. F. T. Plucknett

the said pleas cannot be determined within so short a time, they shall attermine them before the justices of the Bench,[3] except for cases of *novel disseisin*.

2. Further, that the king's writs be sent to the sheriffs, ordering them to have it publicly proclaimed in cities, boroughs, and market towns that all who shall wish to complain of trespasses committed against them in the last seven years, and not previously determined before the justices, and which can be determined without writ, other than pleas of the crown, unless the person appealed or accused shall already be in gaol, shall come before the justices at the days and places named in the royal letters.

3. Further, [the sheriffs] shall cause to come before [the justices] on the same days and at the same places twelve knights or other free and law-worthy men from each hundred, to whom, on the first day, the justices will hand over[4] the articles on which inquiry is to be made; and they will assign to them another reasonable date, the morrow of Epiphany [7 January], on which [the knights] shall reappear before them and return their verdict on the articles.

4. Further, in accordance with the complaints made and the nature of them, let the wrongdoers be summoned or attached to come before the justices on the days and at the places at which the twelve will be appearing with their verdicts; and they shall come without essoin unless there is reasonable cause why they should be essoined, which can be inquired into by neighbours.

5. Further, let it be publicly proclaimed in the manner already described that all who since the last parliament at Oxford have given anything to any of the king's officers or to any other person for obtaining, doing, or deferring justice, shall immediately declare this to the justices, otherwise, if they should be convicted of it by means of others, they will be heavily punished, as it is stated in the provisions made by the council.[5]

6. Further, that it be publicly proclaimed in the manner stated that all who have been bailiffs of the king or bailiffs of magnates within the last seven years shall come before the justices[6] on the[7] morrow of Epiphany.

(1960); H. G. Richardson and G. O. Sayles, *The Governance of Medieval England* and *Law and Legislation from Aethelbert to Magna Carta*.
    [4] M reads: 'the councillors will hand over'.
    [5] This refers to the ordinance for sheriffs, doc. 8.
    [6] N reads: 'of the council when they arrive'. See n. 4.
    [7] M reads: 'when they arrive on the morrow of Epiphany'.

7. Item quod, si aliqui conqueri uoluerint de uicecomitibus uel eorum balliuis de aliquo grauamine uel iniuria illata uel de ospiciis captis aut prisis factis contra eorum sacramentum et contra articulos contentos in prouidencia facta per consilium, tunc, capta securitate de prosequendo, statim fiat conquerenti plena iusticia. Et hoc idem fiat de magnatibus et eorum balliuis si domini illorum requisiti non fecerint de eis conquerenti iusticiam. [g]Similiter fiat si aliquis conqueri uoluerit de iniuria facta contra libertates in magna carta de libertatibus contentas post ultimum parliamentum Oxonie.[g]

8. Item quod inquiratur si balliui magnatum [h]qui custodiunt hundreda que tenentur de rege ad feodi firmam[h] prestiterint sacramentum in omnibus quale uicecomites et alii balliui regis fecerunt anno preterito de seruiendo regi fideliter in hiis que ad ipsum et libertates suas pertinent, et dominis suis in hiis que ad ipsos et libertates et dominica eorum pertinent, et de obseruando alios articulos contentos in literis regis missis anno preterito per comitatus.[i]

9. Item quod inquiratur que libertates et que uille geldabiles seu alia iura subtracta sint regi sine waranto, et a quo tempore et per quos; et habeant predicti iusticiarii secum rotulos [j]de inquisicionibus factis iam tribus uel quatuor annis elapsis in autumpno super iuribus regis. Et similiter rotulos[j]8 de inquisicionibus nuper factis per quatuor milites.

10. Item quod inquiratur de malefactoribus et eorum receptatoribus.

11. Item si aliquis magnatum uel alius pro aliquo dono uel redditu receperit aliquem qui non esset homo suus sub aduocacione uel tuicione sua contra dominum seu uicinum eius aut contra alium post festum Purificationis anno regni regis xliij[o].[k]9

[g-g] Similiter . . . Oxonie, *omitting* uoluerit *follows* comitatus M. *See n. i.*
[h-h] qui . . . firmam *om.* M.   [i] *See n. g.*   [j-j] de inquisicione dumdum factos de iuribus et libertatibus domini regis quando dominus rex ultimo fuit in Scocia et summa M.   [k] NM *add*: die lune proxima post festum sancti Nicholai [anno regni regis Henrici xliii—*thus for* xliv M] liberentur articuli xii de quolibet hundredo et audiantur querele et tunc assignetur eis dies in crastino Epiphanie ad redeundum cum articulis et ad prosequendum querelas.

---

8 M reads: '[the rolls] recently written, of the inquisition concerning the rights and liberties of the lord king when the lord king was last in Scotland and an abstract'. The rolls of the inquisition held when the king was in Scotland in Sept. 1255 (E. L. G. Stones, *Anglo-Scottish Relations, 1174–1328* (1965),

7. Further, that if any wish to complain of the sheriffs and their officers about any grievances or injuries inflicted, or any forced hospitality or any impositions made against their oath and against the articles in the provisions made by the council, then, security of prosecution having been taken, let full justice be done at once to the plaintiff. And the same shall be done with regard to magnates and their bailiffs if the lords of those bailiffs, having been asked, have not done justice to the plaintiff upon them. And let the same be done if anyone wishes to complain of injury inflicted against the liberties in *Magna Carta* since the last parliament of Oxford.

8. Further, let inquiry be made whether the bailiffs of magnates, who have charge of the hundreds which are held of the king at fee farm, have taken an oath in all things, just as the sheriffs and other officers of the king took last year, of serving the king faithfully in those things which pertain to him and to his liberties, and serving their lords in those things which pertain to them and their liberties and domains, and of observing the other articles contained in the royal letters sent last year to all the counties.

9. Further, let inquiry be made to discover what liberties and what geldable townships or other rights have been withdrawn from the king without warrant, and from when and by whom; and let the justices have with them the records of the inquiries made three or four years ago, in the autumn, concerning the king's rights, and also the records of the inquiry recently made by the four knights.[8]

10. Further, let inquiry be made concerning wrongdoers and those who shelter them.

11. Further, whether any of the magnates or anyone else, for any gift or payment, has taken anyone who was not his man, under avowry and protection, against his lord or his neighbour or anyone else since the feast of the Purification in the 43rd year of the king's reign[9] [2 February 1259].

---

pp. 30–4) refer to the eyres held in 1254–5 (*Ann. Mon.* i. 330–3, 337–9). The inquiry by the four knights is that which had been ordered in 1258. See doc. 5, cl. 1.

[9] N and M add: 'On Monday next after the feast of St. Nicholas [in the 43rd year of the reign of King Henry—M 44th] let the articles be handed to the twelve [sworn men] of each hundred and let complaints be heard, and then let them [the twelve] be given a day on the morrow of Epiphany to return with articles and to prosecute the complaints.' See cl. 3.

Queus iustices irrunt en quels cuntes[10]

Norfolch' Suffolch'   Philipp' Basset'[11]
Cantebr' Huntedon'   Will' de Wilton

Wiltesir' Oxon' Berksir'   Nich' de Turr', Hug' le despens'[12]

Gloucestr' Hereford'   H. de Bracton'
Wigorn'   Com Hereford'

Cancia'[13] Susex' Sutht' ⎫
Essex' Hertford' Middel' ⎬   Hugo Bigod
                           ⎭

Sum's' Dorsir'   Ioh' de Weyuile,
Deueness'   Com' Warr, Ioh' de Grey.

Northamthun' Bukingham'   Egidius de Erdington'
Bedeford'   Iacobus de Audel'[14]

Lincoln' Salopesbir'   Gilb' de preston,
Leycest' Staford'   Senescallus de Monte Alto, et I.
Warwyk'   de Verdun'

14

26 JANUARY 1260

Rex Hugoni le Bygod*

[a]Rex Hugoni le Bygod, iusticiario Anglie, salutem. Cum nuper celebrata solempnitate Natalis Domini proposuissemus uersus

[a] Pro rege *in left-hand margin of roll.*

---

* *Text*: Rot. Claus. 44 Hen. III, m. 4d. *Printed*: C.R. *1259–61*, pp. 267–8; *Royal Letters*, ii. 148–50. *See*: *Baronial Plan*, pp. 219–20.

---

[10] This is the heading which appears in N. *C.R. 1259–61*, pp. 142–3 records circuits and names in a letter dated 28 Nov. 1259. There are differences from the list in order of arrangement and in names in N. The plan to have one of the twelve and one of the council on each circuit was not fulfilled. See introduction, pp. 26–7. On 7 Aug. 1259 seven judges with special powers were named. Of this seven, six were among the seven who were named for this eyre. Nicholas de

Counties to be visited by Justices[10]

Norfolk, Suffolk, Cambridgeshire, Huntingdonshire	Philip Basset[11] William de Wilton
Wiltshire, Oxfordshire, Berkshire	Nicholas de Turri Hugh le Despenser[12]
Gloucestershire, Herefordshire, Worcestershire	Henry de Bracton earl of Hereford
Kent,[13] Sussex, Hampshire, Essex, Hertfordshire, Middlesex }	Hugh Bigod
Somerset, Dorset, Devon	John de Weyville, earl of Warwick, John de Grey
Northamptonshire, Buckinghamshire, Bedfordshire	Giles de Erdington James de Audley[14]
Lincolnshire, Shropshire, Leicestershire, Staffordshire Warwickshire	Gilbert de Preston, the steward of Mold [Roger de Mold] and John de Verdun

14

26 JANUARY 1260

The king to Hugh Bigod

The king to Hugh Bigod, justiciar of England, greeting. Although
until lately we had intended making our way back to England after

---

Turri, judge in the Wiltshire circuit, was not named among the seven, while
Roger de Thurkelby did not serve on the eyre (*C.R. 1256–59*, p. 485; *Baronial
Plan*, p. 197 is mistaken).

[11] *C.R. 1259–61*, p. 143 names Henry de Bath not Philip Basset. See *Baronial
Plan*, p. 197, n. 3.

[12] *C.R. 1259–61*, p. 143 states that Despenser was replaced by William de
Englefield as Despenser could not act.

[13] Ibid. does not mention Kent.

[14] Ibid. says that Audley was replaced by Philip Marmion as Audley could
not act.

partes Anglie diuertisse, nos ad instanciam domini regis et regine Francie concessimus quod nuptie Beatricis[1] filie nostre uicesimo die post Natale Domini predictum apud Compend' celebrarentur, ubi prefati rex et regina promiserant interesse, quo quidem die corpus primogeniti prefati regis apud Regalem Montem[2] traditum fuit sepulture, unde occasione mortis eiusdem nupcie predicte filie nostre prorogate fuerunt usque in diem Sancti Vincencii, que eodem die apud Sanctum Dyonisium celebrate fuerunt, propter quod non potuimus adeo cito ut credebamus ad partes Anglie remeare. Preterea, cum quatuor dictatores hinc inde electi ad taxandum peccuniam quam prefatus rex nobis soluere tenetur pro quingentis militibus per biennium tenendis nequiuissent concordare,[3] petebamus ab ipso rege quod Petrus le Chaumberlang quintus esset et iuratus, quod idem Petrus facere recusauit, unde prefatus rex, nolens prefatum Petrum super hoc molestare aut nos offendere in hac parte, respondit quod idem Petrus una cum episcopo Anniciensi in se assumeret negocium supradictum.[4] Ad hec, quia dubitauimus utrum quatuor deputati ad estimacionem terre Agen' faciendam possent concordare, interpellauimus ipsum regem de quinto eisdem adiungendo, qui prefatum episcopum ad hoc nominauit, uerum, cum ex dilacione taxationis dicte peccunie et estimacionis terre Agen' graue dampnum et periculum nobis possit imminere,[5] presertim cum idem rex non teneatur nobis aliquam peccuniam soluere ante taxacionem seu estimacionem predictam, sicut in litteris nostris, quas eidem regi nuper in Anglia fecimus, continetur, nos nolentes predictum negocium totaliter rumpere nec in prefatos episcopum et Petrum in forma predicta sine uestro consilio et aliorum magnatum qui sunt de consilio nostro in Anglia consentire, eo quod idem rex in taxacione predicte peccunie haberet quatuor ex parte sua et nos tantum duos ex parte nostra, uobis mandamus in fide qua nobis tenemini firmiter iniungentes quod, habito super premissis consilio predictorum magnatum qui presentes fuerint, uestrum et predictorum

[1] On 22 Jan. 1260 Beatrice m. John de Dreux, who was to be given the Agenais or a rent equal to the annual value of these lands (*C.P.R. 1258–66*, p. 211; *Diplomatic Documents*, nos. 308, 349; *G.E.C.* x. 813).

[2] A Cistercian abbey, *c.* twenty miles north-west of Paris, founded by Louis IX in 1228.

[3] Negotiations continued until Jan. 1264 when, at Amiens, King Henry, desperately needing money, accepted a final offer of 134,000 *livres Tournois* (*Peace of Paris*, pp. 55–61; *C.P.R. 1258–66*, pp. 243, 379).

the Christmas celebrations, at the pressing request of the lord king
and of the queen of France we agreed that the marriage of our
daughter Beatrice[1] should take place on the twentieth day after
Christmas [14 January] at Compiègne, where the king and queen
promised to be present. But on that very same day the body of the
eldest son of the king [Louis] was borne to burial at Royaumont,[2]
by reason of which our daughter's marriage was postponed to St.
Vincent's day [22 January], when it was celebrated at Saint-Denis:
and for these reasons we have not been able to return to England
as quickly as we had expected.

Moreover, the four arbitrators, chosen from both sides to assess
the money which the king is bound to pay to us for the upkeep
of 500 knights for two years, have been unable to agree.[3] We have
therefore asked the king that Peter the Chamberlain should be
sworn in as a fifth man, but Peter has refused to act, so the king,
not wishing to press Peter on the matter, nor yet to offend us, has
suggested that Peter and the bishop of Le Puy should jointly
undertake the task.[4] On top of this, since we doubted whether the
four men appointed to assess the value of the Agenais could reach
agreement, we put it to the king that a fifth should be joined with
them, and he proposed the bishop of Le Puy for this purpose.
Grave loss and danger may threaten us from delay in the assessment of the money and in the valuation of the Agenais,[5] especially
as King Louis is not bound to pay us anything at all before this
assessment and this valuation have been made, as is stated in the
letters which we lately drew up in England for King Louis. We
do not wish either to break off these negotiations, or to consent to
accepting the bishop and Peter in the terms suggested without
your advice and that of the other magnates of our council who are
now in England, because, in the assessment of this money King
Louis would have four on his side, and we only two on ours.
Accordingly, we now order you, in the fealty in which you are
bound to us, and firmly enjoin you that, having obtained the advice
on these matters of those of the magnates who are present, you

[4] Peter de Villebéon, the chamberlain, was one of Louis IX's closest advisers.
Guy Foulques was, before taking holy orders, a leading royal lawyer and coun-
sellor. He became bishop of Le Puy in 1257, archbishop of Narbonne in 1259,
cardinal-bishop of Sabina in 1261 and was Pope Clement IV, 1265-8. In 1263
he was appointed papal legate in England (*King Henry III, passim*).

[5] Final agreement on the value of the Agenais was reached in Sept. 1261
(*C.P.R. 1258-66*, pp. 124, 169, 174, 189; *Peace of Paris*, pp. 58-9).

magnatum consilium nobis sub omni festinacione qua poteritis rescribatis, quia ante responsum uestrum super premissis, que festino indigent consilio, nichil certum statuere possumus nec debemus. Ceterum, quia intelleximus quod Lewelinus filius Griffini die Sabbati proxima post Epiphaniam Domini cum exercitu suo et machinis obsedit castrum de Beohelt premuniendo suos quod cum uictualibus ad quadraginta dies muniti uenirent ibidem exinde progressuri de Breckinoh et Netherwent uersus partes Marchie nostre ad deuastacionem partium earundem,[6] nos, tam graui et euidenti periculo obuiare uolentes, uobis mandamus quod, omni parleamento postposito et penitus remoto, habito super hiis tractatu cum magnatibus de consilio nostro qui presentes fuerint, ad rescussionem predicti castri et ad tuicionem partium illarum consilium et auxilium efficax sine more dispendio apponi faciatis, nullum parleamentum citra aduentum nostrum in Angliam statuentes aut fieri permittentes, quia, cum ibidem uenerimus, de uestro et predictorum magnatum consilio de parleamento habendo prouidebimus, prout nobis et regno nostro fuerit oportunum.[7] Nos autem et regina nostra sani et incolumes die Conuersionis Beati Pauli de Sancto Dyonisio recessimus, arripientes iter nostrum per Compeyn' et Arraz per dietas moderatas uersus mare, consilium et responsum uestrum super premissis in partibus illis expectantes. Teste apud Lusarch' xvi.[b] die Januarii.

Sub eadem forma scribitur domino R. regi Romanorum et Edwardo filio regis, uerbis tamen competenter mutatis.

[b] *This is a mistake for* xxvi; *the Conversion of St. Paul is 25 Jan.*

---

[6] Brycheiniog and Netherwent were, roughly speaking, the present counties of Brecon and Monmouth. The Welsh problem and the question of the king being advised are mentioned in documents 30 and 31.

should write back to us with all possible speed your advice and that of the magnates, since these matters require the speediest attention, and without your advice on them we neither can nor should decide anything.

Further, we gather that Llywelyn ap Gryffudd, on the Saturday next after Epiphany [10 January], laid siege to the castle of Builth with his army and siege train, notifying his men to come there provided with supplies for forty days, and intending to advance thence through Brycheiniog and Netherwent against our March lands, to the devastation of those parts.[6] We, anxious to avoid so grave and evident a peril, therefore order you to postpone and entirely to set aside all thought of parliament, and, after discussing these matters with those of our council who are present, to cause the most effective counsel and aid to be applied to the rescue of the castle and to the protection of those parts, without wasting any time in delay. Make no arrangements for a parliament and permit none to be held before our return to England, for when we arrive there, we shall arrange, with your counsel and that of the magnates, for holding a parliament as may be best for us and for our realm.[7] We and our queen left St. Denis safe and well on the day of the Conversion of St. Paul [25 January], making our way by easy stages through Compiègne and Arras towards the sea, where we shall await your reply and advice on these matters. Witnessed at Luzarches, 16 [recte 26] January.

Similar letters written to Lord Richard, King of the Romans, and to Edward, the king's son, words having been altered as needed.

---

[7] This order was in direct opposition to that section of the Provisions of Oxford which stated that one of the three annual parliaments should meet on the morrow of Candlemas (3 Feb.) (doc. 5, cl. 21). Simon de Montfort violently opposed the king's order which he saw as a step in the destruction of the independent standing and prestige of parliament. See doc. 29, cls. 29–31.

15

19 FEBRUARY 1260

Rex archiepiscopo Cantuariensi et aliis*

[a]Rex uenerabilibus patribus, B. Cantuariensi archiepiscopo, totius Anglie primati, W. Wygorniensi episcopo et dilectis et fidelibus suis S. de Monte Forti, comiti, R. le Bygod, comiti Norff' et marescallo Anglie, H. de Boun, comiti Hereford' et Esex', Philippo Bassat, Ricardo de Grey, Iacobo de Aldithel' et Petro de Monte Forti[1] salutem.

Super eo quod de statu tranquillo regni nostri[2] nos certificastis et mature regressum nostrum in Angliam totis desideriis affectastis, sicut per litteras uestras et per dilectos et fideles nostros Philippum Marmium et Symonem Passelewe[3] plenius intelleximus, uestre dilectionis et fidelitatis constanciam, quam erga nos geritis, ex hoc attendentes manifeste uobis plurimum regratiamur, quia, quotienscunque de prosperitate predicti regni nostri certitudo nobis nunciatur, ad iucunditatem non modicam excitamur. Ad redeundum uero in regnum nostrum accingimur et diu est quod uenissemus nisi uariis de causis, quarum alique forsitan uos non latent, et aliis impedimentis, que in aduentu nostro uobis plenius poterimus intimare, essemus diutius in regno Francie prepediti. Cum igitur una causa supersit, uidelicet super estimacione peccunie quingentorum militum per biennium tenendorum, quam rex Francie nobis soluere tenetur; et super qua estimatores ex parte sua et nostra ad hoc electi concordare nequiuerant, ac apud eundem regem diligenter instaremus quod quintus ex parte sua et nostra communiter assignaretur, qui controuersiam dirimeret supradictam, et dominus Petrus camerarius esset ad hoc nominatus

[a] Pro rege *in left-hand margin of roll.*

* *Text*: Rot. Claus. 44 Hen. III, m. 3d. *Printed*: *C.R. 1259–61*, pp. 272–3; *Royal Letters*, ii. 153–5. *See*: *Baronial Plan*, pp. 222–3.

[1] The addressees of this letter were members of the Council of Fifteen. The fact that other members of the council accompanied the king to France may explain the absence of their names.
[2] The unrest in England, which is mentioned in documents at this time, derived from the feeling that the king, while in France, was working to restore

15

19 FEBRUARY 1260

The king to the archbishop of Canterbury and others

The king to the venerable fathers, Boniface, archbishop of Canterbury, primate of all England, and Walter, bishop of Worcester, and to his well-loved and faithful subjects, Earl Simon de Montfort, Roger Bigod, earl of Norfolk and marshal of England, Humphrey de Bohun, earl of Hereford and Essex, Philip Basset, Richard de Grey, James de Audley and Peter de Montfort,[1] greeting.

We thank you very much for what you have told us about the peaceful state of our realm[2] and your own eager desire for our speedy return to England, as we have learned from your letters and from our well-loved and faithful servants, Philip Marmion and Simon Passelewe,[3] and we plainly understand from all this the constancy of your love and of the fealty which you bear towards us. Indeed, as often as we receive trustworthy report of the prosperity of our realm, we are moved to no small measure of joy. We are all prepared for returning home, and we would have been home long ago but for various causes, some of which, perhaps, are not unknown to you, and also other hindrances, of which we shall be able to tell you more when we return, all of which things have held us back longer in France. One cause still remains,—that is, the assessment of the money which the king of France is bound to pay to us for maintaining 500 knights for two years, on which the assessors chosen on his behalf and ours have been unable to agree, so that we urgently begged King Louis that a fifth should be assigned commonly for both of us, to put an end to this deadlock, and that Peter the Chamberlain should be named for this, provided he would take the oath. But since he shrank from undertaking this responsibility alone, the king of France wished to join

his power. Leicester and Gloucester were antagonists; Leicester demanded that parliament should meet, protested against the sending of money to France, and spoke of possible armed opposition.

[3] Passelewe was one of the chief royal clerks while Marmion was a royalist 1263–4 (*English Baronies*, pp. 145–6; *C.R. 1256–59, passim*; *C.R. 1259–61, passim*).

dum modo iuraret, cui, pro eo quod hoc onus in se assumere metuebat, dominus rex Francie episcopum Aniciensem adiungere uoluit ut illi duo essent loco quinti, unde nos, istius negocii arduitatem ponderantes, responsionem nostram predicto regi faciendam suspendere decreuimus donec uestrum super hoc consilium haberemus. Quo circa uobis mandamus quatinus, quam dampnosa sit nobis in hac parte dilacio considerantes, in fide qua nobis tenemini quid predicto regi super hoc respondere debeamus, uestrum consilium mature nobis significare curetis; et similiter, si consuletis quod dictum episcopum Aniciensem, quem bonum credimus et fidelem et quem predictus rex Francie nobis optulit, super estimacione ualoris terre Agen' in quintum estimatorem assumamus. Super eo uero quod nobis significastis de colloquio ten⟨en⟩do uobis significamus quod nostre uoluntatis non existit aliquod parliamentum nobis absentibus in regno nostro teneri, cum hoc non deceat nec honori nostro credimus expedire. Verum tamen bene placet nobis quod iusticia communis omnibus et singulis in regno nostro per H. le Bygod, iusticiarium Anglie, cui custodiam predicti regni nostri in absencia nostra commisimus, exhibeatur mediante consilio uestro, dum modo nulla noua mutacio siue ordinacio fiat in regno nostro sine nostra presencia et consensu. Teste ut supra [xix die Februarii anno etc., apud Sanctum Audomarum.] Per ipsum regem, R. comitem Glouc', et I. Mansell'.

16

I MARCH 1260

Rex archiepiscopo Cantuariensi et aliis*

[a]Rex uenerabilibus patribus Cantuariensi archiepiscopo totius Anglie primati, W. Wygorniensi episcopo, et dilectis et fidelibus suis S. de Monte Forti comiti Leyc', H. le Bygod iusticiario Anglie, Philippo Basset et aliis magnatibus de consilio suo salutem.

---

[a] Pro rege *in left-hand margin of roll.*

* *Text*: Rot. Claus. 44 Hen. III, m. 2d. *Printed*: *C.R. 1259–61*, p. 276. *See*: *Baronial Plan*, p. 223.

the bishop of Le Puy with him, that they two should act in place of a fifth assessor; whereupon we, having in mind the difficulty of this matter, decided to withhold our reply to King Louis until we should have your advice on it. Therefore we order you that, bearing in mind how much we are losing by delay in this matter, you should bestir yourselves, in the fealty in which you are bound to us, to let us know quickly your advice on what we ought to reply to King Louis. And at the same time, would you advise us to accept the bishop of Le Puy—whom the king of France has offered to us, and whom we believe to be good and trustworthy—as the fifth assessor in the assessment of the value of the Agenais?

As for what you wrote to us about holding a parliament, we tell you that it is not our will that any parliament should be held in our realm while we are absent, since that would be unfitting, and we think it would not accord with our honour. It is our good pleasure that, with the help of your advice, common justice should be done to each and all in our realm by Hugh Bigod, justiciar of England, to whom we committed the custody of our realm during our absence, provided always that no new change or ordinance be made in our realm without our presence and consent.

Witness as above, 19 February in the year, etc., at St. Omer, by the king himself, Richard, earl of Gloucester, and John Mansel.

16

1 MARCH 1260

The king to the archbishop of Canterbury and others

The king to the venerable fathers, the archbishop of Canterbury, primate of all England, Walter, bishop of Worcester, and his well-loved and faithful [subjects] Simon de Montfort, earl of Leicester, Hugh Bigod, justiciar of England, Philip Basset, and the other magnates of his council, greeting.

Venientes ad presenciam nostram uenerabiles patres Sarisburiensis, Couentrensis et Lichefeldensis[1] episcopi cum litteris
uestris de credencia, nobis nunciarunt regnum nostrum Anglie
plena tranquillitate et pace gaudere, maiores eciam et minores
in nostra deuocione permanere, ac uos aduentum nostrum in
Angliam totis desideriis affectare; de quo non mediocriter gauisi
uobis grates referimus copiosas, ex hoc manifeste propendentes
uoluntatem uestram et fidelitatis constanciam quam erga nos
geritis cum litteris uestris uniformiter concordare; uerum, cum
pro taxacione peccunie quingentorum militum per biennium
tenendorum, quam rex Francie nobis soluere tenetur, necnon et
pro estimacione ualoris terre Agen' facienda, de quibus prefato
regi Francie sub festinacione respondere tenemur, prout alias
uobis mandauimus; et ut consilium uestrum super hiis signi-
ficaretis, quod hactenus facere distulistis, ueniendi in Angliam
hactenus fuerimus prepediti, uobis iterato mandamus quatinus
consilium uestrum cum omni festinacione nobis rescribatis,
peccuniam eciam ad expensas nostras acquietandas et ad iocalia
nostra que sub grauibus usuris impignorauimus liberanda nobis
transmittatis.[2] Expeditis uero negociis nostris supradictis ad
partes Anglie dirigere proponimus gressus nostros, uolentes quod
uniuersis et singulis de regno nostro per iusticiarium nostrum
Anglie plena iusticia exhibeatur. Teste etc. apud Sanctum
Audomarum primo die Marcii anno etc. xliiii.

17

I MARCH 1260

Rex Edwardo filio suo*

[a]Rex Edwardo filio suo salutem. Veniens ad nos dilectus nobis in
Christo frater Iohannes de Derlinton'[1] cum litteris uestris de

---

[a] Pro rege *in left-hand margin of roll.*

* *Text*: Rot. Claus. 44 Hen. III, m. 2d. *Printed*: *C.R. 1259–61*, pp. 276–7.
See: *Baronial Plan*, p. 223.

[1] The bishop of Salisbury, Giles de Bridport, was involved in the king's
negotiations at Rome, in France, and with the Welsh (see Patent Rolls, Close
Rolls, Liberate Rolls). Roger de Longespée, bishop of Coventry and Lichfield,

The venerable fathers, the bishops of Salisbury and of Coventry and Lichfield,[1] coming to our presence with your letters of credence, have told us that our English kingdom enjoys full tranquillity and peace, that both greater and lesser subjects continue in devotion to us, and that you long for our return to England with all your hearts. Greatly delighted by all of this, we return the fullest thanks to you, understanding clearly from this how completely your goodwill and the constant fidelity which you bear to us accords with your letters. However, we are still prevented from coming to England, on account of the assessment of the money for maintaining 500 knights for two years, which the king of France is obliged to pay us, and also of the assessment of the value of the Agenais, on both of which matters we are bound to make an early reply to the king of France, as we have already told you, ordering that you should indicate to us your advice on these things, which hitherto you have delayed in doing. Therefore we now order you again that you should write back to us your advice, with all possible speed, and that you should also send us money to pay our bills and to redeem our jewels, which we have pawned at high interest.[2] We promise that, as soon as our business mentioned above has been settled, we intend to make our way back towards England. We will that full justice be shown by our justiciar of England to each and everyone of our realm of England. Witness, etc., at St. Omer on 1 March, 44th year, etc.

17

1 MARCH 1260

The king to his son Edward

The king to Edward his son, greeting. Our beloved brother in Christ, John de Darlington,[1] coming to us with your letters of

---

1257–95, third son of William de Longespée, was cousin of King Henry (see doc. 4, n. 11).

[2] On 24 Jan. 1260, the king announced that the earl of Gloucester was coming to England to discuss, among other things, the means of giving financial assistance to the king in France (*C.R. 1259–61*, p. 266). The problem of the king's debts, and the attempts of the reformers to control royal expenditure, figure in later documents.

[1] A Dominican friar, the king's confessor. Supporter of Lord Edward in the spring of 1259 (*C.P.R. 1258–66, passim*).

credencia, ea que sibi a uobis iniuncta fuerant nobis prudenter exposuit et discrete, super quibus ipsum diligenter audiuimus et benigne ac de eisdem leti plurimum fuimus et gauisi, propter quod aliquem de nostris specialibus ad partes Anglie in proximo destinabimus ad uidendum si dictis opera correspondeant.[2] Teste ut supra, [apud Sanctum Audomarum primo die Marcii anno etc. xliiii].

18

6 MARCH 1260

*Rex Rogero comiti Norff'**

[a]QUIA R. comes Norff' et marescallus Anglie nec alii magnates regis aliquid regi de statu regni sui significauerunt postquam E. Sarisburiensis et R. Conuentrensis et Lichefeldensis episcopi nuper a rege recesserunt apud Sanctum Audomarum, de quo idem rex non modicum est fastiditus, mandatum est eidem comiti quod statum predicti regni et consilium suum super aduentu suo in Angliam ei sine dilacione significet. Teste ut supra [apud Sanctum Audomarum vi. die Martii, anno etc.].

Eodem modo mandatum est Hugoni le Bygod iusticiario Anglie et Philippo Bassat[1] et tradite fuerunt littere Thome de Kenros,[2] clerico I. Mansell', deferende in Angliam.

[a] Pro rege *in left-hand margin of roll.*

---

* *Text*: Rot. Claus. 44 Hen. III, m. 2d. *Printed*: *C.R. 1259–61*, p. 278. *See*: *Baronial Plan*, p. 224.

credence, has prudently and wisely explained to us the matters which you enjoined on him. We listened carefully and kindly to him on all these matters, and were greatly pleased and rejoiced by them, and so, in the near future, we shall send someone who has our confidence into England to see whether deeds match words.[2] Witness, as above [St. Omer, 1 March 44 Henry III].

18

6 MARCH 1260

The king to Roger, earl of Norfolk

Since neither Roger, earl of Norfolk and marshal of England, nor the others of the king's magnates have told the king anything about the state of his realm after Giles, bishop of Salisbury, and Roger, bishop of Coventry and Lichfield, recently left the king at St. Omer, whereat the king is really disgusted, he now orders the said earl to let him know without delay the state of his kingdom and his advice on the king's return to England. Witness, etc. [6 March, at St. Omer, 44 Henry III].

Similar orders are sent to Hugh Bigod, justiciar of England, and to Philip Basset,[1] and the letters were handed to Thomas de Kinros,[2] clerk of John Mansel, to be taken over to England.

[2] Enmity existed between the Lord Edward and the earl of Gloucester, possibly beginning with conflicting claims to control Bristol castle. This caused Edward to join Leicester, who opposed Gloucester.

[1] Norfolk, Hugh Bigod, his brother, and Philip Basset led a group in the Council of Fifteen which opposed Leicester.

[2] A key royal clerk, at one time bailiff of Stamford, Yorks., Grantham, Lincs., keeper of the honour of Hastings (*C.R. 1259–61*, pp. 444, 448; *C.Lib.R. 1260–67*, p. 74).

19

28 MARCH 1260

*Rex Ricardo de Clare, comiti Glouc'**

aDe statu suo. Mandatum est Ricardo de Clare, comiti Glouc'
et Hertford,[1] quod rex ad plenum conualuit de febre terciana qua
nuper afflictus fuit et quod significet ei statum regni sui et consilium suum de aduentu suo in Angliam per Gilbertum filium
Hugonis,[2] uadlettum suum, qui de statu et beneplacito regis ipsum
plenius poterit uiua uoce certificare. Teste ut supra [apud Sanctum
Audomarum xxviii die Martii].

Item mandatum est Hugoni le Bygod, iusticiario Anglie, et
Philippo Bassat quod statum regni Anglie et consilium suum de
aduentu regis in Angliam eidem regi significent sicut rex eis alias
mandauit.

20

1 APRIL 1260

*Rex Ricardo de Clare, comiti Glouc(estrie)***

Rex Ricardo de Clar' comiti Glouc' salutem.

Sciatis quod dominus rex Francie uenit ad nos usque Sanctum
Audomarum in uigilia Palmarum et morabatur ibi usque ad diem
Iouis sequentem ubi eciam nobis multas curialitates optulit et nos
in magnam specialitatem admisit. Et licet de assensu et uoluntate
prefati regis multos milites et uiros bellicosos inueniamus qui
nobiscum ire uelint in Angliam, pauci tamen aut nulli ausi sunt

---

a Pro rege *in left-hand margin of roll.*

---

* *Text*: Rot. Claus. 44 Hen. III, m. 2d. *Printed*: *C.R. 1259–61*, p. 281. *See*:
Baronial Plan, p. 224.

** *Text*: Rot. Claus. 44 Hen. III, m. 2d. *Printed*: *C.R. 1259–61*, p. 282. *See*:
Baronial Plan, pp. 225–6.

19

28 MARCH 1260

*About his [the king's] realm. The king to Richard de Clare,
earl of Gloucester*

Richard de Clare, earl of Gloucester and Hertford,[1] is informed
that the king has fully recovered from the tertian fever with which
he was recently afflicted, and Richard is ordered to report to him
on the state of his kingdom, with his advice on his return to
England, by means of Gilbert fitz Hugh,[2] his *valettus*, who can
tell him more fully by word of mouth about the king's affairs and
his wishes. Witness as above [28 March at St. Omer].

Similar orders are sent to Hugh Bigod, justiciar of England, and
to Philip Basset, that they should advise the king about the state
of affairs in England and about the king's return to England, as the
king has previously ordered.

20

1 APRIL 1260

The king to Richard de Clare, earl of Gloucester

The king to Richard of Clare, earl of Gloucester, greeting.

This is to tell you that the king of France visited us at St. Omer
on the eve of Palm Sunday [27 March] and stayed here until the
following Thursday [1 April], offering us many courtesies and
treating us with special friendship. But although, with his assent
and goodwill, we can find many knights and warriors willing to
come with us into England, there are few or none bold enough or

---

[1] The leading royalist in the Council of Fifteen.

[2] Called, at different times, king's *valettus*, yeoman, sergeant. Crossed to
France with the king, 1259–60, 1263–4 (*C.P.R. 1258–66, passim*; *C.R. 1256–59*,
p. 403; *C.R. 1261–64*, p. 329).

aut uolunt regnum nostrum ingredi sine nobis,[1] et quia mora nostra extra illud regnum nobis periculosa est propter uarias causas quas recenter intelleximus, uobis mandamus quod statim uisis litteris habitoque super hiis consilio Hugonis le Bygod et Philippi Bassat tam de aduentu nostro quam de aliis circumstanciis nos tangentibus nobis consilium uestrum festinanter significetis; quia probrosum est nobis et toti regno periculosum quod tantam moram fecimus extra regnum nostrum sicut prefatus rex et alii amici nostri nobis dixerunt, propter quod in partibus ubi nunc sumus diutius morari non ualemus, ad hec, cum susceperitis in uos graue onus pro nobis et regno nostro, nos ibidem in proximo ueniemus ad supportandum uobiscum onus illud ut extunc alter alterius onera ualeat supportare. Teste etc. apud Sanctum Audomarum primo die Aprilis anno etc. xliiii.

21

I APRIL 1260

*De summonicione seruicii regis usque London' a die Pasche in tres septimanas**[a]

Memorandum quod die Iouis proxima ante Pascham dominus W. de Merton' mandatum H. le Bygod, iusticiarii regis Anglie, recepit in hec uerba.

H. le Bygod, iusticiarius regis Anglie, dilecto et speciali amico suo domino W. de Merton' salutem quam sibi. Mandatum domini regis recepimus in hec uerba hac die Mercurii ante Pascham.

H. dei gracia etc. Hugoni le Bygod iusticiario Anglie salutem. Mandamus uobis quod omnes illos quorum nomina inseruntur in cedula presentibus inclusa sumoneri faciatis quod sint London' a die Pasche in tres septimanas[1] cum seruiciis que nobis debent, audituri ibidem mandatum nostrum et facturi quod eisdem iniunxeritis ex parte nostra; et hoc sicut honorem nostrum diligitis

[a] *In left-hand margin of roll.*

* *Text*: Rot. Claus. 44 Hen. III, m. 16d. *Printed*: *C.R. 1259–61*, pp. 157–9; 'Baronial Council', pp. 133–4. *See*: *Baronial Plan*, pp. 226–7.

willing to enter our kingdom without us.[1] And since our stay outside our kingdom is dangerous to us, for many reasons which we
have recently learnt, we order you that, as soon as you have read
these letters and taken counsel with Hugh Bigod and Philip Basset
on these matters, you should quickly let us know your advice
about our return and about other matters affecting us. It is shame-
ful to us and harmful to our whole kingdom that we should be
away for so long from our realm, as the aforesaid king and other
friends of ours have told us, and so we cannot delay any longer
where we now are. Moreover, since you took on yourself a heavy
load for us and for our realm, we will come there very soon to bear
that load with you, so that thenceforth each of us may be able to
bear the other's responsibilities. Witness, etc., at St. Omer on
1 April, 44th year.

21

1 APRIL 1260

*Summons of military service for the king, to meet at London
three weeks after Easter*

Memorandum that on the Thursday before Easter [1 April]
Walter de Merton received the mandate of Hugh Bigod, justiciar
of the king of England, in these words:

Hugh Bigod, justiciar of the king of England, to his well-loved
and dear friend Walter de Merton, greeting as to himself. We have
received the mandate of the lord king in these words on the
Wednesday before Easter [31 March]:

Henry, by God's grace, etc., to Hugh Bigod, justiciar of England,
greeting. We order you to have summoned all those whose names
appear on the schedule, enclosed with these presents, to be in
London, three weeks after Easter [25 April][1] with the service which
they owe to us, there to hear our command and to do whatever you
shall order them on our behalf: and this you shall in no wise fail

---

[1] Plans were made to muster men in England to supply the king with an
armed force on his return (see docs. 21, 23). The king used the money which he
received from Louis IX, in 1260 and 1261, to hire mercenaries (*Peace of Paris*,
p. 57).

[1] 'Baronial Council', p. 134, incorrectly dates this meeting on 23 Apr.

nullatenus omittatis. Teste me ipso apud Sanctum Audomarum
xxvij. die Martii[2] anno regni nostri xliiii[to].

Et ideo uobis mandamus ex parte domini regis quatinus, uisis
litteris istis, breuia domini regis fieri faciatis per que omnes
contenti in eadem cedula, quam uobis presentibus inclusam
mittimus, mandentur quod sint London' ad terminum predictum
et sicut predictum est, et eadem breuia sine dilacione mitti
faciatis per nuncios cancellarie, sicut moris est, prouidentes ob
amorem nostrum quod taliter fiat istud negocium quod de pigricie
seu infidelitate redargui non debeamus nec possimus. Datum apud
parcum Windes' die Mercurii predicta.

Cedula custodiatur secretiori modo quo poterit.

[b]Nomina[3,4,5]

Sciendum[c] quod die Iovis proxima ante Pascha, ut predictum
est, recepit dictus dominus W. de Merton' mandatum predictum
et eadem die in mensa. Et eodem die et in mane conscripta fuerunt
et consignata breuia regis ad singulas personas supradictas in
forma predicta apud Maldon'. Et die Sabbati post missam et
mensam statim tradita fuerunt deferenda per nuncios illis quibus
diriguntur una cum breuibus ad uicecomites, ut ipsi propter
breuitatem temporis ea deferri facerent in continenti per nuncios
diuersos. Teste H. le Bygod, iusticiario nostro, apud Westmonasterium xxix[o]. die Martii.[6]

---

[b] Nomina eorum qui London' sunt conuenturi a die Pasche in tres septimanas cum seruicio regis *in left-hand margin of roll.*   [c] *This is a note made
by the chancery clerk.*

---

[2] This letter is calendared in *C.P.R. 1258–66*, p. 123 and dated 28 Mar.

[3] The bishops were those of Salisbury, Exeter (Walter Bronescombe, royal
envoy on several occasions, *C.P.R. 1247–58*, pp. 618, 633; *C.P.R. 1258–66*,
pp. 243, 269), and Norwich (Simon Walton, an active royalist, on occasions
worked with the bishop of Exeter; *Baronial Plan*, pp. 238–9, 260, 287, n. 1;
C.P.R. 1247–58, passim; *C.P.R. 1258–66*, p. 42).

[4] The abbot of Bury St. Edmunds (Simon de Luton, emissary to meet
Richard of Cornwall at St. Omer. *C.Lib.R. 1251–60*, p. 504) and the abbot of
Glastonbury (Roger Forde, see T. S. Holmes, *Wells and Glastonbury* (1908);
Watkin, *Glastonbury Cartulary, passim*). Note the small number of clergy sum-
moned, possibly because they were mostly neutral or sympathetic to Simon.

to do as you love our honour. Witness ourself at St. Omer, 27 March,[2] in the 44th year of our reign.

And therefore, on the behalf of the lord king, we order you that, as soon as you have read these letters, you should have writs in the king's name prepared whereby all who are listed in the schedule, which we are sending to you enclosed with this letter, shall be ordered to be in London at the time and in the manner prescribed; and you shall have these writs sent out without delay by the chancery messengers, in the usual way, making sure, out of your love for us, that this matter is so executed that we neither should nor can be accused of slackness or disloyalty. Dated at Windsor Park on the same Wednesday [31 March]. Keep the schedule as secret as you can.

Names[3,4,5]

Be it known that on the Thursday next before Easter [1 April], as is said above, Walter de Merton received this mandate, on the same day at table. And on that day and on the next the king's writs to each of these persons were written at Maldon in the prescribed form, and were sealed. And on the Saturday [3 April] after mass and breakfast they were immediately handed to the messengers to be delivered to those to whom they were addressed, together with writs to the sheriffs, [instructing them], on account of the shortness of the time, to have them taken out at once by other messengers. Witness Hugh Bigod our justiciar, at Westminster, 29 March[6] [sic].

[5] Seven earls and 99 lay tenants are named. The earls not summoned were Leicester, Derby, who attained his majority in 1260 and was later an opponent of the crown, Hereford, and Richard of Cornwall (*Baronial Plan*, p. 226 and Baronial Council, p. 133 express different opinions). Well-known supporters of Leicester (Peter de Montfort) were not summoned.
[6] This date would appear to be a mistake. If it is correct there may be an explanation in the varied manner for dating chancery documents. See doc. 6, n. 2.

22

10 APRIL 1260

*Rex Hugoni le Bygod et maiori et communitati London'**

Quia rex uellet discordiarum materias elidere et omnes contenciones
et discidii causas extinguere ad unitatem et pacem in ciuitate sua
Lond' et alibi in regno suo confouendam, et audiuit quod Edwardus filius suus disponit cum equis et armis in hoc parleamento[1]
iacere in domibus episcopi London' infra claustrum Sancti Pauli,
de quo ciues Lond' multum timent quod ex hoc possit periculum
iminere, presertim cum parleamentum illud contra uoluntatem
regis captum sit, mandatum est Hugoni le Bygod, iusticiario
Anglie, quod nec ipsum Edwardum nec alium de quo possit aliqua
suspicio mali haberi in regis et ciuitatis predicte periculum
infra muros civitatis predicte iacere uel hospitari permittat;[2]
et hoc in fide qua regi tenetur et sicut indignacionem regis uitare
uoluerit nullatenus omittat. Et dicat Iohanni de Warenn' quod
apud Clerkenwell' uel apud Nouum Templum hospitetur. Teste
etc. apud Sanctum Audomarum x. die Aprilis anno etc. xliiii.
Eodem modo mandatum est maiori et communitati London'.[3]

23

11 APRIL 1260

*Rex comiti Glouc(estrie) et aliis***

Mandatum est comiti Glouc', H. le Bigod iusticiario Anglie et
Philippo Basset quod prouideant quod rex habeat homines cum

* *Text*: Rot. Claus. 44 Hen. III, m. 2d. *Printed*: *C.R. 1259–61*, pp. 282–3.
See: *Baronial Plan*, p. 230.
** *Text*: Rot. Claus. 44 Hen. III, m. 2d. *Printed*: *C.R. 1259–61*, p. 283. *See*:
Baronial Plan, p. 227.

---

[1] See the introduction, pp. 24, 28–31.
[2] At the start of April, Leicester and Gloucester had mustered forces threatening to seize London. Edward was reconciled with his father in the first week of
May 1260 (doc. 17, n. 2; doc. 30, cls. 20, 21).

22

10 APRIL 1260

The king to Hugh Bigod, the mayor and people of London

The king wishes to eliminate all matters of discord and to extinguish all disputes and causes of faction, and to foster unity and peace in his city of London and elsewhere in his realm, and he has heard that during the forthcoming parliament[1] Edward his son proposes to occupy the houses of the bishop of London in St. Paul's Close, with horses and arms, on account of which the citizens of London greatly fear that danger might arise, especially as that parliament is meeting against the king's will. Hugh Bigod the justiciar of England is ordered therefore not to permit either Edward or anyone else of whom suspicion of evil might be entertained, to stay or to be accommodated within the walls of the city to the danger of the king or the city;[2] and this is enjoined in the faith in which he is bound to the king and he shall in no wise fail in it as he shall wish to avoid the king's wrath. And let him tell John de Warenne that he shall be accommodated at Clerkenwell or at the New Temple. Witness, etc., at St. Omer on 10 April, 44th year.

The same order to the mayor and community of London.[3]

23

11 APRIL 1260

The king to the earl of Gloucester and others

Order to the earl of Gloucester, Hugh Bigod, justiciar of England, and Philip Basset that they shall arrange that the king shall have

---

[3] The Londoners were active supporters of the earl of Leicester (*Baronial Plan*, pp. 306, 308, 311, 332; *Simon de Montfort*, pp. 213, 237, n. 1, 250; G. A. Williams, *Medieval London*, and 'London, 1216–1337').

arcubus et sagittis de comitatu Kanc' obuiam regis apud Douor'
cum ibidem uenerit uel alibi in eadem comitatu si opus fuerit et
eis uisum fuerit expedire,[1] uerumptamen rex relinquit hoc ipsorum
discrecioni et prudencie. Teste rege apud Sanctum Audomarum
xi. die Aprilis.

24

18 APRIL 1260

*Rex regi Romanorum**

Rex Anglie regi Romanorum salutem.[1] Sciatis quod pro certo
audiuimus quod quidam de regno nostro miserunt ad diuersas
partes regni Francie pro gente cum armis introducenda in regnum
nostrum contra nos, de quo idem regnum dudum fuisset turbatum
nisi dominus rex Francie transitum ipsorum prohibuisset ad
instanciam nostram; et quod fratres nostri de Pictauia una cum
uicecomite Lemov' dudum, sicut audiuimus, parauerunt se ad
ueniendum in regnum nostrum cum equis et armis contra uoluntatem nostram per portus uestros in comitatu Cornubie.[2] Et, quia
idem comes uendicat sibi ius in predicto comitatu Cornub'[3] et
ex huiusmodi aduentu suo et predictorum tam uobis quam nobis
necnon et regno nostro hiis diebus graue turbacionis periculum
posset iminere, uos rogamus in fide qua nobis tenemini quatinus,
sicut honorem nostrum et uestrum necnon et tranquillitatem
regni nostri diligitis, per terram et potestatem uestram in Cornubia
et alibi in partibus illis firmiter et districte prohiberi faciatis
ne predicti fratres nostri uel uicecomes seu quicumque alii cum
equis et armis sine licencia nostra ingredi permittantur. Scituri

---

* *Text*: Rot. Claus. 44 Hen. III, m. 1d. *Printed*: *C.R. 1259–61*, p. 285. *See*:
Baronial Plan, p. 229.

---

[1] Doc. 20, n. 1.

[1] At this time Richard of Cornwall mediated between Leicester and Gloucester
and between the Lord Edward, Gloucester, and Henry III (*Baronial Plan*,
pp. 233, 238).

[2] Aymer, bishop-elect of Winchester, died in Rome in Dec. 1260; the other
Poitevin brothers came to England in the spring and summer of 1261.

men with bows and arrows from the county of Kent to meet him at Dover when he shall arrive there, or elsewhere in the same county, if need be and if they think fit;[1] but nevertheless the king leaves this to their discretion and prudence. Witness the king at St. Omer, 11 April.

24

18 APRIL 1260

The king to the king of the Romans

The king of England to the king of the Romans,[1] greeting. We have heard for certain that some of our subjects have sent to various parts of the kingdom of France to bring armed men into our realm to oppose us, whereby our kingdom would have been disturbed long ago had not the king of France, at our instance, forbidden their crossing. And some time ago, as we have heard, our Poitevin brothers, with the vicomte of Limoges, were getting ready to enter our kingdom with horses and arms against our will, by way of your ports in the county of Cornwall.[2] And therefore, since the vicomte claims the right to the county of Cornwall,[3] and from his coming and that of the others serious danger of disturbance might threaten, both to you and also to us and our realm, we beg you, in the faith in which you are bound to us that, as you love our honour and your own, and also the peace of our kingdom, you should have it firmly and strictly prohibited, throughout your land and jurisdiction in Cornwall and elsewhere in those parts, that neither our brothers nor the vicomte nor any others with horses and arms should be permitted to enter without our licence.

---

[3] Adémer V, vicomte of Limoges (d. 1199), m. Sara, daughter of Reginald, earl of Cornwall, d.s.p.m. 1175. Adémer V was also half-brother of the count of Angoulême (d. c. 1218) father of Isabella, mother of King Henry III. Adémer, son of Adémer V and brother of Guy, vicomte of Limoges (d. c. 1229), had claimed the county of Cornwall in 1220 (*C. Docs. France*, no. 1299; *G.E.C.* iii. 429; *C.R. 1204–24*, p. 437; Mas-Latrie, *Trésor de Chronologie* (1889), pp. 1537, 1626).

pro certo quod grauius non possetis nos offendere[a] quam ipsos taliter in regnum nostrum uenientes admittere. Teste rege apud Bolon' xviij. die Aprilis.

25

20 APRIL 1260

*Rex regi Francie**

Rex regi Francie salutem. Serenitati uestre intimamus quod nos et regina liberique nostri nobiscum existentes sani et incolumes uenimus usque Wytsand'[1] die Mercurii proxima post quindenam Pasche, parati ad transfretandum in Angliam quamcito prosperam auram habuerimus, cum quibusdam militibus quos nobiscum ducimus de partibus cismarinis, celsitudini uestre significantes quod pro certo intelleximus fratres nostros de Pictauia una cum uicecomite Lemouic' multitudinem armatorum in partibus suis congregasse ad ueniendum in Angliam contra nostram uoluntatem. Qua propter excellenciam uestram quantum possumus deprecamur quatinus duci Britannie[2] uestris dare uelitis litteris in mandatis ut, si ipsos per districtum et potestatem suam transitum facere contigerit, eos modis quibus poterit impediat et repellat. Intelleximus eciam quod quidam magnates de dominio uestro inimicis nostris in hac parte consilium impendunt et fauorem, unde quia post Deum potissime confidimus et speramus, ipsos super hoc ne sua uoluntas impetuosa in actum prodeat cum uobis inde constiterit conpescatis, comes autem Leyc' quosdam dextrarios suos ac eciam arma transire fecit per portum de Wytsand', cum adhuc in partibus illis essemus,[3] pretextu quarundam litterarum uestrarum de conductu ibidem, ut dicitur, exhibitarum, per quod motum animi eiusdem comitis euidentius perpendere poteritis, qualiter erga nos se habeat hiis diebus; super quibus et aliis que nobis obesse poterunt faciatis, si placet, arcius prouideri.

[a] offendare MS.

* *Text*: Rot. Claus. 44 Hen. III, m. 1d. *Printed*: *C.R. 1259–61*, pp. 285–6; *Foedera*, I. i. 396. *See*: *Baronial Plan*, p. 229.

[1] Between Boulogne and Calais.

We want you to be absolutely clear that you cannot offend us worse than by admitting them, coming in this fashion, into our realm. Witness the king at Boulogne on 18 April.

25

20 APRIL 1260

The king to the king of France

The king to the king of France, greeting. We write to tell your serene highness that we and our queen and our children with us have arrived safely and well at Wissant[1] on the Wednesday after the quinzaine of Easter [21 April], ready to cross to England as soon as we shall have a favourable wind, together with some knights whom we are taking with us from this side. We have learnt for certain, as we now inform your highness, that our Poitevin brothers and the vicomte of Limoges have gathered together in their country a multitude of armed men to enter England against our will, and therefore we beg your excellency as strongly as we can, to be good enough to send your written orders to the duke of Brittany[2] that, if they should chance to cross through his land and jurisdiction, he should impede them and drive them back by all means in his power. We have also heard that certain magnates in your dominion are lending counsel and favour to our enemies; wherefore, since we trust and hope in you most strongly, next only after God, we beg that, now you are informed of the matter, you will not look favourably upon them in this business, so that their uncontrolled will shall not advance into action. Moreover, the earl of Leicester has had certain chargers of his, and arms as well, brought over from the port of Wissant at the very time when we ourselves were there,[3] on the pretext of certain letters of safe-conduct of yours which he showed there, as it is said. By this you can clearly deduce for yourself the way in which the earl's mind works, and how he is behaving towards us just now, and we beg you, if you please, to make stricter arrangements in these and all other matters which might impede us. When we have returned

---

[2] John, duke of Brittany (d. 1285), was father of John, count of Brittany, husband of Henry III's daughter Beatrice (*G.E.C.* x. 809–14). Document 29, cl. 23 is incorrect in saying that Beatrice married the son of the count of Brittany.

[3] Henry's complaints against Simon de Montfort may be seen in document 29.

Nos autem, cum in Angliam uenerimus, de statu nostro et regni nostri uos reddemus certiores, parati ea facere que uestris bene- placitis gracia nouerimus et accepta. Teste rege apud Wytsand xx. die Aprilis anno etc. xliiii.

26

23 APRIL 1260

Rex maiori et ciuibus Lond'*

Mandatum est maiori et ciuibus Lond' quod permittant R. de Clare comitem Glouc', R. le Bygod comitem Norff' et marescallum Angl', Iohannem de Warenn', Henricum filium regis Alemannie et alios fideles regis, quos Philippus Bassat et Robertus Walerand' eis dicent ex parte regis,[1] dictam ciuitatem ingredi et ibidem in hospiciis suis hospitari. Teste rege apud Dovor' xxiii. die Aprilis.

27

5 JUNE 1260

De prohibicione itineris iusticiariorum**[a]

Cum per consilium magnatum qui sunt de consilio regis rex nuper prouiderit quod per diuersos comitatus certi iusticiarii mitterentur ad assisas mortis antecessoris et noue disseisine capiendas et ad alias transgressiones et querelas audiendas et corigendas secundum legem terre,[1] et iam tanta karistia ingruerit

[a] *These words appear in the left-hand margin of the roll.*

---

* *Text*: Rot. Claus. 44 Hen. III, m. 1d. *Printed*: *C.R. 1259–61*, p. 287. *See*: *Baronial Plan*, p. 232.
** *Text*: Rot. Claus. 44 Hen. III, m. 14d. *Printed*: *C.R. 1259–61*, p. 172. *See*: *Baronial Plan*, p. 237.

to England, we will let you know about the state of ourselves and of our realm, and you will find us ready to do whatever we know will be welcome and acceptable to your good pleasure. Witness the king at Wissant, 20 April, 44th year.

26

23 APRIL 1260

The king to the mayor and citizens of London

The mayor and citizens of London are ordered to permit Richard de Clare, earl of Gloucester, Roger Bigod, earl of Norfolk and marshal of England, John de Warenne, Henry the son of the king of Germany and other faithful men of the king, whom Philip Basset and Robert Walerand, on the king's behalf,[1] will declare to them, to enter their city and to be accommodated there in their hospices. Witness the king at Dover, 23 April.

27

5 JUNE 1260

Cancellation of the eyre

Whereas, by the counsel of the magnates of the king's council, the king recently provided that certain justices should be sent throughout the different counties to take assizes of *mort d'ancestor* and *novel disseisin* and to hear and correct other trespasses and complaints according to the law of the land,[1] and whereas now such

---

[1] All those named here were trusted royalists.

[1] This is the eyre which was organized in Nov. 1259 (doc. 13). Although famine is mentioned in 1258 and in 1261 the situation in England, in the summer of 1260, suggests that this was not the reason for the cancellation of the eyre. See introduction, pp. 31–2.

per Angliam quod per aduentum iusticiariorum multum graueretur patria hiis diebus, rex pro communi utilitate regni iter predictorum iusticiariorum prorogari fecit usque post festum Santi Michaelis. Et mandatum est uicecomiti Norff' et Suff' quod istud breue in pleno comitatu suo legi et publicari faciat alibi in balliua sua ubi uiderit expedire. Teste rege apud Westmonasterium v. die Junii.

Eodem modo mandatum est uicecomitibus Lincoln', Staff', Salop', Glouc', Wigorn', Hereford', Middilsex', Suthampt'.[2]

28

6 JULY 1260

De scrutacione facienda per omnes portus*[a]

Rex baronibus et balliuis suis Dovor' salutem. Mandamus uobis in fide qua nobis tenemini firmiter iniungentes quod caute explorari et scrutari faciatis si qui, clerici uel laici, Ytalici uel alii cuiuscumque ordinis, cum bullis papalibus nobis aut regno nostro preiudicialibus applicuerint in portu uestro;[1] et, si quos cum huiusmodi litteris ibidem applicare contigerit, ipsos cum litteris illis ibi arestari faciatis donec aliud inde preceperimus. Nullatenus eciam permittatis aliquos cum equis et armis ingredi regnum nostrum per portum uestrum sine licencia nostra speciali; et, si quos cum equis et armis applicare contigerit in portu uestro, ipsos cum equis et armis illis arestari faciatis donec aliud inde a nobis habueritis in mandatis; taliter uos in hac parte habentes quod pro defectu uestri dampnum in hac parte non incurramus quod uobis possit aut debeat imputari. Teste rege apud Westmonasterium vj. die Julii.

Eodem modo mandatum est baronibus per omnes portus.

---

[a] These words appear in the left-hand margin of the roll.

---

* Text: Rot. Claus. 44 Hen. III, m. 12d. Printed: C.R. 1259–61, p. 181; W. Prynne, The History of King John, Henry III and Edward I, ii (1670), 968. See: Baronial Plan, pp. 234, 238, 289.

---

[2] The eyre may have been completed in those counties which are not named. See doc. 13.

a terrible famine has befallen throughout England that the country-side would be grievously burdened by the visit of the justices, the king, for the general good of the kingdom, has caused the eyre of these justices to be prorogued until after Michaelmas [29 September]. The sheriff of Norfolk and Suffolk is ordered to have this writ read and published in the full county court, and wherever else in his bailiwicks he sees fit. Witness the king at Westminster, 5 June [1260].

Similar orders are sent to the sheriffs of Lincolnshire, Staffordshire, Shropshire, Gloucestershire, Worcestershire, Herefordshire, Middlesex, Hampshire.[2]

28

6 JULY 1260

Search to be enforced at all ports

The king to his barons and bailiffs of Dover, greeting. We order you in the fealty in which you are bound to us, that you should cause careful investigation and scrutiny to discover whether any persons, clerks or laymen, Italians or others of whatever degree, shall have landed in your port with papal bulls prejudicial to us or to our realm,[1] and if it should happen that any do land there with such letters, you must cause them to be arrested there with those letters until you shall have received further orders from us about them. Also, you shall in no wise permit anyone to enter our realm with horses and arms by way of your port without our special licence: and if it should happen that any persons do land at your port, with horses and arms, you shall cause them and their horses and arms to be arrested until you shall have further orders from us about them. Act in these matters so that we shall not suffer any harm in these ways, on account of any defect on your part which could or should be imputed to you. Witness the king at Westminster, 6 July [1260].

The same orders are sent to the barons in all the ports.

---

[1] There is evidence that the nobles had agents in Rome in 1261 and this may have been true also in 1260. Such agents may have given Simon the evidence which he used in Oct. 1262 to claim that the pope supported the Provisions of Oxford (*Baronial Plan*, pp. 275-7; doc. 36, n. 1).

29

JULY 1260

*Le Iugement de Simon de Montfort**

1. Nostre seignur le roy dit que conte de Leycestre fu de son conseil et que il li conseillia qu'il treitast de peis au roi de France des terres de la.

Li cuens dit qu'il fu au conseil et li conseillia aueques autres prodes homes de son conseil et de sa terre.

2. Le roy dit que le conte de Leycestre fu son messatge a treiter de peis entre le roy de France et li.

Li cuens dit qu'il en fu messatges ensemble aueques autres prodeshomes de sa terre.

3. Le roy dit que en cele peis fu contenu que la contesse de Leycestre et ses duez fius devoent fere quittance au roi de France.[1]

Li cuens dit que eisint le uout li rois de France.

4. Le roy dit que le roy de France nule quittance ne demanda des fillies le roy[2] ne del puisne fiuz le roy d'Alemagne[3] ne des hoirs l'enpereriz[4] suer einsnee la contesse.

Li cuens dit que ce fu par la uolante le roy de France, ne mie par son porchaz.

5. Li roys dit que le conte per li et par les suens procura et fist procurer, et amentut ei fist amenteuoir au roy de France et a son conseil, par quoi la quittance de la contesse et de ses enfanz fu demandee.[5]

Li cuens dit qu'il ne le procura, ne ne fist procurer, ne n'amentust ne ne fist amenteuoir; et de ce, met il au record le roy de France. Et ce ne fu de rien son pro, quar sa droiture n'en fu de

---

* *Text*: Bibliothèque Nationale (Paris), MS. Latin 9016, no. 5. *Printed*: Bémont, *Simon de Montfort*, pp. 343–53. *See*: *Baronial Plan*, pp. 239–41; E. F. Jacob, 'A proposal for arbitration between Simon de Montfort and Henry III in 1260', *E.H.R.* xxxvii (1922), 80–2.

[1] The Peace of Paris stated that the countess of Leicester, her peers, and children should surrender claims. Eleanor, who as daughter of King John could claim lands in France, bore Simon five sons and two daughters (*Simon de Montfort*, pp. 37 n. 1, 76–7). The mention of only two sons here was probably because, in July 1260, only the two eldest sons, Henry and Simon, were old enough to claim rights from their mother.

29

JULY 1260

The Trial of Simon de Montfort

1. Our lord the king says that the earl of Leicester was a member of his council, and that he advised him to treat for peace with the king of France concerning the lands overseas.

The earl agrees that he was a councillor and that, along with other good men of his council and his land, he did advise the king.

2. The king says that the earl of Leicester was his envoy to treat for peace between the king of France and him.

The earl agrees that, along with other good men of the land, he was an envoy for this.

3. The king says that in the peace-treaty was included a provision that the countess of Leicester and her two sons should make renunciation to the king of France.[1]

The earl says that so the king of France wished it.

4. The king says that the king of France did not demand any renunciation from the king's daughters[2] nor from the second son of the king of Germany,[3] nor from the heirs of the empress,[4] the elder sister of the countess.

The earl says that this was done at the wish of the king of France, and not by his doing.

5. The king says that the earl, both personally and through his agents, arranged and caused to be arranged, and put it into the mind of the king of France, that renunciation should be asked from the countess and her children.[5]

The earl says that he neither arranged nor suggested this, nor did he get anyone else to do so, and on this charge he will stand or fall by the memory of the king of France. And in any case, all this

[2] Margaret m. Alexander, King of Scots; Beatrice m. John, count of Brittany.

[3] Henry of Almain, the elder son of Richard of Cornwall, had renounced his claims in May 1258 and Feb. 1259. Edmund, the second son, d.s.p. 1300.

[4] Isabella, who m. Frederick II in June 1235, d. 1241. She was mother of four children of whom only Henry, d.s.p. 1253, and Margaret, wife of Albert landgrave of Thuringia and margrave of Meissen, survived her.

[5] This clause gave de Montfort a lever to force the king to answer Eleanor's claims. Henry III tried to have this clause excluded from the peace (I. J. Sanders, 'The Texts of the Peace of Paris, 1259', *E.H.R.* lxvi (1951), 83–97).

rien plus clere quant as choses de ca, et sa droiture fu barree quant as choses de la.

6. Le roy dit que la conte granta par sa letre qu'il feret sa fame et ses enfanz fere la quittance si il paiast a la contesse ce que il li deuet, et li amendast les torz fiez a li si fez li eust.

Li cuens dit que ce est uoirs.

7. Le roy dit qu'il fist paie a la contesse de ce qu'il li deuet.

Li cuens dit que bien croit que li rois fist gre a la contesse des arreratges de deniers qu'il li deuet.

8. Li rois dit que des torz feiz a la contesse se fu li rois mis en mise.

Li cuens dit que del doeire la contesse d'Irlande[6] se mistil en mise, ne mie de l'autre tort.

9. Le roy dit que le conte et autres qui donc furent del conseil le roy firent le saremant a Windesore qu'il au conseil ne serent, n'a luer pooir ne seffreroent que li rois meist hors de sa mein rien qui fust de son demeine, ne que eus meismes rien n'en prandraent.

Li cuens dit qu'il fu a Windesore ou il et autres du conseil firent un saremant qui fu tel, a ce qu'il li puet souenir, que les ancieins demeines de la corone ne fussent esloignes en manere que li rois et ses hoirs en fussent deseritez.[7]

10. Le roy dit que le conte defoit a fere la quittance iuesque tant qu'il li eust assigne quatre cenz liurees de terre por quatre cenz liures qu'il solet prandre des contez.[8]

Le conte dit qu'il ne fu pas en Angleterre quant la quittance fu demandee a la contesse,[9] et la contesse ne le uout fere tresques li rois li eust assise la terre si cum il auet en couenant. Et dit li cuens que la contesse monstra au roy que ele ne fu pas tenue a fere la quittance de son heritatge, s'an ne li feist por quoi; et dit que, se li rois li feist l'assise de iiii[c]. liurees de terre, si cum il fu tenuz

---

[6] Eleanor was granted £400 annually as dower from the Irish lands of her first husband, William Marshal, earl of Pembroke. In 1244 an additional 400 m. annually was to be paid and de Montfort was granted 500 m. annually as Eleanor's dower. The king claimed that the 500 m. represented dowry and the increased dower. See *C. Lib. R. 1251–60*, and *1260–67*, *passim*, for payment of these sums by the king.

[7] The councillors planned to control wardships and escheats in order to reduce the king's debts. The 1257 oath of the councillors bound them not to alienate the royal domain (*Ann. Mon.* i. 396). The mention of Windsor is one of the few clues remaining of where the king met his council.

[8] On 5 May 1258 arbitration was planned about the amount of land to be granted to de Montfort. A year later it was agreed that £400 be paid annually

was of no advantage to him, for his rights were not strengthened as regards anything on this side [of the Channel], and his rights to anything on the other side were barred.

6. The king says that the earl granted by his letter that he would make his wife and his children make the renunciation if the king paid to the countess what he owed her, and made good the wrongs done to her if he had done any.

The earl agrees that this is true.

7. The king says he made payment to the countess for what he owed her.

The earl says he can well believe that the king satisfied the countess for the money arrears which he owed her.

8. The king says that as to the wrongs done to the countess he put himself under arbitration.

The earl says that the king put himself on arbitration regarding the countess's dower in Ireland,[6] but not regarding any other wrong.

9. The king says that the earl and others of the king's council at that time made an oath to him at Windsor that they would never advise him, nor within the limits of their power would they allow him, to dispossess himself of any part of his demesne, nor would they themselves accept any part of it.

The earl says he was at Windsor, where he and others of the council swore on oath to the effect that, so far as he can remember it, the ancient demesnes of the crown should not be alienated in any way which would disinherit the king and his heirs.[7]

10. The king says that the earl delayed making the quittance until the king had assigned him £400 worth of land instead of £400 that he had formerly received from the revenues of the shires.[8]

The earl says that he was not in England when the countess was asked for the renunciation,[9] and that the countess was unwilling to make it until the king had assigned the land to her as he had agreed. And the earl says that the countess showed the king that she was not bound to make the renunciation of her hereditary right unless she received compensation; and that she said that if the king would make her a settlement of £400 worth of land, as by his written agreement he was bound to do for the £400 which she received

and lands were granted (*C.P.R. 1247–58*, p. 627; *C.P.R. 1258–66*, pp. 34–5 *C.R. 1256–59*, pp. 381, 426, 433; *C.Ch.R.* ii, 18, 20).

[9] See cl. 22; *Simon de Montfort*, p. 177, n. 3.

par son escrit por quatre cenz liures qu'ele prist en sis contez
et amende d'autres tors et d'autres trespas, que uolantiers feret
la quittance; et por ce que le roy et tot son conseil trouerent que le
roy fu tenu a fere a la contesse l'assise de quatre cenz liurees de
terre, il baillerent au conte et a la contesse iiii^c liurees de terre
en tenance, ce que fu de demeines, si cum le roi l'auet auant leissee
a ses fermiers a tenir au conte et a la contesse et a lor hoirs en
tenance iuesque tant que le roy ou ses hoirs aussent parfet au
conte et a la contesse ou a lor hoirs l'assise de quatre cenz liurees
de terre, d'escheoites ou d'autres terres qui ne soient des demeines;
et bien piert par le fet le roy et par le fet de son conseil que le roy
et son conseil le firent por ce que li roy i fu tenuz ne mie por
destrece. Et en cest fet rien ne descrut au roy, ne rien n'acrut au
conte; et por ce que ce fu en tenance, ne fist il en ce rien contre
son saremant. Et bien piert que uncore ores en prant li rois
taillatges cum deuant.

11. Le roy dit que le conte recut les quatre cenz liurees de terre
des demeines le roy.

Le conte dit qu'il ne tient pas quatre cenz liurees de terre des
demeines; et ce qu'il tient des demeines, tient il en tenance par le
roi et par tot son conseil.[10]

12. Le roy dit que le conte auet son procureor en Angleterre
par se letre ouerte, c'est a sauoir mestre Reymon.[11] Le roy dit que
cil procureres auet plener poer en totes choses qui tocherent les
besognes et les couenances entre le roy et li.

Li cuens dit qu'il ot procureor en Angleterre qui auet pooir
a fere quant que apandet a l'afere de Bigorre,[12] et dit que cil
procureor bailla au roy et a son conseil ses letres de procuracie;
estre ce, dit li cuens que nul autre procureor n'i ot, ne home nul
qui de li eust pooir ne mandemant de quitter ne de relascher ne
de tenir soi a paie de choses que li rois out autres li eussent a fere,
ne n'i ot nul qui mendement ne pooir aust de li de terme aloigner.
Et se par auanture aucuns qui mandement et pooir especial n'aust
del conte a ces choses fere dit on fit riens de tels choses, li cuens ne

---

[10] The lands, which had been granted to de Montfort *in tenentiam*, were subject to tallage, a due levied only on boroughs and on the royal domain.

[11] Raymond Bodini de Aurillac (Bémont, *Simon de Montfort*, p. 346, n. 1).

[12] Petronilla, heiress of Bigorre, married, as her third husband, Guy, brother of Simon de Montfort. By another marriage she was mother of a daughter who married Gaston de Béarn. Henry III had bought the overlordship of Bigorre from the bishop of le Puy while de Montfort had interests in the county because

from six counties, and if he would put right other wrongs and trespasses, she would willingly make the renunciation. And since the king and all his council found that the king was bound to make to the countess a settlement of £400 worth of land, they leased to the earl and countess £400 worth of land on tenancy, these lands being of the demesne, on the same terms as those on which the king had previously leased them to his farmers, to be held by the earl and the countess and their heirs in tenancy until such times as the king or his heirs should have completed the assignment to the earl and the countess and their heirs of £400 worth of land, out of escheats and other lands which would not be part of the demesnes. And it plainly appears from the action of the king and from the action of his council that the king and his council did this because the king was bound to do it, and not under compulsion. And from this transaction the king lost nothing and the earl gained nothing; and since the land was held on lease, he did nothing contrary to his oath. And this plainly appears since even now the king takes tallages from these lands exactly as he did before.

11. The king says that the earl received the £400 worth of land out of the king's demesnes.

The earl says he does not hold £400 worth of land of the demesne; whatever he holds of the demesnes he holds on lease by the grant of the king and all his council.[10]

12. The king says that the earl had his proctor in England— Master Raymond[11]— appointed by his letter patent, and that this proctor had full power in all matters affecting the business and agreements between the king and him.

The earl says that he had a proctor in England who had power to deal with anything relating to the Bigorre[12] affair, and he says that this proctor tendered his letters of procuration to the king and his council: but beyond that, the earl says, he had no other proctor nor any man who had power or authority from him to acquit or to modify or to declare him paid on any matters which the king or anyone else had to settle with him, nor had he anyone there with authority or power from him to prolong the terms. And if by accident someone who had no special authority or power from the earl to do any of these things did or said anything of the sort, the earl never gave his assent to it, nor does he assent now, nor regard it as settled and valid, and he claims that this neither can nor should injure him by law. And on top of all this, the earl says that when

of his brother Guy. In July 1259 the earl agreed to surrender his interests in Bigorre for seven years in return for £1000 annually or lands to that value (*Treaty Rolls, 1234-1325*, pp. 49-51). The genealogy in *Simon de Montfort*, p. 284 is faulty; see *King Henry III*, p. 207.

a'i assanci unques, ne n'assant uncores, ne n'a ferm ne estable;
et dit que ce ne li puet ne ne doit nuire par droit. Et parmi tot
ce, dit li cuens que Reymons sis clers, a son reuenir d'Angleterre,
li reconta qu'il auet tous iours chalangees des defautes des cou⟨en⟩-
ances desus moties; et ce meises dit uncores cil Reymons, et est
prez de ce auerer, se mesciers est. Et fut uncore que ⟨se⟩ li cuens
eust eu tel procureor en Angleterre cum li rois dit en son escrit,
ce qu'il n'ot mie, et cil procurreres se fust tenuz a paiez si cum li
roys dit, ei ne li porret ne deuret ce nuire par droit, quar il offri
a fere la quittance a celi a qui ele deuet estre fete selonc les
couenances, c'est a sauoir au roy de France, et auant la uenue
le roy d'Engleterre en France et en sa uenue, tot ne li fussent mie
ne ne sunt uncores acomplies les couenances par quoi il la deuet
fere, et neporquant si la fist il fere et fist.

13. Le roy dit que le conte auet grante que quel ore que les
diseors eussent pris le dit sur cus et fet le saremant, et les choses
contenues en l'escrit selees del sel au prior des freres Precheors de
Paris fussant accomplies, qu'il feret fere la desus dite quittance.

Le conte dit qu'il granta a fere la quittance quant les choses qui
sunt contenues en l'escrit sele del sel le prior des freres Precheors
de Paris qui parla ou nom del conte et de la contesse li seroent
totes acomplies; et por ce que celes choses ne furent pas acomplies
si cum il estet porparle ne uncores ne sunt, ne fu pas li cuens tenus
a fere fere la quittance.

14. Le roy dit que li diseor auoent pris le dit sur eus et le
saremant auoent fet en presance de l'auant dit procureor le conte.

Le conte dit que bien croit qu'il pristrent le dit sur eus et firent
le saremant, mes a lor saremant recoiure il n'auet nul procureor, si
cum desus est dit.

15. Le roy dit que li diseor furent prest a dire lor dit deuant la
Touz Seinz et qu'il fu prest a recoiure lor dit.

Le conte dit qu'il oi bien dire qu'il en i ot aucun d'eus qui dist
qu'il estet prez de dire son dit, mes bien siet que riens n'en fu fet.

16. Le roy dit que par assentemant de l'auant dir procureor et
par sa proierre et par ses amis qui donc furant de ca, c'est a sauoir
l'euesque de Wirecestre, P. de Montfort, Richard de Grey et
autres, mistrent les diseors lor dit en delay.

Le cont dit qu'il n'i auet nul procureor qui a ce fere eust pooir,
fors a treiter solemant de la besoigne de Bigorre, si cum desus est
dit. Ei dit que il tel pooir ne poet doner a nului, quar il meismes,

he returned to England, his clerk, Master Raymond, told him that
he had consistently challenged the defects of the agreements mentioned above, and that Raymond still says the same, and is ready
to affirm it if required. And even if the earl had had in England
a proctor with the powers which the king asserts in his written
statement, which he never had, and even if that proctor had
declared himself paid as the king says, even so this neither could
nor should harm the earl rightly, for he offered to make the
renunciation to the person to whom, according to the agreements,
it should be made—the king of France, and this he did both before
the king of England came to France and after he had arrived there,
even though the agreements binding him to make it had in no way
been fulfilled and still remain unfulfilled; and nevertheless he had
it done so and he did it himself.

13. The king says that the earl had agreed that as soon as the
arbitrators had undertaken the award and sworn the oath, and as
soon as the things stated in the document sealed with the seal
of the prior of the Dominicans of Paris had been done, he would
make the renunciation.

The earl says that he agreed to make the renunciation when the
things stated in the document sealed with the seal of the prior of
the Dominicans of Paris, who spoke in the name of the earl and the
countess, had been completed; and because these things were not
completed and still are not, the earl was not bound to have the
renunciation made.

14. The king says that the arbiters had undertaken the award
and had sworn the oath in the presence of the earl's proctor.

The earl says that he does not doubt that they undertook the
award and swore the oath, but that, as he already has said, he had
no proctor to receive that oath, as is stated above.

15. The king says that the arbiters were ready to declare their
award before All Saints' [1 November] and that he was ready to
receive their declaration.

The earl says that he did indeed hear that there were some who
said they were ready to declare their award, but that he knows all
too well that nothing came of this.

16. The king says that by the assent of the said proctor and at
his request and by means of his friends who were then on this side
[of the Channel], namely the bishop of Worcester, Peter de Montfort, Richard de Grey, and others, the arbitrators postponed the
making of their award.

The earl says that he had no proctor with power to do this, but
only to deal with the Bigorre affair, as he has already said. And he
says that he could not give such power to anyone, for he himself,

se il fust presanz, ne la peust pas aloigner, por ce qu'il ne fu mie dit en la mise que ele peust estre aloignee; mes en nouele mise se peust il bien estre consantuz se il uousist et eust este presanz.

17. Le roy dit que auant qu'il alast en France, demanda il del procureor le conte se il se teinst a paiez selonc les couenances.

Le conte dit qu'il n'auet nul procureor qui son estat endroit des couenances peust esloigner ne enpirer, fors solemant endroit l'afere de Bigorre, si cum desus est dit.

18. Li rois dit que cil procureor granta que assez fu fet et que plus ne demanda ne ne sauet demander por quoi la quittance remeist a fere.

Le conte dit ausint cum il a dit en la procheine response desue.

19. Le roy dit que quant il uint en France por afermer la pais porueue, le conte desdit a fere la quittance.

Le conte dit qu'il ne desdit mis pleinement a fere la quittance, einz dit qu'il n'estet pas tenuz a fere la quittance por ce que les couenances por qu'il la deuet fere ne li furent pas acomplies, et dit que auant ce que li rois d'Engleterre uenist en France il auet dit au roy de France, et puis mande par bones genz, et dit de bouche qu'il feret fere la quittance quel ore qu'il uoudret, et de ce se met il bien au recort le roy de France, et tot ne l'aust il mie fet et l'aust contredit a fere, si n'aust il de rien trespasse, quar les conuenances por qoi il la deuet fere ne li furent pas acomplies.

20. Le roy dit que por ce qu'il n'ot la quittance, fu il delaie par viii iours et plus.

Le conte dit que par son tort ne fu il point delaie, si cum il a touche en la procheine response de sus.

21. Le roy dit que par cel delaiement de la quittance, li furent xv mile mars arrestez en France.

Le conte dit que le delai de la quittance ne fu pas a son tort si cum desus est dit, ne par son perchaz ⟨les xv mile mars⟩ ne furent point arreste, mes par la uolante le roy de France et de l'outroi le roy d'Angleterre et d'aucuns de son conseil qui la furent; et de ce, se met il ou recort le roy de France.[13]

---

[13] On 3 Dec. 1259 Louis IX announced that he was withholding 15,000 m. of the money which he was to pay Henry III until such time as the disputes between the king and Leicester were solved (*C.P.R. 1258–66*, p. 106). On 4 Dec. Eleanor renounced claims to the lands of her father King John, and de Montfort surrendered claims in Toulouse, Béziers, and Évreux (*Simon de Montfort*, pp. 180–1; *Peace of Paris*, pp. 36–70; Sanders, *E.H.R.* lxvi (1951), 91).

had he been present, could not have prolonged the period of arbitration, since the terms of the arbitration did not provide for postponement; but in a new arbitration that could have been agreed to had he been present and consenting.

17. The king says that before he went to France he asked the earl's proctor if he regarded himself as satisfied according to the agreements.

The earl says that he had no proctor who could prolong or weaken his position with regard to the agreements, but only with respect to the Bigorre affair, as he has already said.

18. The king says that this proctor agreed that enough had been done, and that he asked for no more and did not know how to ask for anything more before the renunciation should be made.

The earl says as before in the preceding reply.

19. The king says that when he came to France to confirm the peace provided, the earl refused to make the renunciation.

The earl says that he did not in any way refuse to make the renunciation, but rather says that he was not bound to make it, since the agreements binding him to make it had not been carried out; and he says that before the king of England came to France, he had told the king of France, and had subsequently informed him by trustworthy men, and had said with his own mouth, that he would have the renunciation made whenever King Louis wanted it, and as to this he is willing to stand or fall by the recollection of the king of France. And even if he had not made it, and had refused to make it, he still would not have done anything wrong, for the agreements binding him to do it had not been carried out.

20. The king says that, since he had not got the renunciation, he was delayed for eight days or more.

The earl says that it was not by any fault of his that the king was delayed, for the reasons given in his last reply.

21. The king says that because of the delay in the renunciation, 15,000 marks of his money were held back in France.

The earl replies that the delay in the renunciation was not his fault, as he has already said, and that it was not by his doing that the 15,000 marks were held back, but by the decision of the king of France and the offer of the king of England and of those of his council who were present: and on all this, he will stand or fall by the recollection of the king of France.[13]

22. Le roy dit que le conte demanda as messatges le roy la partie sa fame de totes les terres qui furent au roy Iehan dela la mer. Le roy dit que par cele demande furent ses messatges destorbez et la peis aloignee.

Li cuens dit que se il la demanda auant que li rois et il fussent a un des demandes qui furent par entre eus, en ce ne cuida il fere nul tort, quar il cuida auoir droit en sa demande; et se il le demanda apres, il n'i fist nul tort, quar les couenances qui li furent feites ne li furent pas acomplies, por quoi il ne se meffit de rien se il demanda son droit.

23. Le roy dit que le conte fu entor por destorber le mariatge sa fillie au fiuz le conte de Bretaigne[14] et dit a celui conte que li rois ni poet doner point de terre aueques sa fillie.

Le conte dit qu'il parla d'auancier le mariatge et ne le destorba mie, et dit li cuens qu'il dit au conte de Bretaigne que li rota auoist grante et outroie a son conseil d'Angleterre qu'il nule grant chose ne donret sanz lor conseil.

24. Le roy dit que les freres le roy furent mis hors de la terre par commun conseil du roy et de la terre, et nomeemant par le conte de Leycestre.

Le conte dit qu'il i fu et assanci aueques li et aueques les autres a ce qui en fu fet a Wincestre.

25. Le rois dit que le conte s'accorda a eus a Paris sanz le gre le roy et son conseil et le comun de la terre.

Le cont dit qu'il feist peis a monseignur W. de Valance de contanz qui estoent antre eus auant que la porueance d'Angleterre fust fete[15] et ne mie de chose que a la comun porueance apartenist, si cum il apiert par un escrit qui fu fet de cele peis ou saeus de prodeshomes pandent; et ce ne cuide mie le conte auoir fet sanz le gre le roy, quar li rois l'en auoist proie auant qu'il partist d'Angleterre.

26. Le roy dit que au parlemant de la seint Michel fu porueu que nuls ne uenist au parlemant a cheuaus et a armes.

Le conte dit qu'il n'i fu mie, mes ce fut bien fet.

27. Le roy dit que quant il ore derreenemant fu en France li cuens de Leycestre i fu.

---

[14] Henry's daughter married the son of the duke of Brittany. See doc. 14.

[15] See *Baronial Plan*, p. 78, n. 7 and *Simon de Montfort*, pp. 49, 132, 151–3 for the quarrel between de Montfort and de Valence. The 'provision concerning England' is the Provisions of Oxford. This complaint is a good example of the king's determination to seize any excuse to accuse the earl. See cl. 28; doc. 30 text comment, p. 211; p. 216, cl. 21.

22. The king says that the earl demanded from the envoys of the king [of France] his wife's share of all the overseas territories of King John, and that on account of this demand the negotiations were upset and the peace-treaty delayed.

The earl says that, if he made this demand before the king and he had come to an agreement on the issues between them, he does not see that he did anything wrong, for he believed he had right in his demand; and if he demanded it after agreement had been reached between the king and himself, he still did nothing wrong, for the promises which had been made to him had not been fulfilled, so that he was doing no wrong if he demanded his rights.

23. The king says that the earl went about to upset the marriage of his daughter to the son of the count of Brittany,[14] and that he told the count that the king could not give any land with his daughter.

The earl says that he spoke to promote and not to upset the marriage, and that what he told the count of Brittany was that the king had granted and offered to his council in England that he would make no great gift without their advice.

24. The king says that his brothers were expelled from the land by the common counsel of the king and the country, and particularly by the earl of Leicester.

The earl says that he was present, and assented with the king and with the others to what was done at Winchester in this matter.

25. The king says that the earl came to terms with them at Paris against the king's will and that of his council and of the community of the realm.

The earl says that he made peace with my lord William de Valence on quarrels existing between them before the provision concerning England was made,[15] and not on any matter pertaining to the common provision, as appears from a document recording this settlement, to which the seals of trustworthy men were attached; and the earl does not believe that this was done against the king's will, for the king had begged him to do it before he left England.

26. The king says that at the Michaelmas parliament it was decreed that none should come to parliament with horses and arms.

The earl says that he himself was not there, but that it was a good decision.

27. The king says that when he was very recently in France, the earl of Leicester was there too.

Li cuens dit qu'il i fu quant li rois i fu, mes li rois i demora plus longuemant que il.

28. Le roy dit que le conte s'en parti d'ileques sanz prandre conge de li, et ala en Angleterre.

Le conte dit qu'il fu aueques le roy a Paris tant qu'il ot pris conge du roy de France; lors si ala li cuens uers Normandie ou la contesse sa fame estet, et de la s'an uint en Angleterre ou il cuida que il rois deust estre ausint tost cum il; et se il uint en Angleterre ou a conge ou sanz conge, il ne cuida de rien mesfere.

29. Le roy dit que tant cum il fu dela, manda il a sa Iustice en Angleterre que nul parlement fust tenu iuesque a sa reuenue.

Le conte dit que bien puet estre qu'il li manda.

30. Le roy dit que la Iustice defandi au conte et as autres del conseil qui donc furent qu'il ne parlementassent, ne parlemant ne tenissent iuesques a la uenue le roy.

Le conte dit que bien puet estre que la Iustice le defandi.

31. Le roy dit que le conte uint a Londre a la Chandelor et parlamenta.

Le conte dit que en la commune porueance fete par le roy et par son conseil, est porueu que trois parlemanz soient tenuz par an, dont l'un est a la Chandelor; et le cont por sauuer son saremant i uint, ausint cum les autres prodeshomes del conseil qui furent en Angleterre firent; et la a primes uint la Iustice et lor dit de part le roy qu'il ne tenissent parlement tresques a la uenue le roy; et li rois auet mande qu'il deuet uenir dedanz trois setmeines, et por ce fu li parlemanz aloignes de jour en jour tresques a trois setmeines.

32. Le roy dit que le conte i uint adonc a cheuaus et a armes.

Le conte dit qu'il n'i uint n'a cheuaus n'a armes, fors en la manere qu'il est constumiers d'aler aual le pais.[16]

33. Le roy dit que le conte itreita de remuer sire P. de Savoe del conseil le roy et metre autre en son lieu sanz le sau le roy.[17]

Le conte dit que mis sires P. de Savoe meimes li dit qu'il se fu demis del conseil. Et a ce que li rois dit qu'il treita de metre autre en son lieu, dit le conte qu'il n'en treita ne ne parla, fors cum les autres del conseil; et se nuls del conseil ueut autremant dire, si le monstre au conte at il i respondra.

[16] See *Baronial Plan*, pp. 220–5; *Simon de Montfort*, pp. 183–7 for discussion of the Candlemas parliament of 1260.

[17] Doc. 31 n. 18.

The earl says that he was there when the king was there, but that the king stayed there longer than he did.

28. The king says that the earl left without taking leave of him, and went back to England.

The earl says that he was with the king in Paris until he took leave of the king of France; then the earl went to Normandy, where the countess his wife was, and then he went to England, where he expected that the king would have arrived as soon as he himself. And whether he came back to England with or without leave, he does not see that he did anything wrong.

29. The king says that as long as he was overseas, he commanded his justiciar in England that no parliament should be held until his return.

The earl says that the king may very well have so ordered him.

30. The king says that the justiciar forbade the earl and the rest of the council then present to hold any parliament until the king's arrival.

The earl says that the justiciar may very well have forbidden it.

31. The king says that the earl came to London at Candlemas [2 February] and held parliament.

The earl says that in the common provision made by the king and by his council, it is provided that three parliaments shall be held every year, of which one is at Candlemas; and to keep his oath the earl came there along with the other sound councillors who were in England; and there, at prime, came the justiciar, and told them, from the king, that they should hold no parliament until the king came, and that the king had sent to say he would be back within three weeks, and therefore the parliament was adjourned from day to day for three weeks.

32. The king says that the earl then came to it with horses and arms.

The earl says that he did not come there with either horses or arms, except in the usual way of travelling about the country.[16]

33. The king says that the earl proposed there to remove lord Peter of Savoy from the king's council and to put someone else in his place without the king's knowledge.[17]

The earl says that lord Peter of Savoy himself told him that he had resigned from the council, and as to the king's charge that he spoke of putting someone else in his place, the earl says that he never proposed or spoke of this except in common with the other councillors, and that if any councillor cares to say otherwise, let him say it to the earl's face, and he will answer it.

34. Li rois dit que le conte atreit genz a li et fist noueles aliances.

Le conte dit qu'il n'atret nules genz ne ne fist aliances en contre la foy le roy ne autrement, fors por la comune emprise.

35. Le roy dit qu'il oi dire de la que le conte n'obeist a ses mandemanz, ne ne cint le defans la Iustice, einz parlemanta et quist aliances.

Le conte dit que li rois ou la Iustice dient en quoi il n'obeist as mandemanz le roy ne ne cint le defans la Iustices, et il i respondra uolanciers par droit au parlemant; et as aliances, dit le conte si cum il a dit desus.

36. Le roy dit que sa terre d'Angleterre fu moult esmoue et troblee par acheison del parlement le conte et de ses aliances.

Le conte dit si cum il a dit auant qu'il ne cint parlemant ne ne fit aliances par ont sa terre deust estre esmoue ne troublee.

37. Le roy dit que par telcs acheisons reuint il en Angleterre esforciblemant a granz genz, en quels genz mener il mist grant coust.[18]

Le conte dit qu'il n'auet fet chose dont li rois aust par reison acheison de mener genz a armes en Angleterre, et de ce qu'il les amena et i mist cost ce poise li, quar il n'en estet nuls mestiers.

38. Le roy dit que le conte dit que l'en pensant de herbergier la gent qui uendroet aueques li de la outre en tele manere que autres n'aussent talant de uenir apres.

Le conte dit qu'il dit moult de paroles por le eneur[a] et por le prue le roy por destorber que li rois n'amenast ciels genz, quar il sauet bien que ce n'estet de riens le pro le roy, einz estet sis domatges et contre l'enuer la roy et la terre communemant, quar il semblet qu'il se fiast plus en genz estranges que en genz de sa terre, et se le conte l'auoit dit en tel manere, il ne l'auret dit fors por le pro et por l'enuer le roy et nuls maus n'en uint.

39. Le roy dit que le conte dit a la Iustice qu'il mandast au roy qu'il n'amenast aueques li gent estrange en Angleterre.

Le roy dit que le conte dit a la Iustice qu'il mandant au roy qu'il ne soffrerret mie que le roy menat en Angleterre gent estrange.

[a] enuer MS.

---

[18] Bémont, *Simon de Montfort*, p. 352, n. 1 refers to Rymer, 28 Apr. This should be 20 Apr. (*Foedera*, I. i. 396).

34. The king says that the earl gathered men to himself and made new alliances.

The earl says that he did not gather any men to himself nor did he make any alliances against his fealty to the king or in any other way, save for the common undertaking.

35. The king says that [while he was overseas] he heard tell that the earl did not obey his commands, and did not observe the justiciar's prohibition, but held parliament and sought allies.

The earl says, 'Let the king or the justiciar say in what ways he disobeyed the king's commands and did not observe the justiciar's prohibition, and he will readily answer to it according to the law in parliament'; and as for alliances, the earl says as he has spoken already.

36. The king says that his English kingdom was greatly upset and troubled by reason of the earl's parliament and of his alliances.

The earl says, as he said before, that he held no parliament and made no alliance whereby the land should have been upset and troubled.

37. The king says that for these reasons he was forced to return to England with a large following, and that in bringing these men with him he was put to heavy expense.[18]

The earl says that he had done nothing which would reasonably have justified the king in bringing armed men into England, and that as to his bringing them and incurring expense, that is his own affair, for there never was any need for it.

38. The king says that the earl said they were thinking of giving such a welcome to the men who came with him from overseas, that others would have no great desire to follow them.

The earl says that he said many things for the honour and profit of the king to dissuade him from bringing such a following, for he well knew that this would not profit the king in the least, but would be harmful and dishonourable both to the king and to the country, for it seemed that he put his trust more in foreigners than in the men of his own land; and so if the earl did say any such thing, he would not have said it save for the profit and honour of the king, and no harm came of it.

39. The king says that the earl told the justiciar to tell the king not to bring foreigners with him into England; that he should tell the king that he would not allow him to bring foreigners into England; that if he did tell the king these things in the manner

Le roy dit que le conte dit a la Iustice que si il eisint mandat au roy cum il est desus dit, bien l'auoeret en cal fet et bien contre tous le meintendret.

Le roy dit que la ou il fu par dela et manda en Angleterre a la Iustice qu'il li enuoiast deniers, la dit le conte a la Iustice qu'il point ne li enuoiast.[19]

Le roy dit que le conte de Leycestre dit a la Iustice que se il li enuoiast deniers il les rendret.

A plusors articles que li rois dit que le conte dit a la Iustice, dit le conte que si il rien en dit, il le dit deuant le conseil et por ce deuant le conseil en respondre au roy, quar autremant se cuideret il meffeire.

30

9 MARCH 1261

*Grauamina pro quibus dominus rex queritur de consilio suo**

*a*Hec sunt grauamina pro quibus dominus rex (scilicet Henricus iiicius) queritur de consilio suo.*a*

a-a *Denholm-Young suggested that this was Dugdale's gloss (E.H.R. xlviii, 572, n. 1), but an asterisk by the word* Hec *and a similar mark by f. 243ᵛ left-hand margin, opposite* Hec *suggest that the words beginning* Hec *were in the MS. from which Dugdale made his copy. See nn. d and g.*

---

* *Text*: Bodleian Library, Dugdale MS. 20, ff. 137ᵛ–138ᵛ (D). *Printed*: N. Denholm-Young, 'Documents of the Barons' Wars', *E.H.R.* xlviii (1933), 572–5; *Collected Papers*, pp. 127–9. *Additional Text*: Muniments of the Dean and Chapter of Durham, Locellus, 1. 62 (incomplete). *See*: *Baronial Plan*, pp. 253–6. The numbers in square brackets refer to similar clauses in doc. 31.

Mr. Denholm-Young suggests that Dugdale copied this document from that part of the Cotton MS. Titus C. ix which is now missing. The folio references in the margin presumably allude to the source from which the copy was made. Furthermore, Denholm-Young claims that the date given at the end of this document—*vii Idus Marcii, anno domini mcclx* (9 Mar. 1260)—is correct, i.e. that this is not contemporary with document 31 which very probably dates from Mar.–Apr. 1261.

The evidence used to assert that document 30 is dated 9 Mar. 1260 is:

1. The original MS. came from Derley (*recte* Darley, co. Derby). The author of the document probably followed the Benedictine custom of dating the Year of Grace from Christmas.

stated, the earl would warrant the justiciar in doing this, and would support him against all comers. The king says that when he was overseas and sent to England for the justiciar to send him money, the earl thereupon told the justiciar that he should by no means send him any,[19] and that if he did send him money, he would have to repay it himself.

On the several charges on which the king says 'the earl said to the justiciar', the earl replies that if he said any of these things, he said them before the council, and before the council, therefore, will he answer the king for them, for he believes that otherwise he would be acting wrongly.

30

9 MARCH 1261

The lord king's grievances against his council

These are the grievances upon which the lord king (i.e. Henry III) complains of his council:

2. The mention, in clauses 20 and 21, which do not appear in document 31, of the Lord Edward's opposition to the king (see doc. 17, n. 2; doc. 22, n. 2).

3. Clause 2 does not mention the fall of Builth castle which appears in clause 21 of document 31. This he explains by the fact that Builth castle fell on 17 July 1260, after the date of this document.

4. Those clauses which appear in document 31 and not in document 30 refer to the decline in reformer–king relations after Mar. 1260.

Many objections against the dating suggested by Mr. Denholm-Young may be argued:

1. King Henry III was in France 14 Nov.–23 Apr. 1260. It is difficult to explain why he should produce a list of complaints dated 9 Mar. 1260. Why did he not wait until he returned to England?

2. Sir F. M. Powicke (*King Henry III*, p. 421, n. 3), who believes that the author of the MS. followed the chancery practice of beginning the Year of Grace on 25 Mar., so that 9 Mar. 1260 on the MS. is 9 Mar. 1261 when the Year of Grace begins on 1 Jan., sees no foundation for Denholm-Young's claim that the writer of the document began his year at Christmas. Furthermore, there is no proof that a document which came from an abbey of Augustinian canons, Darley, followed a possible Benedictine custom.

3. The king, wishing to rake together all possible grievances against the council may well have mentioned any complaints without considering when they

[*Cont. p. 212*]

[19] This is the sole evidence of this action, which de Montfort did not deny.

1 [20]. [b]Inprimis quod illi de consilio domini regis non sunt
prosecuti negotium Sicilie et Apulie cum effectu, nec ad hoc
intenderunt sicut promiserunt. Ita quod dominus Rex indebitatus
est pro hoc ad c. mille marcarum et amplius pro defectu ipsorum.[1]

2 [21]. Item dominus rex exhereditatus est uel quasi, de terra
sua Wallie pro defectu consilii et auxilii ad quam recuperandam
promiserunt se opem et operam efficacem impensuros et nichil
adhuc fecerunt.[2]

3 [1]. Item de debitis suis adquietandis nichil fecerunt et
dominus rex minus expendit quam solebat et nichil dat et parum
habet, ita quod omnes prouentus regni sui quos percipit non
sufficiunt ad tenuem sustentacionem hospicii sui eo quod prouentus
f. 138   et redditus[c] | terre sue et scaccarii sui plus diminuuntur modo
quam prius de x. milia marcarum et amplius.[3]

4 [2]. Item de regno Anglie nulla exhibetur iusticia communis
sed totum regnum depauperatum est plus quam prius.

5 [3]. Item iura domini regis deperiunt cotidie in manibus
prauorum balliuorum quos ipsi de consilio posuerunt qui non
sunt ausi ingredi aliquas terras cuiuscumque de consilio ad
iusticiam faciendam ut deceret.

6. [d]Item de quibus dominus rex conquiritur grauiter, et ipsi
qui dominum regem implacitant sunt de consilio suo contra
rationabilem uoluntatem domini regis et contra conuencionem
habitam inter dominum regem et ipsos.[4]

7 [5]. Item quando dominus rex posuit se in consilio ipsorum
non posuit se in custodia sua cum sit plene etatis ut uidetur

[b] Grauamina Regi H.3 illata per Barones *in margin. The writer seems to have
misinterpreted this document.*   [c] Redditus] Redditus, D.   [d] *Asterisks
by* Item *and f. 244.*

Note * (*p. 211*) *cont.*

occurred. This would destroy Denholm-Young's arguments in points 2–4
mentioned above.

There are several differences between documents 30 and 31:

1. Document 30 is in Latin, document 31 is in French.
2. Document 30 does not record the council's answers as does document 31.
3. Differences in content of the two documents. The text in the Dugdale MS.
(doc. 30) is arranged in paragraphs which have been numbered for ease of
reference. The number in square brackets refers to the similar clause in document 31.

The differences between the two documents, assuming that they both date
from Mar.–Apr. 1261, may be explained if the Latin MS. (doc. 30) was a formal
set of complaints submitted by the king for consideration of the arbitrators who
were appointed in Mar. 1261 (*Flores Hist.* ii, 466). The French document with

1 [20]. First, that the king's councillors have not effectively pro-
ceeded with the business of Sicily and Apulia, nor have they
attended to it as they promised, so that the lord king is indebted
in this matter for 100,000 marks and more, by their negligence.[1]

2 [21]. Next, the lord king is disinherited, or almost so, of his
land of Wales owing to the lack of counsel and aid, for the recovery
of which they promised they would lend help and labour, whereas
they have until now done nothing.[2]

3 [1]. Further, they have done nothing for the acquitting of his
debts, and the lord king spends less than he used to do, gives away
nothing, and has little, so that all the revenues which he receives
from his realm do not suffice for the slender maintenance of his
household, because his receipts and the revenues of his lands and
his Exchequer are now diminished by over 10,000 marks from
what they formerly were.[3]

4 [2]. Again, no common justice is done in the realm of England,
but the whole realm is impoverished more than it used to be.

5 [3]. Further, the king's rights perish daily in the hands of the
wicked bailiffs whom the councillors appoint, and who dare not
enter any of the lands of any member of the council to do justice
as they ought.

6 [—]. Further, those against whom the lord king complains
greatly, and those who implead the lord king are members of his
council against the reasonable wishes of the lord king, and against
the agreement made between the lord king and them.[4]

7 [5]. Again, when the lord king placed himself under their
counsel he did not put himself into their custody, since he is of

the council's answers (doc. 31) forms the minutes of the hearing conducted by
the arbitrators. This would explain the language difference between the two
MSS.—formal documents in Latin and dated, informal memoranda in French.
This linguistic distinction may be seen in document 5 (see introductory comments on text), and in the difference between documents 11 and 12. Thus the
king would refer to the Lord Edward's disloyalty in the past (doc. 30, cls. 20,
21) merely to add to his grievances—there is no reason why he should be
referring to contemporary events. In addition those additional topics in document 31 could have arisen during the examination before the arbitrators.

[1] Doc. 31, cl. 20 estimates the debt at 200,000 m.
[2] Note absence of mention of Builth castle. See comment on text above.
[3] No evidence is known to support or deny this claim. Doc. 31, cl. 1 mentions
no sum.
[4] Although this clause does not appear in document 31 it closely resembles
cl. 16 below and cl. 14 of document 31.

aliquibus, quoniam si ipse rex diceret melius quam ipsi, quod dictum suum staret et quod ipsi non facerent peius quam ipse dixerit⁵ et insuper iniuriatum est domino regi quod cum nominaret bonos et utiles ministros scilicet iusticiarium, cancellarium et thesaurarium ipsi de consilio minus idoneos contra uoluntatem suam prefecerunt, et tales qui officium suum penitus ignorabant.

8 [4]. Item nulla ratio quam rex pretendit potest stare, sed ipsi de consilio sic dicunt: uolumus et decreuimus ita fieri: nullam aliam rationem pretendentes.

9 [7]. Item faciunt tractatus suos et consilia sua in diuersis locis domino rege nesciente super quibus nec requirunt dominum regem super hoc, nec eum uocant ad consilium plus quam minorem regni.

10 [6]. Item constituunt nouos balliuos ad iura domini regis seruanda pro uoluntate sua sine rege, ita quod balliui illi non reputant se cum rege propter quod iura sua dissimulant ut placeant aliis plus quam sibi.

11 [8]. Item alii^e subtraxerunt regi posse suum et dignitatem regalem quod nullus perficit preceptum suum sed minus obedient mandato suo quam minori de consilio.

12 [17]. Item nituntur amouere a domino rege illos quos plus diligit et qui bene sciunt expedire negotia sua ad commodum honorem et uoluntatem domini regis.

13 [18]. Item malefactores et predones discurrentes per patriam uarias depredaciones faciunt ita quod nuper familia domini regis in transitu suo depredata fuit in passu de Alton⁶ et minati sunt depredari carectas domini regis et dare insultas domino regi tales correctiones modo sunt per Angliam et non alie.

14 [22]. Item^f pro defectu ipsorum de consilio prorogata est extenta de Age' ad graue dampnum et dedecus domini regis.

^e alii *Denholm-Young*, alio D.   ^f Item *Denholm-Young*, ita D.

⁵ See doc. 31, n. 8.
⁶ Denholm-Young suggests that this clause could allude to the king's presence at Alton on 1 Oct. 1259. However, as Henry III was at Winchester in Aug. 1260 and in Jan. 1261 this complaint is no direct evidence for dating document 30 in Mar. 1260. In Feb. 1260 the council ordered special watch for malefactors (*Flores Hist.*, ii. 442; *Chron. Majora*, vi. 512).

full age, and it seems to some that if the king proposes something better than they, that his opinion should prevail, and that they should not do something less good than he proposes:[5] and especially is the king deprived of his rights in that when he nominated good and useful ministers as justiciar, chancellor, and treasurer, the councillors, against his wishes, took less suitable men who were wholly ignorant of their offices.

8 [4]. Further, no proposal which the king puts forward can prevail, but the councillors simply say 'We will and decree that it be done so', offering no other reason.

9 [7]. Further, they hold their discussions and meetings at various places without the king's knowledge, not asking the king to attend them, nor summoning him to the council any more than the least person of his kingdom.

10 [6]. Further, they appoint new bailiffs to preserve the king's rights at their own pleasure without consulting the king, so that these bailiffs do not consider themselves the king's agents, and therefore they ignore the king's rights to please others rather than him.

11 [8]. Again, these others have taken away from the king his power and royal dignity, so that no one carries out his orders, and they obey his command less than that of the lowest member of his council.

12 [17]. Further, they try to remove from the lord king those whom he loves best and who know how to discharge his business fittingly, to the honour and satisfaction of the lord king.

13 [18]. Again, malefactors and robbers roving up and down the land inflict many acts of brigandage, as when recently the household of the lord king himself was plundered in passing through the Pass of Alton,[6] and the king's baggage-wagons were threatened with plundering, and insults given to the lord king; and such offences are now common throughout England but not in other countries.

14 [22]. Further, by the fault of the councillors, the making of the extent of the Agenais has been delayed, to the great loss and shaming of the lord king.

15. Item estimatio pecunie recipiende a domino rege Francie in forma pacis pro militibus prorogata est per defectum.[7]

16 [14]. Item quidam de magnatibus minantur domino regi et plebi plusquam prius et de iniuriis per ipsos factis nulle fiunt emende ut deceret.

17 [15]. Item sokemanni et alii tenentes domini regis magis grauantur modo et peius quam alii de regno.

18 [16]. Item domus castrorum et maneriorum domini regis et libertates sue decidunt et deperiunt pro defectu auxilii.

19 [17]. Item de die in diem nituntur artare et diminuere statum regis contra uoluntatem suam nullo alio commodo inde proueniente.[8]

20. [g]Item permittunt Edwardum filium regis distrahere que dominus rex ei dedit in augmentum corone Anglie et que ei tradita[h] | fuerunt ut non separentur a corona Anglie sicut patet per cartas suas.[9]

21. Item per consilium quorundam subtractus est ab amicicia et uoluntate paterna facienda.[10]

22 [9]. Item dominus rex nullam habet potestatem de sigillo suo sed illi de consilio modo disponunt pro uoluntate sua domino rege nesciente.

23 [10]. Item cum placita mota coram domino rege debeant et consueuerunt coram ipso placitari, derogatur honori regis quod placita illa trahuntur post iusticiarium Anglie ubicunque agat in remotis, ita quod nullus aliquod remedium reportat apud regem pro defectu iusticiarii secum existentis unde multi conqueruntur et grauantur ob defectum iusticie consuete.

f. 138[v]

---

[g] *Asterisks by* Item *and by f. 244[v] in margin* D. *See note* [a–a]   [h] Tradita|
Traditur, D.

---

[7] The topic to which reference is made is that clause in the Peace of Paris, 1259, which obliged Louis IX to pay Henry III enough money to maintain five hundred knights for two years (*Foedera*, I. i. 389; *Treaty Rolls, 1234–1325*, p. 371; *Diplomatic Documents, 1101–1272*, nos. 299, 302, 305; not, as Denholm-Young claims, clause 23 of document 31, *E.H.R.* xlviii, 574). The sum of money was to be decided by arbitrators but it was not until Jan. 1264 that a decision was reached—134,000 *livres tournois*. Meanwhile Louis IX made advance payments to King Henry; 39,580 *livres tournois* in 1260 and an additional 30,416 in 1261. In Jan. 1264 the English king recognized that he had received 76,000 *livres tournois* (the only recorded amount is *c.* 70,000) and Louis IX was to pay the balance, half in 1264 and half in 1265 (*Peace of Paris*, p. 61, n. 1; *C.P.R. 1258–66*, pp. 81, 194, 379). The money which King Henry received in 1260 and 1261 made it possible for him to hire mercenary troops to use against his

15 [–]. Further, by their fault, the assessment of the money to be received from the lord king of France under the terms of the treaty for the maintenance of the knights has been delayed.[7]

16 [14]. Further, certain of the magnates menace the lord king and his people more than ever before, and no recompense is made for the injuries which they inflict as there should be.

17 [15]. Further, the socmen and other tenants of the lord king are now more and worse harmed than any others in the realm.

18 [16]. Further, the buildings of the castles and manors of the lord king and of his liberties are decaying and falling into ruin for lack of care.

19 [–]. Further, they daily seek to hedge around and diminish the state of the king against his will, though no good comes of this to anyone else.[8]

20 [–]. Further, they permit Edward, the king's son, to squander the possessions which the lord king gave him for strengthening the crown of England, and which were given to him on condition that they should not be separated from the crown of England, as is evident from his charters.[9]

21 [–]. Further, by the counsel of a certain man, Edward has been seduced from his father's friendship and obedience.[10]

22 [9]. Further, the lord king has no power over his seal, but the councillors now settle matters at their will without the king's foreknowledge.

23 [10]. Further, whereas pleas initiated before the lord king ought to be pleaded before him, the king's honour is diminished in that these pleas are taken before the Justiciar of England, wherever he may be, even in remote places, so that no one can get any redress from the king's court, for lack of justices in attendance on him, so that many are aggrieved and complain of the failure of accustomed justice.

opponents in England (doc. 20, n. 1). See doc. 31, n. 26 for the Agenais. The topic of doc. 30, cl. 15 does not appear in doc. 31.

[8] Denholm-Young is mistaken in suggesting that this clause corresponds to clauses 15 and 17 in doc. 31 (*E.H.R.* xlviii. 574). It resembles cl. 11 above and cl. 8 of doc. 31.

[9] The Lord Edward pawned estates to William de Valence, half-brother of the king, to whom he granted Stamford, Yorks., and Grantham, Lincs., in 1258 (*Chron. Majora*, v. 679).

[10] See comments above on this text.

24 [12]. Item cum rex ab antiquo debeat conferre wardas suas illis maxime qui sibi bene seruierunt et diu, iam adeo restringitur sua potestas quod quicquid ipse de restitucione heredum uel aliis ad hoc spectantibus preceperit mandatum suum non expletur set potius contemnitur tanquam non regnaret et hoc in preiudicium ipsius et heredum suorum.

25 [11]. Item iusticiarius mittit breuia sua per Angliam de ardua gracia inconsulto rege ad placitandum coram iusticiario ubicunque fuerint super hiis que placitari solent coram domino rege et pro quibus consueuit magnam recipere pecuniam et nichil capit per quod sigillum suum deterioratum est de finibus pro graciis concedendis.

26 [24]. Item cum omnes de consilio iurauerunt regi fidelitatem et honorem terrenum sibi et heredibus suis exhibere, ipsi quasi illius iuramenti immemores et obliti ob uoluntatem et gratuitam obligationem domini regis eis factam de stando consiliis ipsorum super releuatione et status regis et regni ipsum cum honore et pristina dignitate regali priuauerunt contra primum iuramentum de homagiis et contra secundum iuramentum de iure et honore regi seruandis prout inter ipsos conuenit, ut in prouerbiis; Qui nimis emungit sanguinem elicit.[11] Dat. vii⁰ idus Marcii, anno domini M°cclx°.[12]

31

c. MARCH–APRIL 1261

Les greuancez dont le roy se pleynt*[1]

Cez sount les greuancez dont le roy se pleynt de son conseil, que luy deuoit auer conseil al honour de Dieu et a le roi et au profit de son reaume.

---

* *Text*: *British Museum*, Cotton MS. Tiberius B. iv, ff. 214ᵛ–18 (T). The MS. text contains no paragraphs. These have been made for ease of reference. *Printed*: E. F. Jacob, 'Complaints of Henry III against the Baronial Council in 1261', *E.H.R.* xli (1926), 564–71. Differences from the MS. are not noted here. The numbers in square brackets refer to the similar clauses in document 30.

This document, unlike no. 30, is not dated but indirect evidence suggests that it may have originated in Mar. or Apr. 1261. The mention of the loss of Builth castle, 17 July 1260 (cl. 21) and the death of Henry de Bath in Aug. or

24 [12]. Again, whereas of old the king was accustomed to grant his wardships especially to those who had served him well and long, now is his power so restricted that whatever he commands concerning restitution of heirs and other related matters, his orders are not fulfilled, but rather despised as though he were not king, and this is prejudicial both to him and to his heirs.

25 [11]. Again, the justiciar sends throughout England his writs of special favour without consulting the king, for pleas to be taken before the justiciar wherever he may be, on matters which are customarily pleaded before the lord king, and for which he used to receive large sums of money, whereas now he receives nothing from this source, so that his seal is worth less by the amount of the fines for granting his grace.

26 [24]. Finally, whereas all members of the council swore fealty to the king, and swore to show temporal honour to him and to his heirs, now, as though forgetful of that oath, by reason of the free and unforced promise which the lord king made to them that he would abide by their advice on the restoration of the state of the king and of the realm, they have stripped him of all honour and of his original royal dignity, against their first oath, that of homage, and against their second oath, that of preserving the king's right and honour,[11] as was agreed between them, as it says in Proverbs, 'The wringing of the nose bringeth forth blood.'[11] Dated 9 March 1261.[12]

31

c. MARCH–APRIL 1261

The grievances of which the king complains[1]

These are the grievances of which the king complains against his council, which ought to give him advice to the honour of God and of the king, and to the profit of the realm.

Sept. 1260 (cl. 10) is direct evidence of the document dating at least in the early autumn of 1260. Indirect evidence suggesting spring 1261 is:

1. The answers to clauses 22 and 23 suggest that the council had ceased meeting. The last order of the council is dated 28 Dec. 1260, while there is indirect evidence of its meeting in Feb. 1261 (see n. 28 below). [*Cont. p. 220*]

---

[11] See doc. 31, n. 29; Proverbs 30 : 33.   [12] See above comment on text.

[1] Taken from first line of MS.

1 [3]. Al comencement, de ceo que de la dette du roy aquiter sez conseillours rien ount fait, et le roi mesmes[a] despent plus qil ne soleit et poy donne, et ad issy que touz les issuez de son regne sount meyndres qe ne lessoloient estre auant qil se obligea a eux del conseil.

A ceo le conseil dit et respount qil fuist purueu que le iustice et aultrez feisont pur pru le roy des gardes et des mariages quant ilz eschairount, et un partie meist as dettes le roi acquitere et une

f. 215   partie a sustenement de | son hostiel, et issy fuit fait en temps S' Hug' Bygot taunt come le roi suffrit,[2] et auxi le fet lem uncore sil pleist au roi. Le conseil dit et respont que de ceo ne sunt ilz nul coupe, kar ils ount souent monstre qil amenusast lez despensez de son hostiel, lez queux[3] illour semble trop grauntez, et il rien ne uoet faire de lour priere.[b] Le conseil dist et respount que le roy sy luy plest, mustre encheson pur quoy ceo est, et qi eu ceste ad coupe et ils se frount amendere uoluntierz com a seigneur.

2 [4]. Derechief, droyture est fayt meys qe ne soleit[4] et le regne est enpoueri pluis qe auant.

Le conseil dit et respount qe lem ueyt par qi droit est destorbee et face lem amendere: le regne est enpouerie par lez felons anez que sount escie, si qe lez gentz morrount par tut de feyme,[5] et ne mye par eux.

3 [5]. Derechief, lez droitures de regne deperisont au meyns des maluois baillifs que conselerez ount mys, qils ne osent entrere en terre de ffraunchise dascun de conseil ou daultre qe les touche, affaire droiture sil apent ou lez droitures del regne demandere ou

---

[a] Mesmes *may be an inaccurate copy of* meyns (meins) *and* plus *was perhaps included in error. The Latin text (doc. 30, cl. 3) states that the king was spending less but the barons' answer in this document suggests that they believed that he was spending more.*   [b] T *adds* que *which appears to be redundant unless a subordinate clause has been omitted.*

Note * (*p. 219*) *cont.*

2. The answer to clause 10 mentions Nicholas de Turri and the Cambridge eyre, to which he was appointed Dec. 1260–Jan. 1261. Furthermore, it was said that the eyre duties had kept de Turri from attending the king 'until this present parliament'—presumably the one which met in Mar. 1261. On 9 Mar. it was stated that Nicholas de Turri was lately in Cambridge (see notes 13, 14; *C.P.R. 1258–66*, p. 144; *Baronial Plan*, pp. 395–6). References for the summons of parliament to meet on 23 Feb. are incorrect in *Baronial Plan*, p. 251, n. 4; *British Chronology*, p. 503.

The text in T follows immediately after a copy of the Provisions of Oxford (doc. 5) which ends, in the list of castles and castellans, with the words *Deuises com. de Warewick*. This document is the last extract in Tiberius B. iv. Folio

1 [3]. Firstly, of this, (a) that his councillors have done nothing to pay off the king's debt, and (b) that the king is now spending even more than he used to, though he gives away little; and moreover that (c) all the receipts from his kingdom are lower than they used to be before he bound himself to their counsel.

To this the council says in reply that (a) it was decided that the justiciar and others should sell the wardships and marriages for the king's profit when they fell in, and should set aside part of the proceeds to reduce the king's debts, and use part for the maintenance of his household; that this was done in the time of Sir Hugh Bigod for as long as the king would allow,[2] and that this would be done again if it pleased the king. (b) The council says in reply that they are blameless in this matter, for they have often shown that the king should reduce his household expenses, which seem to them too great, but that he will do nothing about their request.[3] (c) The council say in reply that if the king will show reason why this is so, and who is to blame for it, they will gladly put matters right as is due to their lord.

2 [4]. Next: (a) justice is less well done than it used to be,[4] and (b) the kingdom is more impoverished than before.

The council says in reply, (a) let it be shown by whom justice is being hindered, and they shall be forced to make amends. (b) The kingdom is impoverished by the evil years they have had, so that everywhere men are dying of famine;[5] it is in no way their doing.

3 [5]. Further, the rights of the crown dwindle away in the hands of the ineffective officers whom the councillors have appointed, and who dare not enter the lands of any liberty belonging to any member of the council, or do anything else which affects councillors, to do justice, when it is necessary either to demand or to pursue the rights of the crown within their county; and nothing

---

218ᵛ has twenty-four short lines of a prayer in Latin. Some sentences are very difficult to translate, mainly because of the corruption of the MS. in copying. Uncertain words and phrases have been marked by obelisks.

---

[2] Doc. 12, cls. 8, 14.   [3] Doc. 37A, cl. 5; doc. 38, cl. 14.
[4] Complaint of the failure to administer justice and attempts at reform are numerous during the years 1258-61 (Docs. 3, 12, 13).
[5] The chronicles record famine, resulting from the failure of the harvest in 1257, and shortage of food is mentioned in doc. 3, cl. 21 (Baronial Plan, pp. 64, 102, 173, n. 2, 237). See doc. 31, cl. 27.

sowire dount tiel contie, qe rien ne rent del corps del countie com
il soleyt, pur ceo qe ne list pas as baillifs en le honour lour franchise
mes taunt soulement sur lur ueynes puruiances.[6]

Le conseil dist et respont qils ne mettent nullz baillifs: il
donnent forme as barons del eschekere coment eux lez deyuent
mettre, cesta sauere par quatre chyualerz de chescun countie qe
par lour serment elisent lez uiscountes[7] et les uiscountes ne facent
ceo qe deyuent se soit amende au roy com a seigneur, et si lem
desterbee les uiscountes ou autrez baillifs qilz ne puisent fere lour
officez, soit enquis par qi cest, et soit amende si come doyt estre au
seigneur. Et sy la manere de eslire lez uiscountez ne soit pas bone,
soit mayntenaunt amende.

4 [8]. Derechief, nul resoune qe le roy dist ne puist estre qe
ceux du conseil ne disunt, nous uoloms qe issy soyt, et autre
resoune ne mettent; et ceo piert qe quant le roy noma bones
ministrez et profitablez justice, tresorer et chauncelere, les
conseillerz meyns couenablez encountre la uolunte le roy mystrent.

Le conseil dist et respount qe bien est droit qe la ou le roy
dit bien, qil soit si pluis auant qe nul autre. Mes en droit de ceo
qilz ne mistrent iustice, tre|sorere, chaunceler, tiels come le roy
noma, respount le conseil qe purueu fuist a comencement qe
tiels ministrez fuissent par elecioun de ceux du conseil et dient
ceux du conseil; qil donerent lour poer a synk de eslire ceux
ministrez, et si nostre seigneur le roy uoet sauer par quoy ceux
qil noma ne furent esluz, fail qe lez cynks elisours soient assois
de la sentence dount le ercheuesque lez lia sils discouerisent parole
qe la fuit dit de nulli persone, et eux li mustrent bone encheson et
uerroy par quoi ils en fyrount.[8]

5 [7]. Derechief, quant le roi se mit en lour conseil il se ne mys
pas en garde, ne qil misent comaundement; qe doit meulz qe son
dit estorroit, et qilz ne feisent auant qe le roy le dit.[9]

Le conseil dit et respount qil nentenderont pas qe lour seigneur
soit en nuli garde, ne ilz ne ueudreyount pas qil fuist, †ne resoun ne

f. 215ᵛ

---

[6] Doc. 5, cl. 1.

[7] Doc. 12, cl. 22 states that sheriffs were to be appointed in the autumn of
1259 by the justiciar and others. Future sheriffs were to be appointed when four
knights, chosen in each county, appeared before the exchequer at Michaelmas.
It is not known if the four knights presented one of their number as sheriff or
if the exchequer chose one of the four to hold this office. There is evidence to
suggest that the four-knight method was used in the spring of 1259 (*Baronial
Plan*, pp. 205–6). See doc. 5, cl. 17; doc. 12, cl. 9.

is returned from the body of the counties as it used to be, because the officials are not allowed within the honours of their [the councillors'] franchises, but only by their permission, which has no basis in law.[6]

The council says in reply that they do not appoint any officials: they give to the barons of the exchequer directions as to how they are to appoint them, that is by four knights from each county who, on their oath, choose sheriffs.[7] Sheriffs who act wrongly shall make amends to the king as their lord, and if anyone opposes the sheriffs so that they cannot discharge their duties, let inquiry be made to discover who is to blame, and it shall be put right, as it should be to their lord. And if the method of choosing the sheriffs is not good, let it be changed at once.

4 [8]. Further, no argument which the king puts forward can prevail: the councillors reply 'We wish it to be thus', without giving any further reason; for example, when the king nominated good and useful persons to be justiciar, treasurer, and chancellor, the councillors appointed less suitable persons against the king's wishes.

The council says in reply that it is indeed right that when the king talks sense he should have his way more than any other person. But as to their not appointing the king's nominees to be justiciar, treasurer, and chancellor, the council says that from the start it was agreed that these ministers should be appointed by election by the councillors, and the councillors say that they committed their power to five men, to choose these officials, and if our lord the king wishes to know why these whom he nominated were not chosen, the five electors must be absolved from the sentence which the archbishop imposed on them should they ever reveal a word of what was spoken by any of them there; then they will show him sound reasons and he will see why they acted as they did.[8]

5 [7]. Again, when the king agreed to accept their counsel he did not make himself their ward, nor did he agree that they should give orders; and if what he says is better, then his proposal should stand, and they should not take action before the king has agreed.[9]

The council says in reply that they have no intention of treating their lord as a ward, and that they do not wish that he should be

[8] Doc. 5, cls. 13–15. This is the first evidence of appointment being made by a committee of five, chosen by the council and bound by an oath of secrecy.

[9] Doc. 30, cl. 7 suggests that the council might fairly prefer its own policy or plan where it was better than that of the king. This text implies that the council should never act until it had the king's consent.

lapartene a nuli comandement†, et dient qil est droit et resoun que
par tut la ou diarra bien, qil soit oie et entendu cum cil qest
seigneur de eux touz.

6 [10]. Derechief il establirent nouels baillifs et nient connuz
du roy a le droiture le roy garder, et issy qe ces baillifs ne se deyent
pas estre de parte le roy, et issynt perisount lez droitures le roy
en lours mayns, kar pluys pleisent a aultrez qe au roy.

Le conseil dit et respount qils ne mettont pas les baillifs;
eux sount ceux del eschekere si come il est desus dit,[10] et cil ad
nul baillif qe ne sawoue par le roy ou die cele parole ou est la
fraunchise le roy deperit, †si le compre† si come deuera solom le
trespas.

7 [9]. Derechief, ils fount lour tretez et lours conseils en diuersez
luez des bosoignes le roy et de regne, noun sachant le roy, ne ils
lez demaundount a lour conseil pluis qe le meyndre du regne, tut
soit il chief del conseil.

Le conseil dit et respount qils tretount meynte foith en lieus
ou il cruident qils soient pluis en pees et hors de noyse[11] pur
myeus entendre as bosoignes le roy, et puys, quant ils ount tretez,
si maundent de roy son asent et sa uolunte come au seigneur e a
chief, mes ils ne fount rien pur soun dit.

8 [11]. Daultre part ount sustret a roy son poer, dignite, reaute,
issint qe poy ou nient est fait pur soun comaundement † et necessarie
et honeste†.

Le conseil dit et respount qils obeirent au roy come a lour
seigneur, ne ils attendent pas qe sa dignite, reaute, ne soun poer
luy soient sustretez, et sil i ad nul qe ne obeise a sez resonablez
comaundement monstre, si plest a luy, ou e en quoy, et lem emendra
come a seigneur.

9 [22]. Daultre part le roy ad nul poer de son seal, mes ceux
fount lour uolontee saunz le sey le roy.[12]

Le conseil dit et respount qe de son seal ne firent unqes sin
a son pru e a son honour, et de ceo qil dist qil nad poer de son

---

[10] See nn. 6, 7, above.

[11] In spring 1259 the meetings were held at the New Temple, in London,
called 'the headquarters of the council' (Baronial Council, p. 123 and n. 3).

[12] Doc. 5, cl. 7. In July 1259 when Henry de Wingham, the chancellor, was
abroad the king used Walter de Merton to issue letters patent, without consult-

so, †or that he should be under any sort of orders†, and they say that it is right and reasonable that whenever he talks sense he should be heard and listened to as the lord of them all.

6 [10]. Further, that they appoint new officials who are not known to the king, to safeguard the king's rights, so that these officials do not regard themselves as the king's agents, and thus the king's rights wither in their hands, since they look to others rather than to the king.

The council says in reply that they do not appoint the officials: they are appointed by the exchequer as has already been explained;[10] and if there be any official who does not recognize himself to be the king's agent, or who says anything whereby the king's liberties are damaged, †let him be punished† as he ought to be, according to the offence.

7 [9]. Further, they hold their business meetings and discussions concerning the business of the king and of his realm in various places without informing the king, and they do not ask for him at their meetings any more than they ask the humblest subject in the realm, although he is the head of the council.

The council says in reply that they meet frequently in places where they think that they will be less disturbed and away from the bustle[11] so as to be able to attend all the better to the king's business, and then, when they have discussed matters, they ask the king for his assent and goodwill, as is due to their lord and to their head, but they do nothing on his sole word.

8 [11]. Further, they have deprived the king of his power, dignity, and regality, so that little or nothing is done at †his necessary and honourable† commands.

The council says in reply that they obey the king as their lord and do not intend that his dignity, regality, or power should be taken from him, and if there is anyone who does not obey his reasonable commands, let the king, if it please him, say who, or in what matter, and they will put this right as is due to their lord.

9 [22]. Further, the king has no control over his own seal, but they do as they like without the king's knowledge.[12]

The council says in reply that they have never done anything with his seal that was not to his profit and his honour; and as

ing the council, for the papal legate Velascus to enter England (*C.P.R. 1258–66*, p. 35; R. F. Treharne, 'An unauthorised use of the great seal', *E.H.R.* xl (1925), 403–11).

f. 216 seal, al lour semble qil ne fait poynt semblaunt, car il donne sez
gardes et sez eschetes et feffes gentz | par sa chartre, la quele il ne
doit pas fere, si lui plest, saunz ceux de conseil, solonc la couenant
qe lour ad feat.

10 [23]. Dautre part come touz plaiez somons deuant le roy
deyuent et soloient deuant luy estre pledez, et cez pleez sount
pledez aillours loyns du roy pur defaute de iustice, si qe nul
pleignant droiture puit auoir pres de roy dount les riches et les
pouerez mult sount greues de trauaille et despensez, et greuement
se pleignent de iustice, et issint perit le honour le roy et le droiture
acustumie.

Le conseil dist et respount qe bien est reson qe iusticez sue le
roy mes pur la mort H. de B.,[13] et par sustrete dautre iusticez, fu
atornee a Nichole de la turre qil deuoit estre as pleez le roy en
le heyre de Cantebrigge, si remist de purueiere justice a siwere
le roy deqes a ceo parlement,[14] et ceo qe ne fust fait donqes
soit fait ore.

11 [25]. Derechief, le justice enuoyt parmy la terre sez briefs
de graunt grace, par qoy le roy soleyt auoir graunt auere pur auer
lez pleez deuant luy, et ore sount tretez apres le iustice la ou il uoet,
et despise le roy, par quoi le seal poy uaut a regard de temps passe
†quant a grauntiere†.

Le conseil respount qe le iustice doit respoundre de cest
chapitre article come de soun fait.

12 [24]. Derechief, come le roy soleit autrement donere sez
wardes nomement a ceux qe longement lauoient seruie, taunt est
restreint le poer le roy qe poy ou nient est fait de ceo pur son
comandement, ne de rendre lez heirs mes dautre chose a ces
apartenant, et issi est le comaundement le roy despit auxi come
mesme ⟨ne⟩[c] regnast.

Le conseil dit et respount qe par le roy mesmes et par le comune
dengleterre fust conseil esluz au roy sil mesmes otrea qiles crerreit
et orreit a lour conseil des gardes et des chetes et dautrez ualuez

---

[c] T *omits* ne *which is present in the Latin version* (doc. 30, cl. 24) *and obviously
required by the sense.*

---

[13] Both Henry de Bath and Roger Thurkelby died in Aug. or Sept. 1260
while Nicholas de Turri was commissioned in the counties of Cambridge and
Huntingdon in Dec. 1260 and Jan. 1261 (*Baronial Plan*, p. 249; *C.R. 1259–61*,
pp. 332, 452; E. F. Jacob, *E.H.R.* xli. 566, n. 4 has an incorrect reference).

regards his complaint that he has no control over his seal, it seems to them far from the truth, for he grants his wardships and his escheats and enfeoffs people by his charters, which, if it please him, he ought not to do without the consent of the councillors according to the covenant which he made with them.

10 [23]. Further, whereas all pleas summoned before the king ought to be, and customarily are, pleaded before him, now these pleas are pleaded elsewhere, far from the king's presence, for lack of justice, so that no plaintiff can obtain justice in the king's presence, whereby both rich and poor are greatly burdened with travel and expense, and complain greatly about justice, so that the king's honour and the accustomed standard of justice are perishing.

The council says in reply that it is indeed right that justice should attend on the king; but owing to the death of Henry de Bath,[13] and the withdrawal of other justices, Nicholas de Turri was assigned to take the king's pleas in the Cambridgeshire eyre, and so he had to give up doing justice in attendance on the king until this present parliament,[14] and what was not attended to then is being attended to now.

11 [25]. Further, the justiciar sends his writs of special favour throughout the land, from which the king used to receive a large income through holding the pleas in his presence; but now these pleas are taken before the justiciar wherever he sees fit, and in despite of the king, whose seal thereby becomes valueless, compared with former times, †in respect of grants of grace†.

The council replies that on this heading the justiciar must answer for his own actions.

12 [24]. Again, whereas the king used formerly to grant his wardships especially to those who had given him long service, now is the king's power so restricted that little or nothing of this kind is done at his orders, neither by way of restoring the heirs nor in any other way pertaining to this matter, and thus the king's command is despised as though he were [not] king.

The council says in reply that by agreement between the king himself and the community of England a council was chosen for the king, who himself granted that he would accept and listen to

Turri's assize roll for Cambridgeshire is Assize Roll 82 (*Reform and Rebellion*, p. 37, n. 6).
[14] Probably the parliament which assembled early in March, 1261 (*Baronial Plan*, pp. 250–3).

de son regne a soun preu et honour, et par eux purueu fust qe les iusticez et autres feisent le preu le roy a ses dettes aquiter si come desus est dit et eyns fu establi par lui par soun conseil.

13[–]. Dautre part par les baillifs des fraunchisez sount ocupiez chescun iour les droitures le roy et de ses fraunchises, et rien nest de ceo fait remedie.[15]

Le conseil dit et respount qe ceo ne sauont ils pas †qe qeun est resoun† qil soit enquis et soit amende, et seyount a ceo atornez ane auenaunt gentz qe ceo sauent.

14 [16]. Derechief, les uns dez grauntz gentz, et nomement ascun de conseil, pluis tort a roy et au people ⟨fount⟩ †ore a par mesmes† quant issy est qe nul amendement est fait ou †resile†.[16]

Le conseil dit et respount qe sil nuli soit, de conseil ou autre, qe eit tre | passe le roy soit sue qe ceux sount, et soit amende come au roy et au seigneur et a autre, com resoun est.

f. 216ᵛ

15 [17]. Dautre part lez soquemans et les propre tenauntz le roy pluis sount greues et pluis sount tretez que autrez du reaume, pur ceo qils nount defense sil ueignent au concles[d] despise, et saunz rien esploiter dispartount.[17]

Le conseil dit et respount qe lez sokemanns le roy ne uindrent unqes deuant eux a pleint faire; si homme lour ad fait tort, ceo soit amende deuaunt les iusticez ou les baronz de leschekere, si come il doit estre, et sil soient malement tretez, soit purueu coment ils serrount defenduz desore en auant.

16 [18]. Derechief, les chasteux du roy et sez maysouns de cez chasteux et de ses maneres e de sez fraunchisez perissent par defaute de eyde.[18]

Le conseil dit et respount que leur mettent amendement, et soit enquis par baillifs et par constables qi est en coupe, et qi lem trouera qil soit en coupes si la mende.

17 [12]. Dautre part le conseil, le roy se peyne, de remuere de luy qil eyme, et les queux il ad troue leaux ieqes ore et bons, les queux seyuent les besoignes le roy expleitere a preu et honour et

---

[d] *This is obviously a mistake. Possible correction:* conseil, il les.

---

[15] See n. 5 above and doc. 10, n. 2; doc. 12, cl. 5; doc. 13, cl. 2.
[16] See doc. 5, cl. 1; doc. 13, cl. 11.
[17] A section of the Provisions of Westminster protected the rights of tenants in socage (doc. 11, cl. 12).
[18] See doc. 3, cls. 4, 5, 15; doc. 4; doc. 5, cl. 8; doc. 12, cl. 27.

their advice concerning wardships, escheats, and other valuable
royal rights to his profit and honour, and that it was provided by
them that the justices and others should, for the king's advantage,
pay off his debts, as has already been said, and as it was formerly
decreed by him on their counsel.

13 [–]. Moreover, the bailiffs of liberties have daily encroached
upon the rights and liberties of the king, and no remedy is provided in this matter.[15]

The council says in reply that they know nothing of this, and
that †if it is true†, that it should be inquired into and put right,
and that last year commissioners were appointed for this purpose
to take cognisance of these things.

14 [16]. Further, that some of the magnates, and particularly
some of the council, do more wrong to the king and to the people
now †than ever before†, since now it is the case that no remedy or
†relief† is provided.[16]

The council says in reply that if anyone, councillor or anyone
else, has done wrong to the king, let it be known who these men
are, and let amends be made to the king as to their lord, or to any
other person, as is right.

15 [17]. Further, the king's socmen and tenants are more
aggrieved and ill-treated than others of the realm, since they have
no defenders if they come to the [council, which despises them]
and so they depart again having achieved nothing.[17]

The council says in reply that the king's socmen never have
come before them to make complaint; if anyone has done them
wrong, let it be amended before the justices or the barons of the
exchequer as it should be, and if they are unjustly treated, let provision be made for their defence in future.

16 [18]. Further, the king's castles, and his living-quarters in
these castles and on his manors and franchises are going to ruin
for lack of attention.[18]

The council says in reply, let remedies be applied, and let
inquiry be made by the bailiffs and the constables to discover who
is to blame, and whoever is found blameworthy shall make amends.

17 [12]. Moreover, the king's council has gone to a lot of trouble
to dismiss from his presence those whom he likes and whom he
has found loyal and good hitherto, and who know how to discharge
the king's business to the king's profit and honour and according

a renable uoluntee le roy, et ceux chescun iour ouztout et mettront
ceux qe le roy ne uodroit.[19]

Le conseil dit et respount et prie qe lem lour face asauer queux
ceux sount, et les queux hommes ount mys countre sa uoluntee, et
si ount fait chose qils ne deyuent il amendrount uoluntierz come
a seigneur.

18 [13]. Derechief, multz de maux et roberiez sount ore feates
par Engleterre, issint qe le nef le roy fuit robee en le paas de
Altone et manacez faitez des chariatz le roy, et a ceo amendre nul
conseil est mys.[20]

Le conseil dit et respount que bien est resoun qe homme mette
graunt peyne a sauer queux ce sount qe ceo firent, et quant homme
sauera les queux ils sount, qe lem en face redde iustice, et soit
purueu que le roy eit tiel compaignie qe neit regarde.

19 [–]. Dautre part com xv. conseillers furent donez au roy par
le comune, ore par conseil de eux pluis est greue le roy despensez
az iustiz, et si pleint uiegne de eux, nul droiture est fait, fors
solement despouerez.

Le conseil et les deux[e] par la comune respount[21] et disunt qe
uoylent bien qil soit a garde et uue qe lez iusticz poent demeynz
estre amenez qil ne sount, et cum il prendrent meyns de roy plus
beal luur serra, for qil facent bien et lealment lour officez, et bien
uolount qe les iusticz facent droit de nous et dez aultrez a touz
gentz, et ceo sunt il touziours elus et uncore uolount.

f. 217   20 [1]. Derechief, ceux | de conseil ne sount point pursui le
bosoigne de Puille si com il promistrent, dount le roy est en dette
pluis de ii. c. ml[22] marcz par defaute † deux ia le pluis tarde †; la terre

---

[e] douze *not* deux.

---

[19] Professor Treharne has claimed that very few changes resulted from the
decision to review the personnel of the exchequer and the royal household, but
the Petyt MS. text of the Provisions of Oxford speaks of the removal of 'divers
of the Household offices' (*Baronial Plan*, pp. 95–6; Richardson and Sayles,
B.J.R.L., xvii (1933), 321). It has been suggested that the king may have been
influenced by his belief that Simon de Montfort forced Peter of Savoy to resign
from the council at the beginning of Mar. 1260 (E. F. Jacob, *E.H.R.* xli. 567,
n. 3; doc. 29, cl. 33).
[20] Doc. 30, n. 6.
[21] Doc. 5, cl. 22; docs. 10, 12, 13. This statement suggests that the twelve to
represent the *commun* still acted in the spring of 1261. Beyond these words the
latest evidence for the twelve meeting comes from autumn 1259 when they
appear to have exercised some influence in the appointment of judges (Baronial
Council, p. 131).

to his reasonable wishes, and these every day they remove; and they put in their places men whom the king does not want.[19]

The council says in reply, and asks, that they should be told who these men are, and what men have been installed against his will; and if they have done anything which they ought not to have done, they will readily put it right as to their lord.

18 [13]. Further, many crimes and robberies are now committed in England, so that the king's train was robbed in the Pass of Alton, and threats made against the king's wagons, and no measures have been taken to remedy this.[20]

The council says in reply that it is very right that great trouble should be taken to discover who they are who committed this crime, and when it is known who they are, let speedy justice be done upon them, and let provision be made for the king to have such a bodyguard that he need fear nothing.

19 [-]. Further, whereas fifteen councillors were given to the king by the community, now, by their advice, the king is more heavily burdened with the costs of the justices than he formerly was, and yet, if any complaint is made against them, no justice is done, but only against poor men.

The council and the [twelve] elected by the community[21] say in reply that they heartily wish that care should be taken to see that the justices can be maintained for less than they now cost, and it will seem better to them when the justices take less from the king, provided that they discharge their office well and loyally; and they wish heartily that the justices should do right against us and against any others to all people, and this they have always wished, and still wish now.

20 [1]. Further, the councillors have not followed up the Sicilian business as they promised, with the result that the king is in debt for more than 200,000[22] marks by their default †at the lowest

---

[22] Doc. 1. This debt is estimated at 100,000 m. and more in doc. 30, cl. 1. In 1257 the pope claimed that Henry owed the Church 135,000 m. while in 1258 the king was commanded to send to Italy an armed force of 8,500 men to be supported by an aid granted by the nobles (*Baronial Plan*, pp. 61, 62, 65). When Henry III presented his case to Louis IX, in preparation for the Mise of Amiens (Jan. 1264), he claimed from the English nobles 200,000 m. in compensation for harm done to him, but no mention was made of Sicily. In the nobles' defence Sicily is mentioned in this matter (doc. 37A, cl. 8; doc. 37C, cl. 8).

est perdue et lesglise defame et sustient galle, et eux promistrent auant cele besoigne, et de fuirer le roy est en graunt perile de le dite damage oue les usurez del dettes.

Le conseil dit et respount qe par eux ne fit unques le roy couenant a lapostoille de lafiere de Puille, et mult lur serra beal qil ce puruayt a cieux qe si male couenant luy fesount faire;[23] et de la promesse qe fust fait au roy sur lafier de Puille, bien poet homme uere par lez condicions qe ples furent entre lapostolie et notre seigneur le roy si eles soient furmes ou noun.[24] Et ceo qe le conseil deuera faire de ceste chose de resoun uoluntierz le fra.

21 [2]. Dautre part le roi est desherite et auxi com desherite de la terre de Gales, et par defaute de conseil, a la qele terre ceux du conseil promistent a eyde de quant qe le roy se obligea a eux, et de ceo rien nest fait, mes perdu est le chastel de Abuelly et plusurez aultrez terres et multz de genz mortz et les targes[f] la ou le roy poeit auere prise m[l]. m[l]. marcz pur trewe grauntiere †fuist purueu† en qele damage sount lez hommes le roy saunz manere et saunz mesure.[25]

Le conseil dit et respount qe le chastel de Abuelly fuist a sir Edward, et il le bailla a sir Roger de Mortimer qe emprist a respoundre la qil deuera,[26] et de m[l]. m[l]. marcz ne oyerent ils unqes parlere; et de damages as marches esti bien droit qe le roi et eus mettent conseil.

22 [14]. Derechief, par defaute de eaux purloigne este le estendre de dageneis a gref damage le roi.[27]

---

[f] *The words* et les targes *are possibly a miscopy of some such phrase as* en les marches *as the council's reply alludes to the Marches.*

[23] The pope cancelled the offer of Sicily and removed the threat of excommunication on 18 Dec. 1258, but Henry reopened negotiations in Jan. 1260 when he was in France (*Foedera*, I. i. 379–80; *C.R. 1259–61*, pp. 265–6).

[24] In Sept. 1259 the king stated that the council had suspended the collection of money, granted to him by the pope, until negotiations with Rome were clarified (*C.R. 1256–59*, p. 485).

[25] Builth castle fell on 17 July 1260 (*C.P.R. 1258–66*, p. 85). Nothing is known of the 2000 m. In Nov. 1259 King Henry stated that Llywelyn ap Gryffydd had offered £16,000 to be paid at £200 annually for eighty years, for a peace treaty, or £700, to be paid at £100 annually, for a truce lasting seven years (*C.R. 1259–61*, pp. 4–5; Lloyd, *History of Wales*, p. 726, correctly quotes *Flores Hist.* ii. 435, but is mistaken in saying that 16,000 m. were offered).

[26] The lordship of Builth formed part of the lands of William de Braose which fell to the control of the crown when Llywelyn ab Iorwerth executed William in 1230. In 1250 Builth was granted to the Lord Edward. Roger Mortimer,

calculation †, and the land is lost, and the Church shamed and humiliated, whereas they promised to advance this business, and in consequence the king is in great danger of suffering this loss together with the interest on the debts.

The council says in reply that it was never by their counsel that the king bound himself to the papacy in the Sicilian affair, and it would be a splendid thing to their minds, if he would take this problem to those who had induced him to make such a bad bargain;[23] and as for the promise which was made to the king on the Sicilian affair, anyone can see, from the conditions that were pledged between the papacy and our lord the king, whether they were firm or not.[24] But whatever the council ought reasonably to do in this business it will willingly do.

21 [2]. Again, the king is disinherited, or practically so, of the land of Wales, and this by the default of the council, for the councillors promised aid in the matter of this land when the king bound himself to them, and nothing has been done about it, but the castle of Builth and many other lands have been lost, and many men slain [in the Marches]. In the very place where the king might have received 2,000 marks for granting a truce † loss was suffered † in which the king's men are damaged beyond description and measure.[25]

The council says in reply that Builth castle belonged to the Lord Edward, and he entrusted it to Sir Roger Mortimer, who undertook to answer for whatever was his responsibility;[26] and as for 2,000 marks, they never heard tell of this offer; while concerning the damage to the Marches it is only too true that the king and they ought to take counsel on it.

22 [14]. Further, by their default the assessment of the Agenais has been postponed, to the king's harm and loss.[27]

---

d. 1282, married Maud daughter of William de Braose. On 30 July 1260 King Henry absolved Roger from all blame but the Lord Edward refused to agree to this (*English Baronies*, pp. 8, 21, 98–9; *C.P.R. 1258–66*, p. 85). Edward may have been suspicious of Roger Mortimer, who had supported the earl of Gloucester in the quarrel between the earl and Edward in the spring of 1260 (doc. 17, n. 2).

[27] In the Peace of Paris, 1259, King Louis agreed to deliver the Agenais to King Henry, if it should escheat to the French crown on the death of the wife of Alfonse, count of Poitou. Meanwhile Henry was to be paid the estimated annual value of the province; in Dec. 1261 a group of arbiters fixed the value at 3720 *livres tournois*, 8s. 6d. (*C.P.R. 1258–66*, p. 194; *Foedera*, I. i. 389; *Treaty Rolls*, *1234–1325*, p. 37; *Diplomatic Documents*, *1101–1272*, nos. 299, 302, 305; I. J. Sanders, 'The Texts of the Peace of Paris', *E.H.R.* lxvi (1951), 81–97; *Peace of Paris*, p. 74; G. P. Cuttino, 'The Process of Agen', *Speculum*, xix (1944), 161–78).

Le conseil dit et respount, uiegne le conseil le roy tout a un lieu[28] semblez euoit lem en qele chose soit de murs si soi amende.

23 [–]. Dautre part, rien ⟨nest⟩ fait del eschange auoir deuer le roi de franche des chosez qe mesme cesti roy ne puit metere hors de sa mayn par agarde iesque le ueisyn qaresme, si come en forme de la pes est tenu, qe deuoit estre fait dedeynz le feste de touz saintz.[29]

Le conseil respount auxi come auant ueygne le conseil ensemble et ueit lem par qi le besoigne est de mere si soit amende.

24 [26]. Derechief, com touz ceux de conseil eient feat homage au roy et feaute iure en terreue honour a luy garder, eus, auxi come de ceo ubliez, par obligacion la qele le roy lour auoit feat de lour conseil usere en amendement lestat du roy et del regne, ount prie

f. 217ᵛ le roy de chescoun honour a luy gardere | † mes par soun assent †[30] le seconde serment fait de treis[31] est lonour de roy sauere si come entre eux doiuent quant le roy se obligea a eux.

Le conseil respount et dit qils nentendent pas qe sa dignite qe a luy apent luy soit rien tolletz, et sil est mustre enqoy et ceo serra bien entendu come a seigneur, et ils nentendent pas qil eyent lour serment [ ]ire a lour seigneur le roy blemie en nul poynt, et sil eyent trepase, soit mustre en quoy et ilz amenderount come a seigneur.

25 [–]. Dautre part, sour larticle de Puille, puisque le roy se obligea a soun conseil, lapostoil pronuncia apertement qe pluis ne fuist tenu a roy de chose qe touche le regne de Puille et qe aillourz se querroit powere, et qil deuoit faire le pru de eglise de Rome de cele regne pur ceo qe couenant ne fuist garde de par le roy, et issi, par defaute de conseil, le roy de totez partz est damage.

[28] These words, together with the answer to cl. 23, suggest that regular meetings of the council had ended. This suggests that the words were spoken possibly in Mar. 1261, for although the last order of the council is dated 28 Dec. 1260 there is some slight evidence of it being in existence in Feb. 1261 (*C.P.R. 1258–66*, pp. 142, 149; Richardson, *T.R.H.S.* 4th ser. v (1922), 61).

[29] By the terms of the Peace of Paris, 1259, King Henry was granted all the lands which the king of France held in fief or in domain in the dioceses of Limoges, Cahors, and Périgueux. The brothers of the king of France and the lords of lands which, it was claimed, could not be granted away from the French crown were to be exempt from the obligation of doing homage to the English king. King Louis promised either to purchase such lands, which would be ceded to King Henry by All Saints (1 Nov. 1260), or to grant other lands in fair exchange (*Foedera*, i. i. 389; *Treaty Roll, 1234–1325*, p. 37; *Diplomatic Documents*, nos. 299, 302, 305; *Peace of Paris*, pp. 68–71). No other reference has been found to agreement being made in Lent.

The council says in reply, let the king's council assemble all together in one place,[28] and they will see where the delay has occurred and will put it right accordingly.

23 [-]. Further, nothing has been done about making the exchange with the king of France of the properties which that king cannot alienate from his crown, until next Lent, whereas in the terms of the peace-treaty it is stated that it should be done before the feast of All Saints[29] [1 November].

The council replies as before, let the council come together, and we will see by whom this business has been held up, and put it right accordingly.

24 [26]. Further, whereas all of the councillors had done homage and sworn fealty to the king, to keep him in worldly honour, they, as if forgetting this, under pretext of the undertaking which the king had given them to make use of their advice in reforming the king's state and that of the realm, have stripped the king of all honour, † but by their assent †[30] the second oath made of the three[31] is to preserve the king's honour as they agreed among themselves, when the king bound himself to them.

The council says in reply that they have no intention of damaging in the slightest degree his proper royal dignity, and if he will show them in what way this has been done, it shall be made good fully, as to their lord; and they do not intend that the oath which they made to their lord the king should be impaired in the slightest degree; and if they have done wrong, let it be shown in what way, and they will make amends as to their lord.

25 [-]. Further, concerning the Sicilian affair, after the king bound himself to his council, the pope declared publicly that he was no longer under any obligation to the king in any matter concerning the kingdom of Sicily, and that he would seek support elsewhere, and that he must take care of the interests of the Roman Church in that kingdom now that the king [Henry] had failed to keep his covenant: and thus, by the council's default, the king has suffered loss on all sides.

[30] The words *mes par soun assent* may read either 'except by his assent', in this case *mes* meaning 'except', or 'but by their assent', *soun* meaning 'their'. The latter reading is suggested by cl. 26 in doc. 30.

[31] Doc. 30, cl. 26 distinguishes between the first and second oaths. The third oath is presumably the councillors' oath (*Baronial Plan*, pp. 31-2, 36, 52, 54, 83, 85 n. 3).

Le conseil respount qe si lapostolie pronuncia qe le roy neust droit en le regne de Poille, pur nulle couenaunt qe entre eaux fuist couenantez, et lez obligementz entre eaux furent faitz auant qe le roy se myst en conseil de gentz de sa terre, et nient gardes, et pur ceo ne ueut il ceo pas.

26 [–]. La roy mustre qe pur amendement de luy et del regne, et pur sez grauntz bosoignes qil auoit a faire, si come il purra mustrer, si se mist il en le conseil de sez gentz, et oultre, apres la Pasche a Londrez, qe ⟨par⟩ lordement de soun conseil ⟨eluz⟩ par le comune de sa terre,[32] freit il amendement de soun regne, uncore ne ueut pas dedire qil ne le tiene fermement quant qe touche le honour die et sa foy et le profit de soun regne, car tout saunz cele oltrie en seroit il tenuz; et par mesme la resoun est il tenu de nun garder ceo qe est outre lo ⟨nour de⟩ Dieu et sa foi et profit de soun regne.

De ceo qe le roy dit qil se mist en conseil de sa gent, et lordement de son conseil fermement tendroit, et uncore le ueuult meyntere, soun conseil luy merci uuult, et sil plest qe le mustrent en qoy lez chosez nount mye estie si bien tenuz come mestre serroit a luy et a soun regne, et serrount[g] au roy come a seigneur qe lez chosez soient amendez al preu et honour de Dieu et de luy.

27 [–]. Le roy mustre qe puis cele ordeynement rien nest fait de soun preu ne del regne, enz est le roy leidement abesse e enpouere et le regne ensement, issi qe dit de gent enpassilent et dedeynz | et dehors, car ceux de denz uient et sentent le mal, et ceux de hors le seyuent par oye dire, par ount le regne est mys en grant desclaundre; car lez foreynz entendront qe le roi est hors de tout poer et de toute terrene seigneurie, et ceo est graunt ledure a touz cez leauz hommes.

f. 218

Le conseil respount qe par les malueis anes entendrount il qe la terre soit enpoueri et si lem nad fait le preu le roy et del regne, mustre en qoy ad defaille, et par qi, et lem amendra come a seigneur.

28 [–]. Le roy mustre qe si ua mal ore, moult pys irra apres, et qe le regne ne puist en nul manere estre solom le manere qe lem le gye, car il dit qe le regne ad este gie auaunt ces heures par treis choses especialment, cest a sauoir par la ley de la terre, ⟨et par le

---

[g] *Some such word as* garantz *is omitted here.*

---

[32] See doc. 1.

The council replies that if the pope declared that the king no longer had any right in the kingdom of Sicily by virtue of any agreement made between them, and the agreements between them were made before the king put himself under the counsel of his own subjects, and now these agreements have not been kept, the council does not now wish to further the matter.

26 [–]. The king says that, for the reform of his own state and of the realm, and for his own great needs which he had to satisfy, as he can show, he placed himself under the counsel of his subjects, and at London after Easter he granted that he would carry out the reform of his realm by the decree of his council [elected] by the community of the kingdom:[32] and even now he does not wish to deny that he should hold to this firmly in everything touching the honour of God, his own good faith, and the profit of the realm, for even had he made no such offer he would still be bound to these ends; but by the same reason he is bound not to keep that which is contrary to the honour of God, his own faith, and the profit of his realm.

As to what the king says of having placed himself under the advice of his subjects and of having promised to observe firmly the ordinances of his council, and of still desiring to maintain this promise, his council wishes to offer him thanks; and if he pleases to show them in what ways things have not been as well managed as they should have been, both as concerns himself and as concerns his kingdom, they will [guarantee] to the king as to their lord that matters shall be put right, to the profit and honour of God and of himself.

27 [–]. The king says that since this ordinance nothing has been done for his good or for that of the realm, wherefore the king is grievously abased and impoverished, and the realm with him, so that the credit of the land suffers, both at home and abroad, for those who are within the realm see and feel the evil, and foreigners know of it by hearsay, whereby the kingdom is put to great shame, for foreigners perceive that the king is stripped of all power and of all earthly lordship, and this is a great scandal to all loyal men.

The council replies that, as they see it, it is by the dreadful seasons that the land has been beggared; and if the good of the king and of the realm have not been achieved, let it be shown where the defect lies and who is to blame and they will put it right as to their lord.

28 [–]. The king says that, if things are going badly now, they will go much worse in future, and that the kingdom can in no wise go on in the way in which it is now being managed, for he says that it has been governed in the past by three things in particular—that

seel⟩ et par leschekere, cest a sauoir par sages et bones gentz qe cestez treis choses gouerneround, et ore troue a le contrarie, car tout seyent il bones en eux, til que sount treis souereynz[h] †en cestz treis choses ne pas apris, car il entrerent en celles baillies la ou dussent lez choses gouerner et les aultrez adresser†,[i] comment qe sour gages qe taunt ne sount tenuz as choses com ils sount les gouernent, et issi sount il disciples la ou il dusent estre mestres.

Le conseil respount et dist qe sy lem ad mys en office gentz nientz couenable qe ne deuont, mustre en quoy, et queux ceux sount, si soit amende par le roy et par soun conseil.

29 [–]. Les uiscontes et lez aultres baillifs qe lem fait ore honysent toute la terre et entrebeysount le droyture le roy et destruyount la pays e su effrount a pur prendre le droyture le roy; et en ceste manere perde le roy et perdra quant qil ad, et la terre ierte destrute.

Le conseil respount et dist qe si homme troue uiscountes et aultres baillifs qe sount partiez al droyture le roy gardere, soient punys si come ils deyuount, ou si destruccioun fount, soient punys sy come auant est dit, et ceo soit enquis hastiuement.

32

13 APRIL 1261

Alexander . . . Regi Anglorum*

Alexander[1] episcopus, seruus seruorum Dei, carissimo in Christo filio regi Anglorum illustri, salutem et apostolicam benedictionem.

Ad audientiam nostram peruenit, quod tu, olim inductus quasi quadam impressione magnatum et hominum regni tui, ad

---

[h] *The text at this point is corrupt: essential words and phrases seem to have been omitted. A conjectural translation is offered.*   [i] T *adds* il (?).

---

* *Text*: British Museum, Cotton MS. Cleopatra E. i. f. 213 (old 198+). Endorsed *Bulla Alexandri pape super* (illegible). An original bull, only the seal cords remain. *Printed: Foedera,* i. i. 405 quotes f. 199. *See: Baronial Plan,* p. 260.

---

[1] Henry III accepted the Sicilian crown for his son Edmund on 6 Mar. 1254 during the pontificate of Innocent IV whose successors faced the problem of

is to say, by the law of the land, by the great seal, and by the ex-chequer, or rather, by experienced and capable men who direct these three things: but now the opposite is found, for, although these things may be good in themselves, in so far as they are three independent powers, †in these three branches the officials are not suitable, for while they undertook these offices, in which they ought to manage affairs and direct others†, they administer them as men working for profit, whereby they are not strictly bound by things as they are, and so they are learners where they ought to be masters.

The council says in reply that if people have been placed in office who are less suitable than they should be, let it be shown in what, and who they are, and accordingly it shall be put right by the king and his council.

29 [–]. The sheriffs and other bailiffs who are appointed now-adays shame the whole land and encroach upon the king's rights and destroy the countryside and allow others to usurp the king's rights, and in these ways the king loses and will go on losing what he has, and the land lies destroyed.

The council says in reply that if sheriffs and other bailiffs are found who have failed to uphold the king's rights, let them be punished as they should be, or if they cause damage let them be punished as has been said above, and let prompt inquiry be made about it.

32

13 APRIL 1261

Alexander [IV] to the king of the English

Alexander, bishop,[1] servant of the servants of God, to his most dear son in Christ, the illustrious king of the English, greeting and apostolic benediction.

It has come to our ears that you, induced some time ago by some sort of tumult among the magnates and men of your realm,

coercing the English king to fulfil the demands of the Church, as well as the opposition of the English nobility (*Baronial Plan, passim*). This bull, and those which form documents 33 and 34, were brought from Rome by John Mansel and mark the culmination of Henry III's work to destroy the power of the nobles.

obseruandum quedam statuta, ordinationes, et colligationes, que
ipsi, sub pretextu reformandi statum eiusdem regni, tuo nomine
fecisse dicuntur et iureiurando firmasse, te iuramento proprio
astrinxisci, in diminutionem potestatis tue, ac depressionem regie
libertatis.[2] Nos igitur, super hoc tue uolentes honorificentie
prouidere, te a iuramento huiusmodi, auctoritate apostolica, ex
nunc prorsus absoluimus, de nostre plenitudine potestatis. Siquid
autem in eisdem statutis et ordinationibus, quod prelatorum,
ecclesiarum et ecclesiasticarum personarum fauorem et commodum
respiciat, continetur, id irritari non intendimus, nec quo ad id
iuramentum predictum aliquatenus relaxare. Nulli ergo omnino
hominum liceat hanc paginam nostre absolutionis infringere, uel
ei ausu temerario contraire. Si quis autem hoc attemptare presumpserit, indignacionem omnipotencis Dei, et beatorum Petri
et Pauli, apostolorum eius, se nouerit incursurum.

Dat' Lateran', id' Aprilis, pontificatus nostri anno septimo.

33

29 APRIL 1261

Alexander . . . archiepiscopo Cantuariensi et aliis*

Alexander episcopus, seruus seruorum Dei, uenerabilibus fratribus
archiepiscopo Cantuarien' et . . . episcopo Norwicen' et dilecto
filio Iohanni Mansello thesaurario Eboracensi, capellano nostro,
salutem et apostolicam benedictionem.

Ad audienciam nostram peruenit, quod nonnulli prelati,
magnates, et alii, tam clerici, quam laici, regni Anglie ad obseruandum quedam statuta, ordinationes, et colligationes *(que
nonnulli ipsorum, sub pretextu reformandi statum ipsius regni,
nomine carissimi in Christo filii nostri regis Anglorum illustris, in
diminutionem et depressionem potestatis et libertatis eiusdem
regis,[1] fecisse dicuntur),* se iuramentis propriis astrinxerunt.

a-a These brackets are in the MS.

* *Text*: P.R.O. SC. 7. 3(29). An original bull, seal intact. Initial letter in black
with yellow facing. *Printed*: *Foedera*, I. i. 406. *See*: *Baronial Plan*, pp. 260–1.

bound yourself with your own oath to observe certain statutes, ordinances, and undertakings which they, on pretext of reforming the state of your realm, are said to have made in your name and to have confirmed with an oath, to the diminution of your power and to the depression of your royal liberty.[2] We therefore, wishing to strengthen your honour in these matters, by apostolic authority and out of the fullness of our power, wholly absolve you, from this moment, from any such oath. If, however, anything is contained in these statutes and ordinances which affects the favour and advantage of prelates, churches, and ecclesiastical persons, we do not intend that this should be invalidated, nor that the said oath should in any way be relaxed in this respect. To no man whatsoever, therefore, is it permitted to infringe this our letter of absolution, or to oppose it with rash daring. If, however, anyone shall presume to attempt this, let him know that he will incur the anger of omnipotent God and of His apostles, Saint Peter and Saint Paul.

Dated at the Lateran, the ides of April (13th), in the seventh year of our pontificate.

33

29 APRIL 1261

Alexander [IV] to the archbishop of Canterbury and others

Alexander, bishop, servant of the servants of God, to his venerable brothers the archbishop of Canterbury and the bishop of Norwich and his beloved son John Mansel, treasurer of York, our chaplain, greeting and apostolic blessing.

It has come to our ears that certain prelates, magnates, and others, both clerks and laymen, of the realm of England have bound themselves with their own oaths to observe certain statutes, ordinances, and undertakings (which some of them, under pretext of reforming the state of the realm, are said to have made in the name of our most dear son in Christ, the illustrious king of the English, to the diminution and depression of his power and liberty).[1] We have also heard that, by a kind of compulsion, they

[2] See doc. 2 and *C.P.R. 1247-58*, pp. 644-5.

[1] On 4 Aug. 1258 the earl of Norfolk, who had been appointed keeper of the East Anglian coast, was ordered to take the oath which the council had ordered throughout the realm (*C.P.R. 1247-58*, p. 649).

Et, quasi per quandam impressionem, ab eodem rege, ac carissima in Christo filia nostra regina Anglie, filiis ipsorum, et a nonnullis aliis, ut ad ipsorum statutorum, ordinationum, necnon colligationum obseruationem similiter se astringerent, exegerunt.

Cum igitur iuramenti religio *ᵃ(qua fides confirmari debet et ueritas)ᵃ* fieri non debeat prauitatis et perfidie firmamentum; nos, uolentes super hoc ipsius regis honorificentie, et aliorum prouidere saluti, discretioni uestre, de qua plene confidimus, per apostolica scripta, districte precipiendo, mandamus quatinus prefatos prelatos, magnates, ac uos ipsos inuicem, si opus fuerit, et alios, uos omnes, uel duo uestrum, aut tu, frater archiepiscope, solus ab huiusmodi iuramentis prorsus curetis absoluere, ac predictas colligationes dissoluere, uice nostra, de nostre plenitudine potestatis. Contradictores per censuram ecclesiasticam, appellatione postposita, compescendo, sicut statui eiusdem regis et regni sui prudenter uideritis, circumspectis omnibus, expedire. Siquid autem in eisdem statutis et ordinationibus, quod prelatorum, ecclesiarum, seu ecclesiasticarum personarum fauorem et commodum respiciat, continetur, id per hoc irritari nolumus, uel quo ad illud, predicta iuramenta ullatenus relaxari.

Dat' Rome, apud Sanctum Petrum, iii. kalendas Maii, pontificatus nostri anno septimo.

34

7 MAY 1261

Alexander . . . archiepiscopo Cantuariensi et aliis*

Alexander episcopus, seruus seruorum Dei, uenerabilibus fratribus archiepiscopo Cantuarian' et episcopo Norwicen' et dilecto filio Iohanni Mansell' thesaurario Eboracen' capellano nostro, salutem et apostolicam benedictionem.

Rationalibus sensibus materiam iuste admirationis importat securim aduersus illum, qui cedit in ea, uel serram contra illum, qui trahit ipsam; eos, uidelicet, quos potioribus legitimus

---

* *Text*: P.R.O. SC. 7. 3 (25). An original bull, seal intact. Initial letter in black with yellow facing. *Printed*: *Foedera*, I. i. 406. *See*: *Baronial Plan*, pp. 260–1.

have exacted from the said king, and from our most dear daughter in Christ the queen of England, and from their sons and from certain others that they should similarly bind themselves to the observance of their statutes, ordinances, and undertakings.

Therefore, since the binding force of an oath (by which faith and truth should be confirmed) ought not to be used to strengthen wickedness and perfidy, we, wishing to do what will bring honour to the said king and salvation to others, give orders to your discretion, in which we have full confidence, firmly commanding by letters apostolic that you shall take care wholly to absolve from these oaths the prelates, magnates, and your own selves in turn, if need be, and others also, whether all three of you, or two of you, or you alone, brother archbishop, perform this absolution; and on our behalf, from the fullness of our power you shall dissolve these undertakings, constraining by ecclesiastical censure, without right of appeal, all who oppose, as you, having considered all the circumstances, shall prudently think best for the state of the king and realm. If, however, anything is contained in these statutes and ordinances which affects the favour and advantage of prelates, churches, and ecclesiastical persons, we do not intend that this should be invalidated nor that the oaths should in any way be relaxed in this respect.

Given at St. Peter's, Rome, 29 April, in the seventh year of our Pontificate.

34

7 MAY 1261

Alexander [IV] to the archbishop of Canterbury and others

Alexander, bishop, servant of the servants of God, to his venerable brothers the archbishop of Canterbury and the bishop of Norwich and his beloved son John Mansel, treasurer of York, our chaplain, greeting and apostolic blessing.

To rational minds it would imply cause for justified wonder that the axe should turn against him who wields it or the saw against him who uses it, or that those, forsooth, whom a lawful order of

subministrationum ordo subiecit, aduersus auctoritatem presidentium eleuari, et principes, legum dominos, quos pre suis participibus celestis ordinatio sublimauit, premi arbitrio subditorum.

Propterea nos mirari coegit publice relationis assertio, auribus nostris insinuans quod nonnulli barones, proceres, magnates, et alii tam clerici quam laici regni Anglie, sub pretextu reformandi statum eiusdem regni, quasdam constitutiones, ordinationes, et colligationes, carissimi in Christo filii nostri regis Anglorum illustris titulo, in diminutionem et depressionem potestatis et libertatis regie factas, iureiurando firmarunt; et ab eodem rege ac plurimis aliis dicti regni, clericis et laicis, ut, ad obseruationem earum, suis se iuramentis astringerent, per quandam impressionis instantiam exegerunt.

Cum igitur idem rex, quem inter ceteros Christianos principes fidei Christiane sinceritas, et catholice deuotionis integritas recommendant, non sit quorumlibet deprimendus studiis, sed omnium fauoribus erigendus, nos, uolentes ipsius honorificentie, aliorumque prouidere saluti, discretioni uestre, per apostolica scripta, districte precipiendo, mandamus quatinus uos omnes, uel duo uestrum, aut tu, frater archiepiscope, solus predictos barones, proceres, magnates, et alios monere attentius, et efficaciter inducere studeatis, ut ^a(non obstantibus huiusmodi iuramentis, a quibus, cum non debeant esse prauitatis uincula, eos alias per uos absolui mandamus)^a prefato regi, tanquam principi suo, adhereant fideliter et intendant; sibi debita prompte fidelitatis, et pacifice subiectionis obsequia exhibentes, nec pretextu constitutionum, ordinationum, uel colligationum predictarum aliquatinus impedientes eundem, quo minus utatur libere priscina in omnibus plenitudine regie potestatis.

Si uero ipsorum aliqui monitis uestris acquiescere fortasse renuerint, uos omnes, uel duo uestrum, seu tu, frater archiepiscope, solus eos, cuiuscumque sint conditionis, et gradus uel ordinis, ad id per excommunicationis in personas et interdicti in terras eorum sententias, remoto appellationis obstaculo, compellatis, sicut statui dicti regis et regni sui uideritis expedire; non obstantibus aliquibus priuilegiis uel indultis, generaliter uel specialiter quibuscumque ab apostolica sede concessis, per que, non expressa presentibus uel totaliter non inserta, mandati nostri execucio impediri ualeat

^{a-a} *These brackets are in the MS.*

subordination have subjected to the more powerful should be raised against the authority of the rulers, and that princes, who are the lords of laws, whom a celestial ordinance has inscribed at the head of their partners, should be curbed by the will of their subjects.

Therefore we are driven to astonishment by a statement of public report, forcing itself on our hearing, that certain barons, nobles, magnates, and others of the realm of England, both clergy and laity, under pretext of reforming the state of that realm, have confirmed with an oath certain constitutions, ordinances, and undertakings, made in the name of our most dear son in Christ, the illustrious king of the English, to the diminution and depression of the royal power and liberty, and have exacted, by a certain threat of compulsion, from the king and many others of the realm, clerks and laymen, that they should bind themselves with their oaths to the observance of these things.

Therefore, since the king, whom the sincerity of the Christian faith and the integrity of his Catholic devotion recommend among the rest of Christian princes, is not to be constrained by the machinations of any persons, but rather to be uplifted by the favour of all, we, wishing to provide for the strengthening of his honour and for the salvation of the others, by letters apostolic now command you in your wisdom, with the most strict orders, that all three of you, or two of you, or you alone, brother archbishop, should do your utmost to warn most carefully the barons, nobles, magnates, and others, and to induce them effectively (notwithstanding these oaths from which, seeing that they should not be made chains of wickedness, we have elsewhere ordered them to be absolved by you) to cleave faithfully to their king as to their chief, and to obey him, showing him the debts of prompt fidelity and the obedience of peaceful subjection, and not, on pretext of these constitutions, ordinances, and undertakings in any way hindering him from using freely in all things the untrammelled fulness of the royal power.

If, however, any should perchance reject your warnings, you all, or two of you, or you alone, brother archbishop, shall compel them, whatsoever may be their condition, rank, or order, by sentences of excommunication against their persons and of interdict upon their lands, taking away all right of appeal, as you shall best think most fitting for the state of the king and his realm; notwithstanding any privileges or indulgences generally or specially granted by the apostolic see to anyone whomsoever, whereby anything not stated and wholly included in these present letters shall be valid to impede or to delay the execution of our mandate, and

uel differri; seu constitutione de duabus dietis[1] edita in concilio generali.

Siquid autem in eisdem constitutionibus et ordinationibus, quod, absque ullo alieni iuris, uel priuilegiorum, seu indultorum, aut mandatorum sedis apostolice preiudicio, ecclesiarum et ecclesiasticarum personarum regni prefati fauorem uel commodum respiciat, continetur, id irritum nolumus, uel, quo ad illud, iuramenta predicta ullatenus relaxari.

Sic itaque sane intelligi uolumus et mandamus, quod sicut in aliis litteris nostris, quas super relaxatione iuramentorum ipsorum, et predictis colligationibus dissoluendis concessimus, est expressum ne dum huiusmodi iuramenta, constitutiones et ordinationes, in quantum utilitatibus ecclesiasticis consonant, relaxari et immutari noluimus, aliquid in illis probasse uel tolerasse credamur, quod aut ius ledat alterius, aut potestati nostre seu gratiis, quas sedes memorata contulit, quomodolibet aduersetur.

Dat' Viterbii, nonas Maii, pontificatus nostri anno septimo.

35

11 SEPTEMBER 1261

*Rex uicecomitibus citra Trentam**

Rex uicecomiti Norff' et Suff', salutem. Cum ex parte episcopi Wigornensis, comitum Leyc' et Glouc' et quorundam aliorum procerum regni nostri uocati sint tres milites de singulis comitatibus nostris quod sint coram ipsis apud Sanctum Albanum in instanti festo Sancti Matthei apostoli secum tractaturi super communibus negociis regni nostri,[1] et nos et predicti proceres nostri in eundem diem apud Windes' conuenerimus ad tractandum

---

* *Text*: Rot. Claus. 45 Hen. III, m. 6d. *Printed*: *C.R. 1259–61*, p. 490; *Royal Letters*, ii. 179. *See*: *Baronial Plan*, pp. 266–7, 271, 353.

---

[1] This alludes to chapter 37 of the Fourth Lateran Council, 1215, which prohibits the summoning of anyone by apostolic letters before a justice who officiates more than two days journey from the defendant's diocese (Mansi, *Concilia*, xxii. 1023). Thus all three of the addressees of this letter, or even one of them,

notwithstanding any constitution *de duabus dietis*[1] enacted in a general council.

If, however, anything is contained in these constitutions or ordinances which, without any prejudice to the right of others, or the privileges, indulgences, or mandates of the apostolic see, redounds to the advantage or profit of churches or ecclesiastical persons in the kingdom, we do not wish it to be invalidated, nor the aforesaid oaths to be in any way relaxed in respect of such an advantage. We therefore will and command it to be soundly understood that, as is stated in our other letters which we have issued regarding the releasing of their oaths, and the dissolution of the [said] undertakings, while we do not wish these oaths, constitutions, and ordinances to be relaxed or changed in so far as they work to the profit of the Church, we shall not be thought to have approved or tolerated anything in them which in any way damages the right of anyone else, or which in any way runs counter to our power or to the graces which the apostolic see has granted.

Given at Viterbo, 7 May, in the seventh year of our pontificate.

35

11 SEPTEMBER 1261

The king to the sheriffs this side of the Trent

The king to the sheriff of Norfolk and Suffolk. The bishop of Worcester, the earls of Leicester and Gloucester, and other noblemen of our kingdom, have summoned three knights from each of our counties to meet them at St. Albans on the feast of St. Matthew the Apostle [21 September] to consider with them the general business of our realm.[1] However, as we and our nobles will be meeting at Windsor on the same day, to negotiate peace between

---

may cite anyone in case of disobedience, or otherwise, wherever he resides, despite the provision of the Fourth Lateran Council. I wish to thank Professor Ullmann, Trinity College, Cambridge for his help in this matter.

[1] The king's policy, by the middle of 1261, reunited the nobles who tried to seek an agreement with Henry III. When they failed they planned summoning, on their own authority, representatives of the counties. See doc. 3, n. 18, for works on knights.

de pace inter nos et ipsos, tibi precipimus quod illis militibus de ballia tua, qui uocati sunt coram eis ad diem predictum, firmiter iniungas ex parte nostra ut, omni occasione postposita, ad nos die predicto ueniant apud Windes',[2] et eis eciam districte inhibeas ne dicto die alibi quam ad nos accedant, sed eos modis omnibus uenire facias coram nobis ad diem predictum, nobiscum super premissis colloquium habituros, ut ipsi per effectum operis uideant et intelligant quod nichil attemptare proponimus nisi quod honori et communi utilitati regni nostri nouerimus conuenire. Teste rege apud Windes' xi. die Septembris.

Eodem modo mandatum est singulis uicecomitibus citra Trentam.

36

25 FEBRUARY 1262

*Vrbanus . . . archiepiscopo Cantuariensi et aliis**

Vrbanus episcopus, seruus seruorum Dei, uenerabilibus fratribus archiepiscopo Cantuarien' et episcopo Norwicen' et dilecto filio Johanni Mansell thesaurario Eboracensi, capellano nostro, salutem et apostolicam benedictionem.

Cum olim, ut nobis innotuit, ad felicis recordationis Alexandri pape predecessoris nostri notitiam peruenisset, quod carissimus in Christo filius noster rex, et carissima in Christo filia nostra regina Anglie, illustres, ac nobiles uiri Edwardus et Eadmundus eorum filii, quasi per quandam baronum suorum impressionem inducti, et nonnulli alii magnates, et alii, tam clerici quam laici, regni Anglie, ad obseruandum quedam statuta, ordinationes et colligationes, que nonnulli ipsorum magnatum, sub pretextu reformandi statum ipsius regni, nomine predicti regis dicebantur fecisse, ac iureiurando firmasse, propriis se astrinxerant iuramentis, in diminucionem potestatis ipsius regis, ac depressionem regie libertatis. Idem predecessor prefatos regem, et reginam, et eorum

---

* *Text*: P.R.O. SC. 7. 33(4). Original bull, seal intact. Initial letter black with yellow facing. In places 33(4) is worn; text checked in duplicates. Duplicates 33(5), 33(6), 33(9), 33(11). *Printed*: *Foedera*, I. i. 416; *Baronial Plan*, pp. 277–8.

us and them, we order that the knights from your counties, who
have been summoned to meet the bishop, earls, and nobles on the
same day be, at our command, strictly warned by you, that, setting
aside all obstacles, they should come to Windsor on that day.[2] You
will firmly forbid them to go elsewhere on the said day, except to
meet us, and you will use all means to cause them to come before
us, on the said day, to have discussion with us on these matters, so
that they may see and understand that we plan to do nothing
except what we will learn is to the honour and good of our realm.
Witnessed the king at Windsor, 11 September.

Similar orders are sent to each sheriff this side of the Trent.

36

25 FEBRUARY 1262

Urban [IV] to the archbishop of Canterbury and others

Urban, bishop, servant of the servants of God, to his venerable
brothers the archbishop of Canterbury and the bishop of Norwich,
and to his beloved son John Mansel, treasurer of York, our chaplain, greeting and apostolic blessing.

Some time ago, as we have learned, it came to the notice of Pope
Alexander, our predecessor of blessed memory, that our illustrious
and beloved son in Christ, the king, and our beloved daughter in
Christ, the queen of England, and the noble men Edward and
Edmund their sons, as it were under the compulsion of a certain
pressure from their barons, together with several other magnates
and others, both clergy and laity, of the kingdom of England, had
bound themselves with their personal oaths to observe certain
statutes, ordinances, and confederacies, which some of the magnates, under pretext of reforming the state of the realm, are said
to have made in the name of the king and to have confirmed with
oaths, to the diminution of the power of the king and to the
depression of the royal liberty. Our predecessor thereupon

---

[2] Presumably because of this order no meeting took place at St. Albans and
there is no evidence of an assembly at Windsor.

natos, extunc per suas absoluit litteras ab huiusmodi iuramento, et uobis per alias diuersas litteras etiam districte precipiendo mandauit, ut prefatos magnates, ac uos ipsos inuicem, si opus existeret, et alios uos omnes, uel duo uestrum, aut tu, frater archiepiscope, solus eiusdem predecessoris uice, ac de ipsius plenitudine potestatis, a iuramento predicto prorsus absoluere, predictasque colligationes dissoluere, atque magnates, barones, proceres, et alios dicti regni ut, non obstantibus huiusmodi iuramentis, prefato regi, tanquam suo principi, adhererent fideliter et intenderent, sibi debita prompte fidelitatis et pacifice subjectionis obsequia exhibentes, nec pretextu constitutionum et ordinationum predictarum, aliquatenus impedientes eundem, quominus uteretur libere pristina in omnibus plenitudine regie potestatis, monere attentius, et efficaciter inducere curaretis, contradictores per excommunicationis in personas, et interdici in terras eorum sententias, remoto appellationis obstaculo, cohercendo.

Sed uos, ut accepimus, ipsius predecessoris morte intercedente, in ipsius mandati executione procedere omisistis;[1] quocirca nos ad eundem regem, ob sue deuotionis merita, intime caritatis affectum habentes, et cupientes fore prosperum et pacificum statum eius, discretioni uestre per apostolica scripta mandamus quatinus, si est ita, prefatos regem, et reginam, ipsorumque filios denuntiantes publice a iuramenti predicti uinculo absolutos, super premissis efficaciter curetis procedere de plano et absque iudicii strepitu iuxta directarum uobis eiusdem predecessoris continentiam litterarum. Non obstante si aliquibus a sede apostolica sit indultum, quod interdici, suspendi, uel excommunicari, aut eorum terre interdicto ecclesiastico supponi non possint, per litteras apostolicas non facientes plenam et expressam, de uerbo ad uerbum de indulto huiusmodi mentionem: aut qualibet alia ipsius sedis indulgencia, per quam effectus presentium impediri possit, seu etiam retardari.

Dat' Viterbii, quinto kalendas Martii, pontificatus nostri anno primo.

---

[1] Alexander IV, who died 25 May 1261, was followed by Urban IV (1261–4). It is not known why this accusation was made, the bulls of Alexander were published on 12 June 1261 and Henry III continued to reassert his power (*Baronial Plan*, p. 261). The opposition which the king had faced in the latter half of 1261, and the election of a new pope, probably caused Henry III to seek a confirmation of the bulls which Alexander IV had issued. These are the documents which, Simon de Montfort claimed, had been cancelled by the pope in a letter which he

absolved the king and queen and their children from this oath by his letters, and also, by various other letters ordered you strictly that all three of you, or any two of you, or you alone, brother archbishop, in the place of our predecessor and with the plenitude of his power, should wholly absolve the magnates, and each other of yourselves should need be, from the said oath, and should dissolve the confederacies, and that you should most carefully warn the magnates, barons, great men, and others of that realm, and take care effectively to induce them, that, notwithstanding these oaths, they should faithfully adhere to and obey the king as their prince, showing him all due obedience of ready fealty and peaceful subjection, in no wise hindering him, on pretext of the aforesaid constitutions and ordinances, from freely exercising in all things the untrammelled plenitude of royal power. And he enjoined you to coerce all who might oppose by excommunication of their persons and sentences of interdict upon their lands, without any appeal.

But you, as we have learnt, owing to the death of our predecessor, have failed to proceed with the execution of his mandate:[1] wherefore we, holding the king, for the merit of his devotion, in the closest love and affection, and desiring his state to be both prosperous and peaceful, order you in your wisdom, by apostolic command, that, if this be so, you should publicly proclaim the king and queen and their children to have been absolved from the bond of the oath, and that you should take care to proceed effectively on all of the commands in full, and without any formality of judicial proceedings, according to the instructions given to you in the letters of our predecessor, notwithstanding any indulgence granted by the apostolic see to anyone that they cannot be interdicted, suspended, or excommunicated, or their lands placed under any ecclesiastical interdict, by apostolic letters not making full and express mention of any such indulgence, word for word; and notwithstanding any other kind of indulgence whatsoever granted by the Holy See, whereby the effect of these present mandates might be impeded or even delayed.

Given at Viterbo, 25 February, in the first year of our pontificate.

produced in Oct. 1262. See doc. 28, n. 1. On 23 Aug. 1263 Urban IV issued another bull in support of Henry III. See *Les Registres d'Urbain IV*, ed. L. Dorez and J. Guiraud. Bibliothèque des Écoles Françaises d'Athènes et Rome, 2nd ser. vol. XIII (1892), no. 345. Copy in the Bodleian Library, MS. Bodley, 91, f. 138^{r-v}, reference in *Ann. Mon.* i. 179.

37A

JANUARY 1264[1]

Per ista subscripta grauatur Rex Anglie*

1. Quod scilicet per constitutiones baronum fit capitalis iusticiarius per eleccionem consili[ari]orum quos posuerunt barones in consilio regis, cum tamen dominus rex et eius antecessores capitalem iusticiarium cum opus esset pro sua uoluntate preficere consueuerunt et amouere, et etiam cum opus non sit huiusmodi iusticiario dum rex egerit in regno. Et pretera onus eiusdem iusticiarii graue est et sumptuosum eidem domino regi.

2. Item quod etiam cancellarius et thesaurarius qui iura regis specialiter conseruare debent, et qui iura ipsius leuiter subuertere pro uoluntate seu commodo aliorum possunt, ponuntur per eosdem consiliarios, cum rex ipse eos eligere et ponere debeat et semper consueuerit quatenus eos sibi meliores nouisset et fideliores.[2] Quod etiam uicecomites qui iura regis externis in suis balliuiis specialiter conseruare debent et quorum permissione poterunt magnates et alii iura regis subtrahere et sibi ipsis appropriare, ponuntur per eosdem consiliarios, cum tamen rex ipse[3] et sui antecessores eos semper ponere et deponere consueuerunt pro uoluntate sua.

3. Item quod etiam iusticiarii minores qui ius reddere debent tam regi quam aliis omnibus de regno in iudiciis suis, ponuntur per eosdem consiliarios cum dominus rex eos ponere consueuerit et amouere ad uoluntatem*a* suam.[4]

---

a uoluntatem *interlineated above* eleccionem *erased.*

---

* *Text*: Paris, Archives Nationales, J.654, no. 29 *bis*. *Printed*: R. F. Treharne, 'The Mise of Amiens, 23 January 1264', in *Studies in Medieval History presented to F. M. Powicke* (1948), pp. 223–39. *See*: *Battle of Lewes*, pp. 87–8. The text is divided into paragraphs. They have been numbered for convenience.

---

[1] Documents 37A, 37B and 37C record the evidence presented to Louis IX, in Jan. 1264, by the king and the reformers. Sir F. M. Powicke has claimed that this document, 37A, which states the *grauamina* and the *peticio* of Henry III, was presented to Louis IX at Boulogne in Sept. 1263 and not at Amiens in Jan. 1264 (*The Thirteenth Century*, p. 179, n. 2).

37A

JANUARY 1264[1]

The king of England has suffered harm in the following ways

1. Firstly, in that, by the constitutions of the barons the chief justiciar is appointed by the votes of councillors whom the barons placed in the king's council, whereas the lord king and his ancestors by custom appointed and removed the chief justiciar, as need might be, at their own pleasure; and further, in that there is no need for a justiciar of this kind, so long as the king stays within the realm; and moreover, the cost of the said justiciar is a heavy expense to the said lord king.

2. Next, that the chancellor and the treasurer, who have a special duty to safeguard the king's rights, and who can easily subvert those rights at the instance or for the profit of others, are appointed by these same councillors, whereas the king himself ought to choose and appoint them, and was always accustomed to choose those whom he knew to be the best and the most faithful to himself.[2] And also that the sheriffs, who especially are bound to preserve the king's rights in their bailiwicks from other people, and by whose connivance the magnates and others will be able to encroach upon the king's rights and to appropriate them to themselves, are appointed by these same councillors, whereas the king himself,[3] and his ancestors, were always accustomed to appoint and to remove them at their own will.

3. Further, even the lesser justices, who are bound to dispense justice both to the king and to all others of the realm in their judgements, are appointed by these same councillors, whereas the lord king was accustomed to appoint and to remove them at his pleasure.[4]

[2] In Mar. 1261 the council said that the justiciar, treasurer, and chancellor were appointed by a committee of five (doc. 31, cl. 4).

[3] See doc. 12, n. 4, for appointment of sheriffs.

[4] There is no evidence of the council appointing judges, but they did both name some judges to exercise special jurisdiction and organize an eyre (doc. 13; *C.R. 1256–59*, p. 485).

4. Item quod castra regis committuntur per eosdem consiliarios cum tamen rex ipse, pro sua et regni sui securitate, ea libere committere consueuit quibus sibi et regno suo uiderit expediri.

5. Item quod senescallus et alii ministri hospicii regis ponuntur per eosdem consiliarios cum tamen rex eos semper posuerit et deposuerit pro sue libito uoluntatis.[5]

6. Item quod potestatem regis quam habet et habere debet cognoscendi et corrigendi facta iusticiarii, cancellarii et thesaurarii atque aliorum ministrorum regni, commiserunt eisdem consiliariis et eam per consequens regi subtraxerunt.

7. Item per hoc quod castra sua et domini Edwardi filii sui et aliorum fidelium suorum in partibus Wallie et alibi capta fuerunt et diruta et depredaciones facta bonorum suorum, regine et liberorum suorum ac aliorum tam clericorum quam laicorum regi adherencium et in personis et rebus ecclesiasticis enormia quamplurima perpetrata, quibus omnibus et aliis malis infinitis occasionem dedit statutum iuramenti illius quod scilicet omnes qui eorum constitucionibus obuiarent ab omnibus de regno inimici capitales haberentur.[6]

8. Sunt etiam alia grauamina suo loco et tempore proponenda, de quibus et supradictis sunt et fuerunt contentiones et discordie inter dominum regem et barones suos.

Vnde[b] petit dictus rex Anglie predictos barones ad interesse suum quod estimat CCC[c] milia libr' sterling' sibi condempnari, et pro iniuriis sibi factis per eosdem in ducentis milibus marc', pro quibus dictas iniurias sustinuisse noluisset.[7]

Petit eciam predictas prouisiones quibus nititur pars aduersa, ordinaciones, statuta et obligaciones, et quicquid ex eis et ob eas secutum est per uestrum arbitrium et ordinacionem, domine rex Francie, cassari et irritari seu cassa et irrita nunciari, et pronunciari ipsum regem Anglie non teneri ad obseruacionem ipsorum et dictum regem per uestrum arbitrium et ordinacionem in eum statum reduci in quo erat dictus rex ante statuta, obligaciones et

---

[b] *The* peticio *is written in another hand.*   [c] centum *deleted*, ccc *written above.*

---

[5] See doc. 4, n. 12; *Baronial Plan*, pp. 95–6, 119, 262.
[6] On 4 Aug. 1258 Henry III issued letters patent binding both himself and the Lord Edward to observe the ordinances of the council. In addition an oath of obedience to obey the council was demanded from all the king's subjects, lay and clerical (*C.P.R. 1247–58*, pp. 644–5, 649).

4. Further, that the king's castles are committed [for custody] by these councillors, although the king personally, for his own safety and that of his realm, was accustomed to commit them freely to whatsoever persons he deemed suitable to his own interests and to those of his realm.

5. Further, the steward and other ministers of the king's household are appointed by these councillors, whereas the king always appointed and removed them at his own free will.[5]

6. Further, that they have committed to these same councillors the power which the king has, and ought to have, of taking cognizance of and correcting the actions of the justiciar, the chancellor, and the treasurer, and of the other ministers of the realm, and thus have taken it away from the king.

7. Further, in this, that his castles, and those of the Lord Edward his son, and of the other faithful men in Wales and elsewhere, have been taken and destroyed, and plundering has been wrought upon his property and that of the queen and of his children, and upon that of others, both clergy and laymen, who have remained faithful to the king, and many outrages have been perpetrated upon ecclesiastical persons and property; all of which, and other infinite evils, have been occasioned by the edict for that oath, by which all who opposed their orders should be treated as capital enemies by all men of the realm.[6]

8. There are, moreover, other injuries to be set out in due time and place, upon which, together with the foregoing matters, contentions and discords have arisen and remain between the lord king and his barons.

Wherefore the king of England asks that the barons shall be condemned to pay compensation to him, which he estimates at £300,000 sterling, also 200,000 marks for the harm done to him by them, for which sums he would not willingly have suffered these injuries.[7]

He also asks that, by your arbitration and ordinance, lord king of France, the provisions, upon which his adversaries rest their case, and all ordinances, statutes, and obligations and everything else which has resulted from them or on account of them, shall be quashed and invalidated, and declared null and void; and that the king of England shall be declared not to be bound to their observance; and that the king, by your arbitration and ordinance, shall be restored to that state in which he was before these statutes,

[7] The reformers answer the claim for 200,000 m. in document 37C, cl. 8. No mention is made of £300,000. In 1261 the king claimed that the nobles had caused him losses of 100,000 or 200,000 marks (doc. 30, cl. 1; doc. 31, cl. 20).

ordinaciones predictas, maxime cum premissa sunt auctoritate
apostolica cassata et irritata et singuli excommunicati qui premissa
obseruant. Hec dicit saluo iure suo in aliis.

dorse Maxime cum[d] dominus rex[e] contra iuramentum suum quod
prestitit in coronacione sua[8] premissa facere uel concedere non
potuit, nec[f] sui subditi uice uersa contra iuramentum fidelitatis
quod eidem domino regi preffecerunt predicta in se suscipere uel
de illis intromittere.

37B

JANUARY 1264*[1]

1. Post hec uero, cum dominus rex attenderet statum regni sui
super prescriptis et aliis grauaminibus quasi infinitis, que longum
esset hic recitare, multiplici reformacione indigere, placuit sibi et
concessit proceribus et magnatibus regni sui quod xii. per ipsum
et alii xii. ex parte procerum eligerentur, et electi ordinarent,
rectificarent et reformarent statum regni secundum quod ad
honorem Dei, fidem regis et regni utilitatem uiderent expedire.
Et quicquid per predictos xxiiii. uel maiorem partem eorum foret
ordinatum, obseruaret, et omnem securitatem quam ipsi uel
maior pars eorum ad huius rei obseruacionem prouiderent, sine
contradiccione faceret et fieri procuraret, iuramento in animam
suam prestito bona fide promisit, sicut in litteris suis patentibus
super hoc confectis plenius continetur. Hoc idem etiam a tota

---

[d] Rex in coronacione sua iurauerit *deleted.*   [e] in sua coronacione *deleted.*
[f] vi *deleted.*

---

* *Text*: Paris, Archives Nationales, J. 654, no. 12 (K). This document, which
consists of three membranes stitched together, records the statement which the
reformers made to Louis IX. The text of the first membrane has been split into
paragraphs (1–6) for ease of reference and reading. The paragraphs in the other
two membranes (membrane 2 contains paragraphs 7–13) are those in the original
text but they have been numbered. Transcript in P.R.O., Transcripts 8/133,
section 4, no. 37. *Printed*: *E.H.R.*, lxix (1954), 421–5 (ed. P. Walne). *See*: *Battle
of Lewes*, pp. 87–8.

---

[8] A bull of Gregory IX, dated July 1235 (not 1236) mentioning Henry's
coronation is printed in *Foedera*, 1. i. 229. The coronation oath has been con-

obligations, and ordinances, especially as these have been quashed
and invalidated by papal authority, and all who observe them are
excommunicate. He says this saving his right in other matters.

orse   Especially as the lord king cannot do or grant the aforesaid
things against his oath which he took at his coronation;[8] and
similarly, on the other hand, his subjects cannot take the aforesaid
matters upon themselves, or interfere with them against the oath
of fealty which they made to the lord king.

37B

JANUARY 1264[1]

1. Eventually, however, when the lord king realized that the state
of his realm required manifold reforms, for the reasons already
given and for an infinity of other causes which it would take too
long to detail here, it pleased him to grant to the leading men and
the magnates of his kingdom that twelve should be chosen by himself and twelve others on behalf of the magnates, and that these
chosen men should set in order, rectify, and reform the state of the
realm accordingly as they should see most fitting to the honour of
God, the faith of the king, and the advantage of the realm. And
whatever should be ordained by the twenty-four or by the majority
of them, he would observe; and he would provide, and cause to be
provided, whatever security they or the majority of them should
lay down for the observance of this, without any demur; and he
promised this in good faith by an oath sworn upon his soul, as is
contained more fully in his letters patent drawn up to record it.

sidered by many scholars: H. G. Richardson, 'The English Coronation Oath',
T.R.H.S. 4th series, xxiii (1941), 129–58; also in *Speculum*, xxiv (1949), 44–75;
H. G. Richardson and G. O. Sayles, 'Early Coronation Records', *B.I.H.R.*
xiii (1936), 129–45; xiv (1937), 1–9, 145–8; L. G. W. Legg, *English Coronation
Records* (1901); P. E. Schramm, *A History of the English Coronation* (1937);
P. L. Ward, 'The Coronation Ceremony in medieval England', *Speculum*, xiv
(1939), 160–78; B. Wilkinson, 'The Coronation Oath of Edward II and the
Statute of York', *Speculum*, xix (1944), 445–69.

[1] See doc. 37A, n. 1.

communitate regni iurari mandauit sicut in aliis ipsius litteris continetur,[2] *hoc adiecto in sacramento singulorum de ipsius mandato, quod si quis contra prouisiones ipsas uenire presumeret pro capitali inimico omnium haberetur,* et nichilominus in omnes qui ordinaciones seu prouisiones eorum infringere attemptarent uel eis quoquo modo contraire per dominum Cantuariensem archiepiscopum et nonnullos suffraganeos suos presente turba hominum non modica ac ipsomet presente et candelam in manu tenente publice et sollempniter excommunicare fecit.[3]

2. Sicque xxiiii[or·], in forma predicta electi et iurati, quia dominus rex uariis a communitate receptis subsidiis tociens eos illusit, cartam de libertatibus Anglie obseruare promittens et post modicum contraueniens expresse, ordinarunt primo de securitate quod castra et municiones regni aliquibus fidelibus et indigenis per consilium electis traderentur ad opus domini regis et heredum suorum saluo custodienda, ita quod nulli nisi eidem domino regi et heredibus suis castra et municiones ipsas redderent, et hoc non nisi de consensu totius uel maioris partis consilii sui, ne forte aliqui processu temporis ordinacionem eorum infringere uolentes ad fomentum sue malicie refugium habere possent in eisdem; et hoc ad xii. annos tantum, infra quod tempus prouisiones ipse seu ordinaciones quas super statu regni facerent, si bene forent obseruate, transsire possent in legem.

3. Demum uero ad reformacionem status regni quedam prouisiones seu ordinaciones facte fuerunt, quas presertim cum dominus rex hiis diebus ante recessum et in recessu suo ab Anglia publice proclamare fecerit se[b] firmiter obseruare uelle, et hoc idem per litteras suas suo et fratris sui domini regis Alemannie[4] sigillis consignatas alias fuerit palam protestatus, petunt barones et communitas regni Anglie et eorum procuratores eorum nomine per dictum uestrum, domine rex Francie illustris, approbari et eidem domino nostro regi Anglie firmiter iniungi et caucionem congruam interponi quod easdem in posterum bona fide obseruet et faciat a subditis firmiter obseruari.

---

a–a hoc adiecto . . . haberetur *ins.* K.　　　*b* K *adds* prouisiones ipsas, *deleted.*

---

[2] See doc. 37A, n. 6.
[3] There is no other evidence of this.
[4] Letter dated 16 July 1263 (*C.P.R. 1258–66*, pp. 269–70).

And he ordered the same to be sworn to by the whole community, as is stated in his other letters,[2] with this addition made by his order to the oath of each subject, that if anyone should presume to oppose these provisions, he should be held to be a capital enemy of all men; and in addition he caused all those who might attempt to infringe these ordinances or provisions, or in any way to oppose them, to be publicly and solemnly excommunicated by the lord archbishop of Canterbury and several of his suffragans before a great assembly of men, he himself being present and holding a candle in his hand.[3]

2. Accordingly the twenty-four, chosen in the way already described, and sworn in, recalling that the lord king had received many subsidies from the community and had tricked them every time, promising to observe the charter of the liberties of England and then speedily and specifically breaking his oath, decreed first of all, for security, that the castles and fortifications of the realm should be entrusted to certain faithful and native-born subjects chosen by the council, to be kept safely for the use of the lord king and his heirs, so that they would give up these castles and fortifications to none save to the king and his heirs, and this only with the consent of his whole council or of the majority thereof, lest perhaps, in the process of time, persons wishing to contravene their orders should be able to find refuge in these places in order to foment their malice; and this for a limited period of twelve years only, during which time their provisions and ordinances, which they would make concerning the state of the realm, if they were truly observed, could pass into the law of the land.

3. Then, for the reform of the state of the realm, certain provisions or ordinances were made, which, especially since the lord king very recently, before and during his recent departure from England, caused it to be publicly proclaimed that he wished to observe them fully, and has openly professed this same on another occasion by his letters sealed with his own seal and with that of his brother the king of Germany,[4] the barons and the community of the realm of England and their proctors in their name, ask should be approved by your award, illustrious lord king of France, and also that our lord the king of England should be firmly enjoined, and suitable guarantees stipulated, that in future he will observe them in good faith, and cause them to be firmly observed by his subjects.

4. Ante omnia autem petunt compromissum integrari ut omnes contenciones et discordie hactenus habite includantur ut super omnibus plena pax et concordia haberi possit submoto omni scrupulo dubietatis.

5. Item et in primis, petunt reuocari et in statum suum reduci omnia que post diem compromissi facti[5] sunt attemptata.

6. Protestantur autem barones et eorum procuratores eorum nomine quod licet compromissum et procuratorium sub certis nominibus expressis sint concepta, intelligunt tamen quod omnes amici et coadiutores et omnes prouisiones Oxonie cum eis obseruare uolentes, quorum nomina et sigilla propter infinitam eorum multitudinem poni non poterant in eisdem, cum eis debeant includi.[6]

7.[7] Ex predictis uero grauaminibus patet manifeste quod propter deffectum iusticie que quodammodo a regno Anglie exstitit relegata, necesse fuit capitalem iusticiarium facere qui potestatem haberet corrigendi omnes excessus minorum iusticiariorum et omnium officialium inferiorum et de comitibus et baronibus et omnibus aliis secundum leges regni; qui iurabit quod singulis tam pauperibus quam diuitibus equalem faciet iusticiam, nec aliquid capiet per quod iustum differatur aut rectum. Quod ut caucius procederet prouisum fuit ut per consilium eligeretur, eo quod sanius et firmius est quod plurimorum hominum consilio roboratur.

8. Et eodem modo propter immensas et immoderatas liberalitates et donaciones domini regis predictas, qui omnia per que suum munire deberet errarium uariis et inmeritis plerumque personis dederat penitus absque causa, et alias causas superius expressas, necesse fuit quod aliquis approbate fidelitatis et industrie per consilium poneretur, qui curam thesauri gereret et ad opus domini regis fideliter conseruaret et iniurias hactenus in scaccario per barones scaccarii et alios factas emendaret, circa quem eo caucius erat procedendum quanto ex ipsius officio maioris periculi iminet formido.

9. De cancellario similiter eligendo necesse fuit prouidere quia, cum omnia placita Anglie in curia domini regis per breuia placitentur, que certam habent et habere consueuerunt formam, multa

---

[5] This probably alludes to the letter mentioned in n. 4.
[6] See doc. 38, cl. 6. [7] Clauses 7–12 mention much that is in doc. 5.

4. Before all else they ask that the arbitration shall cover every issue fully, so that all disputes and disagreements hitherto occurring shall be included, and so that full peace and agreement can be obtained on all points, every scruple of doubt being taken away.

5. Also in the first place, they ask that everything which has been attempted since the day on which the compromise was made[5] should be revoked and restored to the state in which it then was.

6. The barons and their proctors in their name declare that although the compromise and the letters procuratorial are drawn up over certain names there written down, they nevertheless understand that all their friends and fellow workers, and all who with them wish to observe the Provisions of Oxford, whose names and seals, on account of their infinite number, cannot be included in these letters, are to be included with them.[6]

7.[7] From the grievances listed above, it appears clearly that because of the lack of justice, which was virtually shut out from England, it was necessary to create a chief justiciar who should have the power to correct all errors of lesser justices and of all lower officials and of earls and barons and all other persons, according to the laws of the realm; and that he should swear that he would do equal justice to all, both poor and rich, and that he would not take anything whereby justice or right should be set aside. And so that he should proceed with care, it was provided that he should be elected by the council, because it is more sensible and secure that he should have the support of the counsel of many men.

8. And in the same way, because of the immense and uncontrolled liberalities and donations of the lord king, already described, who, entirely without reason, gave away to many undeserving people of one sort or another all that he should use to replenish his treasury, and also for other causes indicated above, it was necessary that someone of approved fidelity and industry should be appointed by the council to undertake the care of the treasure and to keep it faithfully for the use of the king, and to correct the wrongs hitherto inflicted in the exchequer by the barons of the exchequer and others; and for his appointment too it was necessary to go all the more cautiously because fear of even greater danger threatens from the abuse of his office.

9. It was similarly necessary to provide for the choice of the chancellor, since, whereas all the pleas of England in the king's court are pleaded by writ, which have and customarily have had

breuia per deffectum cancellariorum retroactis temporibus de cancellaria exiuerunt contra ius et solitum cursum cancellarie pro curialibus et quibusdam alienigenis et aliis potentibus qui gratiam curie habuerunt, et alia breuia que de iure et regni consuetudine singulis petentibus deberent concedi, contra eosdem nullo modo poterant impetrari, sicut superius expressius dictum est; et similiter multa domino regi preiudicialia sigillabantur, ut puta dona uaria immoderata et irracionabilia, et multa alia per cancellariorum incuriam occurrebant pericula, propter quod necesse fuit huic morbo conueniens remedium adhibere.

10. Similiter de uicecomitibus, qui ad reddendam iusticiam per singulos uicecomitatus sunt deputati, per probos et legales homines de comitatu ipso eligendis et domino regi uel thesaurario scaccarii ad officium ab eis recipiendum presentandis necesse fuit prouidere propter grauamina suprascripta, eo quod firmarii et ignote persone quales esse consuerunt, ut sue satisfacere possent auaricie, iusticiam spernentes, tottaliter intendebant ad predam et quia non nullos deposito officio excusabat inopia ut ad firme sue non sufficerent arreragia persoluenda.

11. De quibus omnibus certa ratione prouisum fuit ipsos esse annales ut ex suis, dum se perpetuos aut longius duraturos congnoscerent, non superbirent officiis ad iniurias proniores, set eo artius ab excessibus se abstinerent quanto certius in fine anni se officium deposituros et administracionis sue se cognoscerent rationem reddituros; quos tamen, si tempore illo bene se haberent et honeste, non negat prouisio iterum ad id officium eligi posse.[c]

12. Propter alia uero multa grauamina et pericula supradicta, que alicuius predictorum officialium specialiter non contingebant officium et super quibus necesse fuit remedium adhibere, oportuit eligere aliquos discretos uiros et fidedignos qui consulerent dominum regem, qui per se solus, quantumcumque sapiens, non sufficeret in hiis que pertinent ad regimen regni sui et ad predictos officiales si in aliquo excederent corrigendos; qui tactis sacrosanctis Ewangeliis iurare debent quod dominum regem consulent bona fide ad honorem Dei, fidem suam et regni utilitatem et quod nichil omnino recipient a domino rege nec alio per se nec per alios,

[c] *A caret mark here shows that paragraph 12, written at the end of the membrane, is to follow.*

a fixed form, owing to the incompetence of chancellors in past times many writs have been issued from the chancery against right, and the customary forms of the chancery, for courtiers and certain aliens and other influential men who had the ear of the court, while other writs, which by right and custom of the realm ought to have been granted to individual plaintiffs, could in no wise be obtained against these people, as is stated above more particularly; and as in the same way many things prejudicial to the lord king were sealed, as, for example, various excessive and unreasonable grants; and as many other perils arose from the carelessness of chancellors, it was necessary, for all these reasons, to apply a suitable remedy to this running sore.

10. Similarly as to the sheriffs, who are appointed to render justice throughout the several counties, on account of the grievances stated earlier it was necessary to provide for their choice by good and responsible men of each separate county, and for their presentation to the lord king or to the treasurer of the exchequer to receive their offices from them; since farmers and unknown persons, such as had become customary in these offices, so that they could satisfy their greed, scorning justice, looked for nothing but plunder, and also because some, on laying down office, were excused by poverty when their means did not suffice to pay the arrears of their farms.

11. For all of these, for a particular reason, it was provided that they should all be annual appointments, so that they should not, through knowing themselves to have perpetual or long-enduring tenure, become arrogant in their offices and the readier to inflict injury, but that instead, they should the more strictly refrain from excesses, since they would know plainly that at the end of the year they would lay down their offices to give an account of their stewardship: but at the same time, if during their tenure they had behaved well and honestly, the provision did not preclude them from re-election to that office.

12. Because of many other grievances, together with these dangers, which did not specially concern the office of any one of the officials, but for which it was necessary to find a remedy, it was necessary to choose certain prudent and trustworthy men to advise the lord king, who alone, no matter how wise he might be, could not suffice to deal with all those things which are involved in the administration of his kingdom, and also to correct these officials if they transgressed in anything: and these councillors, with their hands on the holy gospels, were to swear that they would counsel the lord king in good faith, to the honour of God, to his own faith, and to the advantage of the realm, and that in no way would they

nec wardas nec terras nec escaettas alias nec quicquam nisi consensu tocius consilii aut maioris partis eorum ad hoc accesserit, immo nec expensas; et ideo prouisum fuit quod tales essent qui sufficienter de proprio haberent, unde expensarum huius possent honera sustinere.[8]

13. Vnde patet quod prouisio siue ordinacio ista sancta est et honesta, ad honorem domini regis et communem regni sui utilitatem factam, qui singulis iusticiam reddere tenetur; ad quam succrescente hominum malicia per aliam uiam non potuit perueniri; sed qui prouisionem seu ordinacionem ipsam infringere et dominum regem per decepcionis laqueos in contrariam partem trahere laborant, ipsum confusioni, quod absit, et regnum suum trahere nituntur ad ruinam.

14. Attemptata uero sunt hec:—

In primis cum custodia castri Wintoniensis secundum formam prouisionis siue ordinacionis predicte domino comiti Leycestrie ad hoc per consilium electo tradita fuerit, dominus rex, post compromissum primo factum et sigillis ac sacramento uallatum ad castrum ipsum personaliter accedens, illos qui ex parte comitis predicti illud tenebant eiecit, alium ibidem constabularium quem uoluit preficiendo.[9]

15. Item cancellarium per consilium electum secundum formam prouisionum post idem compromissum amouit, sigillum ab ipso auferendo et alii cui uoluit illud committendo.[10]

16. Item post declaracionem compromissi et sacramentum ultimo factum constituit uicecomites in nonnullis comitatibus per se, in quibus per formam prouisionum prouideri deberet de uicecomitibus per eleccionem bonorum uirorum de comitatu ipso; uidelicet in comitatibus Somerset' et Dorset' dominum Henricum de Alemannia, in comitatu Kencie dominum Rogerum de Leiborn', in comitatibus Norfolchie et Suffolchie dominum Iohannem de

[8] This probably alludes to the Council of Fifteen rather than to the Council of Twenty-four.

[9] Clauses 14–19 record actions of the king which have broken the peace and mention things done on the king's behalf contrary to the truce of July 1263. See doc. 5, n. 23 for Winchester castle. On 9 July 1261 Reginald fitz Peter, Lord of Blaen Llyfni, co. Brecon, a Marcher lord who supported the crown, was appointed constable at Winchester castle by the king, but on 18 July 1263 John de Hay took office 'by council of the magnates'. The nobles are probably referring to the appointment of Reginald fitz Peter (*C.P.R. 1247–58*, pp. 636, 654; *C.P.R. 1258–66*, pp. 163, 271; *C.R. 1261–64*, pp. 241–2; *English Baronies*, pp. 9, 15, 39, 105).

accept, either from the lord king or from anyone else, by their own hands or by those of others, wardships, lands, or other escheats, nor anything else, unless he should obtain it with the consent of the whole council, or the greater part thereof, not even excepting expenses; and therefore it was provided that they should be men who had sufficient means of their own to be able to bear the burden of the expenses of this duty.[8]

13. Therefore it seems that this provision or ordinance is sanctified and honest, and that it is made for the honour of the lord king and for the common advantage of his kingdom, the king being bound to give justice to every one. As human malice grows this purpose could be achieved by no other way; but those who strive to overthrow this provision or ordinance and to draw the lord king by the snares of deception into the opposing party, are seeking to pull him into confusion, which heaven forbid, and his kingdom into ruin.

14. The breaches of the truce are these:

Firstly, whereas, according to the terms of this provision or ordinance, the custody of Winchester castle was given to the earl of Leicester, who was chosen by the council for this duty, the lord king, after the compromise was originally made and confirmed with seals and by an oath, came in person to the castle, threw out those who were holding it on the earl's behalf, and installed another constable of his own choice.[9]

15. Further, after the compromise, he removed the chancellor elected by the council under the terms of the provisions, taking the seal away from him and committing it to another of his own choice.[10]

16. Further, after the declaration of the compromise and the oath finally made, he appointed sheriffs of his own choice in several counties, in which by the terms of the provisions, provision for sheriffs should be made by the choice of the good men of the county itself: namely, in the counties of Somerset and Dorset, lord Henry of Almain; in the county of Kent, lord Roger de Leybourne; in the counties of Norfolk and Suffolk, lord John de Vaux; in the

---

[10] On 12 July 1261 Henry III replaced the baronial chancellor, Nicholas de Ely, by Walter de Merton (see doc. 31, n. 12). On 19 July 1263 Nicholas de Ely resumed office but early in the following November he was replaced by John Chishull. Note coincidence of dates in n. 9.

Vallibus, in comitatu Norhamtonie dominum Alanum la Suche, et quosdam alios in diuersis comitatibus.[11]

17. Item inhibuit baronibus Quinque Portuum ne in aliquo intenderent domino Ricardo de Grey custodi castri Douerie in forma prescripta per consilium deput⟨at⟩o, dominum Rogerum de Leyborn' eis preficiens in custodem, licet semper custodi castri predicti intendere consueuerint.[12]

18. Item post eiusdem compromissi declaracionem dominus Rogerus de Mortuo Mari, qui compromissum ipsum cum aliis obseruare iurauit, litteris domini regis munitus partes Marchie intrauit et hostiliter cum excercitu non modico inuasit terras comitis Leycestrie, uidelicet apud Dilun, Lugwardin et Mawardin,[13] et blada ipsius ibidem inuenta triturari fecit et alia catalla sua uastauit et asportauit et dominium eorundem maneriorum sibi usurpando fidelitatis sacramentum ab hominibus et tenentibus extorsit, redditum de termino Natalis colligendo et asportando. Homines uero et familiares ipsius Rogeri paulo ante aduentum eius constabularium domini comitis predicti municionis sue predicte de Dilun ceperunt et in carcere detinuerunt donec ipsum pro cc. marcis se redimere compulissent. Ita ut, dicto Rogero reuerso, ad prisonam reuerteretur si redempcionem ipsam ratam non haberet, ad uoluntatem suam se iterum redempturus; qui reuersus ipsum ad prisonam redeuntem sub eadem redempcione quam acceptauit ipsum abire permisit.

19. Item idem Rogerus hostiliter inuasit castrum et[d] terras domini Henrici de Penebrigg', coadiutoris et socii baronum prouisiones Oxonie obseruare uolentium, et destruxit [e]et in predam posuit[e] omnia que inuenit in eisdem.[14f]

---

[d] castrum et *ins.* K.   [e-e] et ... posuit *ins.* K.   [f] *On dorse of membrane 1 is written* In quod [rotulo habenda] scripta super statu Regni Anglie.

---

[11] This possibly alludes to appointments made by the king during 1261–3, (*C.P.R. 1258–66*, pp. 163, 300, 327, 333, 357–9; *C.R. 1261–64*, p. 242).

[12] Richard de Grey became constable of Dover castle, as a baronial nominee, on 26 July 1263, but Roger de Leybourne was appointed by the king in the December of that year (*C.R. 1261–64*, pp. 271, 300, 358).

county of Northampton, lord Alan de la Zuche; and certain others in other counties.[11]

17. Further, he forbade the barons of the Cinque Ports to obey in any matter lord Richard de Grey, keeper of Dover castle appointed by the council in the prescribed form, making lord Roger de Leybourne keeper over his head, although they had always, by custom, obeyed the keeper of this castle.[12]

18. Further, after the declaration of the compromise, Roger Mortimer, who swore, with the others, that he would observe the compromise, having been furnished with letters of the lord king, entered the Marches and with a considerable army invaded as an enemy the lands of the earl of Leicester at Dilwyn, Lugwardine, and Marden,[13] causing the corn found there to be threshed, devastating and carrying off his other goods, and usurping to himself the lordship of the manor, extorting an oath of fealty from its men and tenants, and collecting and making off with the rent for the Christmas term. A little before Roger arrived, his men and members of his household seized the earl's constable of his castle of Dilwyn, and kept him in prison until they compelled him to ransom himself for 200 marks, on condition that, when Roger should come back, he would return to prison if Roger did not ratify that ransom, to ransom himself once again at Roger's will; and when Roger returned he put him once more into prison and let him go for the same ransom, which he accepted.

19. Further, the same Roger, as an enemy, invaded the castle and lands of lord Henry de Pembridge, a fellow worker and colleague of the barons wishing to observe the Provisions of Oxford, and destroyed and carried off as booty everything that he found there.[14]

---

[13] Dilwyn, Lugwardine, and Marden were among the lands, valued at £400 annually, which Henry III had granted to de Montfort (*C.P.R. 1258–66*, pp. 34–5, 46; see doc. 29, cl. 10).

[14] Henry de Pembridge had been sheriff of the county of Hereford sometime before 4 Feb. 1262 (*C.P.R. 1258–66*, p. 198; not Hertford as printed in index and loc. cit.). He was a tenant of Mortimer in the lordship of Radnor and also of the barony of Tarrington, Herefordshire. He was captured by the royal forces at Northampton (*C.P.R. 1256–66*, p. 360; *Book of Fees*, pp. 440, 444, 805, 814; *English Baronies*, pp. 8, 21, 86).

37C

JANUARY 1264[1]

*Grauamina quibus terra Anglie opprimebatur**

Grauamina quibus terra Anglie opprimebatur et super quibus necesse fuit statum eiusdem reformare.

1. In primis cum dominus rex Anglie libertates que in cartis suis dudum communitati terre concessis continentur concessisset inuiolabiliter obseruandas, propter quod communitas regni primo quindecimam et postea *a*tam clerus quam populus*a* tricesimam partem omnium mobilium suorum sibi dederunt,[2] et insuper subsidium ad sororem suam imperatori maritandam, uidelicet de quolibet feudo militis xx. solidos[3] idem dominus rex recepta omni huiusmodi pecunia*b* paulisper eos libertatibus predictis uti permisit, et postea peruerso quorumdam ductus consilio contra tenorem cartarum ipsarum ueniens libertates ipsas paulatim infringere attemptauit uidelicet cum concesserit quod ecclesia Anglicana libera sit et habeat iura sua integra et libertates illesas et retroactis temporibus esse consueuerit quod uacantibus episcopatibus, abbaciis et aliis domibus religiosis, quarum aduocacio pertinet ad dominum regem, idem dominus rex habere consueuit custodiam eorumdem quousque in eis de pastore seu prelato prouideretur, recipiendo inde interim tantummodo racionabiles exitus; custodes huiusmodi episcopatuum, abbatiarum et domuum aliarum, per dominum regem positi tempore uacacionum racionabilibus exitibus minime contenti prout deberent eadem

a–a tam . . . populus *ins.* J.   *b* huiusmodi recepta *which follows is cancelled in* J.

---

* *Text*: Paris, Archives Nationales, J.654, no. 17 (J). The paragraphs are as in the MS. Endorsed: *Item Iusticiarii de Banco* (in same hand as text); *Remedia super statu regni anglie tempore Henrici regis*; 293; B (all in French hand contemporary with text); 17, J. 654. *Projet de réformes pour l'Angleterre* (nineteenth-century French hand). Transcript in P.R.O. Transcripts, 8/133, section 6, no. 1. *Printed*: *E.H.R.* lxxiii (1958), 455–9 (ed. P. Walne). *See*: *Battle of Lewes*, pp. 87–8.

This document, which was probably linked with document 37B, records the more general and enduring causes of the breach between the king and his subjects.

37C

JANUARY 1264[1]

Grievances which oppressed the land of England

The grievances by which the land of England was oppressed and on which the state of that kingdom needed to be reformed.

1. In the first place, the lord king of England had granted the liberties which are contained in his charters formerly granted to the community of the land, to be inviolably observed, in return for which the community of the realm first of all gave him a fifteenth, and then both the clergy and the people gave him a thirtieth part of all their movables,[2] and on top of that a subsidy for marrying his sister to the emperor, at the rate of 20s. from each knight's fee.[3] The lord king, having accepted all these payments, for a short time allowed them to enjoy these liberties, and afterwards, led astray by the perverse counsel of certain men, turning against the wording of those charters, sought gradually to whittle away those liberties. In past times it was customary, when vacancies occurred in bishoprics and abbeys, and in other houses of religion, whose advowsons pertained to the lord king, that the said lord king had custody of the same [offices] until provision had been made to them of a pastor or a prelate, meanwhile receiving from these [vacancies] only reasonable issues. Whereas the king had granted that the English church should be free and should have its rights entire and its liberties undamaged, the keepers of these bishoprics, abbeys, and other religious houses installed by the lord king for the duration of the vacancy, in no wise content, as they should be, with the reasonable issues, have wholly

---

[1] See doc. 37A, n. 1.

[2] The fifteenth was granted in 1225, on condition that the charters were confirmed, while the thirtieth marked a new confirmation of the charters (*Taxation*, pp. 160, 215; *P.R. 1216–25*, pp. 560–1; *C.R. 1234–37*, pp. 545–6).

[3] As Isabella, who married Frederick II in 1235, was not King Henry's eldest daughter, the aid levied at 26s. 8d. a knight's fee was not legally due. The levy was variously called *auxilium*, *scutagium*, *tallagium*, *carucagium* (*Taxation*, pp. 208–9; *C.R. 1234–37*, pp. 189–91).

penitus destruxerunt tenentes earumdem tam liberos quam seruos occasionando grauiter et amerciando ac talliando nemora prosternendo et uendendo parcos et uiuaria destruendo. Et nec etiam hiis contenti ad decimas et oblaciones manus sacrilegas extenderunt que ad baroniam nullo modo pertinent et cum sint mere spiritualia a laicis non possunt quoquomodo possideri. In abbatiis uero et prioratibus non solum ad ea que ad ipsos abbates et priores spectabant sed etiam ad ea que conuentuum usibus sunt deputata manus apponendo blada et instaura uendendo et omnia quecumque inuenerunt pro libito dissipando sicque perit hospitalitas et uiri religiosi non habent unde congrue sustententur. Et quod deterius est dominus rex peruersis quorumdam persuasionibus liberam eleccionem quam de iure habere debent et habere consueuerunt ab antiquo per preces et impressiones plerumque abstulit, quod si aliqui preces huiusmodi licet pro indigno forte sibi porrectas non exaudirent dampno rerum temporalium quandoque grauiter afficiebantur, nec aliunde quantumcumque canonice electi ad gratiam admittebantur donec per diutinam uacacionem quicquid esset pinguedinis exhausisset.[4]

2. In eundem modum de wardis et eschaettis nobilium in manus domini regis incidentium quorum bona custodes huiusmodi totaliter dilapidabant nemora uendendo, parcos et uiuaria destruendo, et domos sepes parcorum et fossata et alia que modica reparacione conseruari poterant et debebant tottaliter corruere permittebant. Et etiam nobiles huiusmodi ignobilibus et ignotis personis maritando eos plerumque disparagiarunt contra tenorem carte prenotate.

3. Item cum in carta predicta contineatur quod rex nulli uenderet denegaret seu differret rectum aut iustum,[5] et hoc per aliqua tempora fuisset obseruatum, tamen post aduentum quorumdam[c] alienigenarum quos rex spretis indigenis ad consilium attraxit contra eosdem et quosdam curiales etiam indigenas quantumcumque grauiter delinquerent non poterat iusticia in curia domini regis immo nec breuia de communi iusticia que de consuetudine regni singulis petentibus concedi deberent nec

[c] quorumdam *ins.* J.

---

[4] The king's actions to install Aymer de Lusignan in Winchester shocked Matthew Paris (*Chron. Majora*, v, *passim*). See Moorman, *Church Life in England*; Gibbs and Lang, *Bishops and Reform*.

[5] Magna Carta, cl. 40. *Magna Carta*, p. 326.

destroyed these houses, harrying the tenants, both free and unfree, with amercements and tallages, cutting down plantations, selling parks and destroying fishponds. Not content even with these oppressions, they have stretched out sacrilegious hands to tithes and offerings which are in no wise part of the barony, and which, being purely spiritual revenues, cannot in any circumstances be held by laymen. In abbeys and priories they lay hands, not only on those things which belong to the abbots and priors themselves, but also on those things which are appropriated to the use of the convents, selling corn and stock and dissipating at will all they can find, so that hospitality is starved and monks lack fitting sustenance. And what is still more harmful, the lord king, at the persuasion of certain perverse men, frequently takes away, by prayer or by pressure, the right of free election which by law they ought to have and were accustomed to have from of old, so that if perchance any do not listen to such requests, pressed upon them even for an unworthy candidate, they are often penalized by loss of their temporal goods, or in other instances the persons elected, no matter how canonically, are not admitted to favour until, through prolonged vacancy, everything that was of value has been exhausted.[4]

2. In the same way, concerning wardships and escheats of the nobles falling into the lord king's hand, the goods of which the keepers of these properties completely dilapidate, selling plantations, destroying parks and fishponds, permitting houses, park-fences, ditches and other things which could and should be kept in order by small repairs, to go to utter rack and ruin; even marrying such noble persons to obscure and unknown persons, they [the keepers] often disparage them against the terms of the charter.

3. Again, although in the charter it is laid down that to no one shall the king sell, deny, or delay right or justice,[5] and for some time this was observed, at length, after the arrival of certain aliens whom the king, scorning his native subjects, drew to his counsels, no justice could be obtained in the lord king's court against these men or against certain courtiers, some of them native, no matter how gravely they had offended, nor even could writs of common justice, which by custom of the realm should be granted to every petitioner, nor any other remedy at law be obtained. And if, by

aliqua remedia iuris impetrari. Et si forte super eorum excessibus
breuia de iusticia casu aliquo contingeret contra ipsos impetrari,
non erat qui secundum eas pro conquerentibus iusticiam faceret,
quibusdam eorum qui ius dicere deberent propter fauorem quia
per eos in suis ponebantur et deffendebantur officiis, quorum etiam
aliquibus se tributarios propter hoc constituerunt, quibusdam
propter timorem ne ab eorum*cc* officiis per ipsos amouerentur
parcentibus eisdem. Et quandoque dum placita contra ipsos usque
ad calculum summe diffinitiue essent tractata dominus rex per
litteras suas*d* iudicium proferri uetuit causam in grauem con-
querentium lesionem suspendendo. Et si aliquis zelo iusticie motus
contra tales aliquo de eis conquerente iudicium proferret, statim
per dolos et machinaciones exquisitis occasionibus ipsum amoueri
et alium faccionibus suis consentire uolentem subrogari procura-
bant loco eius, quia omnes fere iusticiarii prece precio uel fauore
ad ydoneitatem persone nullo penitus habito respectu ad ipsorum
procuracionem positi fuerant et in officiis deffensati. Postquam
uero alienigenarum ac curialium huiusmodi potestas et superbia
in tantum excreuerat quod non erat qui contra eos pro minoribus
super eorum excessibus iudicium profferret, nec breuia de communi iusticia poterant contra eos a cancellaria domini regis
optineri, quidam nobiles et magnates regni super hoc indignati
quod dicti alienigene et curiales eis in huiusmodi debebant
preferri, pari iniuria hoc idem ius immo potius iniuriam sibi
uendicarunt, ut nec contra eos seu eorum balliuos ius reddi sed
nec exsecucionem*e* breuium fieri permiserunt sicque subpeditata
iusticia communi potentiores inferiores denegarunt absque
racione et non habita distinccione feudorum quilibet alteri potencior
ipsum pro libito distringebat et quod sibi uisum fuerat faciebat
siue bonum siue malum. Et si contingeret quod aliqui ex predictis
alienigenis seu curialibus aliis uel magnatibus de aliquo inferiori
conqueri uellent statim ad nutum breuia qualia uoluerunt etiam
contra solitum cursum cancellarie et iusticiarios quales petere
uoluerunt quantumcumque sibi fauorabiles et parti aduerse
forent suspecti optinuerunt qui pro eis quales uoluerunt pro-
tulerunt summas siue bonas siue malas, nec erat perperam

cc eorem J.   *d* per litteras suas *ins.* J.   *e sic* J.

chance, it happened that in some cases writs of justice could be obtained against them on account of their excesses, there was no one who would do justice according to the writs for the plaintiffs against these men, for some of those whose duty it was to declare the law would favour these men because they were placed and maintained in their offices by them, and had made themselves clients of some of these men, while others would do the same out of fear lest they should be removed from their offices by them. And sometimes, when suits against these men had been carried as far as the assessment of the definitive sentences, the lord king, by his letters, forbade judgement to be declared, suspending the suit to the grievous damage of the plaintiffs. And if anyone, moved by zeal for justice, declared judgement to someone complaining against these men, then at once by trickery and scheming and ferreting out opportunities, they secured his removal and the appointment in his place of someone willing to take part in their intrigues, for nearly all the judges were placed and kept in their offices by the influence of these men, by prayer, price or favour, no respect whatsoever being paid to their personal suitability. But after the power and pride of these aliens and courtiers had grown so overweening that there was no one who would declare judgement in favour of the humbler men against them and their excesses, nor could writ of common justice be obtained against them from the lord king's chancery, certain nobles and magnates of the realm, indignant that the aliens and courtiers should be preferred to them in these matters, with equal injustice claimed this same right, or, rather, wrong, for themselves, so that they would not permit justice to be done or writs to be executed against themselves or against their bailiffs; and thus, common justice being trampled underfoot, the stronger denied it to the weaker, without reason, and, making no distinction of tenure, any man who was stronger than his neighbour distrained him at will, and did as he saw fit, whether good or evil. And if it chanced that any of the aliens or other courtiers, or any of the magnates, wished to complain of any inferior, then at once, on the merest nod, they obtained whatever writs they wanted, even against the established procedures of the chancery, and whatever judges they chose to ask for, however favourable to themselves or suspect to their opponents they might be, who would pronounce whatever judgements they wanted, whether good or evil, unjustly refusing to the persons thus

condempnatis appellacionem uel supplicacionem nec alicuius alterius remedii locus.

4. Preterea predicti alienigene curiales nobiles et eorum balliui, ubi tenentes eorum nullam sequelam curie facere consueuerunt, ab antiquo ipsos ad huiusmodi sequelas faciendas, nisi hoc in cartis ipsorum foret specialiter exceptum, et ad non nulla alia seruicia indebita et inconsueta contra iusticiam coegerunt, nec poterat super hoc aut aliis eorundem excessibus remedium contra eos impetrari.

5. Item cum de iure et regni consuetudine et sicut in carta predicta continetur mercatores undecumque uenientes et quales- cumque merces defferentes absque prisis et toltis irracionabilibus libere uenire possint in Angliam et quo et quando uoluerint abire, dominus rex et alii curiales sui*ᶠ* sub nomine regis sibi et aliis amicis suis capiunt ultra antiquas racionabiles et consuetas prisas in uino, panno et speciebus et ceteris mercibus quas a mercatoribus huiusmodi ceperunt sine precio, ipsos in prisis et toltis huiusmodi adeo irrationabiliter grauauerunt quod terram fugiunt et cum mercibus suis aliunde se conuertunt in grauem totius regni lesionem.

6. Item cum uicecomitatus et cetere ballie domini regis ad certam et moderatam firmam dudum positi essent, ita quod uicecomites absque subditorum oppressione et aliqua extorsione illicita de firmis huiusmodi poterant bene respondere, thesaurarius scaccarii et ceteri consiliarii et collaterales domini regis in comitati- bus et balliis huiusmodi grauiorem censum constituentes, firmas*ᵍ* ipsas uendiderunt partem precii sibi retinentes incrementum huiusmodi de nouo impositum in perpetuum pro certa firma exigendo et successiue augendo, dum uicecomites et balliui querentes in alieno dispendio lucrum suum quilibet alium per licitacionem superare studebat, sicque impositum et tociens adauctum censum aliter soluere non ualentes *ʰ*ad extorsiones illicitas*ʰ* necesse habebant se conuertere et rapinas per quod tota terra ad incredibilem paupertatem est redacta. Et si qui ab ipsis iniuriose oppressi querimoniam deponerent de eisdem, propter fauttores quos habebant in curia tam scelerati lucri participes uix aut nunquam poterant exaudiri. Nec fuerunt huiusmodi uicecomites milites discreti et sapientes de comitatibus ipsis

ᶠ J *reads* qui.   *ᵍ* firmas *ins.* J.   *ʰ⁻ʰ* ad . . . illicitas *ins.* J.

condemned all opportunity of appeal or petition or any other kind of redress.

4. Moreover, the aliens, courtiers, and nobles and their bailiffs, in instances where their tenants from of old had not been accustomed to do any suit of court, unjustly constrained them to do such suits, unless this was specially excepted in their charters, and forced them to perform other undue and uncustomary services, nor could they obtain against them any remedy on this or other excesses of theirs.

5. Again, by right and by custom of the realm, and as is stated in the charter, merchants coming from any place whatsoever, and bringing any kind of merchandise could freely enter England without unreasonable prices and exactions, and could leave where and when they liked. The lord king, and other courtiers in his name, for themselves and other friends of theirs, take more than the ancient, reasonable and customary prises in wine, cloth, spices, and in other goods, which they have taken from these merchants without payment, and so unreasonably oppressed them with these prises and exactions that they shun the kingdom and betake themselves elsewhere with their merchandise, to the great loss of the whole realm.

6. Again, whereas the shrievalties and other bailiwicks of the lord king were formerly let at a fixed and moderate farm, so that sheriffs could properly answer for these farms without oppressing those subject to them and without any unlawful extortion, the treasurer of the exchequer and other councillors and hangers-on of the lord king, inflicting a heavier burden upon the counties and other such bailiwicks, sold the farms, keeping part of the price for themselves, exacting these newly-imposed increments in perpetuity as part of the fixed farm and increasing them successively; while the sheriffs and bailiffs, seeking their profit at the expense of others, each schemed to outbid the other, and thus, not being able to pay otherwise the payments thus imposed and so frequently increased, of necessity had recourse to illicit extortions and rapine, thus reducing the whole land to an incredible state of poverty. And if any of those who were so harmfully oppressed laid complaint against the oppressors, they could scarcely ever, or never gain a hearing, on account of the protectors whom the oppressors had at court as partners in their ill-gotten gains. Nor were these sheriffs prudent and knowledgeable knights of the counties, as was of old

sicut antiquitus fieri consueuit, set de longinquo uenientes et in
comitatibus ipsis penitus ignoti qui prece uel precio predictorum
graciam curialium optinere potuerunt, qui multociens deposito
officio non habentes unde suum nec domino regi de firma nec
subditis satisfacere poterant de offensis. Vnde multociens urgente
necessitate arreragia uicecomitum et aliorum balliuorum que*hh* ante
recessum a compoto statim solui deberent in scaccario et plerumque
aliquo modico ab eis recepto atterminant ad non modicum tempus,
uel ut aliquod modicum soluat annuatim, ita quod de arreragiis
quadringentarum quingentarum marcarum et supra atterminatur
ut c. solidos uel x. marcas soluat annuatim, in non modicum
domini regis dispendium.

7. Item quidem curiales alienigene et alii sese adinuicem con-
federantes et mutue promouentes eschaettas, wardas et alia
dominum regem contingencia ex quibus suum munire deberet
errarium et non spoliis pauperum intendere sibi inuicem uice
reciproca conferri procurarunt. Insuper et de certis domini
regis redditibus tot et tanta feuda per manus thesaurarii in
scaccarium liberanda sibi et aliis dari procurarunt quod patri-
monium suum per feuda huiusmodi fere tottaliter fuit exhaustum,
set nec ipsi principales maioribus feudis contenti existentes
militibus et aliis familiaribus suis feuda aliqua minora conferri
procurarunt, omni subtilitatis ingenio a domino rege quicquid
poterant emungendo. Et licet dominus rex aliquibus huiusmodi
feuda habentibus usque ad sui feudi equiualenciam annuam uel
supra in terris conferret nichilominus tamen ut feuda ipsa eis
inposterum continuarentur, instare non cessabant quod et
plerumque per importunitatem optinuerunt discussis quoque
thesaurarie racionibus inuenietur quod donarii huiusmodi in
pecunia numerata wardis et eschaettis et aliis a xv. annis citra
summam c. milium marcarum et plus*i* excedent. Ita quod parum
uel nichil remansit penes thesaurarium in usus regis conuertendum
propter quod errario suo*j* tottaliter exhausto dum non haberet
unde uictum cotidianum redimeret necesse habuit se conuertere
ad rapinas, panem, uinum et cetera ad sustentacionem domus
sue necessaria sumens de precio eorundem minime satisfacto,
per quod multi in regno Anglie pauperes effecti sunt et mendici,
et non nulli exulare coacti.

hh qui J.   *i* et plus *ins.* J.   *j* Suo suo J.

custom, but men coming from far away and utter strangers in the counties, who had been able to obtain the support of the courtiers by prayer or by price, and who often on laying down their offices, had not the wherewithal to satisfy the lord king for the farm nor his subjects for their offences. Accordingly, very often, under force of necessity, the arrears of the sheriffs and other bailiffs, which should be paid immediately into the exchequer before the discharge from the account, are instead, on the receipt of some trivial payment from them, attermed for quite long periods or on the promise of some small sum annually, so that out of arrears of 400 or 500 marks or more they were attermed to pay 100s. or 10 marks annually, to the great loss of the lord king.

7. Moreover, certain courtiers, aliens, and others, leaguing themselves together and pushing each others' interests, arranged that escheats, wardships and other perquisites of the lord king, by means of which he ought to replenish his treasury, and not by collecting the spoils of the poor, should be conferred upon themselves in turn. Further, out of the assured revenues of the lord king they procured grants of so many and such large fees to be paid to themselves and others by the hand of the treasurer in the exchequer, that the royal patrimony was almost completely exhausted by fees of this kind; and yet these leading men, not content with their larger fees, obtained for knights and other servants of their households various lesser fees, cheating the lord king of whatever they could by every trick of subtlety. And although the lord king conferred upon some, who held this kind of fee, lands equalling or even exceeding the annual value of their fees, nevertheless, however, so that those fees should be continued to them thereafter, they importuned ceaselessly to this end, and often by their importunity succeeded, for investigations of the treasury documents show that payments of this sort, in coined money, wardships, and escheats and other things over the last fifteen years exceed the total of 100,000 marks or more. As a result little or nothing was left in the treasury for the use of the king, so that, his store of money being utterly spent, having not the wherewithal to pay for his daily food, the lord king had to turn to seizing bread, wine, and other things for the maintenance of his household, seizing what he needed without ever paying the price of it, whereby many of his English subjects were pauperized and beggared, and some driven overseas.

8. Item cum dominus rex in subsidium terre sancte et multi nobiles de regno suo et alii eo pretextu essent crucesignati tandem uoto ipsius et tocius populi contra spem et propositum contra Sarecenorum crucis Christi inimicorum in fratres eiusdem Christiane religionis regnicolas scilicet irracionabiliter commutato, et ad maiorem regni confusionem decima ecclesiasticorum prouentuum ad eorumdem impugnacionem per quinquennium sibi concessa ecclesiis in decimarum huiusmodi solucione, et terra tota per coactam uotorum redempcionem depauperatis et multis milibus marcarum ex huiusmodi preda cum ecclesiarum ac tocius communitatis lesione enormi collectis et in uanum persolutis, demum totum cessit in nichilum ut nec terre sancte ad cuius subsidium omnes uiriliter[k] se accingerant aliquid accreuerit nec ridiculosa commutacio Sicilie in aliquo promota existiteri.[6l] Preter hec uero uiri religiosi preter decimam huiusmodi quam soluere fuerant coacti quidam in cc., quidam trecentis, quidam in quadringentis marcis et ultra ipsis penitus insciis et ignorantibus per [m]episcopum Herefordensem et[m] Robertum Walerandi qui se procuratores eorum fecerant absque mandato fuerant [n]pro eodem negocio Sicilie[n] in curia Romana obligati et non admissa placiti procuracionis excepcione satisfacere coacti, que predicta pecunia cc. milium marcarum summam excedit.[7]

[k] viriliter *ins.* J.   [l] *A paragraph mark here* J.   [m–m] episcopum ... et *ins.* J.   [n–n] pro ... Sicilie *ins.* J.

[6] Henry III took the cross on 6 Mar. 1250 and was granted a tenth for three years on 11 Apr. 1250. He accepted the throne of Sicily for his son Edmund on 6 Mar. 1254 and on 23 May 1254 the tenth was extended to five years.
[7] The barons are asserting that the actions of the bishop of Hereford had committed the religious houses to a debt greater than the 200,000 marks which the king had claimed as recompense for the harm done to him (doc. 37A, cl. 8).

8. Again, the lord king took the cross in aid of the Holy Land and many of his nobles and other subjects were induced to do likewise on the same pretext, but at length his vow and that of his entire people was unreasonably converted, against all hope and expectation, from a crusade against the Saracens who are the foes of Christ's cross into an attack on fellow-subjects of the same Christian religion. And to the greater confusion of the kingdom, a tenth of all ecclesiastical revenues was granted to him for five years for their overthrow, while churches, by payment of these tenths, and the whole land by enforced redemption of the vows, were impoverished, many thousands of marks having been collected in spoils of this kind, with enormous harm to the churches and the whole community, only to be thrown away in vain. In the end it all came to nothing, so that neither did the Holy Land, to whose aid all had manfully girded themselves up, gain anything thereby, nor did the absurd cancellation of the crusade to the Holy Land, in favour of an expedition to Sicily, in any way assist that project.[6] And in fact, over and beyond all this, the monks, on top of the tenth which they were forced to pay, were pledged in the Roman *curia*, completely without their knowledge or awareness, by the bishop of Hereford and Robert Walerand, who without any mandate set themselves up as proctors of the monks, to pay, some of them 200, some 300, some 400 marks or even more, for this same Sicilian business, and, no plea of exception to the procuration being allowed, they were forced to make payments exceeding the aforesaid sum of 200,000 marks.[7]

Mention of the activities of Peter Aigueblanche, a Savoyard, bishop of Hereford, is made in *Ann. Mon.* i. 348–9; iv. 109. See also *Chron. Majora*, v. 511; Lunt, *Financial Relations of the Papacy*, pp. 285–6, and *Valuation, passim*.

38

23 JANUARY 1264

*Reformacio pacis inter Henricum regem Anglie
et barones regni sui . . .**

*ᵃ*Ludouicus, Dei gratia, Francorum rex, uniuersis, presentes litteras inspecturis, salutem.

1. Notum facimus quod carissimus consanguineus noster Henricus, illustris rex Anglie, et subscripti barones Anglie in nos compromiserunt, prout continetur in litteris eorum infra scriptis; tenor autem litterarum ipsius regis talis est.

Henricus, Dei gracia, Rex Anglie, dominus Hibernie, et dux Aquitanie omnibus, ad quos presentes littere preuenerint, salutem.

2. Noueritis quod nos compromisimus in dominum Ludouicum, regem Francorum illustrem, super prouisionibus, ordinationibus, statutis, et obligationibus omnibus Oxoniensibus: et super omnibus contentionibus et discordiis, quas habemus, et habuimus, usque ad festum Omnium Sanctorum nuper preteritum, uersus barones regni nostri, et ipsi aduersus nos occasione prouisionum, ordinationum, statutorum, uel obligationum Oxoniensium predictarum.

3. Promittentes, et per dilectos et fideles nostros, Willielmum Belet*ᵇ* militem, et Robertum Fulconis[1] clericum, de mandato

---

ᵃ In the margin is the heading Reformacio pacis inter H. regem Anglie et barones regni sui facti per Lodouicum, regem Francorum, in quem predictus Henricus et barones sui compromiserunt et consenserunt ad pacem illam reformandam super prouisionibus Oxonie et aliis discordiis inter ipsos habitis.
ᵇ This is an error for Biset *(C.P.R. 1258–66, p. 303; Royal Letters, ii. 251).*

---

* *Text*: P.R.O. E. 36/275. Liber. B, ff. 35–6 (2–3) (O). *Printed*: Foedera, I. i. 433–4 (refers to Liber B, f. 2); Stubbs, pp. 395–7, prints only part of para. 1 and paras. 8–20. *Additional Texts*: i. Bodley MS. 91, ff. 136ᵛ–138 (B). Discussed by N. Denholm-Young, *E.H.R.* xlix (1934), 85–93; *Collected Papers*, pp. 86–93. ii. British Museum, Royal MS. 10 B. vi (R). *Printed*: Foedera, I. i. 434. Papal approval, dated 16 Mar. 1264, for Louis's award in Dorez and Giraud, *Les Registres d'Urbain IV*, no. 708. *See*: Simon de Montfort, pp. 205–8, 247; *Battle of Lewes*, pp. 88–91; *King Henry III*, pp. 451–5; C. T. Wood, 'The Mise of Amiens and Saint Louis' theory of kingship', *French Historical Studies*, vi (1970), 300–10; R. F. Treharne, 'The Mise of Amiens, 23 January 1264', in *Studies in Medieval History presented to F. M. Powicke* (1948), pp. 223–39; J. P. Gilson, 'An unpublished notice of the battle of Lewes', *E.H.R.* xi (1896),

38

23 JANUARY 1264

The re-establishment of peace between Henry, king of England, and the barons of his realm

Louis, by God's grace king of the French, to all who shall read these present letters, greeting.

1. We declare that our dearest cousin Henry, illustrious king of England, and the barons of England named below, have laid their dispute formally in our hands, as is stated in their letters here cited. The terms of the king's letter are as follows:

Henry, by God's grace king of England, lord of Ireland, and duke of Aquitaine, to all whom this present letter shall reach, greeting.

2. Know that we have laid our dispute formally in the hands of the lord Louis, illustrious king of the French, on the provisions, ordinances, statutes, and all other obligations of Oxford, and upon all the disputes and disagreements which we have and have had, down to the feast of All Saints' last [1 November], with the barons of our realm and they with us by occasion of the aforesaid provisions, ordinances, statutes, and obligations of Oxford.

3. Promising, and, through our beloved and faithful knight, William Biset, and clerk, Robert Fulk,[1] by our special command

---

520-2. There are no paragraphs in the MS. The text has been divided and paragraphs numbered to aid reference. The letters of Henry III and the Lord Edward appear in the patent roll (*C.P.R. 1258-66*, pp. 303-4; *Royal Letters*, ii. 251-2) but there is no copy, either of the nobles' letter or of Louis' award, among the chancery rolls.

B places the documents in a different order. After a heading in red, *Dictum domini regis Francorum*, the text continues with para. 1. A rubric in red, *Compromissio domini regis Anglie et Edwardi sui [filii] in regem Francorum de prouisionibus Oxonie*, precedes paras. 2-4. As in O the sentence beginning *confectioni* (see n. *c*) is omitted, paras. 8-20 follow para. 4, while paras. 5-7 end the B text. R is a treatise on canon law by Bernardus Bottonus of Parma, d. 1263. At the end of the MS., added in a late thirteenth-century hand, are (*a*) *Decretum regis Francie super prouisionibus Oxonie factis*, part of the award of Louis IX; (*b*) A narrative of the battle of Lewes, printed by J. P. Gilson in *E.H.R.* xi (1896), 520-2.

[1] William Biset is called one of the king's butlers in Mar. and Aug. 1263, while Robert Fulk was given robes in Dec. 1263 and was called king's clerk in Mar. 1264 (*C.P.R. 1258-66*, p. 254; *C.R. 1261-4*, p. 329; *C. Lib. R. 1260-7*, pp. 121, 135).

nostro speciali, in animam nostram iurantes, tactis sacrosanctis Euangeliis, quod, quicquid idem rex Francie super omnibus predictis, uel eorum aliquibus, de alto et basso, ordinauerit uel statuerit, nos obseruabimus bona fide; ita tamen, quod idem dominus rex Francie dicat super his dictum suum citra Pentecostem proximo uenturam.

In cuius rei testimonium presentibus litteris sigillum nostrum fecimus apponi.

4. Nos autem Edwardus, predicti domini regis Anglie primogenitus; Henricus filius Ricardi regis Alemannie; Rogerus. comes Norfolcie et marescallus Anglie; Iohannes de Warenna; Willielmus de Valencia; Hunfridus de Bohun, comes Hereford et Essex; Hugo le Bygoz; Philippus Basset; Iohannes filius Alani;[2] Robertus de Bruis;[3] Rogerus de Mortuomari; Iohannes de Verdun; Willielmus de Breaus;[4] Iohannes de Baillol; Henricus de Percy;[5] Reginaldus filius Petri; Iacobus de Aldithele; Alanus de la Zuche;[6] Rogerus de Clyfford;[7] Hamo Extraneus;[8] Iohannes de Gray; Philippus Marmyon; Robertus de Nevile; Iohannes de Vallibus;[9] Iohannes de Mouscegros;[10] Warinus de Bassingburn;[11] Adam de Gesemuth;[12] Rogerus de Somery; Richardus Folyot;[13] Rogerus de Leyburn[14] et Willielmus de Latymero;[15] predicto compromisso, per dictum dominum nostrum regem Anglie facte, sicut predictum est, consentimus et iuramus, tactis sacrosanctis Euangeliis, quod, quicquid predictus dominus rex Francie, super omnibus predictis, uel eorum aliquibus, de alto et basso, ordinauerit uel statuerit, obseruabimus bona fide: ita tamen, quod idem dominus rex Francie dicat, super his, dictum suum citra Pentecostem proximo sicut superius est expressum. In cuius rei testmonium presenti

---

[2] Lord of Oswestry and Clun, Salop., Keevil, Wilts. See *Baronial Plan*; *English Baronies*; *G.E.C.* for biographical articles on many of those named in this document.

[3] Died 1262; husband of Isabel, sister of Richard, earl of Gloucester; lord of Writtle, Essex (*English Baronies*, p. 102).

[4] Lord of Bramber, Sussex, and Gower in South Wales. A supporter of Richard, earl of Gloucester.

[5] Lord of Topcliffe, Yorks. A supporter of Richard, earl of Gloucester.

[6] Died 1270; an unchanging royalist, husband of one of the three daughters and coheirs of Roger de Quency, earl of Winchester, who died 1264 (*English Baronies*, p. 62).

[7] Related to the lords of Clifford, Herefordshire, brother-in-law of Roger de Leybourne, an unchanging royalist (ibid., p. 104; see n. 14).

[8] An unchanging royalist, son of John L'Estrange of Knockin, Salop., and Hunstanton, Norfolk (*King Henry III*, pp. 605–6).

taking oath upon our soul, touching the holy gospels, that we will
in good faith observe whatever the lord king of France orders or
decrees upon all of these matters, or on any of them high and low,
provided that the lord king of France shall declare his award on
these things before Whitsuntide next [8 June]. In testimony we
have had our seal placed on this present letter.

4. And we, Edward, firstborn son of the aforesaid lord king
of England; Henry, son of Richard, king of Germany; Roger,
earl of Norfolk and marshal of England; John de Warenne;
William de Valence; Humphrey de Bohun, earl of Hereford and
Essex; Hugh Bigod; Philip Basset; John fitz Alan;[2] Robert Brus;[3]
Roger Mortimer; John de Verdon; William de Braose;[4] John
Balliol; Henry Percy;[5] Reginald fitz Peter; James de Audley; Alan
de la Zuche;[6] Roger Clifford;[7] Hamo L'Estrange;[8] John de Grey;
Philip Marmion; Robert Neville; John de Vaux;[9] John de Mus-
grove;[10] Warin de Bassingbourne;[11] Adam de Jesmond;[12] Roger
de Somery; Richard Foliot;[13] Roger de Leybourne;[14] and William
Latimer[15] have consented and sworn, touching the holy gospel,
to this covenant made by our lord the king of England, that whatever the lord king of France orders and decrees on all of these
things, or on any of them, high or low, we will observe in good
faith, provided that the said lord king of France shall declare his
award on these things before Whitsuntide next [8 June], as is
already said. In testimony we have had our seals fixed to the

[9] Son of the heiress of Freiston, Lincs., a supporter of Richard, earl of
Gloucester.

[10] One of the leaders, together with Warin de Bassingbourne, of the band of
knights who raided Wallingford castle in Nov. 1264 in an attempt to release the
Lord Edward (*King Henry III*, p. 486).

[11] One of the Lord Edward's supporters in March, 1259.

[12] Brother and, in 1278, heir of Ralph de Gaugy, lord of Ellingham, North-
umberland. Royal sheriff of Northumberland and constable of the castle of
Newcastle upon Tyne. Also called Adam de Gesemuth. (*English Baronies*, p. 41;
C.P.R. 1258–66, passim.)

[13] Lord of Fenwick, Yorks. Active on the baronial side in 1261–2 (*King
Henry III*, p. 530, n. 3).

[14] Steward of the Lord Edward, steward of the royal household, 1263–5,
husband of one of the coheiresses of the lordship of Appleby, Westm. (*English
Baronies*, p. 104; see n. 7).

[15] Lord of Corby, Lincs., Scampston, Yorks., active for the king (*G.E.C.*
vii. 460–1).

scripto, sigillo predicti domini nostri regis Anglie signato, sigilla nostra facimus apponi. Datum apud Wyndeles', dominica proxima post festum Sancte Lucie uirginis, anno Domini m° c c° sexagesimo tertio.*c*

Littere uero baronum tales sunt.*d*

5. Vniuersis, presentes litteras inspecturis, H. Londoniensis,[16] W. Wigorniensis episcopi; Simon de Monteforti, comes Leycestrie et senescallus Anglie, Hugo le Despenser, iusticiarius Anglie, Humfridus de Boun iuuenis, H. de Monteforci, S. de Monteforti iuuenis, Adam de Nouo Mercato,[17] Petrus de Monteforti, Radulfus Basset de Sapecot, Baldewinus Wake,[18] Robertus de Ros,[19] Willielmus le Blond,[20] Willielmus Marescallus,[21] Walterus de Colevile,[22] Ricardus de Grey, Willielmus Bandouft, Ricardus de Tanny,[23] Henricus de Hastinggs,[24] Iohannes filius Iohannis,[25] Robertus de Veteri Ponte, Iohannes de Vescy,[26] Nicolaus de Segrave, Galfridus de Lucy, salutem in Domino.

6. Noueritis quod nos compromisimus in dominum Ludouicum, regem Francie illustrem, super prouisionibus, ordinationibus, statutis, et obligationibus omnibus Oxonie, et super omnibus contentionibus et discordiis, quas habemus, et habuimus, usque ad festum Omnium Sanctorum nuper preteritum, aduersus dominum nostrum regem Anglie illustrem, et ipse aduersus nos, occasione prouisionum, ordinationum, statutorum, uel obligationum Oxoniensium predictorum:

7. Firmiter promittentes, et iurantes, tactis sacrosanctis Euangeliis, quod quidquid idem rex Francie, super omnibus

---

c *Foedera adds, in italics,* confectioni istius instrumenti interfuerunt Iohannes de Chishull, Willelmus de Wilton, frater I. de Darlington, magister Ern[aldus] cancellarius Regis Alemannie, Rogerus de Messenden et plures alii. *This paragraph, which is in* Rot. Pat. 48 Hen. III, pt. i, m. 18 (*printed Royal Letters,* ii. 252) *is in neither O nor B. Chishull became chancellor in Nov.* 1263; *Wilton, a judge, died fighting for the king at Lewes; Arnold de Wetzler was Richard of Cornwall's chancellor in Holland; Messenden was a royal clerk. The inclusion of this paragraph in* Foedera *is proof that Rymer consulted the patent roll as well as* O.
d *In the MS. this is included in the text and is not a heading.*

---

[16] Henry de Sandwich, supported Simon de Montfort in 1263 (*Baronial Plan, passim*).
[17] Husband of one of the coheirs of the barony of Redbourne, Lincs., steward of the household 7 July 1264–20 Mar. 1265 (*English Baronies,* p. 75).
[18] Lord of Bourne, Lincs., one of the leaders of the disinherited (ibid., p. 107; *King Henry III, passim*).

present document, sealed with the seal of our aforesaid lord the king of England. Given at Windsor on the Sunday next after the feast of St. Lucy the Virgin [16 December] in the year of our Lord 1263.

The letters of the barons are as follows:

5. To all who shall read these letters, Henry, bishop of London,[16] Walter, bishop of Worcester, Simon de Montfort, earl of Leicester and steward of England, Hugh Despenser, justiciar of England, Humphrey de Bohun junior, Henry de Montfort, Simon de Montfort junior, Adam de Newmarket,[17] Peter de Montfort, Ralph Basset of Sapcote, Baldwin Wake,[18] Robert de Ros,[19] William le Blund,[20] William Marshal,[21] Walter de Colevill,[22] Richard de Grey, William Bardolf, Richard de Tany,[23] Henry de Hastings,[24] John fitz John,[25] Robert de Vipont, John de Vescy,[26] Nicholas Segrave, Geoffrey de Lucy, greeting in the Lord.

6. Know that we have laid our dispute formally in the hands of lord Louis, illustrious king of France, upon the provisions, ordinances, statutes, and all other obligations of Oxford, and upon all the disputes and disagreements which we have and have had, down to the feast of All Saints last [1 November], with our lord the illustrious king of England, and he with us, by occasion of the provisions, ordinances, statutes, and obligations of Oxford.

7. Firmly promising and swearing, touching the holy gospels, that we will in good faith observe whatever the lord king of France

[19] Lord of Wark, Northumberland, brother of William de Ros of Helmsley, Yorks. An active supporter of de Montfort in the latter half of 1264 (*C.P.R. 1258–66, passim; English Baronies*, pp. 53, 149).

[20] Lord of Ashfield, Suffolk, died at Lewes, standard bearer of de Montfort (*English Baronies*, p. 4; *King Henry III*, pp. 449–50).

[21] Son of the coheir of the barony of Hockering, Norfolk, baronial supporter in the Midlands (*English Baronies*, p. 53; *Baronial Plan, passim*).

[22] A small tenant in Lincolnshire, summoned to attend the parliament which met in Jan. 1265 (*Book of Fees, passim*; *C.Mis.Inq.* i, 777; doc. 41A. *Baronial Plan*, p. 335 mistakenly calls him William of Coleville).

[23] Tenant of lands at Stapleford Tawney, Essex; 1261 keeper of Essex and Herts., July 1264 *custos pacis* in Essex (*C.P.R. 1258–66*, pp. 163, 394; *C.R. 1261–64*, p. 390).

[24] One of the leaders of the disinherited (*King Henry III, passim*; doc. 44).

[25] One of the leading opponents of the king in 1261, associated with Robert de Vipont, Nicholas de Segrave, Geoffrey de Lucy, and others. June 1264 sheriff of Westmorland (*C.P.R. 1258–66*, pp. 195, 322; *Baronial Plan, passim*).

[26] Lord of Alnwick, Northumberland, supporter of de Montfort in May, 1263 (ibid., p. 302; *English Baronies*, p. 103).

predictis, uel eorum aliquibus, de alto et basso, ordinauerit uel statuerit, nos obseruabimus bona fide; ita tamen quod idem dominus rex Francie dicat, super his, dictum suum citra Pentecostem proximo uenturam.

Actum Londini, die sancte Lucie uirginis, anno Domini m° c c° sexagesimo tertio.

8. Insuper predictus rex Anglie, ex una parte,[e] et superius nominati, ex alia parte, barones, de omnibus contentionibus, exortis inter eos post predictum festum Omnium Sanctorum usque in preteritum diem sancte Lucie, occasione predicta in nos compromiserunt, et promiserunt per iuramenta, tactis sacrosanctis Euangeliis, praestita bona fide se seruaturos quicquid statuerimus et ordinauerimus de hiis, uel eorum aliquibus; ita tamen quod citra Pentecostem proximo uenturam, dicamus, super hiis, dictum nostrum, et super omnibus que super rebus, in compromissum deductis, uel circa ipsas interim contigerit attemptari.

9. Nos uero, partibus propter hoc conuocatis Ambianis dicto rege personaliter, et quibusdam de baronibus per se, et aliis per procuratores comparentibus coram nobis; auditis hinc inde propositis, et etiam defensionibus, ac rationibus partium plenius intellectis, attendentes per prouisiones, ordinationes, statuta, et obligationes Oxonienses, et per ea, que ex eis, et occasione eorum subsecuta sunt, iuri et honori regio plurimum fuisse detractum, regni turbationem, ecclesiarum depressionem, et depreditationem, et aliis personis ipsius regni, ecclesiasticis et secularibus, indigenis, et alienigenis, grauissima dispendia prouenisse; et quod uerisimiliter timebatur ne grauiora contigerint in futurum, communicato bonorum et magnatum consilio.

10. In nomine Patris, et Filii, et Spiritus Sancti, predictas prouisiones, ordinationes, et obligationes omnes, quocumque nomine censeantur, et quidquid ex eis, uel occasione eorum subsecutum est, per dictum nostrum, seu ordinationem nostram cassamus et irritamus; maxime cum appareat summum Pontificem eas per suas litteras cassas et irritas nunciasse;[27] ordinantes quod tam dictus rex, quam barones, et alii quicumque presenti

[e] Ex una parte *om.* B.

[27] Docs. 32–4, 36.

shall have ordained or decreed upon all of these matters, or on any
of them, high or low, provided that the lord king of France shall
declare his award on these things before Whitsuntide [8 June]
next. Done at London, on the day of St. Lucy the Virgin [13
December] in the year of our Lord 1263.

8. Moreover the king of England on the one side, and the
barons on the other side have agreed to accept our [Louis IX]
arbitration in all disputes which have arisen by occasion of these
issues between them since the feast of All Saints' [1 November],
down to the day of St. Lucy [13 December] recently past, and
have promised on oaths, sworn touching the holy gospels, that
they will observe in good faith whatever we ordain or decree upon
the above matter or on any of them, provided we shall declare
before Whitsuntide [8 June] next our award on these matters
and upon all others which may happen meanwhile to have been
attempted, arising out of the matters submitted to our award or in
connection with them.

9. Accordingly we, for this purpose, summoned the parties to
Amiens, and the king appeared before us in person, and certain
of the barons appeared personally and others by proctors; and
we heard the proposals of both sides and fully understood the
replies and counter-arguments of the parties. We concluded that
through the provisions, ordinances, statutes, and obligations of
Oxford and through those issues which had arisen from them or
had followed in consequence of them, the rights and honour of the
king had been greatly harmed, the realm disturbed, churches
oppressed and plundered, and that very heavy losses had befallen
other persons of the realm, both ecclesiastical and secular, native
and alien, and that there was good reason to fear that still worse
would follow in the future; and we received the counsel of good
and great men.

10. In the name of the Father, and of the Son, and of the Holy
Spirit, by our award or ordinance we quash and invalidate all
these provisions, ordinances, and obligations, or whatever else they
may be called, and whatever has arisen from them or has been
occasioned by them; especially since it is apparent that the pope,
by his letters, has already declared them quashed and invalid;[27]
and we decree that both the king and the barons, with all others
who agreed to the present compromise, and who in any way had

compromisso consenserunt, et de predictis obseruandis se quoquo modo astrinxerunt, se de eisdem quietent penitus, et absoluant.

11. Addicimus etiam quod, ex ui, seu uiribus predictarum prouisionum, siue obligationum, seu ordinationum, uel alicuius iam super hoc concesse potestatis a rege, nullus noua statuta faciat, neque iam facta teneat uel obseruet, nec propter non obseruanciam predictorum debeat aliquis alterius capitalis, uel aliter inimicus haberi, uel penam propter hoc aliquam sustinere.

12. Decernimus etiam, quod omnes littere, super premissis prouisionibus, et eorum occasione confecte, irrite sint et inanes; et ordinamus, quod ipsi regi Anglie restituantur a baronibus et reddantur.

13. Item, dicimus et ordinamus, quod castra, quecumque fuerint tradita custodienda ad securitatem, seu occasione predictorum, et adhuc sint detenta, libere a dictis baronibus eidem regi reddantur, tenenda ab eodem rege, sicut ea tenebat ante tempus dictarum prouisionum.

14. Item, dicimus et ordinamus, quod libere liceat predicto regi capitalem iusticiarium, cancellarium, thesaurarium, consiliarios, iustic' minores, uicecomites, quoscumque alios officiales, ac ministeriales regni sui, ac domus sue, preficere, instituere*f*, destituere, et amouere, pro sue libito uoluntatis, sicut faciebat, et facere poterat ante tempus prouisionum predictarum.

15. Item, retractamus et cassamus illud statutum factum, quod regnum Anglie de cetero per indigenas gubernetur, necnon ut exirent alienigene, non reuersuri; exceptis illis quorum moram fideles regni communiter acceptarent.

16. Ordinantes per dictum nostrum quod liceat alienigenis morari in dicto regno secure; et quod rex possit alienigenas et indigenas uocare secure ad consilium suum, quod sibi uiderit utiles et fideles, sicut facere poterat ante tempus predictum.

17. Item, dicimus et ordinamus, quod dictus rex plenam potestatem et liberum regimen habeat in regno suo, et eius pertinentiis; et sit in eo statu, et in ea plenaria potestate, in omnibus et per omnia, sicut erat ante tempus predictum.

18. Nolumus autem, nec intendimus per presentem ordinationem derogare in aliquo regiis priuilegiis, chartis, libertatibus, statutis, et laudabilibus consuetudinibus regni Anglie, que erant ante tempus prouisionum ipsarum.

f instituere B; *om.* O.

bound themselves to observe them, shall now entirely acquit and absolve themselves from them.

11. And we also add that no one shall make new statutes in virtue of these provisions, obligations, or ordinances, or in virtue of any power hitherto granted by the king in consequence of them; nor shall anyone hold or observe any enactments hitherto made by virtue of them, nor by reason of the non-observance of them ought anyone to be held the mortal enemy, or any other kind of enemy, of anyone, nor suffer any penalty therefore.

12. We also decree that all documents made concerning or by occasion of the provisions are invalid and of no effect, and we command that they shall be restored by the barons to the king of England, and handed back to him.

13. In particular, we declare and ordain that whatever castles were handed over to be kept as security, or by reason of the provisions and are still held back, shall be freely restored by the barons to the king, to be held by the king as he held them before the time of the provisions.

14. Next, we declare and ordain that the king shall freely be allowed to appoint, institute, dismiss, and remove at his own free will the chief justiciar, the chancellor, the treasurer, the councillors, the lesser justices, sheriffs, and all other officials and servants of his realm and of his household, as he did and had the power to do before the time of the provisions.

15. Further, we reject and quash the statute made declaring that the realm of England should in future be governed by native-born men, and that aliens must depart, never to return, save those whose stay the faithful men of the realm might in common accept.

16. And we decree by our award that aliens shall be allowed to stay in the realm securely, and that the king can safely call to his counsel both aliens and natives whom he may think useful and faithful to him, as he had power to do before this time.

17. Further, we decree and ordain that the said king shall have full power and free authority in his kingdom and in all that pertains to it, and shall be in that same state and fullness of power, in and for all things, that he enjoyed before this time.

18. But we do not wish or intend, by the present ordinance, to derogate in any way from the royal privileges, charters, liberties, statutes and laudable customs of the realm of England which were in force before the time of the provisions.

19. Ordinamus etiam quod idem rex predictis baronibus indulgeat et remittat omnem rancorem, quem habet aduersus eos occasione premissorum, et similiter barones eidem; et quod unus alterum occasione premissorum, de quibus in nos extitit compromissum, per se uel per alium de cetero non grauet in aliquo, uel offendat.

20. Hanc autem ordinationem nostram seu dictum nostrum protulimus Ambianis, in crastino beati Vincentii Martiris, anno Domini m. cc. sexagesimo tertio mense Ianuario.[g] In cuius rei testimonium presentibus litteris nostrum fecimus apponi sigillum. Actum anno, mense, die et loco predictis.

39

4 JUNE 1264

*De custodibus pacis et de parliamento summonendo**

Rex Adae de Nouo Mercato, salutem. Cum iam, sedata turbatione nuper habita in regno nostro, pax inter nos et barones nostros, divina cooperante gratia, ordinata sit et firmata;[1] ac ad pacem illam per totum regnum nostrum inuiolabiliter obseruandam, de consilio et assensu baronum nostrorum prouisum sit, quod in singulis comitatibus nostris per Angliam, ad tuitionem et securitatem partium illarum, custodes pacis nostre constituantur donec per nos et barones nostros de statu regni nostri aliter fuerit ordinatum;[2] cumque nos, de uestra fidelitate simul et industria fiduciam gerentes, uos de consilio dictorum baronum nostrorum custodem nostrum assignauerimus in comitatu Lincolnie quamdiu nobis placuerit. Vobis mandamus, in fide qua nobis tenemini firmiter

---

[g] mcclxiii mense Ianuario in cuius rei testimonium B. *This, in modern dating, is 1264. See doc. 10, n. 5; doc. 30, n.* *

---

* *Text*: Rot. Pat. 48 Hen. III, m. 12d. *Printed*: *C.P.R. 1258–66*, p. 360 (abstract); *Foedera*, I. i. 442; Stubbs, pp. 399–400; Hennings, pp. 179–80, translates part of this document. *See*: *Baronial Plan*, pp. 317–18, 335–6; A. Harding, 'The Early History of the Keepers of the Peace', *T.R.H.S.* 5th. ser. x (1960), 85–109; H. Ainsley, 'The Problems relating to the maintenance of Law and Order in Thirteenth Century England, with particular reference to the *custos pacis*'.

19. We decree that the lord king shall fully pardon the barons, and shall renounce all rancour which he may have against them by reason of these disputes, and that the barons shall do likewise to him, and that in future neither shall harm nor offend the other, either by himself or through another, in any matter which was submitted to our arbitration.

20. We have declared this our ordinance or award at Amiens on the morrow of St. Vincent the Martyr [23 January], in the month of January in the year 1263. In testimony of this we have had our seal affixed to these present letters. Done in the year, month, day and place aforesaid.

39

4 JUNE 1264

Concerning keepers of the peace and the summoning of parliament

The king to Adam de Newmarket, greeting. Now that the recent disturbances in our realm have been settled, and, by the help of God's grace, peace has been decreed between us and our barons;[1] and, for the inviolable observance of that peace throughout our whole realm, it has been provided with the counsel and assent of our barons, that in each of our counties in England, for the protection and safety of those parts, keepers of our peace should be appointed until other arrangements shall be made by us and our barons for the state of our realm;[2] and we, having trust in your fidelity and also in your industry, with the counsel of our barons have appointed you to be our keeper in the county of Lincoln for as long as we shall please. We order you, firmly enjoining on the

---

[1] The peace here mentioned is the Mise of Lewes. See doc. 40, n. 1.

[2] The control of sheriffs was a point of controversy between the king and the reformers. In July 1263 Simon de Montfort appointed *custodes pacis* despite the existence of royal sheriffs. The *custodes* named by the Montfortians in 1264 were to consolidate the victory of Lewes. The words 'our barons' refer to the supporters of Simon de Montfort.

iniungentes, quatenus custodie pacis nostre ibidem et hiis que ad conseruationem pacis nostre pertinent, diligenter intendatis, ut predictum est; firmiter et publice per totum comitatum predictum inhibentes, ex parte nostra, ne quis sub pena exheredationis et periculo uite et membrorum super aliquem currat nec aliquem depredetur, nec homicidia uel incendia, roberias, toltas, seu alia huiusmodi perpetret enormia, nec cuiquam damnum aliquod inferat contra pacem nostram; nec eciam de cetero arma portet in regno nostro, sine licentia nostra et mandato nostro speciali. Et si quos huiusmodi malefactores et pacis nostre perturbatores, uel eciam, ut predictum est, arma portantes, inueneritis, eos sine dilatione arestari et saluo custodiri faciatis donec aliud inde preceperimus. Et ad hoc si necesse fuerit, totum posse dicti comitatus, cum toto posse comitatuum adiacentium, uobiscum assumatis, custodibus ipsorum comitatuum ad consimilia, cum opus fuerit, uiriliter auxiliantes. Et si forte ipsos malefactores euadere contingat, quod nulla ratione uellemus, tunc de nominibus eorum nobis constare faciatis, ut quod iustum fuerit de ipsis fieri faciamus. Et quia instanti parliamento nostro, de negotiis nostris et regni nostri, cum prelatis, magnatibus et aliis fidelibus nostris tractare necessario nos oportebit, uobis mandamus quatenus quatuor de legalioribus et discretioribus militibus dicti comitatus, per assensum eiusdem comitatus ad hoc electos, ad nos pro toto comitatu illo mittatis, ita quod sint ad nos Londoniis in octauis instantis festi Sancte Trinitacis ad ultimum, nobiscum tractaturi de negotiis predictis.[3] Vos autem in hiis omnibus exsequendis tam fideliter et diligenter uos habeatis, ne per negligentiam uestri ad uos et uestra grauiter capere debeamus. Teste rege apud Sanctum Paulum Londoniis, iiii° die Junii.[4]

[3] See doc. 3, n. 18.

[4] Similar letters were sent to twenty-six people who were appointed to the office of *custos pacis* for twenty-eight counties. *Foedera*, I. i. 422 omits John de Aure, who was to act in Dorset, and the order of naming differs from the patent roll.

faith in which you are bound to us, that you should diligently undertake the keeping of our peace there, and all those things which pertain to the keeping of our peace, as is said above, firmly and publicly prohibiting throughout the county, on our behalf, that anyone, under pain of disherison and peril of life and limbs, shall assault anyone else, or plunder anyone, or perpetrate manslaughters, arson, robbery, exactions, or any other outrages, or that anyone shall inflict loss upon anyone else against our peace, nor in future shall anyone bear arms in our realm save by our licence and on our special command. And if you shall find any such evildoers and disturbers of our peace, or also, as is aforesaid, any bearing arms, you shall have them arrested immediately and kept in safe custody until we give further orders concerning them. And if it should be necessary for this, you shall take with you the entire force of the county, and all the forces of the neighbouring counties, and you shall manfully aid the keepers of those counties in the same way, whenever need shall be. And if by chance it should happen that such evildoers escape, which we do not wish by any means to happen, then you shall inform us of their names, so that we may cause whatever may be just to be done to them.

And since, at our forthcoming parliament, it will be necessary for us to treat with our prelates, magnates, and other faithful subjects, concerning our business, and the business of our realm, we order you to send to us, for the whole of your county, four of the more law-worthy and prudent knights of the said county,[3] chosen for this purpose by the assent of the county, so that they shall be with us in London on the octave of the forthcoming feast of Holy Trinity [22 June] at the latest, to treat with us on the aforesaid matters. In carrying out all these things, you shall bear yourself so faithfully and diligently that we shall not be forced by any negligence on your part to deal severely with you and yours. Witness the king at St. Paul's, London, on 4 June [1264].[4]

40

22–28 JUNE 1264
c. 15 AUGUST 1264

*Forma pacis a domino rege et communitate approbata**

Hec est forma pacis a domino rege et domino Edwardo filio suo, prelatis et proceribus omnibus, et communitate tota regni Anglie, communiter et concorditer approbata; uidelicet, quod quedam ordinatio, facta in parliamento London' habito circa festum Natiuitatis beati Johannis Baptiste proximo preteritum, pro pace regni conseruanda, quousque pax inter dictum dominum regem et barones apud Lewes,[1] per formam cuiusdam mise prelocuta compleretur, iuratura omnibus diebus predicti domini regis, et eciam temporibus domini Edwardi postquam in regem fuerit assumptus, usque ad terminum quem ex nunc duxerit moderandum, firma maneat, stabilis et inconcussa;[2] dicta autem ordinatio talis est.

Ad reformationem status regni Anglie[3] eligantur et nominentur tres discreti et fideles de regno,[4] qui habeant auctoritatem et potestatem a domino rege eligendi seu nominandi, uice domini regis, consiliarios nouem;[5] de quibus nouem, tres ad minus

---

* *Text*: Rot. Pat. 48 Hen. III, pt. 1, m. 6d. *Printed*: *C.P.R. 1258–66*, p. 365 (abstract); *Foedera*, I. i. 443; Stubbs, pp. 400–3; Hennings, pp. 170–4 (translated). *Additional Texts*: i. Bodleian Library, Bodley MS. 91, ff. 139ᵛ–140 (B). Variations in word order differ more from *Foedera*, I. i. 443 than is suggested by Denholm-Young, *E.H.R.* xlix (1934), 93. ii. Rot. Chart., 49, H. III, m. 5. *Printed*: *C.Ch.R.* ii, 54; *Foedera*, I. i. 451–2. *See*: N. Denholm-Young, 'Documents of the Barons' War', *E.H.R.* xlviii (1933), 558–75, and 'The Winchester-Hyde Chronicle', *E.H.R.* xlix (1934), 85–93; J. P. Gilson, 'The Parliament of 1264', *E.H.R.* xvi (1901), 499–500; *King Henry III*, pp. 467–78.

---

[1] A reference to the Mise of Lewes, the agreement between de Montfort and the king immediately after the battle. No text of the Mise has survived. See introduction, pp. 47–8.

[2] This preamble was obviously written at the same time as the August section of this document. See n. 9. In Aug. 1264 Henry III was fifty-six years old while the Lord Edward, twenty-five years old, was violently opposed to the reformers. It was necessary to create machinery of administration which would survive the death of the king and control an autocratic successor.

40

22–28 JUNE 1264
c. 15 AUGUST 1264

*The form of peace accepted by the king and the community
of the realm*

This is the form of peace commonly agreed upon and approved
by the lord king and the Lord Edward his son, by the prelates, and
all the great men and the community of the whole realm of
England; namely, that a certain ordinance made in the parliament,
which met at London about the feast of the Nativity of St. John
the Baptist last [24 June], for preserving the peace of the realm
shall remain in force, stable, and unshaken until the peace between
the lord king and the barons, promised at Lewes in the terms of
a certain agreement, shall be completed.[1] Should this agreement
not be completed the ordinance is to last throughout the life of
the lord king, and also during the reign of the Lord Edward
when he shall have become king, until a date which shall be settled
hereafter.[2] The ordinance is as follows:

For the reform of the state of the realm of England[3] three prudent and faithful men of the realm shall be chosen and nominated,[4]
who shall have authority and power from the lord king to choose
and to nominate, on behalf of the lord king, nine councillors:[5] of

[3] The failure of Louis IX to arbitrate caused the reformers to put forward
their own plan of administration which was meant only to last until the French
king intervened.

[4] The three were de Montfort, Gilbert de Clare, earl of Gloucester, and
Stephen Bersted, bishop of Chichester, a staunch Montfortian.

[5] The names of the nine appear only in B (*E.H.R.* xlix, 93). They were Henry
de Sandwich, bishop of London, Humphrey de Bohun, junior (son of the earl
of Hereford), Adam de Newmarket, Peter de Montfort, Roger de St. John (of
Lageham, Surrey, killed with de Montfort at Evesham), Ralph de Camoys
(of Torpel, Northants., aided the crown in the siege of Kenilworth), Giles de
Argentin, Thomas Cantilupe (chancellor, nephew of Walter Cantilupe, bishop
of Worcester), Henry, abbot of St. Radegund, Bradsole, Kent (treasurer in 1263
when de Montfort had power, steward of the lands of the archbishop of Canterbury up to 1261, acted in this office under Kilwardby and Peckam).

alternatim, seu uicissim semper sint in curia presentes.[6] Et
dominus rex, per consilium eorundem nouem, ordinet et disponat
de custodia castrorum et omnibus aliis regni negotiis: preficiat
etiam dominus rex, per consilium predictorum nouem, iustitiarium,
cancellarium, thesaurarium, et alios officiales maiores et minores, in
hiis que spectant ad regimen curie et regni.[7] Iurabunt autem primi
electores siue nominatores quod, secundum conscientiam suam,
eligent uel nominabunt consiliarios quos credent honori Dei et
ecclesie, domino regi et regno, utiles et fideles. Consiliarii quoque
ac omnes officiales, maiores et minores, in sua creatione iurabunt
quod officia sua pro posse suo, ad honorem Dei et ecclesie et ad
utilitatem domini regis et regni, absque munere, preter esculenta
et poculenta que communiter in mensis presentari solent, fideliter
exsequentur. Quod si predicti consiliarii uel aliqui seu aliquis
eorum, in administratione sibi commissa, male uersati uel uersatus
fuerint aut fuerit, seu ex alia causa mutandi fuerint, dominus
rex per consilium priorum trium electorum seu nominatorum
quos amouendos uiderit, amoueat, et loco eorum, per eosdem,
alios fideles et idoneos subroget et substituat. Si autem officiales
maiores uel minores in officiis suis male uersentur, dominus rex
per consilium predictorum nouem ipsos amoueat et alios sine
dilatione per consilium predictorum,[a] loco eorum, substituat.
[b]Quod si primi tres electores seu nominatores in electione uel
nominatione consiliariorum, aut forte consiliarii in creatione
officialium uel aliis negotiis domini regis et regni gerendis seu
disponendis, discordes fuerint, quod a duabus partibus concorditer
factum fuerit uel ordinatum firmiter obseruetur; dummodo de
illis duabus partibus unus sit prelatus ecclesie in negotiis ecclesiam
contingentibus. Et si contingat duas partes dictorum nouem in
aliquo negotio non esse concordes, de discordia illa stabitur
ordinationi primorum trium electorum uel nominatorum aut
maioris partis eorundem.[b] Et si uideatur communitati prelatorum
et baronum concorditer expedire, quod aliqui uel aliquis, loco
aliquorum aut alicuius primorum trium nominatorum subrogentur
uel substituantur, dominus rex, per consilium communitatis
prelatorum et baronum, alios uel alium substituat. Omnia autem

---

[a] consilium predictorum sine dilatione B.   [b–b] B *places* Quod . . .
eorundem *after* substituat, *at the end of the next sentence.*

[6] There is no evidence of rotation of attendance at court.

these nine councillors three at least, in rota and turn, shall always be in attendance at court.[6] And the lord king, by the counsel of these nine, shall settle and dispose of the custody of castles and all other affairs of the realm. By the counsel of these nine, the lord king shall appoint the justiciar, chancellor, treasurer, and other officials, great and small, in all those things which concern the government of the court and of the realm.[7] The first electors or nominators shall swear that, according to their knowledge they will choose or nominate councillors whom they believe to be useful and faithful for the honour of God, of the Church, of the lord king, and of the realm. The councillors and all officials, great and small, will swear at the time of appointment that they will faithfully discharge their offices to the best of their ability, for the honour of God and of the Church, and the good of the lord king and of the realm, without any reward, beyond such food and drink as are commonly brought to table. If any of the councillors or any of their household, in the duties committed to him, shall have behaved badly, or for any other cause ought to be changed, the lord king, by the counsel of the three first electors or nominators will remove those whom he shall see fit to remove, and in their place, by the counsel of the same three, he shall appoint and substitute other suitable and faithful men. If the officials, higher or lower, behave badly in their offices, by the counsel of the nine the lord king shall remove them, and without delay shall, by the same counsel, put others in their places. If the three first electors or nominators disagree in the election or nomination of councillors, or if the councillors disagree in the appointment of officials, or in handling or settling any other business of the lord king or of the realm, whatever shall be agreed or ordained by two-thirds shall be firmly observed, provided that, of those two-thirds, one shall be a prelate of the Church in any matters affecting the Church. And if it should happen that two-thirds of the nine disagree on any matter, the decision of the three first electors or nominators, or of the majority of them, shall hold good in the matter of dispute. And if it shall seem necessary to the community of the prelates and barons that anyone should be put forward and substituted in the place of any of the three first electors, the lord king, by the counsel of the prelates and barons, shall substitute others for them. The lord king shall do all these things by the

---

[7] All surviving evidence indicates that de Montfort and his justiciar Hugh Despenser controlled the government; the power of the Council of Nine seems to have been nominal.

predicta faciat dominus rex per consilium predictorum nouem in forma supradicta, uel ipsi uice et auctoritate domini regis, presenti ordinatione duratura, donec misa apud Lewes facta, et postea a partibus sigillata, fuerit concorditer consummata; uel alia prouisa quam partes concorditer duxerint approbandam. Hec autem ordinacio facta fuit Londoniis de consensu, uoluntate et precepto domini regis, necnon prelatorum, baronum ac etiam communitatis tunc ibidem presentis. In cuius rei testimonium domini R. Lincolniensis et Hugo Eliensis episcopi, R. comes Norfolcie et marescallus Anglie, R. de Veer comes Oxoniensis, Humfredus de Bohun, Willelmus de Monte Canisio, et maior Londoniensis, signa sua huic scripture apposuerunt. Actum in parliamento Londoniis, mense Iunii anno Domini mcclxiv.[8]

Item ordinatum est[9] quod status ecclesie Anglicane in statum debitum reformetur. Item ordinatum est quod predicti tres electores et consiliarii, de quibus fit mentio in predicta ordinatione London', et castrorum custodes, et ceteri balliui domini regis, semper sint indigene; alienigene uero pacifice ueniant, morentur et redeant; et tam laici in suis possessionibus quam clerici in suis beneficiis residere uolentes; mercatores etiam et alii omnes pro suis negotiis procurandis, libere ueniant et pacifice commorentur; dum tamen pacifice sine armis et suspecta multitudine ueniant. Et quod nullus eorum ad aliquod officium uel balliuam in regno uel hospitio domini regis aliquatenus assumatur. Carte uero libertatum generalium et foreste indigenis a domino rege dudum concesse, et statuta super grauaminum reuocationibus, de turnis uicecomitis, sectis curie et aliis, que dominus rex anno preterito in singulis comitatibus per suas litteras patentes fecerat publicari, cum laudabilibus regni consuetudinibus et diutius approbatis, in perpetuum obseruentur, et prouideatur qualiter melius et fortius ualeant obseruari.[10] Item prouisum est quod dominus rex

---

[8] *in uigilia apostolorum Petri et Pauli anno domini mcclxiii* B (28 June). The dating of this document is a source of much controversy. The mention of the three *fideles* suggests some time before 23 June when the three were authorized to act (*C.P.R. 1258–66*, p. 326). This is possibly why Jacob dates the document 22 June (*Simon de Montfort*, p. 223). Denholm-Young and the Annals of Winchester support the date in B but there was a strong link between the last two (*Ann. Mon.* ii. 102; *E.H.R.* xlviii, 561, n. 3; ibid., xlix, 85–93).

[9] This addition to the administrative arrangements made in June 1264 was necessary because Louis IX continued to delay acting as an arbitrator. This section of the document, together with the earlier part, came to be called 'the peace provided at Canterbury' (*C.P.R. 1258–66*, p. 370; introduction, pp. 49–50).

counsel of the nine in this form, or they shall do them in place of and on the authority of the lord king, as long as the present ordinance shall last, until the agreement made at Lewes, and afterwards sealed by both parties, shall have been completed by agreement, or other arrangements provided which the parties shall have approved in common. This ordinance was made at London with the consent, will and precept of the lord king, and of the prelates, barons and also of the community at that time present. In testimony whereof the lord bishops Richard of Lincoln and Hugh of Ely, Roger, earl of Norfolk and marshal of England, Robert de Vere, earl of Oxford, Humphrey de Bohun, William de Montchenesy, and the mayor of London, have affixed their seals to this record. Done in the parliament at London, in the month of June, in the year of our Lord 1264.[8]

It is also ordained[9] that the state of the English Church shall be restored to its due condition. It is ordained also that the three electors, and the councillors mentioned in the ordinance of London, and the keepers of the castles, and the other bailiffs of the lord king shall always be natives; aliens, however, may peacefully come, stay, and go away again, both laymen wishing to live in their possessions and clergy wishing to reside in their benefices, and merchants and all others may freely come to conduct their business and may stay in peace, provided they come peacefully, and not in arms or in suspiciously large companies, and provided that none of them may be at any time appointed to any office or bailiwick in the realm or in the king's household. The charters of general liberties and of the forest, previously granted to his native subjects by the lord king, and the statute on the redress of grievances, concerning tourns of the sheriff, suits of court, and other things, which last year the lord king had publicly proclaimed by his letters patent in all shire courts, together with the laudable customs of the realm long approved, shall be observed in perpetuity, and let provision be made for their better and firmer observance.[10] Also it is provided that the lord king and the Lord

---

[10] These clauses presumably refer to the king's promise on 2 May 1262 to observe the charter of liberties and the charter of the forest; while in Jan. 1263 Henry III had reissued the Provisions of Westminster (*C.R. 1261–64*, p. 123; *C.P.R. 1258–66*, p. 253; *Reform and Rebellion*, pp. 76, 121–2, 124–5; *Baronial Plan*, pp. 295–6).

et dominus Edwardus baronibus, et hiis qui cum eis steterunt, omnem iniuriam et rancorem remittant, ita quod nullum ipsorum, occasione eorum que facta sunt in turbatione preterita, grauent uel a suis grauari permittant, et faciant omnes balliuos suos in assumptione balliue iurare quod nullum occasione predicta grauabunt, sed omnibus equaliter iustitiam exhibebunt, et prouideatur bona securitas quomodo hec omnia firmiter obseruentur.

41A

14 DECEMBER 1264

*Summonitio pro parliamento**

Henricus Dei gracia rex Anglie, dominus Hibernie et dux Aquitannie, uenerabili in Christo patri R. eadem gracia episcopo Dunelmensi[1] salutem. Cum post grauia turbacionum discrimina dudum habita in regno nostro carissimus filius Edwardus primogenitus noster pro pace in regno nostro assecuranda et firmanda obses traditus extitisset, et iam sedata, benedictus Deus, turbacione predicta super deliberacione eiusdem salubriter prouidenda,[2] et plena securitate tranquillitatis et patis ad honorem Dei et utilitatem totius regni nostri firmanda et totaliter complenda, ac super quibusdam aliis regni nostri negociis que sine consilio uestro et aliorum prelatorum et magnatum nostrorum nolumus expediri, cum eisdem tractatum habere nos oporteat; uobis mandamus, rogantes in fide et dilectione quibus nobis tenemini, quod omni occasione postposita et negociis aliis pretermissis, sitis ad nos Lond' in octabis Sancti Hillarii proximo futuris, nobiscum et cum predictis prelatis et magnatibus nostris quos ibidem uocari fecimus super premissis tractaturus et consilium uestrum impensurus. Et hoc sicut nos et honorem nostrum et uestrum necnon

---

* *Text*: Rot. Claus. 49 Hen. III, m. 11d., schedule. *Printed*: *C.R. 1264–68*, pp. 84–7; *Foedera*, I. i. 449; *Dignity of a Peer*, iii, appendix i, pt. i, 33–5; Stubbs, pp. 403–4; Hennings, 180–1. *See*: M. McKisack, *The Parliamentary Representation of the English Boroughs during the Middle Ages* (1932); D. Pasquet, *An Essay on the Origins of the House of Commons* (1925); K. M. E. Murray, *The Constitutional History of the Cinque Ports* (1935); *Simon de Montfort*, pp. 227–31; *Battle of Lewes*, pp. 100–2.

Edward shall remit to the barons and to those who supported them, all injury and rancour, so that they will not harm any of them, or permit any of them to be harmed by their men, by occasion of what was done during the recent disturbances; and they shall cause all officials, on taking up their bailiwicks, to swear that they will not harm anyone for these matters, but will show justice equally to all men; and let good security be provided for the firm observance of all these things.

41A

14 DECEMBER 1264

Summons to parliament

Henry, by God's grace king of England, lord of Ireland and duke of Aquitaine, to the venerable father in Christ Robert, by the same grace bishop of Durham, greeting.[1] After the grave perils of the recent disturbances in our realm our dearest firstborn son Edward was delivered as a hostage for securing and confirming peace in our realm, but now, blessed be God, the disturbance has been settled. To provide happily for his deliverance,[2] and to confirm and finally complete the full security of tranquillity and peace, to the honour of God and the advantage of the whole realm, and also for certain other matters concerning our realm, which we do not wish to settle without your counsel, and that of our other prelates and magnates, it is necessary that we should have discussion with them. Therefore, we order you, asking in the faith and love in which you are bound to us, that, setting aside every other matter or reason, you should be with us at London on the octave of St. Hilary next [20 January 1265], to treat on these things, with us and with our prelates and magnates, whom we have caused to be summoned there, and to lend us your counsel. And this you shall in no wise fail to do, as you love us and our honour and your own,

---

[1] Robert Stichill, active in negotiations with the northern barons and in defence of northern England in the summer of 1264 (*C.P.R. 1258–66, passim*).

[2] Reference to the Mise of Lewes (doc. 40, n. 1) and to the agreement and release of the Lord Edward from the custody of Henry de Montfort on 8 and 10 Mar. 1265 (*Foedera*, I. i. 451–2, 452; *C.Ch.R.* ii. 54).

et communem regni nostri tranquillitatem diligitis, nullatenus
omittatis. Teste rege apud Wygorniam xiiii.*a* die Decembris.

Eodem modo mandatum est episcopo Karleolensi.[3] . . .

Eodem modo mandatum est subscriptis.[4] . . .

In forma predicta scribitur abbatibus prioribus subscriptis[5]
sub hac data. Teste rege apud Wodest' xxiiii. die Decembris. . . .

Item in forma predicta mandatum est comitibus et aliis subscriptis.[6] Data de Wodestok'. . . .

Item mandatum est*b* singulis uicecomitibus per Angliam quod
uenire faciant duos milites de legalioribus, probioribus et di⟨s⟩cre-
tioribus militibus singulorum comitatuum ad regem Lond' in
octabis predictis, in forma supradicta.[7]

Item in forma predicta scribitur ciuibus Eboraci, ciuibus
Lincolnie et ceteris burgis Anglie quod mittant in forma predicta
duos de discretioribus, legalioribus et probioribus tam ciuibus
quam burgensibus suis.[8]

Item in forma predicta mandatum est baronibus et probis
hominibus Quinque Portuum, prout continetur in breui inrotulato
inferius.

   a xiii *C.R.*; *see doc.* 42, n. 6.   *b* et *C.R.*

---

[3] Twenty-one names follow: the archbishop and dean of York together with
nineteen abbots and priors.
[4] Fourteen names follow; nine bishops, the bishop-elect of Bath and Wells,
and four deans.
[5] Eighty-three names follow; eighty-one abbots and priors, the prior of the
Hospitallers, the master of the Temple.
[6] Twenty-three names follow: five earls, eighteen noblemen.

and also the common tranquillity of our realm. Witness the king at Worcester on 14th day of December.

In the same way orders were sent to: the bishop of Carlisle. . . .[3]

In the same way orders were sent to the following: . . .[4]

In the same form orders were sent to the following abbots and priors under this date. Witness the king at Woodstock on 24 December: . . .[5]

Further orders were sent in the same form to the earls and others written below: Dated from Woodstock. . . .[6]

Each of the sheriffs throughout England was ordered to send two of the more law-worthy, honourable and prudent knights from each of the counties to the king at London on the said octave, in the form given above.[7]

In the same form letters were written to the citizens of York, the citizens of Lincoln, and to the other boroughs of England that they should send, according to the same aforesaid form, two of their most prudent, law-worthy and honourable fellow-citizens or burgesses.[8]

In the same way the barons and good men of the Cinque Ports were instructed, as is contained in the writ enrolled below.

[7] In the thirteenth century the number of knights summoned from each shire varied from two to four (*Rot. Litt. Claus.* i. 165; *C.C.R. 1288-96*, p. 481; doc. 35; C. H. Jenkinson, 'The First Parliament of Edward I', *E.H.R.* xxv (1910), 231-42).
[8] This is the first known parliament to which borough representatives were summoned. See introduction, pp. 51-2 and doc. 22; *Baronial Plan*, pp. 270, 310, 327, 354-5.

41B

20 JANUARY 1265

*Summonitio baronibus de Sandwico pro parliamento**

Rex baronibus et balliuis portus sui de Sandwico salutem.[1] Cum
prelatos, magnates et nobiles regni nostri, tam pro negocio liberacionis Edwardi primogeniti nostri quam pro aliis communitatem
regni nostri tangentibus, ad instans parliamentum nostrum, quod
erit Lond' in octabis Sancti Hillarii, conuocari fecerimus, ubi
uestra et aliorum fidelium nostrorum presencia plurimum in-
digemus; uobis mandamus, in fide et dilectione quibus nobis
tenemini firmiter iniungentes, quod omnibus aliis pretermissis
mittatis ad nos ibidem quatuor de legalioribus et discretioribus
portus uestri, ita quod sunt ibi in octabis predictis, nobiscum et
cum prefatis magnatibus regni nostri tractaturi et super premissis
consilium impensuri. Et hoc sicut honorem nostrum et uestrum
et communem utilitatem regni nostri diligitis nullatenus omittatis.
Teste rege apud Westmonasterium xx. die Ianuarii.

Similiter mandatum est singulis portubus per se.

41C

15 FEBRUARY 1265

*Summonitio uicecomiti de comitatu Eboracensi***

Rex uicecomiti Ebor' salutem. Cum nuper uocari fecerimus duos
de discretioribus militibus singulorum comitatuum nostrorum
Anglie, quod essent ad nos in parliamento nostro apud Lond' in
octabis Sancti Hillarii proximo preteritis ad tractandum nobiscum

---

* *Text*: Rot. Claus. 49 Hen. III, m. 11d. *Printed*: *C.R. 1264–68*, p. 89.
** *Text*: Rot. Claus. 49 Hen. III, m. 10d. *Printed*: *C.R. 1264–68*, p. 96.

[1] This is the only text of the writs which were issued to the Cinque Ports.
This summons is noteworthy as the Portsmen became enthusiastic supporters
of de Montfort in 1263–5. The importance of the Cinque Ports is shown by the

41B

20 JANUARY 1265

Summons to parliament for the barons of Sandwich

The king to the barons and bailiffs of his port of Sandwich, greeting.[1] Whereas we have summoned the prelates, magnates, and nobles of our realm, both for the matter of the liberation of Edward our firstborn son and for other matters touching the community of our realm, to our forthcoming parliament, which will be in London on the octave of St. Hilary [20 January 1265], where we greatly need your presence and that of our other faithful subjects; we order you, in the faith and love in which you are bound to us, firmly enjoining that, setting all other business aside, you shall send to us there four of the more law-worthy and prudent men of your port, so that they be there on the aforesaid octave, to treat with us and with the magnates of our realm and to give your counsel on these matters. And in this you shall in no wise fail as you love our honour and yours and the common good of our realm. Witness the king at Westminster, 20 January.

Similar orders sent to each of the individual ports separately.

41C

15 FEBRUARY 1265

Summons to the sheriff of the county of York

The king to the sheriff of York, greeting. We recently summoned two of the more prudent knights of each of our counties of England, to be with us in our parliament at London on the octave of St. Hilary last [20 January], to treat with us and with our council

fact that each one sent four representatives as compared with two from each of the other towns. Representatives of the Ports appeared on only one occasion in the reign of Edward I when they were litigants rather than deputies (*Baronial Plan*, p. 270; Pasquet, *An Essay on the Origins of the House of Commons*, pp. 50, 56; Murray, *The Constitutional History of the Cinque Ports*, p. 30; idem, 'Faversham and the Cinque Ports', *T.R.H.S.* 4th ser. xviii (1935), 53-84).

et cum consilio nostro super deliberacione Edwardi filii nostri carissimi et securitate inde facienda necnon et aliis arduis regni nostri negociis, ac iidem milites moram diuturniorem quam credebant traxerint ibidem, propter quod non modicas fecerunt expensas; cumque communitates dictorum comitatuum uarias hoc anno fecerunt prestaciones ad defensionem regni nostri et maxime partium maritime contra hostilem aduentum alienigenarum, per quod aliquantulum se nimium sentiunt grauatas;[1] tibi precipimus quod duobus militibus qui pro communitate dicti comitatus prefato parleamento interfuerunt de consilio quatuor legalium militum eiusdem comitatus racionabiles expensas suas in ueniendo ad dictum parleamentum, ibidem morando et inde ad partes suas redeundo, prouideri et eas de eadem communitate leuari facias, prouiso quod ipsa communitas occasione prestacionis istius ultra modum non grauetur.[2] Teste rege apud Westmonasterium xv. die Februarii.

41D

23 FEBRUARY 1265

*Summonitio uicecomiti de comitatibus Salopie et Stafford**

Rex uicecomiti Salop' et Staff' salutem. Cum prelatos, magnates et nobiles regni nostri tam pro negocio liberacionis Edwardi primogeniti nostri et securitate inde facienda, quam pro aliis communitatem regni nostri tangentibus, nuper uacari fecerimus, quod essent ad nos London' in quindena[1] Sancti Hillarii proximo preterita nobiscum super hiis tractaturi, et tibi sicut aliis uicecomitibus nostris per Angliam preceperimus quod de utroque comitatuum predictorum ad nos uenire faceres ad predictos diem

---

* *Text*: Rot. Claus. 49 Hen. III, m. 9d. *Printed*: *C.R. 1264–68*, pp. 98–9.

---

[1] After his victory at Lewes de Montfort faced continued opposition from the lords of the Welsh March, from some northern noblemen and from forces assembling in France. *Custodes pacis* were appointed to enforce peace in the realm and levies were mustered to protect the coasts (*C.P.R. 1258–66*, pp. 337, 360–5; *C.R. 1261–64*, pp. 398–401).

on the liberation of Edward our dearest son and also on the provision of security for this, and for difficult matters touching our realm. The knights have spent a longer time there than they had expected, and accordingly have been put to considerable expense; and this year the communities of our counties have made various payments for the defence of our realm and especially of the coastal districts, against the attacks of aliens, by which they feel themselves somewhat excessively burdened.[1] And so we order you that, by the counsel of four law-worthy knights of the said county, you should pay to the two knights who attended the parliament on behalf of the community of the shire their reasonable expenses in coming to the parliament, staying there, and returning thence to their own home, and you shall cause the sum to be raised from the said community provided that the community is not burdened beyond measure by this payment.[2] Witness the king at Westminster on 15 February.

41D

23 FEBRUARY 1265

Summons to the sheriff of the counties of Shropshire and Staffordshire

The king to the sheriff of Shropshire and Staffordshire, greeting. Whereas we recently summoned the prelates, magnates, and nobles of our realm to be with us at London in the quinzaine[1] of St. Hilary [27 January 1265] last for arranging the liberation of our firstborn son Edward, and for providing security for this, and also for other things touching the community of our realm, to treat with us on these matters; and we ordered you, like all our other sheriffs in England, to send to us from both of the counties, at

---

[2] Details of the financial burden of attendance at parliament may be seen in Pasquet, op. cit., pp. 166 et seq.; McKisack, *Parliamentary Representation* ch. v).

[1] This date is an error for octave. See docs. 41A–C. The sheriff of Shropshire and Staffordshire on 14 Dec. 1264, when knights of the shire were summoned, was Hamo L'Estrange who was replaced at the start of Feb. 1265 by Robert de Grendon (*Lists and Indexes*, ix. 117; *C.R. 1264–68*, p. 29).

et locum duos de discretioribus et legalioribus militibus eorundem comitatuum, nobiscum et cum predictis magnatibus ex parte communitatum comitatuum illorum super premissis tractaturos et consilium suum impensuros, ac de partibus predictis iuxta mandatum nostrum ibidem non uenerint aliqui milites, super quod miramur quamplurimum et mouemur;[2] tibi precipimus iterato firmiter iniungentes quod dictos milites ad nos uenire facias, ita quod modis omnibus sint ad nos a festo Cathedre Sancti Petri in quindecim dies ubicunque tunc fuerimus in Anglia, nobiscum et cum magnatibus qui sunt de consilio nostro super premissis negociis locuturi. Et ita te habeas in hoc mandato nostro exequendo quod pro defectu tui ad te minime capere debeamus. Teste rege apud Westmonasterium xxiii. die Februarii.

42

14 MARCH 1265

De forma pacis et iuramento regis prestito super eodem[*a]

Rex omnibus de comitatu Eboracensi,[1] salutem. Cum propter hostilem turbationem habitam in regno nostro, de unanimi assensu et uoluntate nostra et Edwardi filii nostri primogeniti, prelatorum, comitum, baronum et communitatis regni nostri, pro regni ipsius pace pro cuius securitate dictus Edwardus et Henricus filius regis Alemannie nepos noster obsides dati fuerunt, concorditer sit prouisum, quod quedam ordinatio de unanimi assensu nostro, prelatorum, comitum ac baronum predictorum super nostro et regni nostri statu Londoniis, mense Iunii anno regni nostri xlviii° facta, inuiolabiliter obseruetur,[2] uniuersitatem uestram scire uolumus quod nos ordinationem ipsam et pacem et tran-

---

[a] *In the left hand margin.*

---

* *Text*: Rot. Chart. 49 Hen. III, m. 4. *Printed*: *C.Ch.R.* ii. 54; *S. of Realm*, i. 32–3; W. Blackstone, *The Great Charter and Charter of the Forest with other authentic instruments* (1759), pp. 74–8; Adams and Stephens, *Select Documents*, p. 68. *Additional MS.*: British Museum, Cotton MS. Claudius, D. ii, f.124 (C). *Printed*: *Foedera*, I. i. 453; Stubbs, pp. 404–6 quotes Blackstone, loc. cit. but evidently used C. *See*: *Simon de Montfort*, p. 229.

that day and place, two of the more prudent and law-worthy knights of each of the counties, to treat with us and with the magnates, on behalf of the communities of those counties, concerning these affairs and to give their counsel; and whereas no knights have come there from these counties as we ordered, which has greatly astonished and angered us;[2] we order again with firm injunctions, that you should send the said knights to us, so that they should be by all means with us in the quinzaine of the feast of St. Peter's Chair [8 March], wherever we may then be in England, to talk with us and the magnates of our council on these matters stated above. And in discharging this our command you shall act in such a way that we shall not need to punish you for any default on your part. Witness the king at Westminster on the 23rd day of February.

42

14 MARCH 1265

Concerning the form of peace and the king's oath in this matter

The king to all of the county of York,[1] greeting. Because of the wars and disturbances which recently troubled our realm, by the unanimous agreement of ourselves, and of Edward our firstborn son, and also of the prelates, earls, barons, and of the community of our realm, it is by agreement provided for the peace of the realm, for the security of which Edward and our nephew Henry, the son of the king of Germany, had been given as hostages, that a certain ordinance made at London in June in the 48th year of our reign [1264] with the unanimous assent of ourselves, the prelates, earls, and barons concerning our state and that of our realm should be observed inviolably.[2] We now wish you all to know that we have sworn, on the holy gospels of God, that we will observe in good faith that ordinance and peace, and will maintain the tran-

---

[2] The absence of knights from these counties is explained by the fact that they were dominated by the lords of the Welsh March, some of de Montfort's most bitter opponents.

[1] The text in *Foedera* taken from D is addressed to Middlesex.

[2] This is the first part of document 40. See doc. 40, n. 8.

quillitatem regni bona fide obseruare et in nullo contrauenire ad
sancta Dei Euangelia iurauimus; hoc adiecto in eodem sacramento
specialiter et expresse, quod occasione factorum precedentium
tempore turbationis aut guerre precedentis neminem occasionabi-
mus aut inculpabimus de illis aut de parte illorum quos tanquam
inimicos diffidauimus, puta comites Leycestrie et Gloucestrie
et alios sibi adherentes, ac barones siue ciues nostros Londoniarum,
et Quinque Portuum, nec alicui de predictis dampnum faciemus
aut fieri procurabimus nec per balliuos nostros aliquatenus fieri
permittemus. Iurauimus insuper quod ea omnia que pro liberatione
dictorum filii nostri ac nepotis sunt prouisa et sigillo nostro sigillata,
quantum ad nos pertinet, inuiolabiliter obseruabimus et ab aliis
pro posse nostro faciemus obseruari. Volentes et consentientes
expresse quod si nos uel dictus Edwardus filius noster contra
predictam ordinationem, prouisionem nostram, seu iuramentum,
quod absit, in aliquo uenire, seu pacem et tranquillitatem regni
nostri turbare, seu occasione factorum precedentium tempore
turbationis ac guerre precedentis, aliquem de predictis, aut de
parte predictorum quos diffidauimus, occasionare seu alicui de eis
dampnum facere aut fieri procurare presumpserimus, liceat
omnibus de regno nostro contra nos insurgere et ad grauamen
nostrum opem et operam dare iuxta posse. Ad quod ex presenti
precepto nostro omnes et singulos uolumus obligari fidelitate et
homagio nobis factis non obstantibus; ita quod nobis in nullo
intendant sed omnia que grauamen nostrum respiciunt facient ac
si in nullo nobis tenerentur, donec quod in hac parte transgressum
fuerit seu commissum cum satisfactione congrua in statum debitum,
secundum predictarum ordinationis et prouisionis nostre seu
iuramenti formam, fuerit reformatum; quo facto sicut prius
intendentes existant. Et si aliquis alius de regno nostro contra
predicta uenire seu pacem et tranquillitatem regni nostri turbare
presumpserit, seu nobis uel Edwardo filio nostro aut alicui alteri
contra predicta uel aliquid predictorum uenientibus opem,
consilium, consensum, uel auxilium quoquo modo prestiterit, si
hoc notorium fuerit aut de hoc per considerationem consilii nostri
et magnatum terre nostre conuictus fuerit,[3b] siue non, tam ipse

---

[b] *After* fuerit D *adds* de unanimi assensu nostro, Edwardi filii nostri, comitum,
baronum, et communitatis regni nostri, prouisum est (et statutum quod corpus
ipsius, si inuentus fuerit, capiatur; alioquin a regno nostro utlagetur; et siue
inuentus fuerit) siue non ... *The words* de unanimi ... prouisum est *may be
derived from the sentence which follows* fieri consueuit (*note c*) *but no origin is*

quillity of our realm, and will in no way work against them; with this addition specially and expressly made in the said oath, that we will not proceed against or seek to blame, by reason of whatever was done in the time of the said disturbances or of the war, any of those whom we denounced as enemies, or any of their supporters, that is to say, the earls of Leicester and of Gloucester and others supporting them and our barons and citizens of London, and of the Cinque Ports, nor to any of them will we do harm or order harm to be done, or permit harm to be done to them in any way by our bailiffs. We have sworn also that we will inviolably observe all those things which were provided for the release of our son and nephew, and which were sealed with our seal, so far as they concern us, and that we will to the best of our power cause them to be observed by others. And we wish and expressly agree that if we, or Edward our son, should in any way oppose our ordinance, provision, or oath, which Heaven forbid, or should disturb the peace and tranquillity of our realm, or, on pretext of things formerly done in the time of disturbances or of war, should proceed against any one of the aforesaid whom we denounced, or of their following, or should presume to inflict any harm upon any of them or cause them to be harmed, then it shall be lawful for all our realm to rise up against us, and to lend help and labour to our discomfiture, as much as they can. And we wish that by our present command each and every one shall be bound to this, notwithstanding the fealty and homage which they have done to us, so that they shall obey us in nothing, but do all that can work to our harm, as if they were in no way bound to us, until whatever in this matter has been wrongly done or committed has been restored to its due state, according to the terms of our ordinance, provision, and oath; and only when that is done should they obey as of old. And if anyone else of our realm should presume to oppose these orders, or to disturb the peace and tranquillity of our realm, or to give help, counsel, consent, or any manner of aid to us, or to our son Edward, or to anyone else opposing the orders or any part of them, if this became known or if anyone be, or be not, convicted of this by the judgement of our council and the magnates of our land,[3] he and

known for the words which have been placed in brackets. Blackstone mentions the D *variations in a footnote. Stubbs includes the variations in his text.*

---

[3] D adds: 'it is provided (and ordered) by the unanimous assent of ourselves, of Edward our son and of the earls, barons and community of our realm (that if he can be found he shall be arrested. If he cannot be found he shall be outlawed from our realm, and whether he be found or not)'.

quam heredes sui imperpetuum exheredentur; ac de terris et tenementis ipsorum fiat prout de terris eorum qui de felonia conuicti sunt secundum leges et consuetudines regni nostri fieri consueuit.[4c] Ad hec de unanimi assensu et uoluntate nostra, Edwardi filii nostri, prelatorum, comitum, baronum et communitatis regni nostri concorditer prouisum est, quod carte antique communium libertatum et foreste, communitati regni nostri per nos dudum concesse, in quarum uiolatores ad petitionem nostram sententia excommunicationis dudum lata est et per sedem apostolicam specialiter confirmata,[5] necnon et omnes articuli de nostro et magnatum terre nostre communi assensu dudum prouisi, quos nuper apud Wigorniam existentes per singulos comitatus sub sigillo nostro transmisimus, inuiolabiliter obseruentur imperpetuum;[6] ad quorum obseruationem sacramento ad sancta Dei Euangelia prestito sponte nos obligamus; et omnes iusticiarios, uicecomites et quoscunque balliuos de regno nostro tam nostros quam aliorum simili sacramento uolumus obligari, ita quod nullus teneatur alicui balliuo obedire donec sacramentum prestiterit. Et si quis contra cartas ipsas uel articulos predictos in aliquo uenire presumpserit, preter periurii reatum et excommunicationis sentenciam que incurret, per considerationem curie nostre grauiter puniatur; saluo in premissis prout decet priuilegio clericali. Et quia uolumus quod hec omnia firmiter et inuiolabiliter obseruentur, uniuersitati uestre iniungendo ac precipiendo mandamus, quatinus uos omnes et singuli predicta omnia et singula, sicut superius scripta sunt, faciatis, teneatis et inuiolabiliter obseruetis, et ad ea omnia facienda, tenenda et obseruanda ad sancta Dei Euangelia sacramento corporaliter prestito, ad inuicem uos obligetis. In cuius rei testimonium cartas et ordinationes predictas cum presentibus litteris patentibus uobis sub sigillo nostro transmittimus in comitatum nostrum sub custodia fidedignorum ad hoc electorum ad rei memoriam saluo custodiendas. Contra quas ne quis ignorantiam pretendere possit in futurum, ad minus bis in anno in pleno comitatu ipsas precipimus publicari,

---

[c] *See note b.*

---

[4] Note the king's oath in document 2 and the sanction clause of Magna Carta (*Magna Carta*, pp. 333–7).

[5] On 2 May 1262 Henry promised to observe the charters (*C.R. 1261–64*, p. 123).

his heirs shall be perpetually disinherited, and their lands and property shall be dealt with as are the lands of those convicted of felony, according to usual practice under the laws and customs of our realm.[4] And further to this, by the unanimous assent and will of ourselves, of Edward our son, of the prelates, earls, barons, and community of our realm, it is in agreement provided that the ancient charters of common liberties and of the forest, formerly granted by us to the community of our realm, against the violators of which, at our petition, a sentence of excommunication was formerly proclaimed and was specially confirmed by the apostolic see,[5] shall in future be observed inviolably;[6] and also all the articles formerly provided by the common consent of ourselves and of the magnates of our realm, and which, when we were lately at Worcester, we sent out to all counties under our seal, for the observance of which we have, of our free will, bound ourselves by an oath taken in person on the holy gospels of God; and we will that all justices, sheriffs, and all other kinds of officials in our realm, whether our own or those of others, shall be bound by the same oath, so that no one shall be obliged to obey any official until he has taken that oath. And if anyone shall presume to oppose these charters or the articles in any way, in addition to the penalty of perjury and the sentence of excommunication which he will incur, let him also be punished severely by consideration of our court, saving in these matters, as is fitting, the privilege of clergy. And since we will that all these orders should be faithfully and inviolably observed, we order you all, firmly enjoining and commanding, that each and every one of you shall do, keep, and inviolably observe each and every one of the things as they are written above, and shall bind yourselves by a personal oath taken on the holy gospels of God, to do and observe all these things. In testimony of which we send you the charters and ordinances, with these present letters patent, under our seal, to be kept safely, as a constant reminder of this, in our county court in the custody of trustworthy men elected for this purpose. And so that in future no one may assert ignorance of these things, we order them to be read

[6] On 14 Dec. 1264, at Worcester, the king reissued the Provisions of Westminster (*Registrum Malmesburiense*, i. 50; *Reform and Rebellion*, p. 77, mistakenly mentions 13 Dec.). See doc. 41A, n. *a*.

ita quod fiat prima publicatio in proximo comitatu post instans festum Pasche, secunda uero fiat in proximo comitatu post festum Sancci Michaelis, et sic deinceps fiat annuatim. Volumus insuper quod, saluis omnibus supradictis, omnes alie ordinationes et articuli per nos et consilium nostrum hactenus prouisi, qui poterunt ad honorem Dei et ecclesie, fidem nostram et regni nostri commodum, obseruari, inuiolabiliter obseruentur et teneantur. Vt autem premissa omnia et singula firma maneant et inconcussa, reuerendi patres episcopi per regnum constituti ad instantiam nostram sententiam excommunicationis fulminarunt in omnes illos qui contra premissa uel aliquod premissorum scienter uenerint aut uenire temptauerint cum effectu, quorum iurisdictioni seu cohercioni spontanea uoluntate quantum ad premissa nos submittimus; priuilegiis nostris omnibus impetratis aut impetrandis seu proprio motu domini pape nobis concessis aut in posterum concedendis in hoc pure renunciantes, prout in litteris super hoc confectis penes dictos prelatos residentibus plenius continetur.[7] In cuius rei etc. Teste rege apud Westm(onasterium).[d]

43

15 MAY 1265

De parliamento apud Wintoniam*

Rex decano et capitulo Ebor' salutem. Cum prelatos et magnates regni nostri iam uocari fecerimus quod sint ad nos apud Wint' primo die Iunii proximo uenturo,[1] ad tractandum nobiscum super nostris et regni nostri negociis que sine eorum presencia finaliter expleri nolumus; uobis mandamus in fide et dilectione quibus

---

[d] *Enrolled between documents dated 8 Mar. and 14 Mar. Blackstone notes that D adds xiiii die Marcii anno regni nostri xlvi (see doc. 10, n. 6).*

---

* *Text*: Rot. Claus. 49 Hen. III, m. 6d. *Printed*: *C.R. 1264–68*, pp. 116–17; *Dignity of a Peer*, iii, appendix i, pt. i, 36; Stubbs, pp. 406–7.

---

[7] No example of the letters deposited with the bishops remains. Reference to the pope is a precaution against papal bulls. See docs. 32–4, 36.

aloud in full county court at least twice every year, so that the first publication shall take place in the first county court after the forthcoming feast of Easter [5 April] and the second in the first county court after Michaelmas next [29 September], and so henceforth every year. And we also will that, saving all that is said above, all other articles and ordinances hitherto provided by us and our council, which can be observed to the honour of God and of the church, to our own faith and to the profit of the realm, shall be inviolably observed and kept. And so that each and every one of the above enactments shall remain firm and unshaken, the reverend fathers, the bishops appointed to this realm, at our instance, have launched a sentence of excommunication against all who shall knowingly oppose or in effect attempt to oppose the orders or any of them, and with respect to the said things we, of our own free will, submit ourselves to their jurisdiction and coercion, entirely renouncing in these matters all our privileges obtained or to be obtained, granted or in future to be granted to us by the lord pope on his own initiative, as is more fully declared in the letters drawn up for this and deposited with the bishops.[7] In which matter etc. Witness the king at Westminster.

43

15 MAY 1265

Concerning the parliament at Winchester

The king to the dean and chapter of York, greeting. Whereas we have now summoned the prelates and magnates of our realm to be with us at Winchester on the first of June next,[1] to treat with us on our affairs and those of our realm, because we do not wish to settle these matters without their presence, we order you, in the

---

[1] Faced with the opposition of the lords of the Welsh March de Montfort ordered his forces to muster at Gloucester on 3 May, where he remained until c. 20 May. The threat from the Marches probably explains the change of the venue of parliament, on 15 May, from Westminster to Winchester. Unlike the parliament summoned to meet in Jan. 1265, town representatives do not seem to have been called to this parliament which, because of the crisis in the west, did not meet.

nobis tenemini, firmiter iniungentes quatinus modis omnibus duos de discretioribus concanonicis uestris ad dictos diem et locum mittatis,[2] qui plenam habeant potestatem uice uestra ad tractandum nobiscum una cum prefatis prelatis et magnatibus super negociis antedictis, et ad ea facienda nomine uestro que uos ipsi facere possetis si presentes ibidem essetis. Et hoc sicut nos et utilitatem regni nostri diligitis nullatenus omittatis. Teste rege apud Glouc' xv. die Maii.

De uinis ad opus regis prouidendis.—Quia rex instans parliamentum habiturus est apud Westmonasterium, propter quod rex multis uinis indigebit ibidem, mandatum est Reginaldo de Suff', camerario Lond', quod sine dilacione prouideat regi in ciuitate London' de centum doliis uini tam de empto quam de prisa et ea liberet uicecomitibus London' carianda usque Westmonasterium ponenda in celario regis ibidem. Et hoc nullatinus omittat. Et mandatum est thesaurario regis quod uina illa acquietet uel terminos capiat a mercatoribus a quibus uina illa capta fuerint ad quos eis satisfacere possit pro uinis predictis. Teste ut supra.[3]

44

30 OCTOBER 1266

*Incipit Dictum de Kelenworthe**

In nomine sancte et indiuidue Trinitatis, amen. Ad honorem et gloriam omnipotentis Dei Patris et Filii et Spiritus Sancti, et

---

* *Text*: British Museum, Cotton MS. Claudius, D. ii., ff. 122ᵛ–124ᵛ (old 119ᵛ–122ᵛ) (C). *Printed*: *S. of Realm*, i. 12–18. *Additional Texts*: i. British Museum, Claudius, D. ii, ff. 250ᵛ–252ᵛ. ii. British Museum, Cotton MS. Appendix xxv, ff. 15–20ᵛ (A). iii. British Museum, Harley MS. 1033, ff. 21–23ᵛ (F). iv. Bodleian Library, Oxford, Rawlinson MS. C. 820, ff. 10–13 (E). v. Guildhall Record Office, London, MS. Liber Horn, ff. 16–19ᵛ (H). vi. Christ Church Cathedral, Dublin, MS. Liber Niger, ff. 168–70. vii. Public Record Office, London, Liber X, also called the Statute Book of the Exchequer, ff. 51ᵛ–53 (formerly 20ᵛ–22). viii. Trinity College Library, Cambridge, MS. o.3.20, ff. 6–8. *See*: *Reform and Rebellion*; *King Henry III*; *Rotuli Selecti*; A. Lewis, 'Roger Leyburn', *E.H.R.* liv (1939); H. G. Richardson and G. O. Sayles, 'The Early Statutes', *Law Quarterly Review*, l (1934); C. H. Knowles, 'The Disinherited, 1265–80'; M. Hoyle, 'The Judicial Proceedings under the Dictum of Kenilworth'.

faith and love which bind you to us, firmly enjoining that by all means you should send two of your more prudent fellow-canons at the same day and place,[2] who shall have full power in your name to treat with us, together with the prelates and magnates on the matters, and to do in your name all those things which you your-selves could do if you were present there. And in this you shall in no way fail as you love us and the good of our realm. Witness the king at Gloucester on 15th day of May.

Note on the provision of wine for the king's use. Because the king is to hold his forthcoming parliament at Westminster, so that he will require many wines there, Reginald of Suffolk, the chamberlain of London, is ordered to secure for the king, without delay, in the city of London 100 tuns of wine, both by purchase and by prise, and to hand them over to the sheriffs of London to be carried to Westminster and placed in the king's cellar there. And let him not for any reason fail to do this. And the king's treasurer is ordered either to pay for this wine or to arrange with the merchants from whom the wine is bought suitable dates at which he will pay them for the said wines. Witness as above [at Gloucester on 3rd May].[3]

44

31 OCTOBER 1266

Here begins the Award of Kenilworth

In the name of the Holy and Undivided Trinity, amen. To the honour and glory of Almighty God, the Father, the Son, and the

No original copy of the *Dictum* has survived. Those texts which remain are to be found in late thirteenth- or fourteenth-century collections of legal texts, being placed between the statute of Merton (1236) and the statute of Marl-borough (1267). The *Explanacio Dicti*, which records the decisions of the two umpires (cl. 23) and the *Addicio Dicti*, resulting from modifications and inter-pretations of the text of the *Dictum*, are printed in *S. of Realm*, i. 18.

The final text of the *Dictum* was to consist of the recommendations of the committee of twelve modified, on disputed points, by the decisions of the two

---

[2] The later practice, both for convocation and parliament, was for chapters to nominate one and diocesan clergy two, representatives (*Parl. Writs*, i, *passim*).

[3] *C.R. 1264–8*, pp. 52–3. The intention of de Montfort to hold a parliament in London on 1 June was reached as early as 19 Mar. and the dating of this letter indicates that this plan remained at the start of May (ibid., p. 36).

gloriose et precelse Dei genitricis Virginis Marie et omnium
beatorum quorum in terris meritis et intercessionibus guber-
namur; sacrosancte Catholice atque apostolice Romane ecclesie
que est omnium fidelium mater et magistra; sanctissimi patris et
domini nostri Clementis ipsius uniuersalis ecclesie summi ponti-
ficis; ad honorem et bonum, prosperum, et pacificum statum
Christianissimi principis domini Henrici regis Anglie illustris
et tocius regni et ecclesie Anglicane; nos vero W. Exoniensis,[1a]
W. Bathoniensis et Wellensis,[2] N. Wygorniensis[3] et R. Meneuensis
episcopi,[4] Gilbertus de Clare comes Gloucestrie et Hertford,
et Humfridus de B. comes Herford', P. Basset, Iohannes
de Baillol, Robertus Walraund, Alanus de la Suche, Rogerus de
Someri, et Warinus de Bassingbourne, prouidendi super statum
terre, nominatim super facto exheredatorum,[5] habentes a domino
rege predicto et ab aliis baronibus, consiliariis regni, et proceribus
Anglie plenariam potestatem, secundum formam conscriptam in
litteris puplicis sigillis predictorum regis et aliorum munitis;[6b]
ea quidem gracia diuina fauente prouidimus que secundum iuris
et equitatis[c] Dei beneplacito et paci regni putauimus conuenire,
nullius in hac parte acceptantes personam, sed habentes pre oculis
solum Deum, ante omnia igitur tanquam in conspectu Dei
omnipotentis facientes et ex ordine capud membris aptissime
premittentes:

---

[a] Exoniensis AH. W. Oxoniensis *in later hand* C.   [b] FE *and other texts
proceed* uolumus secundum equitatis tramitem incedere ... *nearly as in clause 12,
omitting the intervening section except for clause 12. See n. ee below, p. 336.*   [c] equitatis semitas A. *Gap in* H *and* C, normam *in margin of* C.

Note * (*pp.* 316–17) *cont.*

umpires. These conditions are not to be found in any of the surviving texts of
the *Dictum*, all of which fail to incorporate the decisions of the umpires, while
texts C, i and H alone have the *Explanacio* as a separate document. Furthermore,
the surviving texts of the *Dictum* vary in arrangement. Text C falls clearly into
two parts. Clauses 1–11 restore royal power and petition the king on different
matters; the second part, beginning with clause 12, records the ways in which
redemption could take place. All the other texts begin with clause 12 and omit
almost entirely the first eleven clauses of text C. The fact that the order of clauses
is very much the same in all texts of the *Dictum* has led Jacob (*Reform and
Rebellion*, p. 176, n. 2) and F. M. Powicke (*King Henry III*, p. 534, n. 2) to claim
that clause 12 of text C was the first clause of the original *Dictum*. It is possible,
however, as texts of the *Dictum* have only survived in MSS. dealing with the law,
that the first eleven clauses were omitted as they were considered unnecessary
for use in court.

No attempt has been made to record all the variant readings; only the most
important have been noted.

Holy Ghost, of the glorious and most excellent Mother of God
the Virgin Mary, and of all saints by whose merits and inter-
cessions we are governed on Earth. To the honour of the Holy
Catholic and Apostolic Roman Church, which is the mother and
ruler of all the faithful; to the honour of the Most Holy Father
and our lord Clement, ruler of that universal Church; to the honour
and good prosperous and peaceable estate of the most Christian
prince, lord Henry, illustrious king of the whole realm of England,
and of the English Church. We, Walter, bishop of Exeter,[1] Walter,
bishop of Bath and Wells,[2] Nicholas, bishop of Worcester,[3] and
Richard, bishop of St. David's,[4] Gilbert de Clare, earl of Gloucester and Hertford, and Humphrey de Bohun, earl of Hereford,
Philip Basset, John Balliol, Robert Walerand, Alan de la Zuche,
Roger de Somery, and Warin de Bassingbourne have been given
full power from the lord king, from other nobles, counsellors of
the realm, and from the leading men of England according to the
terms enrolled in letters published and sanctioned by the seals of
the king and others,[6] to provide for the state of the realm especially
in the matter of the disinherited,[5] favouring no person in this
matter, but having God alone before our eyes, doing all things
as in the sight of Almighty God and in order, rightly preferring
the Head to the Members.

[1] Walter Bronescombe, elected to Exeter Feb. 1258, d. July 1280.
[2] Walter Giffard, appointed chancellor immediately after the battle of
Evesham. Archbishop of York, Oct. 1266–Apr. 1279.
[3] Doc. 37B n. 9. Walter Cantilupe d. Feb. 1266. Nicholas of Ely elected to
Worcester June 1266, translated to Winchester Feb. 1268, d. Feb. 1280.
[4] Richard de Carew, canon of St. David's, called *Theologus et philosophus
optimus*. Consecrated bishop of St. David's Feb.–Mar. 1256, d. 1 Apr. 1280.
One of the twelve to execute the terms of the *Dictum*, justice in the special eyre
Oct. 1267 (*Annales Cambriae*, pp. 90, 103, 105; *Menevia Sacra*, ed. F. Green
(1927); *C.P.R. 1266–72*, p. 161).
[5] On 31 Aug. 1266 the king appointed six counsellors who were to co-opt an
additional six (*C.P.R. 1258–66*, pp. 671–2). There were no extremists on the
committee; many had links with the rebels. The earl of Gloucester had been
de Montfort's main ally; Somery's daughter was widow of Ralph Basset of
Drayton, Staffs., who had died with de Montfort at Evesham. Basset's sons-in-
law, John fitz John and Hugh Despenser fought for the earl of Leicester at
Evesham where Despenser died. The bishop of Exeter had negotiated with the
rebels earlier in 1266, while the other bishops and the earl of Hereford were
moderate in their opinions. The most loyal were John Balliol, Warin de
Bassingbourne, Robert Walerand, and Alan de la Zuche. These twelve
counsellors also witness and seal the *Explanacio* (*S. of Realm*, i. 18). See n. 35.
[6] 'we wish to proceed along the path of justice' DE.

1. Dicimus et prouidimus quod serenissimus princeps dominus Henricus rex Anglie illustris dominium suum, auctoritatem et regiam potestatem habeat, plenarie optineat, et libere excerceat sine cuiuscumque inpedimento uel contradictione per quam contra iura approbata et leges ac regni consuetudines diu optentas, dignitas regia offendatur; atque ab uniuersis et singulis maioribus et minoribus ipsius regni hominibus, ipsi domino regi et mandatis ac preceptis suis licitis plene obediatur et humiliter intendatur. Et omnes et singuli per breuia ad curiam domini regis iusticiam petant et in iusticia respondeant, sicut ante tempus huius turbacionis hactenus fieri consueuit.

2. Rogamus eciam ipsum dominum regem et ipsius pietati cum reuerencia suademus, ut tales ad iusticiam faciendam et reddendam proponat, que non sua sed ea que Dei et iusticie sunt querentes, subiectorum negocia secundum leges et consuetudines regni laudabiles recte component, et ex hoc roboratum iusticia reddant solium regie maiestatis.

3. Rogamus pariter et suademus eidem domino regi ut libertates ecclesiasticas, cartas libertatum et foreste, quas seruare et custodire tenetur expresse et proprio iuramento, plene custodiat et obseruet.

4. Prouideat eciam dominus rex quod concessiones quas fecit hactenus, spontaneus non coactus, obseruentur,[7] et alia necessaria que per suos ex eius beneplacito sunt excogitata, stabiliat duratura. Et eciam Anglicana ecclesia suis libertatibus et consuetudinibus, quas habuit et habere debuit ante tempus huiusmodi turbacionis, plene restituatur et eis uti permittatur.

5. Dicimus et prouidemus ut prefatus dominus rex uniuersis et singulis qui, ab inicio presentis turbacionis regni et occasione ipsius usque ad hoc tempus, in ipsum uel in coronam regiam commiserunt iniuriam quamlibet uel offensam, et qui ad pacem ipsius uenerunt infra xl. dies post publicacionem huiusmodi nostre prouisionis, omnino remittat et parcat; ita quod nullo modo nullaque causa uel occasione propter huiusmodi preteritas inurias uel offensas, in eosdem offensores nullam excercet ulcionem; aut ipsis penam uite, membri, carceris, uel exilii aut peccunie inferat uel uindictam; exceptis hiis qui in presenti nostra prouisione inferius continentur.

6. Dicimus eciam et prouidemus ut omnia loca, iura, res, et alia ad coronam regiam pertinencia, ipsi corone et domino regi restituantur, per eos qui ea detinent occupata, nisi ostendant se

1. We declare and provide that the most serene prince, lord Henry, illustrious king of England, shall have, fully receive, and freely exercise his dominion, authority, and royal power without impediment or contradiction of anyone, whereby the royal dignity may be offended contrary to approved rights, laws, and long established customs, and that full obedience and humble attention be given to the same lord king, to his lawful mandates and precepts, by one and all, greater and lesser men of the kingdom. And one and all shall, through writs, seek justice and be answerable for justice at the court of the lord king as was the custom before the time of the disorder.

2. Furthermore, we ask the same lord king, and with reverence urge him in his piety, that he appoint, for doing and rendering justice, such men as, seeking not their own interests but those of God and right, shall justly settle the affairs of subjects according to the praiseworthy laws and customs of the kingdom and thereby strengthen the throne and royal majesty with justice.

3. Likewise we ask and urge the lord king that he fully protect and observe the liberties of the Church, and the charters of liberties and of the forest, which he is expressly bound to keep and hold by his own oath.

4. Also the lord king shall provide that the grants which, up to the present, he has made freely and not under compulsion shall be observed;[7] and he will establish firmly other necessary measures which are devised by his men at his pleasure. Furthermore, the English Church shall be fully restored to its liberties and customs which it had and should have had before the time of such disorders, and shall be permitted to exercise them.

5. We declare and provide that the lord king shall completely excuse and pardon each and all of those who, from the beginning and up to the present time, because of the present disorders of the realm, have offended against or done any injury to him or the royal crown and who return to his peace within forty days after the publication of this our ordinance. The lord king shall in no way for any cause or reason, because of these past injuries or offences, bear any vengeance against these offenders nor shall he inflict any penalty or revenge against them in life, limb, imprisonment, exile, or fine. Excluded are those mentioned below in this our present ordinance.

6. We also declare and provide that all places, rights, goods, and all other things pertaining to the royal crown shall be restored to that crown, and to the lord king, by those who detain them in their

---

[7] An allusion to the Provisions of Westminster, doc. 11.

illa per racionabilem warantiam ab ipso domino rege uel a suis antecessoribus possidere.

7. Dicimus eciam et prouidemus quod uniuersa scripta,/ obligaciones, et instrumenta, que prefatus dominus rex, uel dominus Edwardus eius primogenitus, uel alii fideles fecerint, seu exposuerint hactenus, prouisionum[d] Oxon(ie) uel occasione turbacionis in regno habite, ad instanciam quondam S. de Monteforti, comitis Leycestrie, et suorum conplicium, penitus adnichilentur et cassentur, et pro cassis et pro nullis penitus habeantur. Facta eciam dicti Simonis et conplicium suorum preiudicialia et iudicialia et dampnosa, et contractus super rebus inmobilibus ab eis facti dum essent in suo potentatu adnichilentur et pro nullis habeantur.

8. Rogantes humiliter tam dominum legatum quam dominum regem ut ipse dominus legatus sub districtione ecclesiastica prossus inhibeat, ne S. comes Leycestrie a quocumque pro sancto uel iusto reputetur,[8] cum in excommunicacione sit defunctus, sicut sancta tenet ecclesia; et mirabilia de eo uana et fatua ab aliquibus relata nullis unquam labiis proferantur; et dominus rex hec eadem sub pena corporali uelit districte inhibere.[9e]

9. Supplicamus reuerenter et humiliter uenerabili patri nostro domino O. sancti Adriani diacono cardinali et apostolice sedis legato, ut cum tam domino regi expedire cognouerit quam aliis hominibus maioribus et minoribus[10f] de regno qui cartas iuratas minime obseruarunt,[11] ad quas obseruandas omnes per excommunicacionis sentenciam iam latam inde non obseruantes tenebantur, beneficium absolucionis inpendant.

10. Rogamus eciam et suademus quod nullus cuiuscumque condicionis existat blada aut uictualia quelibet uel alia quecumque bona sub nomine mutui uel prouisione future solucionis capiat, sine licencia eorum quorum res seu bona sunt, saluis regni consuetudinibus approbatis.

11.[g] De Londoniis[12] laudamus et prefatum dominum regem hortamur et rogamus ut ipse prouideat per consilium suum de

---

[d] hactenus, occasione prouisionum A.   [e] sub pena . . . inhibere] sub districcione temporali uelit districtissime prohibere A.   [f] ut cum tam . . . minoribus] ut tam domino regi si sibi ipsi expedire contigerit, quam omnibus aliis tam maioribus quam minoribus A.   [g] See below, n. ee, p. 336

---

[8] See 'Miracula Simonis de Montfort' in *Rishangers' Chronicle*.
[9] 'prohibit most strictly under pain of temporal punishment' A.

possession unless they can show that they hold them by reasonable warrant from the lord king or from his ancestors.

7. Also, we declare and provide that all bonds, deeds, and instruments which the lord king, his eldest son the Lord Edward, or other faithful subjects have hitherto made or drawn up by reason of the Provisions of Oxford or because of the disorder present in the realm, at the instance of the late Simon de Montfort, earl of Leicester, and his accomplices, are absolutely nullified and destroyed and shall be held completely annulled and valueless. The injurious and damnable acts of the said Simon and his accomplices, together with the agreements about land made by them when he exercised power, are nullified and have no force.

8. Humbly begging both the lord legate and the lord king that the lord legate shall absolutely forbid, under distraint of the Church, that Simon, earl of Leicester, be considered to be holy or just[8] as he died excommunicate according to the belief of the Holy Church. And that the vain and fatuous miracles told of him by others shall not at any time pass any lips. And that the lord king shall agree strictly to forbid this under pain of corporal punishment.[9]

9. We reverently and humbly beseech our venerable father Lord Ottobono, cardinal deacon of St. Adrian and apostolic legate of the Holy See, that, since he knows it expedient for the king, he should announce that benefit of absolution may be given both to the lord king and to other men of the realm both great and small,[10] who have made little effort to observe the sworn charters, to the observation of which all are bound by the sentence of excommunication pronounced against all who do not observe the said charters.[11]

10. Likewise we beseech and urge, saving the approved customs of the realm, that no man of any condition shall take corn or any manner of victual, or any other goods under guise of borrowing or provision of future payment, without licence of those who own the things or goods.

11. We commend London[12] and urge and beseech the lord king that he provide, by his council, for the reform of the state of the

[10] 'that if he should consider it expedient... both to the lord king and to others both great and small' A.

[11] See doc. 42.

[12] No provison was made for London as the problem of the city was still under discussion. See G. A. Williams, 'Social and Constitutional Developments in Thirteenth Century London' (1952).

statu reformando ciuitatis, quoad terras, redditus, dominium et
libertates, et huiusmodi prouisio cito fiat.

12. Super statu et negocio exheredatorum, inter cetera que
ordinauimus et statuimus, uolentes secundum Deum et equitatis
tramitem incedere, ita duximus prouidendum, de assensu uenera-
bilis patris O. sancti Adriani diaconi cardinalis et apostolice sedis
legati et nobilis H. de Alemannia similiter habentium potestatem,
quod non fiat exheredacio sed redempcio,[13] uidelicet, quod incipientes guerram et perseuerantes usque nunc;[14h] item uiolenter
et maliciose detinentes Norhampton'[15] contra regem; item ex-
pugnantes et debellantes regem apud Lewes; item capti apud
Kenilworth qui uenerunt de predacione Wyntonie, uel alibi
fuerint contra regem, quibus rex non remisit; item bellantes apud
Euesham; item qui fuerunt apud Cestrefeud in bello; item qui
gratis et uoluntarie miserunt seruicia sua contra regem uel filium
eius; item balliui et ministri comitis Leycestrie et uicinos depredati
sunt, et homicidia, incendia et mala alia procurauerunt, soluent
quantum ualet terra eorum per quinque annos,[16] et si isti soluant
redempcionem, rehabeant terras suas; ita quod, si terra uendi
debeat, nullus eam emat nisi ille qui eam tenet ex dono domini
regis, si tantum uelit dare quam quilibet communiter emens, et
eisdem terminis; similiter[i] si ad firmam debeat dari, nullus sit
propinquior ea quam ille qui eam tenet ex dono domini regis, si
tantum uelit dare quam quilibet alius pro eo ad firmam uelit dare,
et eiisdem terminis habeat;[17j] similiter satisfaciens pro tota terra

---

[h] usque nunc] A *adds* quidam nostrum prouident, dicunt et ordinant quod
exheredacio debet fieri et alii quod non fiat exheredacio set redempcio; quidam
dicunt quod si debeat fieri exheredacio, quod detur exheredatis uita sine muti-
lacione menbrorum ex exilio et cum escaetis que eis possent contingere per
successionem hereditariam et tercia pars tercie eorum; et alii quod medietas
detur exheredatis; quidam dicunt, proui dent et diffiniunt quod redempcio debeat
fieri, et incipientes guerram et perseuerantes.   [i] *om*. FE.   [j] similiter...
habeat] quod si redimens terram satisfecerit pro tota terra sua a principio statim
totam terram suam habeat FE.

---

[13] The policy of redemption, rather than disherison, the key point of the
Dictum, was favoured by the umpires (*S. of Realm*, i. 18).
[14] 'some of us provide, say, and ordain that disherison be enforced, others
demand ransom and not disherison. Some of us claim that if disherison be
enforced the disinherited be granted their life in exile without loss of limb and
one ninth of escheats which may fall to them by inheritance; others assert they
should be given one half. Some provide and specify what ransom should be paid
by those who fought at the start of the war and are still in arms' A.

city in the matter of lands, rents, power, and liberties, and that provision of this kind be made immediately.

12. Concerning the condition and business of the disinherited, among other things which we have ordained and established, wishing to proceed in the way of God and the path of equity, we have been led to provide, by assent of the venerable father Ottobono cardinal deacon of St. Adrian and apostolic legate of the Holy See and by assent of the noble Henry of Almain, having similar power, that there be no disherison but rather ransom,[13] as follows. Those who fought at the start of the war and are still in arms;[14] those who violently and maliciously held Northampton against the king;[15] those who fought against and assailed the king at Lewes; those captured at Kenilworth after having sacked Winchester; those who have in other ways opposed the king and have not been pardoned; those who fought at Evesham; those who were in the battle at Chesterfield; those who freely and of their own will sent their followers against the king or his son; the bailiffs and officers of the earl of Leicester who robbed their neighbours and caused murder, arson, and other evils to be committed shall pay five times the annual value of their lands.[16] If they pay this redemption they shall recover their lands. Furthermore, if any one shall be forced to sell land, only he who holds it by gift of the lord king may buy it, if he offer as much as any other buyer and on the same terms. Similarly, if he who wishes to redeem his lands be forced to place the land to farm no one shall have greater right to farm the land than he who holds it of the gift of the lord king, and he shall have it on these terms that he be willing to give as much as anyone else to hold it at farm. He who gives satisfaction for all his land shall have full possession;[17] if satisfaction be given for a half or

[15] Captured by the royal forces 5 Apr. 1264. The period of the war, in the opinion of the judges, was from 4 Apr. 1264 until 16 Sept. 1266, when peace was declared by Henry III at the parliament which met at Winchester c. 14–23 Sept. (*King Henry III*, pp. 506–7). The dates are mentioned at the end of the text of F. See *S. of Realm*, i. 18, where reference is made to f. 10ᵛ of the MS.

[16] The umpires agreed with the choice of five years (*S. of Realm*, i, 18). The garrison on the Isle of Ely, which did not surrender until July 1267, was included within the five year group. Furthermore, the period within which the *Dictum* was to be accepted was extended from forty days after 31 Oct. 1266 until 1 Aug. 1267.

[17] 'that if he who pays the ransom for his lands from the beginning gives satisfaction for all his lands, he shall immediately be granted possession of his lands' FE.

habeat totam, pro medietate medietatem habeat, et pro tercia
parte statim terciam partem habeat. Quod si ultimo termino
statuto redimens non satisfecerit, medietas[18] terre remanentis
remaneat illis quibus terre collate sunt per dominum regem;[19k]
liberum autem sit redimenti infra illum terminum uendere totum
uel partem terre secundum formam uendicionis superius anno-
tatam, et similiter ad firmam tradere.[20]

13. Et si aliqui habeant nemora et uelint uendere ad redempcionem suam, ille qui tenet iam ex dono domini regis habeat
f. 123ᵛ fidelem suum / qui reciperat inde peccuniam, et exheredatus ille
qui uendit siluam habeat unum de quo confidat; et isti duo
recipientes soluant in conspectu illorum denarios quos recipiunt
de nemore illis quibus debet dari redempcio.[21,22l]

14. Item comes de Ferrariis[23] puniatur quantum ualet terra
sua per vii. annos; et[24m] milites autem et armigeri qui fuerunt
predones, et cum principalibus predonibus in bellis et depre-
dacionibus, si non habeant terras et habeant bona, soluant pro
redempcione sua medietatem[25n] bonorum suorum, et inueniant
fideiussionem conpetentem quod pacem regis et regni amodo
conseruabunt. Qui uero nichil habuerint iurant ad sancta Dei

---

[k] alii dicunt quod due partes remanent eis *added in* A.   [l] AFE *add*
Solucio istius redempcionis fiat per tres annos. A *continues* ut quidem dicunt alii
infra duos annos quamuis illi de Kenill' respondeant infra octo dies post
puplicacionem dicti si uelint istam pacem seruare; alii dicunt infra tres dies,
aliter sint extra formam pacis, si uelint sint in forma quinque et sex.   [m] Item
. . . et *om.* FE. De comite Ferariensi, si ad hoc extendi possit dictum nostrum,
quidam dicunt quod puniatur in octo annis, alii dicunt in septem annis, quantum
ualet terra eius A. *See n. ee, p. 336*   [n] *Explanacio Dicti* tertiam partem.

---

[18] The umpires favoured one half. Originally two thirds of the lands were to
remain with those to whom they had been granted (*S. of Realm*, i. 18).
[19] 'others say that they should keep two thirds' A.
[20] This clause is fully discussed in *Reform and Rebellion*, pp. 174–5, 190.
A fine could be paid in different ways: (*a*) Instalments paid over a fixed period.
The rebel holds all his lands except those which may be surrendered as
guarantee for payment of the instalments. (*b*) Part of the rebel's lands may be
allotted on long lease instead of a fine being paid. (*c*) Grantee holds all lands
until the accrued revenue liquidates the fine due. The choice of method of payment of the fine was agreed upon by the grantee and the rebel. See Knowles
'The Disinherited', iii. 49.
[21] The umpires' suggestion, that a time limit of three instead of two years
be demanded, was accepted. The point from which the three years was to be
calculated was undecided; was it to be from the time of the recognisance of the
debt or from the time of the publication of the *Dictum*? In practice the time
limit was often waived ('The Disinherited', iv. 71, 73–4; *S. of Realm*, i. 18).

a third part he shall immediately have a half or a third part. If the person redeeming his lands has not fulfilled his obligations at the last appointed term, half[18] the remaining land shall remain with those to whom[19] the land has been granted by the lord king. The person redeeming the land shall be free, within the said term, to sell all or part of the land in the manner above mentioned, and similarly he may place the land to farm.[20]

13. If any one has woods and wishes to sell them for his ransom, he who holds them by gift of the lord king shall appoint a trustworthy representative who shall receive the money while the disinherited tenant, who sells the woods, shall name a representative whom he trusts. These two receivers shall, in their presence, pay the money which they have received for the woods to those to whom the ransom is due.[21,22]

14. Be it noted that earl Ferrers[23] shall be punished by a ransom of seven times the annual value of his lands.[24] Knights and squires who were robbers and collaborated with the leading robbers in skirmishes and plundering raids, if they have no lands but have goods shall pay as ransom one half of their goods.[25] Furthermore they shall find a trustworthy surety that they will henceforth preserve the peace of the king and of the realm. Those who have no possessions shall swear on the Holy Gospel of God, and find

---

[22] 'Payment of this ransom shall be made within three years' ADE. A continues 'that certain others say within two years, provided that those who are in Kenilworth answer within eight days after the publication of the said terms, if they wish to accept this peace. Some say within three days, otherwise they are outside the form of the peace, others say within five or six days if they wish to be within the form of the peace.'

[23] The earl of Derby, who had robbed and plundered indiscriminately, was defeated at Chesterfield; his lands were granted to Edmund of Lancaster. After the publication of the *Dictum* the earl lost the bulk of his estates by trickery; for that part which he redeemed he paid £50,000 ('The Disinherited', iv. 58).

[24] 'In the matter of earl Ferrers, if our award may include this topic, some claim that he should be punished by paying eight times the annual value of his lands, others assert that he should pay seven times the annual value' A.

[25] The recommendation of the umpires that one third be charged was not accepted ('The Disinherited', iv. 4, 7, 64; *S. of Realm*, i. 18). In most cases the decisions of the umpires were accepted. The reference to landless knights suggests that baronial households still contained a landless element. It was possibly the landless knights of Gilbert de Clare's *familia* who joined de Montfort when he was deserted by Clare in 1265 (R. F. Treharne in *Proc. of the British Academy*, xl (1954), 75–102).

euangelia, et inueniant fideiussionem conpetentem quod pacem regis et regni amodo seruabunt, et subeant satisfaccionem conpetentem et penitenciam secundum iudicium ecclesie, exceptis bannitis quibus solus rex potest remittere.

15. Ceterorum domini heredum infra etatem et in custodia existencium soluant pro eis, et cum uenerint heredes ad legitimam etatem soluant redempcionem dominis eiisdem terminis per[o] tres uel per duos annos[26] quibus alii soluerunt, ita quod domini terre habeant custodias heredum cum maritagiis usque ad legitimam etatem heredum. Si autem domini terre nolunt soluere redempcionem illis quibus terre date sunt per dominum regem, iidem habeant custodes heredum cum maritagiis sine disparagacione usque ad legitimam etatem heredum et tunc heredes soluant prout alii soluerunt eis eiisdem terminis.

16. Custodie autem que debentur domino regi maneant illis quibus concesse sunt per dominum regem, et cum peruenerint ad legitimam etatem soluant redempcionem eiisdem terminis quibus alii, et nullam faciant destruccionem ab hiis qui habent custodias; sin autem fiat iusticia contra illos, secundum quod continetur in Magna Carta.[27]

17.[p] Omnes de castro sint in communi uia et forma pacis, exceptis Henrico de Hastinges et mutilatoribus nuncii domini regis, qui sunt de vii. annis puniantur[28q] uel in misericordia domini regis se ponant.[29]

18. Si quis ante bellum de Lewes steterit cum domino rege et post bellum sit exheredatus qui noluit uenire ad filium regis et eius adiutorium, dicat rex uoluntatem suam de eo per fidele dictum suum.

19. Nemora ab eis qui tenent nunc non uendantur nec destruantur aliquo modo nisi post terminum ultimum non obseruatum; necessaria tamen ad custodiam uel restauracionem domorum habeant illi quibus terre locate sunt per regem, sin autem grauiter puniantur.[30]

[o] *Explanacio Dicti* per duos annos. [p] *om* FE, *see n. ee* p. 336.
[q] de vii . . puniantur] in octo uel septem annis A.

[26] The umpires favoured two years ('The Disinherited', iv. 81–2; *S. of Realm*, i. 18). [27] This is cl. 4 of Magna Carta (Holt, pp. 318–19).

[28] 'of eight or seven years' A.

[29] The original text of the *Dictum* demanded seven or eight years, the umpires suggested seven. In many cases only five years was demanded ('The Disinherited', iv. 58–9). Henry de Hastings was leader of the Kenilworth garrison which cut off the hand of a royal messenger. The Dunstable annalist states that John de la

a trustworthy surety that henceforth they will preserve the peace of the king and of the realm. Furthermore, they shall suffer fitting and satisfactory penance under judgement of the Church. Excepted are the banished whom the king alone may remit.

15. The lords of heirs under age and in ward shall pay ransom for them to the grantee. When the heirs attain their majority they shall pay the ransom to their lords according to the terms under which others pay in two or three years.[26] The lords of such lands shall have custody of the heirs with rights of marriage until the majority of the heirs. If, however, the lords of the lands refuse to pay the ransom to those to whom the lands were given by the lord king, these shall have custody of the heirs with rights of marriage without disparagement until the full age of the heirs who should then pay ransom to the grantee as others have paid and on the same terms.

16. Wardships which belong to the lord king shall remain with those to whom they have been given by the lord king. When the heirs shall come of full age they shall pay ransom at the same terms as others and no waste shall be made by those who have custody. If such waste be made justice shall be enforced against them as is contained in Magna Carta.[27]

17. All persons in the castle shall be in the common way and form of peace, except Henry de Hastings and those who mutilated the king's messenger. These shall be punished by a ransom of[28] seven times the annual value of their lands[29] or they shall place themselves at the king's mercy.

18. The king shall by just award pronounce his pleasure concerning any one who supported the lord king before the battle of Lewes and was disinherited after the battle because he was unwilling to support the king's son and come to his aid.

19. Woods shall not be sold or wasted in any way by those who hold them now except after failure to make payment at the last term. Those to whom the lands have been given by the lord king shall have necessaries for the maintenance or restoration of dwellings. If they act otherwise they shall be severely punished.[30]

Ware, constable of Bristol, May and June 1265, captured at Evesham and released in Oct. 1266, was with Hastings (*C.R. 1264–68*, pp. 240–1; *C.P.R. 1258–66*, pp. 425, 429, 649; *Ann. Mon.* iii. 243).

[30] See n. 20; doc. 3 cl. 1. Despite this prohibition there is much evidence of waste by grantees ('The Disinherited', iv. 103).

20. Si aliquis sit de quo timetur quod uelit guerram facere seu procurare, prouideant se domini legatus et rex securitatem quam uiderint expedire, mittendo extra regnum ad tempus uel aliter sicut expedire uiderint; ita tamen quod, si contingat illum impediri a solucione sue redempcionis, propter hoc non exheredetur.[31]

21. Si aliquis non[r] ista prouisione, subeat iudicium in curia domini regis infra festum sancti Hillarii; extra regnum uero existens habeat inducias transmarinas secundum legem et consuetudinem terre,[32] ita tamen quod teneat se in pace, aliter non sit in forma pacis.

22. Quia rex tenetur multis qui eum iuuerunt et ei fideliter assuerunt, quibus de terris non prouidit, et quidam plus habent quam habere debent, prouideat dominus rex de redempcione capienda quod habundanter eos respiciat, ne sit materia noue guerre.[33]

23. Prouideant eciam se domini legatus, rex, et Henricus de Alemannia, quod eligant xii.[34][s] qui ista diligenter et fideliter exequantur,[35] et illa faciat dominus rex et heredes sui firmiter obseruari et manuteneri. Isti inquirant et conpleant qui a supradictis xii. electis sunt ordinata, secundum formam ordinacionum que iam facte sunt; sin autem faciant estimaciones racionabiles et uerraces secundum quod xii.[36][t] prouidebunt executores.

---

[r] sit contentus *added* AF.   [s] quod rex eligatur, alii quod xii A.
[t] xii . . . executores] dominus rex uel xii executores prouidebunt A.

[31] The fairness and justness of this decision is worthy of note.
[32] Respite was for forty days. *Reform and Rebellion*, p. 175, discusses why an eyre was held when the king's court was to act in grievances. G. O. Sayles, *Select Cases in the Court of King's Bench* (1936, 1938, 1939), discusses this court. 'The Disinherited', iv. 38–48, considers the work of the Court of King's Bench after Kenilworth.
[33] Many lands had been seized by the *seisitores* of 1265 and by royal officials after that time (*Reform and Rebellion*, p. 175).
[34] These words make little sense. A possible meaning is that another twelve be elected by the king.
[35] The twelve were named late in Jan. 1267 (*C.R. 1264–68*, p. 361). They were the bishop of St. David's; Henry de Bracton, a judge; Richard de Middleton, a judge, chancellor 1269; the abbot of Tintern, active for the crown *post* Aug. 1265, called Sir John in 1267, may be John le Breton, a judge (*C.P.R. 1258–66, passim; C.P.R. 1266–72, passim; C.Ch.R.* ii. 304); Robert de Neville; Eustace Balliol, brother of John Balliol, lord of Kirklington, co. Cumb., sheriff of Cumberland and constable of Carlisle castle, who took the cross with Henry of Almain and the Lord Edward; Roger de Somery; John Lovel, sheriff of the counties of Cambridge and Huntingdon, constable of Northampton castle; Alan de la Zuche; William de St. Omer, a judge; Adam de Gesemuth, sheriff of

20. If there be anyone about whom it is feared that he wishes to cause or wage war the legate and the lord king shall provide for themselves such security as they shall deem expedient, sending him out of the realm for a fixed time or otherwise as they shall see fit. Nevertheless if it so happens that such a person be hindered from paying his ransom he shall not on this account be disinherited.[31]

21. If there be anyone ⟨who is dissatisfied⟩ with this ordinance let him submit to the judgement of the court of the lord king before the feast of St. Hilary [13 January 1267]. If any man be out of the kingdom he shall have the respite granted to those across the sea according to the law and custom of the land,[32] provided he remain in peace, otherwise he shall not be in this form of peace.

22. As the king is bound to many who have aided him and have faithfully stood by him, for whom he has provided no lands, and some have more than they should have, the king shall provide for them from the ransoms which are collected, lest this be a cause of further unrest.[33]

23. Furthermore let the legate, the king, and Henry of Almain stipulate that there be chosen twelve[34] who will diligently and faithfully execute these things[35] and let the lord king and his heirs cause them to be firmly observed and maintained. Let them examine and fulfil the ordinances made by the twelve selected, in the manner of the regulations which have already been enacted. Otherwise they shall make true and reasonable estimates according[36] to what the twelve executors shall provide.

Northumberland, constable of the castle of Newcastle upon Tyne, custodian of the lands of the earl of Derby; Simon de Creye, constable of Canterbury castle, warden of the Cinque Ports. *Reform and Rebellion*, p. 176, n. 2 is wrong in stating that the entry in *C.P.R. 1258–66*, pp. 671–2, records the terms of reference for those who were to supervise the enforcement of the *Dictum*. See n. 5. E. F. Jacob confuses the twelve who were to draw up the *Dictum* with the twelve who were to execute the terms of the *Dictum* (*Reform and Rebellion*, p. 176, n. 2). The commission appointed in Jan. 1267 was superseded by a special eyre, appointed on 17 Sept. at Shrewsbury. Many of the judges of the eyre, which lasted until 1272, had been nominated in Jan. (*C.P.R. 1266–72*, p. 160). 'The Disinherited', appendix iii and Sayles, *Selden Soc.*, lv (1936), xli–lxxviii give biographical details of the judges. *Reform and Rebellion*, pp. 182–3 lists the *capitula itineris*, which were preserved in *Lib. de Ant. Leg.* p. 96, but alludes to only three circuits (p. 179). The fourth was in the W. and S.W. of England. Details of the eyre are considered in 'The Disinherited', iv. 18–37.

[36] 'the lord king or the twelve executors shall provide' A.

f. 124   24. / Firmarii qui fuerunt contra dominum regem careant firmis suis, saluis iuribus dominorum quibus reddant censum annuum detinentes firmas et elapso termino reuertantur ad ueros dominos.[37]

25. De castris edificatis qui per cartas domini regis et per consensum eius sine consensu exheredati, dicimus quod dominus terre soluat custum que ponebatur[38u] ante publicacionem dicti per consensum regis uel racionabile escambium terre.[39]

26. Laici manifeste procurantes negocia domini comitis et conplicium suorum, attrahendo homines per mendacia, per falsitates insidiando partem comitis et conplicium suorum, et detrahendo partem domini regis et filii sui,[40] puniantur quantum ualet terra eorum[41v] per duos annos.

27. Coacti uel metu ducti qui uenerunt ad bellum, qui non expugnauerunt nec malum fecerunt; impotentes qui ui uel metu miserunt seruicia sua contra regem uel filium suum; coacti uel metu ducti qui fuerunt predones et cum principalibus predonibus depredaciones fecerunt, et quando commode poterant, a predacionibus cessauerunt et ad domos suas redierunt, existentes in pace, redimantur quantum ualet terra eorum per unum annum.[42,43w]

28. Emptores scienter rerum alienarum ualorem bonorum que emerunt restituant et sint in misericordia domini regis qui contra iusticiam fecerunt quia illud inhibuit dominus rex iam dimidio anno elapso.

29. Illi qui ad mandatum comitis Leycestrie ingressi sunt Norhampton' nec pugnauerunt nec malum fecerunt, si ad ecclesiam fugerunt quando regem uenientem uiderunt et hoc sit attinctum

---

    [u] dicimus quod . . . ponebatur] quidam dicunt quod solui debent da(m)pna et sumptus et alii dicunt quod nichil; qui dicunt quod dampna et sumptus solui debent, quod post redempcionem solutam tempore trium annorum soluat dominus terre infra sex annos custum qui (im)ponebatur A.   [v] puniantur... eorum] quidam dicunt quantum ualeant terre eorum per tres annos, quidam dicunt quantum ualeant A.   [w] redimantur ... annum] moderate redimantur isti; tres quidam dicunt quantum ualent terre eorum et bona infra duos annos; alii dicunt quantum ualeant terre eorum et bona infra unum annum A.

---

    [37] There is no evidence of this claim being applied in court ('The Disinherited', iv. 96).
    [38] 'some say that they should pay damages and costs while others say that they should pay nothing. Those who say that damages and costs should be paid demand that after paying the ransom within three years the lord of the land shall pay, within six years, the cost which was imposed' A.

24. Those holding lands at farm, who were against the lord king, shall lose the farms; those who keep the farms, saving the rights of the lords of the lands, shall pay an annual rent and at the end of the term the lands shall revert to the true lord.[37]

25. Concerning castles which were built by charter, and by consent of the lord king, without the consent of the disinherited.[38] We ordain that the lord of the land pay the cost, which was imposed before the proclamation by consent of the king or make reasonable exchange of land.[39]

26. Laymen who openly supported the interests of the earl and his supporters, gaining followers by lies and false tales, rousing them to the side of the earl and his accomplices and withdrawing them from supporting the lord king and his son,[40] shall be punished by the payment of twice the annual value of their lands.[41]

27. Those who were coerced or driven by fear to battle but who neither fought nor did evil; weaklings who because of force or fear sent their military following against the king or his son; those who were coerced or driven by fear to be robbers and made plundering raids with the leading robbers but who, when possible, ceased plundering and returned to their homes, remaining there at peace, shall pay a ransom of one year's value of their lands.[42,43]

28. Those who knowingly bought the goods of others shall restore the value of the things which they bought. They are at the mercy of the lord king for they did this unjustly, as the lord king forbade this six months ago.

29. Those who, at the command of the earl of Leicester, entered Northampton but neither fought nor did harm, if they fled to the church when they saw the king coming and this is proved by

[39] The umpires agreed with this demand but there is no evidence of its enforcement ('The Disinherited', iv. 96). See cl. 36.

[40] The umpires agreed with these demands. Cases arising from the enforcement of this clause covered a wide range of wrongs in addition to those specified ('The Disinherited', iv. 62).

[41] 'some say at three times the annual value of their lands, some say at the annual value' A.

[42] 'that they shall pay a moderate ransom; three, however, assert that they shall pay less than twice the annual value of their lands and goods, others assert that they shall pay less than one year's value of their lands and goods' A.

[43] The original text of the *Dictum* was undecided between one and two years. The umpires favoured less than one year (*S. of Realm*, i. 16, 18).

per bonos; illi qui ⟨non⟩ tenebant[x] de comite Leycestrie et uenerunt ad mandatum eius soluent quam ualent terre eorum per dimidium annum.[44,45][y] Isti qui ex feodo comitis tenebant solum sint in misericordia domini regis.

30. Impotentes et illi homines qui malum non fecerunt statim rehabeant terras suas et recuperent dampna sua in curia domini regis; et puniantur accusatores quod[46][z] amodo rex non credat eis de facili; et talis pena fiat eis qualis debet fieri illis qui iniuste fecerunt fideles regis exheredari, sine tamen periculo mutilacionis[47][aa] et exheredacionis; maliciose accusati statim rehabeant terras suas et recuperant dampna sua in curia regis ut supra.[48]

31. Mulieres autem habeant hereditates suas et dotes de primis dominis; de terris autem maritorum habeant[49][bb] secundum quod rex statuit et redimantur.[50]

32. Redempcio eorum qui fuerunt contra dominum regem stet; set in illis qui in nullo fuerunt contra regem nec stet redempcio sed statim rehabeant terras suas et recuperent dampna sua ut supra.

33. De maliciose accusatis dictum est, et recipiantes[cc] puniantur ut supra. Submissio facta est domino regi uel aliorum dominorum per uos uel per concordiam uel pacem factam stet in robore suo.

34.[dd] De Simone de Monteforti et comitissa et filiis comitis nichil dicimus, quia dominus rex Anglie factum eorum posuit in manus regis Francie.[51]

35. Omnes recepti in pace per illos qui habuerunt potestatem remaneant in statu in quo recepti sunt.[52] Omnes qui redempti

[x] non tenebant AFE.   [y] per . . . annum] per unum annum alii dicunt quantum ualeant per dimidium annum A.   [z] accusatores penes dominum regem quod AF.   [aa] uito et mutilacionis AF.   [bb] maritorum qui fuerunt contra regem habeant ADE.   [cc] accusantes F.   [dd] See below, n. ee, p. 336.

44 'for one year, others say the value of half a year' A.
45 The umpires agreed with this clause. There was very considerable variation and modification in the application of the rules of redemption ('The Disinherited', iv. 65).
46 'accusers in the household of the lord king' AD.
47 'of life and mutilation' AF.
48 The provisions of this clause which, together with clauses 32 and 33, protected those disinherited by mistake or malice, were often applied in the courts ('The Disinherited', iv. 93).
49 'husbands who were against the lord king' ADE.
50 Concessions for the wives or widows of opponents were made by de Montfort and the king (C.P.R. 1258–66, pp. 334, 337, 558; C.R. 1264–68, pp. 199–

lawful men; those who did not hold lands of the earl of Leicester but obeyed his command shall pay a half year's value of their lands.[44,45] Those who held lands of the earl are in the mercy of the king.

30. Powerless people and others who did no harm shall immediately recover their lands and receive their damages in the court of the lord king. Let the accusers[46] be punished so that henceforth the king will not easily believe them and let them be punished as were those who unjustly caused the king's faithful subjectsto be disinherited, nevertheless without danger of mutilation[47] or disherison. Those who are maliciously accused shall immediately have their lands and recover their damages in the king's court, as mentioned above.[48]

31. Women shall have their heritages and dowers of their first husbands. They shall have the lands of their husbands[49] in the manner in which the king has ordained, and the lands shall be ransomed.[50]

32. The ransom of those who opposed the king shall be paid. No ransom shall be paid by those who were not against the king, instead they shall immediately recover their lands and recover damages as mentioned above.

33. Mention has been made of those maliciously accused, and receivers shall be punished as mentioned above. Submission has been made to the king, either by the other lords through you or let it prevail in its own right through a friendly or imposed peace.

34. We say nothing of Simon de Montfort, the countess, and the sons of the earl, as the lord king has placed their case in the hands of the king of France.[51]

35. All those who have been received in peace by those so appointed shall remain in the condition in which they were so received.[52] All who have been ransomed shall not be bound to answer for damages and for trespasses committed by them against

200). The problem of dower rights arising from redemption is discussed in 'The Disinherited', iii. 32-6; iv. 75.

[51] King Louis IX wrote to Henry III on 12 May 1266 asking him to make peace with the countess of Leicester and her children, while on 25 Sept. 1266 Henry III wrote to Louis IX about Eleanor de Montfort and her son Simon (C.P.R. 1258-66, p. 678; Royal Letters, ii. 304-5). See Simon de Montfort, pp. 249, 258-73.

[52] This clause covered men who had become loyal after opposing the king at Northampton and Lewes. Especially favoured were those who had aided the earl of Gloucester at the time of his break with de Montfort. All were granted letters of protection to cover them if they were summoned to answer in the courts for trespasses committed during the period of the disturbances ('The Disinherited', iv. 91-2).

sunt non teneantur respondere de dampnis et transgressionibus per eos factis super illos qui inpugnauerunt tempore turbacionis predicte, sed dampna et transgressiones ex utraque parte remittantur, salua tamen accione cuique de dicta turbacione non intromittet, set saluo ei quod ad ecclesiam pertinet.

36. Et quia periculosum uidetur quod castra essent in potestate eorum qui male egerunt contra regem, dicimus et prouidimus de castris de Erdeal', Bitham', et Cortesleye quod pro ipsius detur racionabile excambium.[53]

37.[ee] Omnes decetero teneant firmam pacem et nullus faciat homicidia, incendia, roberias, nec aliquas transgressiones contra f. 124ᵛ pacem, / et qui fecerit et conuictus fuerit habeat iudicium et legem secundum consuetudinem regni.

38. Item omnes quorum interest iurent super sancta ewangelia quod nullus capiet uindictam nec procurabit nec consentiet nec fieri sustinebit quod uindicta capiatur occasione turbacionis. Et si aliquis uindictam capiat puniatur per curiam domini regis, et satisfaciant ecclesie hii qui eam leserunt.

39. [54ff]Insuper quicumque isti dicto non consenserit sit puplicus inimicus domini regis et filiorum suorum et communitatis; populus et clerus quam canonica iura[55gg] permittant prosequantur eum tanquam inimicum pacis ecclesie et regni.

40. Inprisonati seu incarcerati, prestita sufficienti et racionabili securitate, liberentur per obsidem uel per aliam securitatem competentem et racionabilem, secundum prouisionem dictorum legati et regis.

Datum et publicatum in castro apud Kenilworthe, secundo[56hh] kalendas Nouembris anno gracie m.cc.lxvi. regni uero domini Henrici regis Anglie anno quinquagesimo primo.[57ii]

[ee] *In E clauses 34, 11, 14 and 17 are inserted between 36 and 37; in F clauses 34, 11, 17 and 14 appear between 38 and 39.*   [ff] AFE *start* Si quis eciam non uelit dictam istud tenere uel iudicium curie domini regis per pares subire, et sic exheredati qui se dicunt tales, nullum ius habeant ad recuperandam terras. Et si aliquis qui tenet terras exheredatorum rebellet dicto nichil iuris per donum domini regis uendicare possit in terra uel redempcione.   [gg] clericus quantum canonices et iura AFE.   [hh] pridie E.   [ii] Nullus preterea occasione preterite turbacionis possit aliquem exheridare qui sibi aliquo iure succedere debeat *before dating clause* A, *after dating clause* FE.

---

[53] The umpires agreed with this demand (*S. of Realm*, i. 18). Little reason is known why these three castles are mentioned. Peter d'Aigueblanche, the Savoyard bishop of Hereford, had been taken as a captive to Eardisley in 1263,

those whom they fought at the time of the unrest. Mutual damages and trespasses are excused, saving, nevertheless, the right of action of each man who was not involved in the unrest and saving, as far as he is concerned, that which pertains to the Church.

36. Furthermore, as it is considered to be most dangerous that castles be in the control of those who acted evilly against the king, we award and ordain concerning the castles of Eardisley [Herefordshire], Bytham [Lincs.], and Chartley [Staffs.] that a reasonable exchange be given for them.[53]

37. Henceforward all shall keep a firm peace and none shall commit murder, arson, robbery, or any other violation of the peace. He who shall do this and shall be convicted shall have judgement and law according to the custom of the realm.

38. Furthermore all of those whom it concerns shall swear on the Holy Gospels that they will not, on account of the disorders, take revenge nor procure, consent to, nor support such action. If anyone takes revenge he shall be punished by the court of the lord king and let those who have harmed the Church make satisfaction to it.

39. [54]Furthermore, he who does not consent to this decision shall be a public enemy of the king, of his sons and of the community. Laymen and clergy, allowed by canon and lay law,[55] may prosecute him as an enemy of the peace of the church and of the realm.

40. Those who are imprisoned or in custody, having found a sufficient and reasonable surety, shall be liberated by pledge or by another competent and reasonable surety according to the ordinance of the legate and of the king.

Given and published in the castle at Kenilworth, on the second[56] day before the kalends of November [31 October], in the year of grace 1266, the fifty-first year of the reign of the lord Henry, king of England.[57]

Chartley had been held by the earl of Derby but nothing of note is known about Bytham. Eardisley and Bytham were recovered by their lords ('The Disinherited', iv. 94–5).

[54] 'Also, if any one does not wish to abide by this decision or submit to judgement by his peers in the court of the lord king, such persons, so declaring themselves, shall be disinherited and shall have no right to recover their lands. And if any man, holding lands of a disinherited person, rebels against the decision he shall have right, by gift of the lord king, to claim the lands or the ransom for it' AFE.

[55] 'clergy, within the limits of canon and lay law' AFE.

[56] 'the day before' E.

[57] 'Henceforward no man, by reason of the past unrest, may disinherit anyone who by law should be his successor' AFE.

APPENDIX I

The relation between the Petition of the Barons, the Provisions of the English Barons, the Provisions of Westminster (Legal) and the Provisions of Westminster (Administrative)

THE following table shows the extent to which the grievances mentioned in the Petition of the Barons (document 3) were answered in the enactments of the reformers.

The table also indicates the close link between the clauses of document 9 (Provisions of the English Barons, probably dating from autumn 1258–March 1259) and the Provisions of document 11 (the legal resolutions of the Provisions of Westminster) which were enacted in the October parliament of 1259.

Certain clauses of documents 9 and 11 do not appear on the table as they dealt with problems of administration of law not mentioned in document 3. Thus clause 19 of document 9, dealing with the rights of patrons of churches, appears in clause 7 of document 11; clause 24 of document 9, concerning essoins, forms clause 15 of document 11, while clauses 21–3 of document 9 are concerned with the technicalities of writs of entry and *mort d'ancestor*.

Petition	Provisions	Provisions of Westminster (Legal)	Provisions of Westminster (Administrative)
Document 3 Clause	Document 9 Clause	Document 11 Clause	Document 12 Clause
1^1	25^1	9, 10, 12^1	14^1
2 } 3 }			8, 14, 16, 17
4^2			27
5^2			
6^3			
7 } 8 } 9 }			24, 25
10 } 11 }		14	
12			17
13		4, 13	
14	17	5, 21	
15^2			
16^4		19,	9, 20, 22
17 } 18 }	14, 15, 16	4	
19		13, 23	
20^5			
21		22	
22 } ^{6} 23 }			
24	1–13	1–3	
25 } ^{7} 26 }			23
27	18	6	
28	20	8	
29		16	

¹ The first clause of document 3 mentions three topics; right of the eldest son or daughter to inherit father's lands, relief, queen's gold. Queen's gold is mentioned in cl. 14 of document 12. Clauses 22 and 25 of document 9 consider problems associated with the writ of *mort d'ancestor* while clauses 9, 10, 12 of document 11 provide concerning inheritance.

² See documents, 4, 5.   ³ See document, 4.   ⁴ See document, 5.

⁵ Although no laws were made to remedy this abuse the appointment and work of sheriffs was a great concern of the reformers.

⁶ See document, 3, n. 14.   ⁷ See documents, 4, 5.

APPENDIX II

*The relation between the Provisions of Westminster (Legal),
the Provisions issued in January 1263, Bodley MS. 91,
ff. 133-5 and Cam. U.L. MS. Mm.1.27. ff. 75-6*

Provisons of Westminster (Legal)	Provisions of Westminster Jan. 1263[1]	Bodley MS. 91.[1]	Cam. U.L. MS. Mm.1.27[3]
Document 11 Clause	Clause	Clause	Clause
1	1	1	1
2	2	2	2
3	3	3	3[4]
4	4	4	
5	5	5	
6	6	6	
7	7	7	
8	24	9	
9	10	}11	}4
10	11		
11	9	10	
12	12	12	5
13	13	13	6
14[2]			
15	14	14	7
16	15	15	8
17	16	16	9
18	23	23	10
19	17	17	11
20	18	18	12
21	19	19	13
22	20	20	14
23	21	21	15
24	22	22	16
	25	{24 25	{17 18
	26	26	

[1] Clause 8, which is the same in both documents, is not in document 11. This clause appears in the Statute of Marlborough cl. 13 (*S. of Realm*).

[2] This clause does not appear in any of the following documents.

[3] This document is not divided into paragraphs. Division has been made to enable comparison with document 11.

[4] Only half of clause 3 of document 11 appears in C. See document 11 note *c*.

GENERAL INDEX

Because of the great number of topics mentioned, both in the introduction and in the texts, the Subject element in this index is selective.

Basset, Ralph, of Drayton, co. Staffs., 318–19
— — w. of, da. of Roger de Somery, 319
— — of Sapcote, co. Leics., 112–13, 284–5
Bassingbourne, Warin de, 282–3, 318–19
Bath, Henry de, 152–5, 218, 226–7
Bath and Wells, b. of, see Giffard, Walter
Béarn, Gaston de, 198
— w. of, da. of Petronilla of Bigorre, 198
Beatrice, see Henry III
— see Raimond-Berengar
Beaudesert, co. Warws., 101
Bedfordshire, 164–5
Belet, William, see Biset, William
Bémont, C., 4, 11, 38, 41, 57, 194, 208
Berkshire, 164–5
Bersted, Stephen, b. of Chichester, 49, 295
Besill, Mathias de, 112–13
Beverley, co. Yorks., 74
Béziers, dept. Hérault, 202
Bigod, Hugh, 4–6, 9, 10, 12, 19, 23, 24, 26–31, 34–5, 38, 54, 83, 90–1, 100–1, 103–5, 110–13, 159, 164–5, 172–3, 176–81, 184–5, 220–1, 282–3
— Roger, e. of Norfolk, 100–1, 104–5, 110–11, 118–19, 156–7, 170–1, 176–7, 190–1, 241, 282–3, 298–9
Bigorre, 33, 198–9, 200–3
Biset, William, 280–1
bishop, 16, 126–7, 140–3, 182, 248–9, 294–7, 314–15
bishoprics, 268–9
Blackstone, Sir William, 308, 311
Blaen Llyfni, co. Brecon, 264
Blund, William le, 284–5
Bodini, Raymond, 198–9
Bohun, Humphrey de, e. of Hereford, 26, 100–1, 104–5, 118–19, 164–5, 170–1, 183, 198–9, 282–3, 318–19
— — (probably e. of Hereford), 298–9
— — junior, 284–5, 295
Boniface, ab. of Canterbury, 10, 32–3, 37, 47, 73, 100, 104–5, 118–19, 170–3, 240–3, 248–9, 295
Bosham, Sussex, 54
Boulogne-sur-Mer, dept. Pas-de-Calais, 43–4, 50, 188–9, 252

Bourne, co. Lincs., 284
Bracton, Henry de, 164–5, 330
Bradsole, Kent, see Henry, prior of St. Radegund
Breconshire, 41, 168
Breton, John le, 330, see John, Sir
Brickendon, co. Herts., 54
Bridgnorth, co. Salop., castle, 112–13
— town, 42, 51, 54
Bridport, Giles de, b. of Salisbury, 11, 104–5, 174–5, 177, 182
Bristol, co. Glos., castle, 19, 177
— constable of, see Ware, John de la
— town, 19, 51, 53, 55
Brittany, c. of, see John
— d. of, see John
Bronescombe, Walter, b. of Exeter, 33, 56, 182, 318–19
Bruges, Belgium, 48
Brus, Robert, 282–3
— Isabel, w. of, 282
Buckinghamshire, 164–5
Builth, co. Radnor, castle and lordship, 211, 213, 218, 232–3
burgesses, 51, 52, 54, 302–5
Burgh, Hubert de, e. of Kent, 6
Burgundy, 41
— duke of, see Hugh
Burton, co. Staffs., 6, 149
— annals of, 4, 6, 9, 13, 14, 20, 105, 118
Bury St. Edmunds, co. Suff., 43
— — abbot of, see Luton, Simon de
Bytham, co. Lincs., 336–7

Cahors, dept. Lot, 87
— diocese, 234
Cahorsins, 86–7, 96–7
Calais, dept. Pas-de-Calais, 188
Cam, H. M., 14, 57, 128
Cambridge, co. Cambs., 220
Cambridgeshire, 164–5
— eyre in, 220, 226–7
— sheriff of, 11, 330
Camoys, Ralph de, 295
Canterbury, Gervase of, 57
Canterbury, Kent, ab. of, see Boniface; Kilwardby, Robert; Peckham, John
— castle, 112–13, 331
— — constable of, see Creye, Simon de
— peace provided at, 50–1, 298
— town, 50, 55
Cantilupe, Thomas, 49, 295